Fatima in Twilight

Mark Fellows

Marmion Publications
Niagara Falls
Canada • U.S.A.

ISBN 0-9733763

On the Cover: The Basilica at Fatima, Portugal

Marmion Publications

In Canada:
P.O. Box 694
Niagara Falls, Ontario
L2E 6V5

In U.S.A:
M.P.O. Box 743
Niagara Falls, New York
14302

716-691-7091

Printed in Canada

This book is dedicated to
the Immaculate Heart

Fatima in Twilight

Chapter Listing

Chapter One

What the Children Saw

The Fatima Message began like many revelations in Sacred Scripture — with the appearance of an angel.

It was the spring of 1916. A sudden strong wind on a calm day startled three peasant children out of a game they were playing in the hill country of Portugal. Turning to the wind the children saw "a light whiter than snow in the shape of a transparent young man, who was more brilliant than a crystal struck by the rays of the sun."

"As he approached," Lucy, the oldest child, recalled, "we began to see his features. He was a young man of great beauty, about fourteen or fifteen years old. We were surprised and ecstatic. We did not utter a word."

He stopped in front of the children and said, "Fear not. I am the Angel of Peace. Pray with me." The angel prostrated himself, his forehead touching the ground. Lucy and her two cousins, Francisco and Jacinta, instinctively imitated him, and repeated the angel's prayer three times: "My God, I believe, I adore, I hope, and I love Thee! I beg Thee forgiveness for those who do not believe, do not adore, do not hope, and do not love Thee!"

He rose and said, "Pray thus. The Hearts of Jesus and Mary are attentive to the voice of your supplications." Then he disappeared, leaving a "supernatural atmosphere" described by Lucy as:

> "So intense that for a long time we were scarcely aware of our own existence, remaining in the same posture in which he had left us, and continually repeating the same prayer. The presence of God made itself felt so intimately and so intensely that we did not even venture to speak to one another. Next day, we were still immersed in this supernatural atmosphere, which only gradually began to disappear."

The children told no one what they had seen.

The Angel Returns

It was mid-summer when the angel returned. The day was so hot that Lucy, Francisco, and Jacinta returned early from the hills to shelter the sheep they tended in a barn. Then the children lounged in the shade of a fig tree. "Suddenly," Lucy remembers, "we saw the angel right beside us." He admonished them: "What are you doing? Pray, pray very much! The Holy Hearts of Jesus and Mary have merciful designs concerning you. Offer prayers and sacrifices constantly to the Most High!"

"How must we sacrifice?" Lucy asked. The angel replied:

"Offer God a sacrifice of anything you can as an act of reparation for the sins with which He is offended, and as a supplication
for the conversion of sinners. Draw peace upon your country by
doing this. I am its Angel Guardian, the Angel of Portugal. Above
all, accept and endure with submission whatever suffering the
Lord sends you."

The angel disappeared, but his words "were impressed upon our souls
like a light that made us understand who God is, how much He loves us
and wishes to be loved, the value of sacrifice and how it pleases God, and
how He converts sinners because of it," Lucy wrote in her memoirs.
Again, the children told no one what they had seen.

In the fall of 1916 the angel appeared to the children for the third and
last time. He found them prostrate in a rocky hollow in the hills, praying
the prayer he had taught them on his first visit.

"An extraordinary light shone upon us," recalls Lucy. "We sprang up
to see what was happening, and beheld the angel. He was holding a chalice in his left hand, with the Host suspended above it, from which some
drops of blood fell into the chalice. Leaving the chalice suspended in the
air, the angel knelt down beside us and made us repeat three times:

"'Most Holy Trinity, Father, Son, and Holy Spirit, I adore Thee
profoundly, and I offer Thee the Most Precious Body, Blood, Soul,
and Divinity of Jesus Christ, present in all the tabernacles of the
earth, in reparation for the insults, sacrileges, and indifference
with which He is offended. And through the infinite merits of His
Most Sacred Heart, and of the Immaculate Heart of Mary, I beg
Thee for the conversion of poor sinners.'"

The angel rose and gave the Host to Lucy, which she consumed. He
gave the chalice to Francisco and Jacinta, saying: "Take and drink the
Body and Blood of Jesus Christ, Who is horribly insulted by ungrateful
men. Make reparation for their crimes and console your God."

After Communion the angel and children prostrated themselves and
repeated three times the "Most Holy Trinity" prayer. The angel disappeared, but the children remained prostrate in prayer for hours afterwards. At nightfall they returned home with the sheep.

Says Lucy:

"In the third apparition, the presence of the angel was still
more intense ... It seemed to deprive us even of the use of our
bodily senses for a long period of time. For several days after-
ward, we performed our physical actions as though sustained by
that same supernatural being who compelled us to do them. The
peace and happiness we felt were great, but intimate, as our souls
were entirely concentrated on God."

For some reason Francisco, who had been present at all three apparitions, had been unable to hear the angel's words. Lucy explained each

angelic message to him. He said, "I love to see the Angel, but the trouble is that later on, we are incapable of doing anything. I could not even walk anymore, I didn't know what was the matter." Lucy agreed: "The physical weariness that overwhelmed us was great."

It is not surprising the children were exhausted. They had joined the ranks of a select group of saints who were granted the grace of receiving Holy Communion from an angel. And no ordinary angel, for Portuguese historians are convinced that the Angel of Peace who prepared the children to meet the Blessed Virgin was none other than the Guardian of Portugal, St. Michael the Archangel.

The Children

At the time of the angel's appearances Lucy was nine, Francisco was eight, and Jacinta was six years of age. Lucy's father, Antonio dos Santos, was the brother of Olimpia Marto, mother of Francisco and Jacinta. It was Lucy's mother, Maria Rosa, and Francisco and Jacinta's father, Manuel ("Ti Marto"), however, who provided the strongest Christian examples to their children.

Lucy was the sixth and last child born of Antonio and Maria dos Santos. She came into the world on March 22, 1907. Like Lucy, Francisco was the sixth child of Ti and Olimpia Marto, born June 11, 1908. Jacinta, born March 11, 1910 was the Martos' last child.

The two families lived in a hamlet called Aljustrel, minutes away from the village of Fatima, which is located about eighty miles north of Lisbon, in a range of rocky hill country called Aire. There is a legend that Fatima was a Moslem princess captured by Crusaders during the reconquest of Spain. She married a Crusader named Goncalo, converted, and was baptized. Fatima died young, however, and the widowed Goncalo joined a monastery. He took his wife's remains with him, and the town that developed around the monastery adopted the name of the converted Moslem princess.

Lucy, Francisco, and Jacinta lived lives typical of peasant children in rural Portugal. They learned to work and pray very early on. In her memoirs Lucy writes, "The first thing I learned was the Hail Mary because my mother had the habit of taking me in her arms while she would teach (the prayer to) my sister Caroline ..."

Life in rural Portugal did not turn on political events, or even newspaper reports on the Great War in Europe. Of greater import were the agricultural seasons (animals and crops were primary sources of income), and the liturgical calendar. There was a tendency to blend the two calendars together, which occasionally caused confusion. For instance, near the feast of Pentecost Lucy overheard her mother asking Antonio what crops were ready to eat. He replied: "The fruits of the Holy Spirit (i.e., the fruits that will be ready for Pentecost) are broad beans, peas and cherries." On Sunday Lucy attended a catechism class, and when the priest asked the children, "What are the fruits of the Holy Spirit?", Lucy confidently replied, "Broad beans, peas, and cherries," to the amusement of all present.

Feast days were village events nearly everyone participated in. On Easter Sunday the parish priest visited each house to give every family a blessing "in the name of the Risen Lord Jesus." Lucy remembered binding the legs of a small lamb, tying a bow and silk ribbon around its neck, and placing it in a wicker basket full of flowers, to present to the priest on his Easter visit. In return the priest let Lucy fill up her dress pockets with sugared almonds before blessing her entire family.

The Rosary, Scripture, and catechetics were the basis of education. In this classroom the stars, as Lucy explained to another girl, were "the candles that Our Lady and the angels light and place at the windows of Heaven to light us on our way." The Portuguese hills helped preserve a way of Christian life that may sound quaint and outdated to modern ears. In 1916 Fatima was a remnant of a fast disappearing Christian civilization, one of the few places left in the world with enough living faith to hear and respond to the intentions of God, as expressed by the Queen of Heaven Herself.

Lucy was a social girl. Affectionate and generous, she liked to entertain by singing and dancing. Thanks to her mother Maria, one of the few women in Fatima who could read, Lucy was precocious in her religious education. She was permitted to receive First Communion at age six, which was unusual for the time. Equally unusual was her loud first Confession: "When my turn came round, I went and knelt at the feet of our dear Lord, represented there in the person of His minister, imploring forgiveness for my sins. When I had finished I noticed that everyone was laughing. My mother called me to her and said, 'My child, don't you know that confession is a secret matter and that it is made in a low voice? Everybody heard you!'"

Her First Communion was quieter. Upon receiving Our Lord Lucy felt herself "bathed in such a supernatural atmosphere that the presence of Our Dear Lord became as clearly perceptible to me as if I had seen and heard Him with my bodily senses":

> "I then addressed my prayer to Him: 'O Lord make me a saint. Keep my heart always pure, for You alone.' Then it seemed that in the depths of my heart Our Lord distinctly spoke these words to me: 'The grace granted to you this day will remain living in your soul, producing fruits of eternal life.' I felt as though transformed in God ... After this I lost the taste and attraction for the things of the world, and only felt at home in some solitary place where, all alone, I could recall the delights of my First Communion."

Francisco and Jacinta Marto loved Lucy, but otherwise they were as unlike each other as any brother and sister could be. Calm and quiet like his father, Francisco tended to avoid the noisy games and dancing of his companions by retiring to high places in the rocky hills to play the flute. He had an indiscriminate love of animals. Ti Marto said his son "played with lizards, and when he came across any snakes he got them to entwine themselves around a stick, and even poured sheep's milk into the holes in the rocks for them to drink." He often brought his reptile companions home with him, a habit that must have delighted his mother.

Despite his peaceful exterior, at times Francisco "could lose his patience and fuss like a young calf." He would tease Jacinta, and she learned how to get even. Their father remembers, "When the two were quarreling and I couldn't tell where the right lay I gave them both a box on the ear for their pains. To put sense into them I had to be a bit strict." Yet Ti Marto admitted Jacinta was his favorite: "She was always so gentle! In this respect she was really remarkable. From the time her mother nursed her she was always like that. She never got angry at anything. We never raised another child like that! It was a natural gift with her."

Jacinta felt things deeply. She wept when Lucy told her of Christ's crucifixion. Lucy wrote, "Many times later she would come and ask me to tell the story again. She would weep and grieve, saying, 'Our poor dear Lord! I'll never sin again. I don't want Our Lord to suffer more.'"

It was Jacinta who pestered her mother into allowing her and Francisco to accompany Lucy's sheep tending duties. Jacinta named the sheep ("Dove", "Star", "Beauty", and "Snow" were some of them). "She used to sit with them," Lucy recalled, "holding and kissing them on her lap. At night she would attempt to carry a little one home on her shoulders, to save it from tiredness, as in pictures of the Good Shepherd she had seen."

Jacinta didn't always wear a halo, however. She could be moody and unpredictable, and as selfish as any other child. The smallest disagreement "was enough to put her into a fit of the sulks", and she tried to shorten the Rosary by saying just the first two words of the Our Father and Hail Mary prayers. Although Jacinta was possessive of Lucy's time, Lucy was less than overjoyed with her company. In her memoirs she recalls, "I sometimes found Jacinta's company quite disagreeable on account of her oversensitive temperament." As for Francisco, Lucy's affection "was just one of kinship ... I myself did not always feel too kindly disposed towards him."

They were, then, normal children, related by blood but with distinct personalities. Although each child accepted without question the faith of their parents to be as right and natural as the air they breathed, it was the Angel of Peace that cemented the friendship between Lucy, Francisco, and Jacinta. Their shared experience, and the profound impression it left on them made the three cousins inseparable companions. There were no more shortcut Rosaries. The children prayed and sacrificed almost continually, and regularly practiced physical mortifications that would have been difficult for healthy, willing adults.

The Lady of Light

While the children practiced a piety beyond their years Europe was changing too, but not in the direction of Heaven. The non-Christian rulers of Portugal involved their country in the Great War. As the killing continued into the spring of 1917, Lucy's brother, Manuel, enlisted in the army and left Aljustrel. Lucy's two older sisters married and also moved out. Lucy's father Antonio had a reputation for liking his wine, a reputation Lucy disputed in her fifth Memoir. In any event, Maria Rosa dos Santos missed her children deeply, and her health failed. Lucy helped as best she could. Saddened by her family's turn of fortune, she often wept and prayed alone. Francisco and Jacinta consoled her. So did the words of the angel: "Above all, accept and endure with submission the suffering the Lord will send you."

Pope Benedict XV was suffering too. On May 5, 1917, he lamented "the cruel war, the suicide of Europe." He invoked "the most holy Virgin" for peace, and added the invocation "Queen of Peace, pray for us" to the Litany of Loreto. He concluded, "We wish the petitions of Her most afflicted children to be directed with lively confidence, more than ever in this awful hour, to the great Mother of God ... that Her most tender and benign solicitude may be moved and the peace we ask for be obtained for our agitated world."

The Pope's letter was as yet unpublished on Sunday, May 13, when Lucy, Francisco, and Jacinta attended morning Mass at St. Anthony's parish in Fatima. Afterwards they herded their sheep towards the hills. It was a beautiful, cloudless spring day spotted with blooming wildflowers. The children drove the sheep about a mile and a half outside Fatima, to a small property owned by Lucy's parents, called Cova da Iria.

As the sheep grazed, the children ate lunch and prayed the Rosary, accompanied by the bells of St. Anthony's. Then they decided to "make a house" out of a small thicket by closing its opening. As Lucy and Jacinta lugged stones for Francisco to pile at the opening, they were all startled by a brilliant flash of light. The stones dropped, and the children ran to a large oak tree for protection against what they thought was a sudden storm. Under the tree they saw a second brilliant flash of light. The children realized now that there were no clouds in the sky. Confused and frightened, they wandered from their shelter. They hadn't gone far when they saw something that stopped them dead in their tracks.

Lucy, Francisco, and Jacinta were standing in front of a holm oak tree, a small evergreen with glossy, sharp foliage that stood about three feet high. On top of the tree, as if resting upon it, was a ball of light. In the center of the ball of light stood a Lady.

She was, said Lucy, "all dressed in white, more brilliant than the sun, and radiated a light more clear and intense than a crystal glass filled with sparkling water, pierced by the burning rays of the sun." She wore a white tunic. A white veil edged with gold covered Her head, hiding Her hair and ears, and descending to Her feet. Her hands were pressed together over Her breast in prayer, and a rosary hung from Her right hand. Standing a yard away from Her, the children were also bathed in the light of the Lady. So dazzling was She that it was difficult to gaze at Her face, which Lucy remembers looking "neither sad nor happy, but serious."

"Do not be afraid. I will not harm you," the Lady said in greeting. Lucy and Jacinta heard Her, Francisco did not. Jacinta did not speak to the Lady, but Lucy did. "Where does Your Grace come from?" she asked. "From Heaven," the Lady replied. "What does Your Grace want from me?" Lucy asked. The Lady answered: "I have come to ask you to come here for six months in succession, on the thirteenth day, at this same hour. Later I will tell you who I am and what I want. Afterwards, I will return here yet a seventh time."

Lucy asked if the children would go to Heaven too. The Lady said she and Jacinta would; Francisco "will go there too, but he will have to say many Rosaries." Lucy asked about two older girls she knew who had recently died. The Lady said one was in Heaven, the other "will be in Purgatory until the end of the world." Then the Lady asked: "Are you willing to offer yourselves to God to endure all the sufferings He may be pleased to send you, as both an act of reparation for the sins with which He is offended, and an act of supplication for the conversion of sinners?"

"Yes, we are willing," answered Lucy. "Well then," said the Lady, "you will have much to suffer. But the grace of God will be your comfort." At these last words the Lady opened Her hands for the first time. From them came "a most intense light that penetrated our breasts reaching the innermost part of our souls, and making us see ourselves in God, Who was that light," Lucy said later. Moved by an inward impulse, the three children spontaneously knelt and prayed: "O Most Holy Trinity, I adore Thee! My God, my God, I love Thee in the Most Blessed Sacrament."

The Lady waited for them to finish the prayer, then said, "Pray the Rosary every day to obtain peace for the world and the end of the war." Then rising in the air and moving eastward, "She disappeared in the immensity of space," said Lucy, adding, "the light that surrounded Her seemed to open up a path before Her in the firmament." The children were alone again.

Reaction

They spent the rest of the afternoon reliving the Lady's appearance. Francisco asked again and again for details of the conversation, and became more and more thoughtful. Unlike the apparitions of the angel, the children were not exhausted after the Lady's visit. As Lucy describes it, "Instead of bodily exhaustion we felt a certain physical strength. In place of annihilation before the Divine Presence, we felt exultation and joy; in place of difficulty of speaking we felt a certain communicative enthusiasm."

Lucy thought it best to keep things a secret, and the other children agreed. On the way home Lucy pressed Jacinta on this point, and her little cousin solemnly assured her she would tell no one about the Lady, not even her own mother. Jacinta's resolve lasted until she saw Ti Marto and Olimpia returning from market. She raced towards them, and her "communicative enthusiasm" eclipsed her promise to Lucy. "Mother!" she burst out, "I saw Our Lady at the Cova da Iria!"

Olimpia laughed. "I believe you, child! Oh, yes, you are such a good saint that you see Our Lady!" Jacinta persisted, breathlessly relating the events of the afternoon. Olimpia questioned Francisco, who confirmed Jacinta's story. After supper Jacinta was questioned again, with occasional interruptions of high humor by her older brothers. Olimpia became annoyed when Jacinta stuck to her story. Ti Marto sat silently by the fireplace, sipping cabbage soup and listening. He knew his children and studied them carefully. He thought to himself, "From the beginning of the world Our Lady has appeared many times in various ways. It was certainly possible She would do so again." He thought about his children: "I always found Francisco truthful, and Jacinta even more so." Moreover, neither child could read or write. How could they repeat such big words they had probably never heard before? How could they dream up, even as a prank, the theological concepts expressed by the Lady? They had received no instruction on these matters. "Why should they lie so outrageously now, when they had always been truthful children?" he asked himself. At the end of the evening of May 13, 1917, Ti Marto quietly made up his mind. Nobody's fool, he was the first to believe the Blessed Virgin Mary had actually come to Cova da Iria.

Lucy awoke the next day to find her secret the talk of the village. She was teased by her older sister, and scolded by Maria Rosa for being such a liar. "She was determined to make me confess that I was telling lies," Lucy wrote, "and to this end she spared neither caresses, nor threats, nor even the broomstick. To all this she received nothing but a mute silence, or the confirmation of all that I had already said."

Maria Rosa proved as stubborn as her daughter. She went to the parish priest, Father Ferreira, who interrogated the children. He was unimpressed by their story. Jacinta didn't help matters. She was so mortified over the trouble Lucy was in because of her own broken promise that she tearfully swore: "I won't ever tell anyone anymore!" This included Father Ferreira, before whom Jacinta was mute.

The reaction of the majority of townsfolk was to dwell on the entertainment value of the story. "Hey, Lucia, is Our Lady going to walk over the roofs today?" laughed the other children. Such remarks drove Maria dos Santos to the brink. She saw Lucy's story as a blow to the family honor. "If you don't say it was a lie," she threatened Lucy, "I will lock you up in a dark room where you will never see the light of the sun again!" She seemed to mean it.

Under these circumstances it is understandable that the children preferred their own company, where they quietly made heroic sacrifices for the conversion of sinners. Only the mysterious vision of God granted the children when the Lady opened Her hands can explain their subsequent love of suffering. Every day they gave their lunch away and ate pine cones and bitter berries instead. They gave up drinking water, even on hot days when their throats were parched. These and other severe penances were practiced every day, and when one of the children weakened, the other two were there for encouragement. Lucy, Francisco, and Jacinta responded to the Lady's question — would they suffer in reparation to God and for sinners? — as if it were the most important question in the world.

The Lady Comes Again

June 13, the day the Lady said She would come again, was also the feast day of St. Anthony of Lisbon (better known as St. Anthony, the wonder worker of Padua). Aside from Christmas and Easter, it was the biggest feast day in Fatima. St. Anthony was one of their own, born in Portugal's capital, Lisbon, Patron Saint of Portugal, and patron of the Fatima parish. Second only to the Blessed Virgin in veneration, St. Anthony's feast day was routinely accompanied by a day-long festival the children of Fatima particularly enjoyed.

Lucy remembers, "My mother and my sisters, who knew how much I loved a festival, kept saying to me: 'We'll see if you leave the festival just to go to the Cova da Iria and talk to that Lady!'" Lucy, Francisco, and Jacinta never wavered. With all due respect to St. Anthony, they were going to see the Lady. After attending morning Mass they set out for Cova da Iria in their best clothes. Their departure was not ignored. Lucy's brother came along to bribe Lucy not to go to Cova da Iria. This hurt her more than the taunts and gibes of passersby. Angry and tearful, she refused the money. Jacinta was also sad; she begged her mother to come to Cova da Iria, and Olimpia refused. When they reached the Cova, the children were dismayed to find about fifty people waiting for them. Expecting more mockery, the children cautiously approached the small holm oak tree.

The adults waiting for them were not believers or unbelievers. They lived in various villages around Fatima, had heard of the Lady's visit, and decided to see for themselves whether anything was really happening at the Cova da Iria. One of them, Maria Carreira, gave the children food, which they took but did not eat. After praying the Rosary the Litany of Loreto was begun, but was interrupted by Lucy, who said there was no time for it. Then Lucy stood and exclaimed: "Jacinta, Our Lady must be coming. There's the lightning!" Only the children saw the lightning, which was actually a reflection of the approaching light. Everyone gathered around the holm oak tree.

Remembers Lucy, "The next moment Our Lady was there on the holm oak, exactly the same as in May." She asked, "What does Your Grace wish of me?" The Lady answered: "I wish you to come here on the thirteenth of next month, to pray the Rosary each day, and to learn to read. Later, I will tell you what I want."

The onlookers saw Lucy kneel at the holm oak tree, and heard her question. They did not see the Lady, and most did not hear her. Maria Carreira was one of the few who, as the Lady spoke to Lucy, heard "the sound of a very faint voice; but we could not understand what it was saying; it was like the buzzing of a bee."

Other witnesses noticed the branches of the holm oak tree were bent down, as if pressed upon by a greater weight. Everyone heard Lucy say: "I would like to ask You to take us to Heaven." The Lady replied: "Yes, I will take Jacinta and Francisco soon. But you are to stay here some time longer. Jesus wishes to make use of you to make Me known and loved. He wants to establish in the world devotion to My Immaculate Heart. To whoever embraces this devotion I promise salvation; these souls shall be dear to God, as flowers placed by Me to adorn His throne."

These remarkable statements were not immediately welcomed by Lucy, for her own nine-year-old heart was broken. She could not go to Heaven with Jacinta and Francisco! What would she do without the only people who understood her? "Am I to stay here alone?" she asked sadly. "No, my daughter," the Lady said. "Do you suffer a great deal? Don't lose heart. I will never forsake you. My Immaculate Heart will be your refuge and the way that will lead you to God."

Lucy recalls, "As Our Lady spoke these words, She opened Her hands, and for the second time She communicated to us the rays of that immense light. We saw ourselves in this light, as it were, immersed in God. Jacinta and Francisco seemed to be in that part of the light that rose to Heaven, and I in that which was poured out on the earth."

The final thing Lucy saw was the Immaculate Heart itself: "In front of the palm of Our Lady's right hand was a heart encircled by thorns which pierced it. We understood that this was the Immaculate Heart of Mary, outraged by the sins of humanity, and seeking reparation."

The onlookers saw none of this, but they saw Lucy stand very quickly, and heard her shout, "Look, there She goes, there She goes!" Maria Carreira heard a sound "somewhat like a rocket, a long way off, as it goes up". And she saw "a little cloud" that "went up gently in the east, until it finally disappeared completely." Only a few others saw this, but everyone observed that after Lucy said the Lady had left, the branches of the holm oak tree "picked up and leaned in the same direction, as if Our Lady, as She left, had let Her dress rest upon the boughs." It was several hours before the branches returned to their original position.

Years later Lucy believed the purpose of Our Lady's second visit was "to infuse within us a special knowledge and love for the Immaculate Heart of Mary, just as on the other two occasions (with the Angel of Peace, and the Lady's first appearance) it was intended to do, as it seems to me, with regard to God and the mystery of the Holy Trinity."

The infusion occurred when the Lady opened Her hands and divine light flooded the children's senses. "From that day onwards," Lucy wrote, "our hearts were filled with a more ardent love for the Immaculate Heart of Mary."

The Next Visit

On the way back home Lucy told Francisco what the Lady had said, for once again he had seen but not heard the Lady. All three agreed that the vision of the Immaculate Heart would be kept secret, and this time Jacinta, her little heart overflowing with love for the beautiful, serious Lady, was as good as her word.

This didn't keep Lucy out of trouble, however. Maria Rosa was very annoyed she had gone to Cova da Iria again, and furious that many of the onlookers believed the Blessed Virgin had appeared. When Lucy timidly asked to learn to read, her good mother blew a gasket. "A lot it matters to Our Lady whether the likes of you can read and write," she huffed. The next day Maria Rosa strode to St. Anthony's rectory. Lucy labored behind her, struggling to keep up. When they arrived Maria Rosa ordered Lucy to tell Father Ferreira she had lied about the Blessed Virgin appearing at Cova da Iria.

Once more Father Ferreira listened to Lucy's account of the apparitions. He concluded that Lucy was sincere, but suggested the apparitions might be "a deceit of the devil." Lucy was terrified, and Maria Rosa was appalled: not only had her youngest child become a pathological liar, she was consorting with demons as well. The long walk home was made even longer for Lucy by her mother's blows, kicks, and hard words.

Later she was consoled and encouraged by Francisco and Jacinta. The two younger children had received their own cross to bear from Father Ferreira, who reluctantly heard their First Confessions, but told them they would have to wait a year to receive First Communion. But Francisco and Jacinta's parents, particularly Ti Marto, were kinder to them than Lucy's family were to her. And unlike Lucy, the two younger children were not having nightmares of the devil grabbing them and dragging them down to hell. After a month of anguish Lucy, on the evening of July 12, told Francisco and Jacinta she was not going to Cova da Iria the next day as the Lady had requested. Lucy's two cousins wept, and Maria Rosa, after calling Lucy "a fine little plaster saint", heaved a sigh of relief.

On the morning of July 13, "when it was nearly time to leave", Lucy recalls, "I suddenly felt I had to go, impelled by a strange force that I could hardly resist." She ran to the Marto house, and found her cousins weeping and praying in their room. Francisco and Jacinta had prayed through the night that Lucy would change her mind, and on seeing her implored her to come with them to Cova da Iria. "Yes, I'm going," Lucy said. They sped out of the house and into the Portuguese summer heat.

Olimpia saw them leave and told Maria Rosa, who sagged at the news. Neither mother believed the Blessed Virgin was appearing at Cova da Iria, but they resolved to follow the children there. To guard against "deceits of the devil" Maria Rosa and Olimpia took, as weapons, blessed candles and matches, intending perhaps to give the devil a hot foot if he appeared. Within the hour, they had joined a surprisingly large crowd (about five thousand) on Cova da Iria.

Ti Marto was there too; he had seen the crowds and wanted to protect the children. He fought through the crush of people to position himself near Jacinta. Lucy led the Rosary and some of the crowd answered. When it ended Ti Marto saw Lucy rise "so quickly that it seemed as if she were pulled up." Lucy looked to the east and Ti Marto heard her call: "Our Lady is coming!" "I looked as hard as I could," he remembers, "but could see nothing."

As the apparition began, however, Ti Marto saw "what looked like a little grayish cloud resting on the oak tree, and the sun's heat lessened, and there was a delicious fresh breeze. It hardly seemed like the height of summer." Others close to the three children also saw the cloud on the tree, and felt the temperature cool. Still others noticed the sun seem to decrease in brightness, and the atmosphere appear to turn golden yellow.

After Lucy asked, "What does Your Grace want of me?", Ti Marto heard a "buzzing" sound. What Lucy and Jacinta (but again, not Francisco) heard was the Lady's response: "I want you to come here on the thirteenth of next month, and to continue praying the Rosary every day in honor of Our Lady of the Rosary, in order to obtain peace for the world and the end of the war, because only She can help you."

Lucy asked the Lady Her name, and requested She work a miracle so everyone would believe the Lady was really there. She replied, "Continue to come here every month. In October, I will tell you who I am and what I want, and I will perform a miracle for all to see and believe."

Then the Lady instructed the children: "Sacrifice yourselves for sinners, and say many times, especially when you make some sacrifice: O Jesus, it is for love of Thee, for the conversion of sinners, and in reparation for the sins committed against the Immaculate Heart of Mary."

The Secret

After She spoke these words the Lady opened Her hands as She had done on Her previous visits. Today, however, there was no divine light revealing the love of God and His sorrow for sin (the first apparition), or the Immaculate Heart of Mary, wounded by thorns of sin (the second apparition). Instead the children saw the rays of light from the Lady's hand penetrate the earth to reveal a sea of fire. It was hell.

Lucy remembers the vision vividly. "Plunged in this fire were demons and souls in human form, like transparent burning embers" floating, rising, and falling "without weight or equilibrium, amid shrieks and groans of pain and despair, which horrified us and filled us with fear. The demons could be distinguished by their terrifying and repellent likeness to frightful and unknown animals, black and transparent like burning coals."

Years later Lucy said the terrible vision lasted only an instant, "thanks to our Good Mother in Heaven, Who in the first apparition had promised to take us to Heaven. Were it not for that I believe we would have died out of fright and fear."

The vision ended, and the Lady, in tones serious and tender, told Lucy, Francisco, and Jacinta what has become known as the Secret of Fatima.

"You have seen hell, where the souls of poor sinners go. To save them God wishes to establish in the world devotion to My Immaculate Heart. If what I say to you is done, many souls will be saved and there will be peace. The war is going to end, but if people do not cease offending God, a worse one will break out during the reign of Pius XI. When you see a night illumined by an unknown light, know that this is the great sign given you by God that He is about to punish the world for its crimes by means of wars, famine, and persecution of the Church and of the Holy Father.

"To prevent this I shall come to ask for the consecration of Russia to My Immaculate Heart, and the Communion of Reparation on the First Saturdays. If My requests are heeded, Russia will be converted and there will be peace; if not, she will spread her errors throughout the world, causing wars and persecutions of the Church. The good will be martyred, the Holy Father will have much to suffer, various nations will be annihilated ...

(It is likely that the Third Secret appears at this point in the Blessed Virgin's prophecy. It begins "In Portugal the dogma of the faith will always be preserved etc." and was first revealed in Sister Lucy's memoirs, tacked discreetly onto the end of the Blessed Virgin's message.) "In the end, My Immaculate Heart will triumph. The Holy Father will consecrate Russia to me, and a certain period of peace will be granted to the world."

After revealing the Secret the Lady concluded Her instructions to the children: "Do not tell this to anybody. Francisco, yes, you may tell him. When you say the Rosary, say after each mystery, 'O my Jesus, forgive us, save us from the fire of hell. Lead all souls to Heaven, especially those most in need."

The Lady ascended toward the east, and the crowd heard what Ti Marto called "a large clap of thunder." The onlookers, who were remarkably silent during the apparition, considering they couldn't see or hear the Lady, now threatened to overwhelm the children. Ti Marto grabbed Jacinta and elbowed his way roughly through the crowd, his youngest daughter clinging to his neck. Lucy and Francisco escaped by and by, and were reunited with Jacinta at the bottom of the hill. Here they were offered their first ride in a mysterious new invention called the automobile. They accepted, and a kind and curious out-of-towner drove the exhausted children (and Ti Marto) back to Aljustrel.

NOTES

There is little disagreement among Fatima scholars and researchers about the central facts of the Fatima apparitions. The primary source is, of course, Sister Lucy's Memoirs. The other sources listed below were also used for Chapters 1-4 of this work, but to avoid repetition will only be listed once, here.

Barthas, Canon, *Our Lady of Light*, World Wide Message of Fatima, The Bruce Publishing Company, 1947.

Borelli, Antonio A., John R. Spann, Plinio Correa de Oliveira, *Our Lady at Fatima: Prophecies of Tragedy or Hope for America and the World?* The American Society for the Defense of Tradition, Family and Property, 1985.

Haffert, John, *Meet The Witnesses*, Ave Maria Institute, 1961.

Johnston, Francis, *Fatima: The Great Sign*, Tan Books and Publishers, Inc., 1980.

Kondor, Father Louis, Editor. *Fatima In Lucia's Own Words* (Sister Lucia's Memoirs), 9th Edition, Ravengate Press, 1995. In this edition Father Kondor asserts that the consecration of Russia to the Immaculate Heart of the Blessed Virgin Mary had been successfully performed by Pope John Paul II. Fatima experts dispute this claim. For what it's worth, so do I.

De Marchi, John, *The Immaculate Heart, The True Story of Our Lady of Fatima*, Farrar, Straus, and Young, New York, 1952.

De Marchi, John, *The Crusade of Fatima, The Lady More Brilliant Than The Sun*, English translation by Fathers Branco and Kelly, P.J. Kenedy & Sons, New York, 1948.

Thomas McGlynn, O.P., *Vision of Fatima*, Little, Brown And Company, Boston, 1950.

Frère Michel de la Sainte Trinité, *The Whole Truth About Fatima*, Volume I, *Science and Facts*, CRC 1984, English translation published by Immaculate Heart Publications, 1989. (Hereinafter referred to as TWTAF, Vol. I).

Frère Michel de la Sainte Trinité, *The Whole Truth About Fatima*, Volume II, *The Secret and the Church*, CRC 1984, English translation published by Immaculate Heart Publications, 1989. (Hereinafter referred to as TWTAF, Vol. II).

Joseph Pelletier, A.A., *The Sun Danced at Fatima*, *A Critical Story of the Apparitions,* The Caron Press, Worcester, Mass., 1951.

Monsignor Finbar Ryan, O.P., *Our Lady of Fatima*, Browne and Nolan Limited, 1940.

Walsh, William Thomas, *Our Lady of Fatima*, The MacMillan Company, 1947.

Chapter Two

The Divine Seal

After the Lady's third appearance, the events at Cova da Iria were noticed by the press. The Catholic press was reserved and skeptical. The secular press was happier about the apparitions, as they provided not only entertainment, but fodder for anti-Catholic editors as well. For instance, after thoroughly ridiculing the apparitions, the Lisbon daily newspaper *O Seculo* advanced a remarkable conspiracy theory: the dastardly Jesuits had duped three illiterate peasant children into manufacturing a supernatural sideshow in order to fleece the faithful, and line Church coffers with the profits.

Less fantastic but equally insulting were the attempts of some journalists to portray the children as demented, psychotic, or epileptic, and to explain away what was seen at Cova da Iria as mass hypnosis. These themes would increase in intensity as the appearances of the Blessed Virgin reached their tremendous, fable-shattering conclusion on October 13. Only then would the secular press be forced, for the moment anyway, to print a semblance of the truth. Back at Aljustrel, Lucy, Francisco, and Jacinta spent much of their time hiding or fleeing from curiosity-seekers, pilgrims, and the idle rich. With a few exceptions, relatives and neighbors became even more hostile towards the children as the apparitions became publicized.

Lucy, in particular, became a lightning rod for abuse. She was punched, kicked, threatened, and insulted when she appeared alone in public. Curiously, much of this ill treatment came from the women at St. Anthony's parish in Fatima. At home Lucy continued to get the business end of a broomstick from her mother. Even her father, previously indifferent to the events at Fatima, now turned against her. Antonio was understandably upset that the crowds (and horses) at Cova da Iria had not only destroyed the family's vegetable gardens but had trampled the ground so thoroughly that it was beyond cultivation. The appearances of the Lady had, indirectly, hit the dos Santos family hard in the pocketbook.

Consequently, when Lucy dared ask for a piece of bread at meal times her sisters would snap, "Go and eat what you find growing at Cova da Iria!" And Maria Rosa would add, "Yes, ask that Lady to give you something to eat." Lucy got used to going to bed hungry. Her only solace was the time she spent with Francisco and Jacinta, although the vision of hell turned their conversations quite somber. The three reminded themselves that the Lady had told them they would "have much to suffer", and with a spiritual maturity beyond their years offered their trials to God, for the conversion of sinners, and in reparation for offenses against the Immaculate Heart of Mary. Little did Lucy, Francisco, and Jacinta know that they were about to enter a new phase of suffering, courtesy of a Freemason unaffectionately nicknamed "the Tinsmith."

The Masonic Interlude

His real name was Arturo de Oliveira Santos. Baptized Catholic, at one time he made a living as a smithy. He joined the Grand Orient Lodge in Leiria (a little north and west of Fatima) just as the Masonic revolution of 1910 was toppling the Portuguese government. Robbing the Church has often been a profitable business, and so it was with the Tinsmith. After seizing Church property and imprisoning or exiling hundreds of priests and nuns, the revolution rewarded the promising Arturo by making him chief administrator of the Portuguese district that included Fatima and Aljustrel.

The Tinsmith had a printing press at his headquarters in Ourem (several miles north and east of Fatima), from which he published *The Voice of Ourem*, a fiercely anti-Catholic journal of enlightened opinion. Arturo was barely thirty when he was appointed to Ourem, a post which appeared to be a stepping stone to bigger and better positions within the Brotherhood. His only stumbling stone was the strange occurrences at Cova da Iria, and the unaccountable attraction they held for thousands of people in his district. Santos promised his superiors he would — in the name of Liberty and Freedom — stamp out these last vestiges of medieval superstition by making an example of Lucy, Francisco, and Jacinta. He commanded the children to appear before him at Ourem on August 11, two days before the next apparition.

Ti Marto disobeyed the summons. He refused to make Francisco and Jacinta walk nine miles to Ourem, but went there himself to tell this to the Tinsmith in person. Antonio dos Santos was less concerned about Lucy, and put her on a donkey. It was a rough road and Lucy fell off several times. She arrived at Ourem bruised and dirty. A formal court proceeding awaited her. The Tinsmith was unhappy that Francisco and Jacinta failed to appear, but he was unable to intimidate Ti Marto. Then it was Lucy's turn. She remembers: "The Administrator was determined to force me to reveal the Secret and to promise him never again to return to Cova da Iria. To attain this end he spared neither promises, nor even threats. Seeing that he was getting nowhere, he dismissed me, protesting however, that he would achieve his end, even if this meant that he had to take my life."

It was quite an ordeal for a ten-year-old. So was the long trip back home on the rough roads, with her father berating Lucy for being such a troublemaker. The difference between her father and Ti Marto could not have been clearer to Lucy, or more painful. "But I must be patient," she told herself, "since this means I have the happiness of suffering more for the love of You, O my God, and for the conversion of sinners."

Two days later, on the morning of August 13, 1917, Arturo Santos unexpectedly appeared at the Marto house. Lucy was fetched. A smiling Tinsmith told the children that he too wished to view the miracle on Cova da Iria. But first he took the children, in a carriage, to Father Ferreira's rectory to be interrogated. Afterwards he ordered them back in the carriage, and started down the road to Cova da Iria. At the opportune moment a sharp turn off the road was made, the horse was whipped, and the carriage disappeared in a cloud of dust. The children had been kidnapped.

Arturo's plan was audacious, but simple. Without the children the event at Cova da Iria would be a failure. The wrath was likely to fall on Father Ferreira, at least at first. Meanwhile, he would have the time and the means to force a confession from the children, without the strong presence of Ti Marto. The interrogation he had in mind took some time to set up, so Lucy, Jacinta, and Francisco spent their first day of captivity at the Tinsmith's house. His wife fed the children, and they played with the Tinsmith's children, who were also three, with the interesting names of "Democracia", "Republica", and "Libertade". Unbeknownst to the Tinsmith, his wife was enough of a Catholic to have had the three children with the unfortunate names baptized.

The next morning, August 14, Lucy, Francisco, and Jacinta were interrogated by an elderly lady. Then they were interrogated separately by the Tinsmith, who unsuccessfully tried to bribe each of the children. Next he tried to enlist a doctor to diagnose the children as mentally ill. This failed too, and the Tinsmith lost his temper and put the children in the public jail. They wept and offered their sufferings to God, as the Lady and the Angel of Peace had instructed them. Most heartbreaking for the three was the thought that they had missed their appointment with the Lady. Jacinta also wept because she was sure she would never see her parents again.

While in prison Lucy, Francisco, and Jacinta were again interrogated separately, in a private room. Reunited again in the prison cell, the children were informed they would be fried alive in boiling oil unless they told the Secret. The other prisoners took pity on the young, weeping waifs and urged them to tell the Secret. "Never!" Jacinta snapped. The children began praying the Rosary. After a few decades the prisoners knelt and joined the prayer. Most likely they were a collection of drunks, vagabonds, and petty criminals; Lucy describes them as "young thieves", but notes, "they were polite with us."

The children were removed from the cell and taken to the Tinsmith's office. He melodramatically asked a stooge if the oil was boiling, and was told it was. Then he asked again about the Secret. The children refused to tell. The Tinsmith ordered Jacinta thrown in the cauldron. She cried and prayed as the police guards grabbed her and took her away. Francisco prayed an *Ave Maria* "so that Jacinta won't be afraid" and confided to Lucy: "If they kill us as they say, we will soon be in Heaven. How wonderful! Nothing else matters!"

The guard came back and snarled, "She's fried, now for the next one!" He grabbed Francisco and hauled him away. The Tinsmith bore down on Lucy, now all alone. Terror drove away the Lady's remark that Lucy would live longer than her young cousins. Convinced she was about to die, she nevertheless refused to tell the Tinsmith the Lady's Secret. She too was seized and taken out of the room to ... another room holding Francisco and Jacinta. Astonished to be alive, the children now knew there was no boiling cauldron, excepting perhaps the flushed countenance of the Tinsmith.

Arturo's failure was complete. The young Freemason had tried nearly everything: kidnapping, bribery, imprisonment, and terroristic threats; yet he had been unable to wrest a secret from three illiterate peasant children. Worse yet, he had not even been able to get the children to contradict each other. Not once. The forces of enlightenment had been routed by three unwashed Catholic kids. Score one for medieval superstition.

The Tinsmith returned the children to Father Ferreira on August 15, the feast of the Assumption. Forgetting for the moment their own ill treatment of Lucy, Francisco, and Jacinta, the citizens of Fatima picked up sticks and stones and headed for Arturo, whose quick departure saved him from being thrashed, or worse. In the canonical investigation that followed, the Tinsmith did not deny his kidnapping of the children, or his threats to boil them in oil. The extraordinary way in which the children conducted themselves whilst in his clutches disappointed Arturo de Oliveira Santos, but did not cause him to question his loyalty to the occult Brotherhood. He returned to Ourem to bide his time.

The August Apparitions

Although the children were not present at Cova da Iria on August 13, an estimated eighteen thousand people gathered to wait for the Lady. As news of the kidnapping spread, the restless crowd became angry and loud. They were silenced by a clap of thunder and a flash of lightning. Maria Carreira recalled, "We began to see a little cloud, very delicate, very white, which stopped for a few moments over the (holm oak) tree, and then rose in the air and disappeared."

Many witnesses noticed a change in atmosphere that caused everything to reflect the colors of the rainbow, and made leaves on trees appear to be flowers. These unusual events caused the large crowd to believe that the Lady had indeed come, but not finding the children, had left. This reminded them of their anger at the Tinsmith. In his absence, the crowd accused Father Ferreira of conspiring to abduct the children. Feelings were so strong the priest published a letter denying the charges, and stating, for the first time, that there may actually be something supernatural happening at Cova da Iria.

After Mass the following Sunday, August 19, Lucy, Francisco, and his older brother John were tending sheep at a place called Valinhos, very near to Aljustrel. After a time Lucy noticed the air had cooled. Looking up she saw the sun was dimmed. She felt the familiar feeling she had prior to the Lady's other appearances. Lucy turned to Francisco, who looked at her with the same awareness on his face. But this wasn't Cova da Iria, and Jacinta wasn't with them!

They asked John to run and fetch Jacinta. He refused, wanting to stay and see the Lady. Lucy promised John four pennies (a lot of money at the time) if he went and got Jacinta. John sprinted off as a flash of lightning rent the air. A few minutes later lightning flashed again. Lucy and Francisco turned and saw, in the distance, little Jacinta running towards them, arms flailing and legs pumping. She and John arrived, breathless. As if waiting for Jacinta, the brilliant Lady immediately appeared to them, standing just above yet another holm oak tree. She looked very beautiful, and as serious as always, but Her gaze was tender.

Lucy asked her usual question: "*Que e que Vocemece me quere?*" What is it that You want of me? The Lady answered, "I want you to continue going to the Cova da Iria on the thirteenth, and continue praying the Rosary every day. In the last month I will perform a miracle so that all may believe."

Lucy asked what to do with the money given by pilgrims. The Lady told her and the other children to carry litters in a procession, and to use the money in the litters for a chapel for Our Lady of the Rosary. Lucy asked for the healing of some sick people she knew. The Lady said that some of the people Lucy mentioned would be cured that year. Here the Lady looked sadder, and Lucy writes, "She recommended anew the practice of mortification, saying lastly, 'Pray, pray very much, and make sacrifices for sinners; for many souls go to hell because there are none to sacrifice and to pray for them.'"

Then She rose and disappeared into the east. John was disappointed because he had seen nothing. As usual, Francisco had seen the Lady but had not heard Her. Lucy and Jacinta saw and heard the Lady, but Lucy was the only one who spoke to her. Jacinta's silence was out of character; a chatterbox much of the time, in the presence of the Lady she tended to be tongue-tied.

September 13, 1917

In the weeks before the Lady's next appearance, the hostility towards the children lessened. The many credible witnesses of the unusual events at Cova da Iria began to have an impact on the people of Fatima.

In addition, the children's courage under the captivity of the Tinsmith endeared them to many. Others figured that any enemies of the Tinsmith couldn't be all bad. The insults and blows decreased.

Ti Marto had quietly believed Francisco and Jacinta from the first apparition. Now Olimpia began to trust her children more as well. Their abduction had devastated her, and given her a new appreciation of her two youngest ones. The only remaining obstacle for Olimpia Marto was a conviction that her family was not worthy of the honor being bestowed upon them by the Queen of Heaven.

Lucy's lot improved too. Maria dos Santos was not a tender woman; softness was a luxury she could ill afford. The kidnapping of little Lucy changed her though, and upon her daughter's return Maria was noticeably more protective of her youngest child. As Lucy put it, "My mother also began during this month to find a little more peace." Her older sister, Maria dos Anjos, agrees: "Our mother began to be shaken up, and our father also began to be less opposed to Lucy."

The lives of Lucy, Francisco, and Jacinta would never be care-free again, however. The Tinsmith sent three thugs to Aljustrel to intimidate the children, and remind them of his threat to murder them. And a certain Jose do Vale, a journalist and Freemason, organized a large group of like-minded progressives to meet at Fatima to demonstrate against the Jesuit plot at Cova da Iria. The Sunday before September 13 the group gathered outside St. Anthony's parish. There was no one to insult, however, as Father Ferreira had gotten wind of their plan and had Sunday Mass said at a church two miles away.

Irritated at being outfoxed, the friends of progress stalked to Cova da Iria and labored uphill. Hot and dusty at the summit, they found themselves outfoxed once more. A thoughtful peasant had tied a pack of burros to a tree near where the Lady appeared. Upon seeing the well-dressed out-of-towners, the peasant set them to braying madly, about as raucous and unpleasant a welcome as can be imagined. To make sure the liberals got the point, the peasant had piled straw and feed near the little holm oak tree — "as if to welcome a delegation of asses."

A group of Catholics, led by Maria Carreira, began heckling the would-be hecklers, calling out: "*O burros, o bestas!*" "Burros, beasts!" This was the last straw, so to speak, and the progressives began hollering back, "*Botas de serra!*" "Mountain clodhoppers!" The sophisticated debate ended with the arrival of the police, and the forces of enlightenment trudged away, grumbling about Jesuits and peasants.

The apparition of September 13 drew the largest crowd yet to Cova da Iria. Some 30,000 gathered there before noon. Many had arrived the previous day and spent the night outdoors. Just before midday Lucy, Francisco, and Jacinta were helped through the crowd, and knelt at the holm oak tree. Lucy led the Rosary, and the crowd answered with more devotion than ever before. Then a roar went up, and hundreds of hands pointed to the cloudless sky. A priest, Monsignor Joao Quaresma, recalled: "To my great astonishment I saw clearly and distinctly a luminous globe that moved from the east toward the west, slowly and majestically gliding down across the distance ... all those who were near us observed what we did, for on all sides were heard manifestations of joy and greetings to Our Lady."

As the globe of light neared the holm oak tree the sun dimmed so noticeably that stars could be seen. The atmosphere turned golden yellow. The globe of light disappeared and the shortest of all the apparitions began.

"What do You want of me?" Lucy asked. The Lady replied, "Continue to say the Rosary to obtain the end of the war. In October Our Lord will come, as well as Our Lady of Sorrows and Our Lady of Carmel. Saint Joseph will appear with the child Jesus to bless the world."

The Lady continued, "God is pleased with your sacrifices. He does not want you to sleep with the rope on, but only to wear it during the daytime." This was a reference to a thick, rough-fibered cord Lucy found in the streets of Aljustrel. The children divided it in thirds, and each wrapped the coarse rope under their shirts and around their waists. The constant chafing often made Jacinta weep, and gave the children little rest at night. This was only one of the mortifications regularly practiced by the little seers.

Lucy then mentioned to the Lady the many requests for healings she had received. The Lady answered, "Yes, I will cure some, but not others, because Our Lord does not trust them." Lucy presented some gifts, asking: "I have been given these things. Do You want them?" The Lady replied, "These are not needed in Heaven." After reminding the children that "In October I will perform a miracle so that all may believe", She rose and disappeared into the heavens. A shout went up as many in the crowd bid farewell to the luminous globe in the sky, visible once more as it moved eastward.

During the apparition a majority of the crowd witnessed a "rain of flowers" — thousands of small, white, petal-like forms floating down from the sky that disappeared when they neared the ground. Those close to the holm oak tree during the apparition saw a "pleasant looking cloud" above the holm oak tree. The cloud rose, disappeared, then re-appeared to rise again, almost as if "some invisible thurifers were incensing the vision liturgically."

Not everyone saw these things, but the many who did spread the news. Lucy told the crowd the Lady intended to perform a miracle at Her next visit. For the next few weeks the tension grew unbearable as believers and non-believers, Catholics and "Free-Thinkers" alike anticipated October 13 with hope and fear.

The Last Apparition

As the great day approached the fondness Antonio and Maria dos Santos had rediscovered for Lucy vanished like smoke before a stiff breeze. They had never believed the Blessed Virgin was appearing to their daughter, so when the family was threatened with violence if the miracle was a failure, Antonio and Maria descended on Lucy like goblins. Her sister Maria dos Anjos recalls: "As the thirteenth of the month drew closer we kept telling Lucy that she should forget all these wild stories she had invented, because otherwise all of us would suffer. My father was difficult with her, and especially when he was drinking, he was very, very bad, except that he did not beat her. It was my mother who did that."

Much of Portugal was becoming unhinged, and all the loose cannons began rolling towards Fatima. Thoughtless pilgrims invaded the Marto home looking for relics. Masonic journalists artfully laughed the whole thing to scorn, yet somehow could not stop writing about Fatima, often in violent fashion. The threat of violence hung everywhere. Maria dos Anjos says, "We kept hearing reports that if the miracle was a failure our house would be bombed. We were terror-stricken, and our neighbors believed it too. In our fear it seems that we believed everything, and everyone, but Lucy ... only the children remained unexcited."

On October 11 a hard rain began to lash Portugal. With it came a gale wind that tore at the wet skin of the tens of thousands slogging to Fatima in ankle-deep mud. Despite the wretched conditions, they camped out early at Cova da Iria in anticipation of the great event. At night the crowd noise could be heard in Aljustrel. Perhaps Maria Rosa heard it too, for at dawn on October 12 she woke Lucy and insisted they go to confession immediately. Prodding her sleepy daughter, Maria Rosa persisted: "We will probably be killed tomorrow in the Cova da Iria — do you hear me! If your Lady does not perform Her miracle the people will attack us!"

"Oh, Momma, please," Lucy groaned.

Maria Rosa raised her voice. "*Kill* us, I said, daughter. And so we had better go to confession. We had better be prepared." At this point Maria Rosa's anxiety lapsed into deep fatigue. Helpless from nervous exhaustion, she awaited the next day with bleakest dread.

The rain and tree-bending wind woke Maria Rosa on October 13. Convinced it was Lucy's last day on earth, Maria Rosa was very kind to her. When the time came for Lucy to go to Cova da Iria, Maria Rosa drew herself up and announced she was going too: "If my daughter is going to die, I want to die with her."

She apparently wanted Antonio to die as well, for she dragged him along, with Lucy, to the Marto house. It was already filled with muddy pilgrims and Olimpia's shrieking. Everyone was wet, cold, muddy, and hysterical — except for the three children and Ti Marto. They set out for Cova da Iria, "into such a rain as you never did see," he remembered.

Unlike Antonio and Maria Rosa, Ti Marto was unimpressed by threats of violence against him: "I'm going, because I have faith in all the children have said." Good as his word, he chaperoned Jacinta all the way to the holm oak tree, laden with rain-pelted flowers and soaked, drooping ribbons to honor the Blessed Virgin. "The crush of people here was so great and frightening that Jacinta began to cry," he remembered. Some well dressed ladies knelt down in the mud as the children passed, as if worshipping them. Ti Marto shook his head: "My good people, you must leave the children alone." A man came at him with a stick, was restrained by the crowd, and disappeared.

Lucy and Francisco joined Jacinta. Ti Marto stood nearby, calm and alert. Also near the children was the other early believer in the apparitions, Maria Carreira; it was she who had placed the bouquets on the holm oak tree. As minutes passed and nothing happened, a priest begin to badger Lucy about when she had said the Lady would appear. Then he announced: "It is past noon now. Cannot all you people see that this is just a delusion? That it is nonsense? Go home everyone, go home!"

He began pushing the children. Lucy wept, but stayed put. The crowd murmured restlessly. In the background a soft chorus of *Ave Marias* kept time with the plunking of raindrops on raised umbrellas. More minutes passed. Lucy abruptly called out for people to close their umbrellas. Most did, although it was still raining. More waiting. Then Lucy called: "Oh, Jacinta, get on your knees, Our Lady is coming. I already saw the lightning!"

Maria Rosa dos Santos, who had struggled to the inner circle around her daughter, gripped her bottle of holy water more tightly and wailed, "Watch out, daughter! Don't let yourself be deceived!" Lucy never heard her. She and Jacinta and Francisco were kneeling at the holm oak tree. The rain fell on their upturned faces. They were in ecstasy. The apparition had begun.

The next voice was Jacinta's. Poking Lucy she said, "Speak Lucy, Our Lady is already here!" Overcome by the beauty and brilliance of the lady of light, Lucy had to take some deep breaths before asking her usual question: "What do You want of me?" The Lady answered, "I want a chapel built here in My honor. I want you to continue saying the Rosary every day. The war will end soon, and the soldiers will return to their homes."

"Yes," Lucy echoed. Then, remembering the Lady's promise, she asked, "Will You tell me Your name?" "I am the Lady of the Rosary." There was a long, reverent silence. Then Lucy said, "I have many petitions from many people. Will you grant them?" "Some I will grant, and others I must deny," the Lady replied. "People must amend their lives and ask forgiveness for their sins." Sadness passed over Her face. "They must not offend Our Lord anymore, for He is already too much offended."

"Do you want anything more?" Lucy asked. "Nothing more," said the Lady. She rose slowly, almost as if She did not want Her last visit with the three children to end. Then She opened Her delicate hands, and Her palms faced the dark sky. The rain stopped and the clouds scattered, revealing the sun. Rays of light issued from Her hands, and streamed directly into the sun. Although transfixed by the Lady's majestic ascent, Lucy was moved by "an inner impulse" to shout, "Look at the sun!"

Thousands of pairs of eyes did just that for the next ten minutes. There was not one destroyed retina, for as Ti Marto explained, "We looked easily at the sun, which did not blind us." Avelino de Almeida, journalist, Freemason, and Editor in Chief of the Lisbon daily *O Seculo*, agreed: "It is possible to fix one's eyes on it without the least damage to the eye. It does not burn the eyes. It does not blind them."

Almeida described the sun as "a dull silver disc." Another witness, Portuguese university science professor Dr. Almeida Garrett, disagreed. The sun, he said, "was a clearer, richer, brighter color ... it looked like a glazed wheel made of mother-of-pearl." This was all remarkable enough: the sudden ending of the rain, the dispersion of the clouds, and the mother-of-pearl sun that could be viewed without retina damage. Yet it was merely a prelude to the miracle that the Lady of the Rosary had been predicting for the past three months.

What happened next almost defies imagination. Maria Carreira said the sun "shook and trembled." The Masonic editor Almeida wrote: "the sun trembled, (and) made sudden incredible movements outside all cosmic laws." Ti Marto recalled, "the sun seemed to stop and then began to move and dance." The phrase used most often, by Catholics and unbelievers alike, to describe this phenomena was that "the sun danced." It did so three times in succession.

Then the sun "spun round upon itself in a mad whirl," according to Dr. Garrett. "It seemed like a wheel of fire," said Maria Carreira. A reporter for another Lisbon daily, *O Dia*, wrote that the sun "was seen to whirl and turn in the circle of broken clouds." Yet another secular newspaper, *Ordem*, reported that the sun "seemed to be in an exceedingly fast and whirling movement, at times appearing to be loosened from the sky ..." A priest, Father Manuel Pereira da Silva, said the sun "came down as if to the height of the clouds and began to whirl giddily upon itself like a captive ball of fire."

(In passing, let it be noted that Father da Silva came to Cova da Iria only to satisfy himself that the apparitions were a complete fraud. Prior to the miracle of the sun he was a hostile critic of the Fatima seers. His skepticism was widely shared among the clergy, as evidenced by the priest who berated the children prior to the appearance of the Blessed Virgin on October 13, 1917. The Church had been badly scarred by the Masonic revolution in Portugal, and in the ensuing years the Masonic press seemed intent on keeping the wounds open by its continual baiting and slandering of Christ's Church. Consequently the clergy were defensive, and perhaps overly sensitive to anything resembling the "medieval superstition" lampooned so effectively, and so repeatedly in the secular press.)

After watching the sun "dance" for "about eight minutes", Father da Silva said, "the atmosphere darkened, and the features of each became yellow." Maria Carreira said the sun "produced different colors: yellow, blue, white ..." Dr. Garrett at first saw "everything an amethyst color". Then "everything both near and far had changed, taking on the color of old yellow damask ... My own hand was the same color." Ti Marto said the sun "shot rays in different directions, and painted everything in different colors."

The colors were everywhere: on people, on the earth, in the air. Even shadows donned, in succession, all the colors of the rainbow, courtesy of the sun that the Lady of the Rosary had opened Her palms toward. This phenomenon was witnessed not only by the tens of thousands of witnesses overflowing Cova da Iria, but 40 kilometers away from Fatima as well. Half that distance away one Inacio Lourenco remembers: "During those long minutes of the solar phenomenon objects all about us reflected all the colors of the rainbow. We saw ourselves blue, yellow, red, etc. ..." Then, as the secular reporter from *Ordem* noted, the sun appeared to "detach itself from the sky, to approach the earth and to radiate strong heat." In this understated account of the sun hurtling itself towards the earth at high speed, we have an objectivity that borders on surrealism. Another witness, the science professor Dr. Garrett, remembers the fall of the sun a bit more vividly: "Then, suddenly, one heard a clamor, a cry of anguish breaking from all the people. The sun, whirling wildly, seemed to loosen itself from the firmament and advance threateningly upon the earth as if to crush us with its huge and fiery weight. The sensation during those moments was terrible." "It was a terrible moment," Ti Marto agreed. The sun "was being detached from the sky and was falling on us." The sun was "a wheel of fire which was going to fall on the people," Maria Carreira remembered. Another witness, Alfredo Santos, saw the sun "hurtle upon us like a wheel of flame." His wife fainted and he fell to his knees in the mud. Yet another witness, Father John Gomes Menitra, remembers "seeing the sun fall on us." Jose Joaquim da Assuncao said, "The sun began spinning as though in a sort of box. All the people cried: 'It comes down! It comes down!'"

Believers and unbelievers saw the same thing. Mario Godinho, an agnostic engineer, took his pious mother to Cova da Iria, but remained in his car. He saw the sun, "like a disc of smoked glass illuminated behind and turning over itself, giving us the impression that it was coming down over our heads ... Then I believed. I was sure I had not been the victim of suggestion. I saw that sun as I never saw it again."

Miles from Cova da Iria, Inacio Lourenco saw the sun "come down in a zigzag, menacing the earth. Terrified, I ran and hid myself among the people, who were weeping and expecting the end of the world at any moment. Near us was an unbeliever who had spent the morning mocking the simpletons who had gone off to Fatima ... He now seemed to be paralyzed, his eyes fixed on the sun. Afterwards he trembled from head to foot, and lifting up his arms fell on his knees in the mud, crying, 'Nossa Senhora! Nossa Senhora!' Our Lady! Our Lady!"

And at Fatima, the once skeptical Father Manuel da Silva said, "When I saw the sun fall zigzag, I fell on my knees. I thought the end of the world had come." This was the nearly unanimous reaction of the tens of thousands of onlookers: they were witnessing the end of the world. Nearly everyone fell to the mud, either in a faint or on their knees in prayer, begging God to forgive them their sins. Even decades later witnesses would describe the falling of the sun with a shudder.

When the falling sun neared the horizon line it stopped, and returned to its normal position, "tracing a sort of winding ellipse as it went," according to another former skeptic, one Baron de Alvaiazere. "When the people realized that the danger was over," Inacio Lourenco recalls, "there was an explosion of joy, and everyone joined in thanksgiving and praise to Our Lady." The Miracle of the Sun — and there is absolutely no question that this was indeed a miracle — was over, to the vast relief of all. Only then was it noticed that, despite the hours (and for many, the days) spent in the rain, everyone's clothes were now bone dry.

The Fatima Message

The seers were nearly torn limb from limb by excited witnesses. The Freemason Almeida noted, not unkindly, that Jacinta was "closer to passing out than to dancing." Someone cut off Lucy's braids, she never found out who. Eventually the children departed, with great difficulty, from Cova da Iria. As Lucy was carried away, she seemed inspired and addressed the crowd in a loud voice with dramatic gestures: "Do penance! Do penance! Our Lady wants you to do penance! If you do penance the war will end!"

For the next week they were questioned night and day by Church officials, reporters, and others. The unrelenting interrogations were often designed to catch the children in contradictions. After several days of this Lucy, probably because of exhaustion, began saying that the Lady told her the war would end on October 13. It is the only significant contradiction Lucy has ever made, and the mistake is in all likelihood due to the duress she was put under. Jacinta said the Lady had said, "If people would atone for their sins, the war would end today." In her fatigue Lucy seems to have forgotten the conditional nature of the Lady's statement. On seeing the children on October 19, Canon Formigao noted that Lucy's "state of exhaustion causes her to respond to questions put to her without attention and the desirable reflection ... unless somebody is careful to spare the children the fatigue of too frequent and prolonged interrogations, their health runs the risk of being profoundly shaken." Despite such brutal treatment, the children's stories remained remarkably consistent. Nor did the children reveal the Fatima Secret told them on July 13. Penance, conversion, and praying the Rosary was the Lady's message, they said. The only new information garnered during the week of endless questioning concerned what the children saw during the dance of the sun. Lucy recalls:

"After Our Lady had disappeared into the immense distance of the firmament, we beheld St. Joseph with the child Jesus and Our Lady robed in white with a blue mantle, beside the sun. St. Joseph and the child Jesus appeared to bless the world, for they traced the sign of the cross with their hands.

"When, a little later, this apparition disappeared, I saw Our Lord and Our Lady. It seemed to me that it was Our Lady of Sorrows. Our Lord appeared to bless the world in the same manner as St. Joseph had done. (Lucy has also stated that Our Lord appeared from the waist up, dressed in red, and appeared to be approaching Calvary).

"This apparition also vanished, and I saw Our Lady once more, this time resembling Our Lady of Carmel."

These living images corresponded to the mysteries of the Rosary, thus emphasizing the title of the beautiful Lady, Our Lady of the Rosary. The series of apparitions represent the Joyful, Sorrowful, and Glorious mysteries of the Rosary. Daily recitation of the Rosary was an instruction the Blessed Virgin gave in each of Her six appearances to Lucy, Francisco, and Jacinta. The point could not have been made any clearer; the celestial apparitions the children witnessed on October 13 were an exclamation point.

The other themes of the six appearances of the Blessed Virgin at Fatima were equally clear. In the first apparition (May 13) She asked the children to endure sufferings in reparation for the sins of the world, and for the conversion of sinners, and allowed them an interior vision of God's love and mercy, and His indignation of sin. In the second apparition (June 13) She revealed God's will to establish in the world devotion to the Immaculate Heart of Mary, and showed the children a vision of the Immaculate Heart, encircled by piercing thorns. In the third apparition (July 13) the Blessed Virgin encouraged the children to make sacrifices for sinners and showed them a horrifying vision of hell. The remedy against hell was devotion to the Immaculate Heart.

This devotion was not revealed for many years. Neither was the Fatima Secret, which was also given to the children on July 13. Here the Virgin predicted the First World War would soon end, that a second World War would erupt during the reign of Pius XI, and that this war would be preceded by an "unknown light" in the sky. All these predictions came to pass as the Virgin had prophesied.

She warned that unless the Holy Father and all the bishops consecrated Russia to Her Immaculate Heart, Russia would scourge the world and the Church. Eventually this would be done, Her Immaculate Heart would triumph, and there would be a period of peace. In the fourth apparition (probably August 19) the Blessed Virgin told the children to pray and sacrifice much for the many sinners headed for hell. She also predicted the miracle of October 13.

In the fifth apparition the Virgin again predicted a miracle on October 13 and, as in all Her appearances, ordered daily recitation of the Rosary. On October 13 the Lady in light revealed Herself as Our Lady of the Rosary, and warned sinners to "offend Our Lord no more, for He is already too much offended." The great Miracle of the Sun occurred, as if to put the seal of divine authority on the words of the Blessed Virgin, and to underscore the importance of Her message. The fall of the sun seems about as clear a warning to heed the Fatima Message as one could expect. We may pray that it too was not a prophecy.

Conversion, penance, sacrifice and reparation for sinners, the mercy and exhausted patience of God, the prominence of the Queen of Heaven in the designs of Heaven and man, the threat of eternal damnation of millions of souls, the lifeline of the Rosary and devotion to the Immaculate Heart, all these sober, serious themes punctuated by unexplained phenomena, and climaxed with a stupendous, undeniable miracle that is a fact of history attested to by thousands of eyewitnesses, believers and atheists, at Fatima and as far as 30 miles away. Heaven had visited earth and delivered an unmistakably ominous warning to three rustic peasant children on a Portuguese hillside near the beginning of the most enlightened, godless, murderous and bloodstained century in human civilization. Was anyone listening?

Chapter Three

Lucy Alone

The first of many miraculous healings at Cova da Iria occurred on October 13, 1917, during the last apparition of the Blessed Virgin. For five years Maria do Carma had suffered from a bloody cough, and severe chest and body pains. Doctors said it was tuberculosis. By 1917 she was unable to eat, and subsisted on small amounts of milk. In July she was given two weeks to live.

Maria lived eighteen miles from Fatima, in a village called Arnal. She had heard of the Blessed Virgin's appearances at Cova da Iria, and prayed to Her for healing. In return, Maria promised to walk to Cova da Iria four times, barefoot. Her husband, Joaquim, warned her she would not make it to Fatima alive, but Maria persisted, so at one o'clock in the morning of August 13 husband and wife set off on foot for Fatima, rosaries in hand. Maria made it there alive, and stated she felt her condition had improved, despite the 36 mile hike.

They walked to Fatima again on September 13. Once more Maria noticed a slight improvement. On October 13, although chilled to the bone by the rain and wind, Maria believed she was cured. Her cough and pains disappeared, and her appetite returned. It was not a temporary improvement. On November 13 Maria, in gratitude and thanksgiving, returned to Fatima for the fourth time in fulfillment of her promise to the Blessed Virgin. She was cured. (Later, her case was formally investigated, and her recovery was declared unexplainable.)

Reaction

Maria do Carma was not the only pilgrim to return to Cova da Iria after October 13. Nearly every day at least a handful of visitors would gather at the little holm oak tree the Lady had appeared on, even though by now the little oak was more stump than tree — most of its branches had been taken as relics.

Many of the visitors to Cova da Iria also visited Aljustrel to talk to, pray with, or plead intercession from the three seers. Although the apparitions had stopped, the events at Fatima had acquired a momentum of their own. The attraction increased over the years, despite violent attacks in the Masonic press, the presence of armed troops at Cova da Iria, and the fact that within four years of the last apparition, none of the little seers lived at Fatima anymore.

Back at Lisbon, Freemason and Editor-in-Chief of *O Seculo*, Avelino de Almeida, was raked over the coals by his fellow leftists for daring to report the Miracle of the Sun as it actually occurred. It was thought that such a public concession to reality only encouraged the forces of reaction, and consequently imperiled the revolutionary cause in Portugal. In Ourem, no one needed to instruct Arturo Santos ("the Tinsmith") about the party line. To his dying day he denied anything miraculous had ever occurred at Cova da Iria — although he never set foot there. On October 23, 1917, however, some of his henchmen did.

The Tinsmith's agents were joined by members of the Grand Orient Lodge of Santarem (about forty miles south of Fatima). Under cover of darkness they entered Cova da Iria to cut down the holm oak tree, and remove the rustic wooden arch built over it, from which hung lanterns perpetually lit in honor of the heavenly Lady. They also took a table and the small altar resting on it, and an image of the Blessed Virgin. The carload of booty was driven to Santarem, where the thieves displayed the stolen items the next day. For a small fee one could view the arch and a small hatcheted tree, and receive a Masonic harangue on medieval superstition. That night the Freemasons staged a public procession with their display, "singing blasphemous litanies to the accompaniment of drums."

Adding salt to the wound was the fact that the Portuguese government had outlawed Catholic religious processions. The Masonic "procession" was so fanatical in its anti-Catholicism that even the secular press was critical of the event. On the morning of October 24 Maria Carreira hurried to Cova da Iria. Her heart sunk when she saw the arch and lanterns missing, then rose when she saw the little stump of the holm oak tree still sticking up out of the ground. The vandals had cut down the wrong tree.

Lucy went to investigate too. "I then asked Our Lady to forgive these poor men," she wrote in her second Memoir, "and I prayed for their conversion." The next ploy of the "poor men" was to post armed cavalry around Cova da Iria to intimidate pilgrims. The crowds only seemed to increase.

Publicly dismissing the apparitions at Fatima as a "shameful spectacle staged as a ridiculous comedy" (as one hyperventilating Brother put it), an implacable hatred of the one true God gave Freemasonry no rest. Truth to tell, the revolution in Portugal was menaced. But it was not, as the Masons supposed, the dark plotting of the Jesuits or Portuguese clerics that would stall the forces of progress. Most clergy maintained a prudent silence regarding the apparitions, and more than a few were downright skeptical. Rather, it was the prayers, penances, and sacrifices inspired by the beautiful Lady at Cova da Iria that posed the real threat to Masonic authority. Before this onslaught of religious fervor Freemasonry could only sputter impotently, and flee.

On December 8, 1917, the Blessed Virgin began to grind Her heel on the spiteful head of the revolution. Portugal's government was over-thrown by one of its own, a Freemason named Sidonio Pais. The day af-ter his coup d'etat Pais allowed the Portuguese bishops to return from exile. Two weeks later he allowed worship in the churches the revolu-tion had confiscated from the Church. Diplomatic relations with the Vatican were reopened, and other measures were taken to allow free-dom of worship in Catholic Portugal. Obviously Pais was no ordinary Freemason. He knew that by his actions he was signing his own death warrant. It is said he felt protected by the Blessed Virgin, and had even received "encouraging visions" from Her. Had he lived long enough, it is likely he would have converted. But he had made himself a marked man, and he knew the Masonic reputation for vengeance was justified.

Nevertheless, Pais persisted. His efforts to allow the Jesuits to re-en-ter Portugal were rewarded by an assassination attempt. Undaunted, Pais had the police raid the Masonic headquarters in Lisbon. On Decem-ber 14, 1918, he attended a Mass for fallen Portuguese soldiers. After-wards, he was gunned down at a train station in Lisbon. He died there, his body riddled with bullets, a crucifix resting on his bloody chest.

It was another glorious victory for the champions of liberty, equality, and fraternity. Yet Freemasonry had only killed a messenger; they were powerless against the message, and they knew it. Their days were num-bered.

Death of Francisco

One month before Sidonio Pais was assassinated the war ended, as the Lady from Heaven had promised. As peace began an epidemic of in-fluenza ravaged Europe. The modern plague hit Portugal hard. Lucy was the only one to escape it in her family. Ti Marto was the only one to escape it in his. In Fatima the sound of funeral bells became so common they were silenced in order to prevent a general panic. Francisco and Jacinta developed pneumonia and were confined to bed.

"When he was ill," Lucy remembers, "Francisco always appeared joy-ful and content. I asked him sometimes: 'Are you suffering a lot, Fran-cisco?' 'Quite a lot, but never mind! I am suffering to console Our Lord, and afterwards, within a short time, I am going to Heaven!'"

His greatest anguish in the last year of his life was that he had gotten mixed up reciting the Credo, and was not allowed First Communion. This troubled Francisco far more than the daily harassment he suffered at school. The boys were goaded on by their teacher, a man who considered the Marto boy a lazy charlatan. It is true that Francisco was a frequent truant (schooling was not then mandatory). He was absent not because he feared ill treatment, but because he felt impelled to console the "hidden Jesus", as he called the Blessed Sacrament at St. Anthony's parish in Fatima.

In the morning Francisco would say to Lucy and Jacinta, "Look, you go to school and I will stay here in church near the hidden Jesus. It isn't worth the trouble for me to learn to read. I'm leaving here soon for Heaven. When you come back, call me." The girls proceeded to school, where Lucy was learning to read as the Lady from Heaven had requested. After school they went to St. Anthony's parish, "and there I found him," Lucy remembers, still kneeling in front of the tabernacle. The boy's naturally calm and quiet personality began to reflect the presence of a truly contemplative spirit.

Another development in Francisco's personality was his outspokenness for the truth. Curious adults asked him what he wanted to be when he grew up. A carpenter? A soldier? A doctor? A priest? "I don't want to be anything. I want to die and go to Heaven," Francisco told them. Then there was the time Francisco came home to find his house full of gawking pilgrims. A woman was blessing a table full of rosaries, medals, and other religious items. She asked Francisco to assist her. "I could not give a blessing," he replied, "and neither should you! Only priests do that." He also reprimanded Lucy for giving in to the insistent pleas of her friends to join them for games and dancing. Lucy accepted the rebuke and cancelled her plans. Her friends began asking to pray the Rosary with the seers at Cova da Iria.

Francisco was as kind as he was blunt. He helped Maria Carreira round up her stray sheep so often she called Francisco her "dear guardian angel." His compassion for the sufferings of others at times overwhelmed him, but he faithfully interceded on their behalf with prayers and sacrifices. During his short life he obtained many notable cures and conversions. Above all, however, he sought to console Jesus and Mary. Out of all the appearances of the angel, the brilliant Lady, the messages and the Secret, and all the miracles, what seems to have made the deepest impression on Francisco was the sadness of God's Son over the sins of the world. To console His Heart was Francisco's quiet passion.

When his illness made him too weak to walk he was deprived of visiting the "hidden Jesus". Like all his sufferings, he offered this to God in reparation for the sins that sorrowed Him. The stream of visitors to his bedside was at times consoling, but more often a trial. It was all the same to Francisco, but his visitors seemed to gain a hidden benefit from their time with him. "I don't know what it is about Francisco," one visitor said, "but it feels so good to be here!" Another remarked: "When we go into Francisco's room, we feel just as we do when we go into a church!"

In January, 1919, he rallied for two weeks, and dragged himself to Cova da Iria to kneel at the holm oak tree until he fell over from weakness. Then he relapsed, and never left bed again. Fever parched his skin and cracked his lips. Olimpia Marto remembers: "The meanest medicines he swallowed without making a face. He was so good and cheerful that we kept feeling he was getting better, but he always smiled and told us it was no use — Our Lady was coming to take him to Heaven, he would say."

In the last weeks of his life Lucy visited Francisco often. When Jacinta was well enough she joined them, and they prayed together. Mindful of the Lady's admonition that he "would have to say many Rosaries" to get to Heaven, Francisco commonly prayed up to eight Rosaries a day. Now he struggled through one. Near the end he asked Lucy and Jacinta to pray the Rosary for him. The prayers and presence of his best friends became a vigil as the three children waited for the Lady's promise to come true: "I shall take Jacinta and Francisco soon ..."

Towards the end he gave Lucy his penitential cord, whispering, "I can't manage it any more, Lucy. Please take it from me before my mother finds out." In April he stopped eating. Ti Marto went to Fatima to fetch Father Ferreira for last rites. Lucy and Jacinta helped Francisco prepare his confession. On the morning of April 3, remembered as "a beautiful spring day", the hidden Jesus came to Francisco in his first and last communion at the hand of a priest. Afterwards Francisco remained motionless for a long time, his eyes closed. He did not speak of what transpired during this time, but told his friends: "I am happier than you are, because I have the hidden Jesus within my heart. I'm going to Heaven, but I'm going to pray very much to Our Lord and Our Lady for Them to bring you both there soon."

Lucy and Jacinta stayed with Francisco that night, and prayed the Rosary for him. "I shall miss you terribly in Heaven", the dying boy told them. He became upset at the thought that he might forget to pray for Lucy and Jacinta when he reached Heaven: "I'm afraid I'll forget when I see Our Lord. (For) then, more than anything else, I want to console Him."

Finally Lucy said goodnight and, practical girl that she was, good-bye as well. "Don't forget to pray for me when you get there," she reminded him. "No, I won't forget. Be sure of that", he answered. Then realizing that this really *was* good-bye, Francisco seized Lucy's hand with surprising strength. "He held it tightly, for a long time," Lucy remembers. He stared wordlessly at her as tears ran down his hollow cheeks. She stared back silently until Francisco became a blur behind her own tears. In the face of death and judgment there were, finally, no words left to say, but Lucy found some. "Good-bye, Francisco, till Heaven. Good-bye till Heaven." She ran, weeping, from the Marto home.

He died the next evening, first Friday, April 4, 1919, around ten o'clock. There was no final agony as his soul passed on. In death, as in life, Francisco's last moments were calm and quiet. "He seemed to smile," Olimpia said, "then he stopped breathing." Ti Marto agreed: "He died smiling." The next day his body was placed in a simple coffin. After a short ceremony he was buried under a simple wooden cross in the Fatima cemetery, one year and a half after the last apparition at Cova da Iria. He was ten.

The Price of Heaven

After Francisco "took his flight to Heaven in the arms of his heavenly Mother," as Lucy put it, Jacinta was moved into her brother's bed. She had been too sick to attend Francisco's funeral, and this grieved her. Lucy writes: "She suffered keenly when her brother died. She remained a long time buried in thought, and if anyone asked her what she was thinking about, she answered: 'About Francisco. I'd give anything to see him again!' Then her eyes brimmed over with tears."

Like her brother, Jacinta's health would not improve. After becoming ill she, like Francisco, took off her penitential rope and secretly gave it to Lucy, saying, "Keep it for me; I'm afraid my mother may see it. If I get better, I want it back again." The cord had three knots tied in it, and was bloodstained.

Unlike Francisco, who sought continually to console Jesus and Mary, Jacinta was "solely concerned with the one thought of converting sinners and saving souls from going to hell," Lucy said. Early in her illness Jacinta told Lucy the Blessed Virgin had visited her and asked if she wanted to convert more sinners. "I said yes," Jacinta related, then explained: "Our Lady wants me to go to two hospitals, not to be cured, but to suffer more for love of Our Lord and for sinners."

In early July, 1919, Jacinta went to the first hospital, in Ourem. "Lucy," she wept, "if only you could come with me. The hardest thing for me is to have to go without you." Jacinta's only other trip to Ourem had been two summers ago, when the Tinsmith had kidnapped and imprisoned her, Francisco, and Lucy. Ti Marto fastened the frail, feverish nine year old to a donkey and traveled the dusty road to Ourem as gently as possible.

While Jacinta was at Ourem, Lucy's father died. "My father was a healthy man, and robust," wrote Lucy. "But in less than 24 hours an attack of double pneumonia carried him off into eternity." On July 31, 1919, Antonio dos Santos died cradled in the arms of Maria Rosa and his sister, Olimpia Marto, who coached him to repeat religious ejaculations. The parish priest was slow in coming, and Antonio died without Viaticum. Lucy recalls: "My sorrow was so great that I thought I would die as well ... 'My God! My God!' I exclaimed in the privacy of my room. 'I never thought You had so much suffering in store for me! But I suffer for love of You, in reparation for the sins committed against the Immaculate Heart of Mary, for the Holy Father and for the conversion of sinners.'"

The doctors in Ourem were unable to help Jacinta and she returned to Aljustrel. Her pneumonia had turned into pleurisy, and an open wound in her side wept pus. The wound became infected and Jacinta's temperature rose. Canon Formigao, who had interrogated the three seers after the Miracle of the Sun, visited Jacinta in October. He wrote:

"The child is like a skeleton. Her arms are frighteningly thin ... She always has a fever. Looking at her moves one to pity. Poor child! Only last year full of life and health, and now already like a wilted flower, with one foot in the grave."

Trapped in bed, she was the unwilling recipient of numerous visitors. "Jacinta had to undergo detailed and exhausting interrogations," Lucy remembers. "She never showed the slightest impatience or repugnance, but simply told me later: 'My head aches so much after listening to all those people! Now that I cannot run away and hide, I offer more of these sacrifices to Our Lord.'"

Fatally ill as she was, there was in Jacinta something that consoled her visitors. Her favorite visitor, of course, was Lucy. "When Lucy came in, joy and sunshine entered my house," said Olimpia Marto. Lucy would bring Jacinta wild flowers, which reminded her of the summer afternoons she, Lucy, and Francisco would play on the hills outside Fatima while tending sheep.

The sheep were all gone now. Lucy and Jacinta's parents had sold them off after the apparitions because the children were too besieged by visitors and inquisitors to tend them. Jacinta would never tend the sheep she loved and called by name again. She would never play in the hills with Lucy and Francisco, or dance to Francisco's flute-playing either. But there were still flowers for an ardent young heart to admire, and Lucy remembers how Jacinta would "pick the flowers from her bouquet, and count the petals of each one."

Maria Rosa

After Jacinta came back from Ourem, and before she left Fatima for the last time, Lucy's mother fell seriously ill. It was her heart, the doctor said. Maria Rosa's children gathered around the dying woman's bed to receive her blessing. Upon seeing Lucy, Maria Rosa hugged her and exclaimed: "I am dying with my heart pierced through because of you." As Maria Rosa sobbed, Lucy was harshly rebuked by her sisters: "Mother is going to die of grief because of all the trouble you've given her."

"I knelt down, put my head on a bench, and in a distress more bitter than any I had ever known before, I made the offering of my sacrifice to Our Dear Lord," Lucy wrote. Her two older sisters told Lucy to go to Cova da Iria and ask the Blessed Virgin to cure their mother. This was said more out of desperation than faith, as Lucy's sisters, like Maria Rosa, still had trouble believing Heaven had visited Lucy.

Lucy did as they requested. When she returned home, "my mother was already feeling somewhat better. Three days later she was able to resume her work around the house," Lucy wrote. Lucy brought back some earth from Cova da Iria and asked her sisters to make an herbal drink out of it for their mother. Maria Rosa drank the "dirty water", and Lucy's sister says, "The cardiac problems disappeared on the spot."

Lucy and her sisters made a nine-day Rosary novena to Cova da Iria in gratitude for the miraculous cure. They covered the distance from the roadway to the holm oak tree on their knees (a custom still used by pilgrims to Fatima). Lucy's sister, Maria dos Anjos says, "Our mother also made the novena, walking behind us."

Jacinta Dies

Shortly after her mother's recovery Jacinta told Lucy the Blessed Virgin had visited her again.

"She told me that I am going to Lisbon to another hospital; that I will not see you again, nor my parents either, and after suffering a great deal, I shall die alone. But She said I must not be afraid, since She Herself is coming to take me to Heaven."

Jacinta hugged Lucy and wept: "I will never see you again! You won't be coming to visit me there. Oh please, pray hard for me, because I am going to die alone." This thought tormented Jacinta, but her love overcame even this fear. Clinging to the Blessed Virgin's promise to take her to Heaven, Jacinta offered her anguish for the conversion of sinners. Lucy remembers: "At times, she kissed and embraced a crucifix, exclaiming, 'O my Jesus, I love You, and I want to suffer very much for love of You!' "How often did she say: "O Jesus, now You can convert many sinners, because this is really a big sacrifice!'"

The prophecy of Jacinta dying away from home seemed impossible of fulfillment. Ti Marto had depleted his finances on Jacinta's hospitalization at Ourem. Feeling their options were exhausted, he and Olimpia resigned themselves to Jacinta languishing in her own bed until the Virgin took her to Heaven. Through an unlikely series of events, however, the prophecy was fulfilled to the letter.

First, a prominent Lisbon doctor, Dr. Lisboa, visited Fatima, and through his acquaintance with Canon Formigao, was able to pray the Rosary at Cova da Iria with Lucy. Afterwards, he visited Jacinta and examined her. He persuaded a reluctant Ti Marto and Olimpia to send their daughter to Lisbon, to be treated by their best doctors. Canon Formigao arranged the transportation, and the cost of the trip and the treatment was covered by the Baron of Alvaiazere. The Baron was a skeptical pilgrim to Cova da Iria on October 13. The Miracle of the Sun had changed his life, and made him a fast friend of Ti Marto, who recalled, "Everything I did for the child (the Lisbon arrangements for Jacinta), I did by means of the Baron, who was so good to me."

In January, 1920, Jacinta made her final visit to Cova da Iria — on a donkey, as she was too weak to walk. Then she said good-bye to Lucy. "It was a heart-rending farewell," Lucy wrote years later. "For a long time, she clung to me, with her arms around my neck and sobbed: 'We shall never see each other again! Pray a lot for me, until I go to Heaven. Then I will pray a lot for you. Never tell the Secret to anyone, even if they kill you. Love Jesus and the Immaculate Heart of Mary very much, and make many sacrifices for sinners.'" They never saw each other again.

Olimpia, Jacinta, and her oldest brother, Antonio, took the train to Lisbon. Upon arriving they discovered that the woman who agreed to care for Jacinta until her admission to the hospital had changed her mind, probably because of the extreme state of the young girl's illness. Olimpia, who had never been to Lisbon, searched fruitlessly for other lodging. "Nobody would take us in," she recalled. Finally, "we came to a house of a good woman who opened her doors to us and could not have given us a better welcome." The good woman was Mother Godinho. The house was an orphanage called "Our Lady of Miracles".

Here the exhausted Jacinta was well cared for. The orphanage was right next to the chapel it was named after, and Jacinta was able to attend Mass and go to Confession. Olimpia, who lingered there for some days, accompanied her youngest daughter, and would carry her in her arms to the Communion rail to receive the hidden Jesus. It was at Our Lady of Miracles Orphanage that the Blessed Virgin again appeared to Jacinta, to tell her the date and hour of her death, and entrance into Heaven.

On February 2, the Feast of the Presentation, Jacinta was transferred to the children's ward of Dr. Lisboa's hospital. On February 5 Olimpia returned to Fatima. On February 10 Jacinta was operated on. Two of her ribs were removed, leaving a gaping wound that required daily dressings. Her doctor recalled: "The daily dressings were excruciating agony, but Jacinta's only cries were repetitions of Our Lady's name when the pains were worst. She bore her sufferings with the resignation of a saint, and no one ever heard her complain."

Shortly after the operation Ti Marto visited Jacinta. It was a very brief visit. He left and Jacinta was, as the Lady had prophesied, "all alone." Humanly speaking, that is, for Jacinta said the Blessed Virgin visited her at the hospital and took all her pain away. The absence of pain was confirmed by Dr. Lisboa. Greatly encouraged, he wrote Ti Marto and Olimpia that Jacinta was recovering. All it meant, however, was that the young seer had drained the chalice of suffering offered to her by Heaven for the conversion of sinners. The end was near, but only Heaven and Jacinta knew the day and the hour.

On February 20, the Friday before Ash Wednesday, Jacinta asked for last rites. Father Reis, from the nearby parish of the Church of Holy Angels, was called to hear her confession. He did not give her Viaticum, however, as he judged her not to be near death. Jacinta persisted, saying she was soon to die. She asked again for Viaticum, and Father Reis again declined, telling her he would come the next morning to give her Holy Communion. Two hours later she quietly died, alone.

Her body was placed in an open coffin at the Church of the Holy Angels. Dr. Lisboa made arrangements for Jacinta's remains to be transferred to the vault of Baron Alvaiazere in Ourem. Portugal had a law requiring all bodies to be buried within 24 hours of death, and Father Reis fretted as day after day more pilgrims came to see Jacinta's corpse. Father had a reputation as a good priest, and no doubt he was; but he didn't care much for this apparition business, and scolded some of the pilgrims for what in his opinion was excessive veneration of Jacinta's body. Yet even Father Reis admitted what many visitors observed with reverence: Jacinta's skin was a soft, fresh pink color, and her body seemed to give off the most beautiful aroma. This was even more unusual given the nature of Jacinta's illness; purulent (i.e., pussy) pleurisy gives off a notoriously bad odor even from a living body.

Three days later the arrangements for the transfer of Jacinta's body were completed. The undertaker, one Antonio Almeida, came to take the body. Since he dealt with corpses for a living, Mr. Almeida's remarks about Jacinta are significant:

"I seem to see Jacinta still (he wrote later), looking like a little angel. In her coffin she seemed to be alive; her lips and cheeks were a beautiful pink. I have seen many corpses, large and small, but I have never seen anything like that. The beautiful perfume which the body exhaled could not be explained naturally, and the hardest skeptic could not doubt it. One remembers the smell which so often makes it repugnant to remain near a corpse, yet this child had been dead three days and a half, and the smell of her body was like a bouquet of flowers ..." Not for nothing is Jacinta known as "the Flower of Fatima."

Lucy

Ti Marto waited in Ourem for the train carrying the body of his youngest daughter. He had worn himself (and his pocketbook) out caring for his large, sick family, including Olimpia. Despite his efforts Francisco had died. His hopes for Jacinta's recovery had been raised by Dr. Lisboa's letter, and now she — his favorite child — lay before him in a coffin that was soldered shut. He remembers: "When I saw the people gathered around the coffin that held my Jacinta — well, I just broke down, and I cried, believe me, as I have never cried before or since. It seemed such a sad, sad, waste for her to have gone off all the way to Lisbon only to die without us, all alone." Lucy was twelve, and seemed to suffer no less bitterly than Ti Marto. It was one thing to sincerely rejoice over Francisco and Jacinta being taken to Heaven by the beautiful Lady; it was quite another to be deprived of their companionship. She visited the places she and her cousins used to pray, and, "There, alone with God, I poured forth my grief and shed tears in abundance." Once the memory of her friends was so strong that Lucy went to the Marto home "and made for Jacinta's room, calling out to her. Her sister, Teresa, seeing me like that, barred the way, and reminded me that Jacinta was no longer there!"

Lucy's loneliness was in sharp contrast to the attention given her. She was a national celebrity, and pilgrims and Freemasons alike had designs on her. The pilgrims wanted to make Lucy a saint, and saw in her the symbol of a religious movement to combat Portugal's Masonic government. The Freemasons heaped scorn, lies, and slanders on Lucy, and the threat of physical harm was seldom far away. The spiritual dangers were even more ominous.

In addition, many in Fatima were still skeptical of Lucy. Her fiercest opponent, aside from various family members, was the parish priest. "Father Ferreira," Ti Marto recalled, "was the last person in the whole country to believe in the apparitions." Outspokenly skeptical, he became openly hostile to young Lucy. Father complained — with some justification — that Catholics spent more time prostrate in the fields of Cova da Iria than before the Blessed Sacrament. He was also quite exasperated that while the renovation of St. Anthony's parish had stalled for lack of funds, a short distance away generous pilgrims helped finance a new chapel on Cova da Iria.

It all became too much for Father Ferreira. He left Fatima in June, 1919, before a successor had been named. Rumors spread that he left because of Lucy. As a result, Lucy remembers, "several pious women, whenever they met me, gave vent to their displeasure by insulting me; and sometimes they sent me on my way with a couple of blows or kicks."

The official Church reaction to the Fatima apparitions was an appropriate, but definite silence. It would be some years before enough evidence had been gained to begin assessing the merits of the occurrences at Cova da Iria. Meanwhile, the Church waited. Unofficially, many clergy shared Father Ferreira's skepticism; some, his hostility.

Thus it was that Lucy found herself a national figure, the center of attention, with nary a true friend in the world. It was a tough spot for a fatherless twelve year old, but she didn't complain. She saw the ill treatment as God's way of keeping away "the little worm of vanity which has the habit of gnawing its way into everything." She used to tell herself: "They are all mistaken. I'm not a saint, as some say, and I'm not a liar either, as others say. Only God knows what I am."

The forces swirling around the vortex Lucy had become manifested on May 13, 1920. Pilgrims came to Cova da Iria from all over Portugal to honor the anniversary of the first appearance of the Blessed Virgin. In Ourem, Arturo Santos vowed to "put a stop to this ridiculous fairy tale!" He and the other regional powers of Freemasonry met to "neutralize this shameless Jesuitical trick." Their solution was armed force.

Squadrons of Republican Guard calvary blocked all roads into Fatima, forcing back thousands of pilgrims. The Tinsmith arrived around noon, resplendent in a white straw hat, and ordered troops to block the road leading from Fatima to Cova da Iria. Canon Formigao was there, and remembers, "There were infantry, cavalry, machine-guns, and I know not what besides. A general offensive seemed to be in progress, but against what, in the name of God!"

It may have been around this time that Lucy set out for Cova da Iria to pray the Rosary. She was stopped by two mounted soldiers. They asked her name and she told them. "Let's cut off her head," said one soldier to the other, "and leave her here dead and buried. Then we'll be finished with this business once and for all." Lucy remembers, "I thought that my last moment had really come, but I was as much at peace as if it did not concern me at all." After some more harassment the soldiers took her home and told her to stay there. By sunset of the same day, however, Lucy was at Cova da Iria, praying the Rosary, "accompanied by hundreds of people."

Despite the intimidation, and the pouring rain, thousands honored the Blessed Virgin at Cova da Iria on May 13. No one was killed, but there were many blows and a few beatings dealt out by the frustrated soldiers, many of whom did not appear to like their duty. Afterwards, the Tinsmith claimed victory, writing that "reaction suffered a complete reverse". He vowed to continue to "combat lies and defend liberty."

To return to facts, the Tinsmith had lost another round. Once again he had been unable to outbluff simple, pious Catholics. Although he left his prominent post at Ourem shortly after failing to stop the anniversary pilgrimage, it does not appear that Arturo Santos pondered these defeats in his heart. He surfaced a few years later when the Masonic government was overthrown. He was injured while making a home-made bomb to heave at Portugal's new Catholic rulers. The bomb, like many of Arturo's plans, blew up in his face. It is tempting to say he went out with a bang — but he didn't. After lingering on the fringes of the revolution for decades, the unrepentant Freemason met Judgment in Lisbon in 1955.

The Warnings

Just before her death Jacinta received two messages from the Blessed Virgin that she entrusted to Canon Formigao. The first message was about Lucy, a warning of the "grave dangers" that threatened her, now and in the future. In 1917 Canon Formigao had recommended the seers be removed from Fatima for their own protection. Now he acted decisively. He persuaded Lucy and Maria Rosa to consider sending Lucy to boarding school to continue her education. In July, 1920, Maria Rosa and Lucy traveled to Lisbon. An offer was made to pay for Lucy's education as long as she remained in a boarding school in Lisbon. She accepted. At the last minute, "when everything was ready, and the day arranged for my entering the boarding school, I was informed that the government was aware that I was in Lisbon, and was seeking my whereabouts ..."

Lucy was spirited out of Lisbon just as the Masonic authorities began to close in. She was hidden at Canon Formigao's house in Santarem for a week, "without even being allowed out to Mass." She ended up back at Fatima. The plan had failed.

The second message from the Blessed Virgin warned that Portugal would suffer "a terrible cataclysm of the social order" in which sinful Lisbon would "become a real image of hell". The instrument of chastisement would be "a civil war of an anarchist or communist character" with "plundering, killing, arson, and all sorts of devastation." Mercifully, this plague could be averted "if there were souls who would do penance and make reparation for the offenses done to God ..."

In the sixteen years following the Masonic revolution of 1910, there were sixteen violent revolutions and over forty changes in government. Much of the violence was between Freemasons and Portuguese Bolsheviks. The situation in Portugal was similar to that strange and terrible revolution in Russia, where the monarchy was overthrown by the Freemason Kerensky, who was in turn deposed by the Bolshevik Lenin. The second message of the Blessed Virgin could not have described the political situation in Portugal more accurately. The remedy was the known part of the Fatima Message: practice penance and reparation for sins against God.

Portugal was a microcosm of Europe, where Bolshevism infiltrated everywhere, instigating violence and upheaval. While Lucy was in Lisbon, Pope Benedict XV warned:

> "Morals are much more depraved and corrupt than formerly ... The fond hope and wish of every renegade is the speedy rise of some universal state which is based on the complete equality of men and women and common ownership of property as a fundamental principle, in which neither any distinctions of nationality nor authority of parents over children, nor of public authority over citizens, nor of God over man living in society, is acknowledged. If these principles are put into practice, dreadful horrors must necessarily follow."

Although the Church was officially silent regarding Fatima, regarding the state of the world the Church and Our Lady of the Rosary were of one accord.

Lucy Leaves Fatima

On August 5, 1920, when Lucy was secretly being taken from Lisbon to Santarem, the diocese of Leiria (which contains Fatima) witnessed the consecration of its first Archbishop. His name was Dom Jose Alves Correira da Silva. He had been imprisoned by the Freemasons in 1910. They tortured him by making him stand in icy cold water day and night, an experience that crippled him permanently.

When he was released he left Portugal, and with other refugees, made pilgrimages to Lourdes to plead for mercy for Portugal. Eventually he returned to Portugal to teach at the seminary. He was known for his orthodoxy and gracious personality. The articles he wrote for the Catholic press were also orthodox and graceful, and widely read. Dom Jose was devoted to the Mother of Sorrows, and when he became Archbishop of Leiria he formally consecrated his diocese to the Mother of God on the Feast of the Assumption. Then he began studying the "Fatima problem".

The good people of Fatima were happy to have a holy bishop. A number of them assured Lucy that the new bishop would expose her lies once and for all. In fact, after studying all the evidence, and after being bombarded and besieged by Lucy's supporters and detractors, Dom Jose wasn't sure what to think. What he felt most certain about was that if Lucy did not leave Fatima soon she would either be canonized or murdered. Her departure would be a worthy test for the validity of the apparitions. Would the enthusiasm of pilgrims continue in Lucy's absence? How would she react to the lack of attention? It was time to find out. Dom Jose met with Lucy in Leiria on June 13, 1921. He asked her if she would like to leave Aljustrel and continue her education. Lucy was pleased at the idea. Dom Jose suggested a school run by the Dorothean Sisters in Porto, on the northern coast of Portugal, and said Lucy could go there very soon. Lucy agreed. Dom Jose then gave explicit orders. She was to tell no one where she was going. She was to tell no one at the school who she was. And she was to say nothing to anyone about the apparitions at Fatima. Lucy agreed to everything without hesitation. Dom Jose told her to start packing.

Maria Rosa consented to the bishop's proposal. Lucy could not say good-bye to people, but she visited her father's and Francisco's tombs. Then she went to each of the places the Angel of Peace and the beautiful Lady had appeared to her. She longed to say good-bye to Maria Carreira, who had become her best friend. And her heart ached for Ti Marto and Olimpia, who had lost two more children, Florinda and Teresa. Four deaths in less than two years had devastated the Marto home, but their faith remained intact.

At two o'clock on the morning of June 16, 1921, Lucy and her mother left Fatima for Leiria. They stopped one last time at Cova da Iria to pray the Rosary. Years later Lucy revealed that after praying on that quiet, dark, star studded night, she saw someone at the bottom of the hill. It was the beautiful Lady. Motionless and silent, She regarded Lucy. Was Her appearance a reward for the young seer's fidelity? An encouragement to go with God? Or perhaps the Virgin appeared to remind Lucy that She was someone Lucy would never have to say good-bye to. Had She not written Her words in the young girl's heart? "I will never forsake you. My Immaculate Heart shall be your refuge and the road that shall lead you to God ..."

It really was time to go. "As long as this place was still in sight, I kept turning around to say a last goodbye," Lucy wrote. Then the Cova disappeared, and Lucy wondered if she would ever see it again.

NOTES

In addition to sources listed below, see Chapter 1 Notes for other sources.

Cirrincione, Msgr. Joseph A., *Venerable Francisco Marto of Fatima*, Tan Books and Pubilshers, Inc., 1994.

De Oliveira, Rev. Joseph Galamba, *Jacinta, The Flower of Fatima*, AMI Press, 1973.

De Oca, Rev. V. Montes, *More About Fatima*, The Newman Bookshop, 1945.

There is an alternative version of Arturo Santos' later years, which appeared in a Portuguese religious magazine, *Stella*. Here is the account as it appears in Haffert, op. cit., p. 63:

"A pious woman approached Santos in June, 1920, to install a statue in the little Chapel at Fatima. After hesitating, suddenly he gave permission, stipulating that it be done when there were no crowds and that she should not reveal that he had given permission. (This was revealed by the woman in question to the Baron of Alvaiazere, who described it in a letter to the Viscount of Montelo on June 5, 1920).

"On April 7, 1942, when this same statue was being carried in triumphant procession from Fatima to Lisbon, Santos was in the crowd when it passed through Ourem, and he was heard to declare: 'I am not at all in favor of religion and of priests ... but when I saw the image of the Vision I felt inwardly something which I cannot explain ...'"

Chapter Four

Pontevedra and Tuy

Lucy, Jacinta and Francisco were no longer at Fatima but the crowds continued to come. After inspecting the chapel built on Cova da Iria, Bishop da Silva authorized Mass to be said there. Realizing there was no water available for the thousands of pilgrims, he ordered a well dug.

There were few places less likely to hold water than the rocky hills outside Fatima. The laborers began digging a hole at the bottom of the Cova, but struck stone too large to break up. Dynamite was sent for, but before the charges were laid water began pooling over the rock in the ground. Declared by pilgrims to be a miracle, the improbable well provided an abundant source of water in the otherwise dry lands. And then there were the miraculous cures. "Never," recalls Jose Alves Carreira (husband of Maria), "did Our Lady work so many miracles as at that time ..."

"They came here with their bottles and their pitchers which they filled and took home for their sick to drink and to wash their wounds in. Everyone had the greatest faith in Our Lady's water, and She used it to cure their wounds and their pains ... I saw people with terrible legs that were running with pus, but when they washed themselves with the water they were able to leave their bandages behind, because Our Lady had cured them. Other people knelt down and drank that earthy water, and were cured of serious internal diseases."[1]

Then there was the case of the young newlywed who discovered she had advanced tuberculosis. She recommended herself to Our Lady of Fatima, and began using a small quantity of Fatima water she had. When the water was all gone so were her symptoms, which never returned. Her doctor in Lisbon called her recovery "inexplicable."

Had these cures been the product of simple hysteria or exaggeration, the enemies of Fatima would have exploited them at the Church's expense. Instead they responded with violence. Portuguese Freemasons placed four bombs in the chapel at Cova da Iria, and one on the holm oak tree. On the evening of March 5-6, 1922, the bombs were detonated.

The bomb on the holm oak tree failed to explode, but the others badly damaged the chapel. Fortunately no one was injured. Two months later over sixty thousand pilgrims attended a Mass of reparation on May 13. Forty thousand attended on October 13. By the end of the year the chapel was being rebuilt. The Freemasons' usual weapons — slander and violence — seemed to have no effect on the crowds coming to Cova da Iria.

It was now clear to the prudent Bishop da Silva that the attraction of Cova da Iria had little to do with the children. Events had convinced him there was more to Fatima than the personality cult that surrounded Lucy. Confirmation of his conclusion came two years later on May 24, 1924. Over two hundred thousand thronging the hills outside Fatima witnessed flower petals drifting slowly down from Heaven, disappearing before touching the ground – a repeat of the September 13, 1917 apparition.

Pontevedra

Since leaving Fatima in 1921 Lucy had lived a life of anonymity at the college of Vilar, obeying Bishop da Silva as well as the Blessed Virgin, Who had told Lucy to learn to read and write. The school was run by the Sisters of St. Dorothy (a congregation approved by Pope Pius IX in 1863). The Mother Superior gave Lucy a new name — Maria das Dores, Maria of Sorrows — and forbade her from talking about Fatima.

Lucy obeyed. The only time she spoke of Fatima was in 1924, when she was given permission to respond to an interrogation that was part of the canonical process for approving the apparitions. It was around this time that she read the autobiography of St. Thérèse of Lisieux. Inspired by the book and the recent canonization of Thérèse, Lucy asked her Mother Superior about the Carmelites. She was told the Order was too demanding for her. Lucy then decided to become a Dorothean. On October 25, 1925, she began her postulancy at the Dorothean convent in Pontevedra, Spain.

It was here that the Blessed Virgin appeared as She had said She would on July 13, 1917: "I will come to ask for ... the Communion of Reparation on the first Saturdays of the month." On December 10, 1925, eighteen-year-old Lucy was visited in her cell by the Blessed Virgin. By Her side, "elevated on a luminous cloud, was the Child Jesus." Putting Her hand on Lucy's shoulder, Mary "showed her a heart encircled by thorns". Jesus told Lucy:

> "Have compassion on the heart of your most holy Mother, covered with thorns, with which ungrateful men pierce it at every moment, and there is no one to make an act of reparation to remove them."[2]

Then the Blessed Virgin said:

> "Look, My daughter, at My heart, surrounded with thorns with which ungrateful men pierce Me at every moment by their blasphemies and ingratitude. You at least try to console Me and an-

nounce in My name that I promise to assist at the hour of death, with the graces necessary for salvation, all those who, on the first Saturday of five consecutive months, shall confess, receive Holy Communion, recite five decades of the Rosary, and keep Me company for fifteen minutes while meditating on the fifteen mysteries of the Rosary, with the intention of making reparation to Me."[3]

The Blessed Virgin was requesting a refinement of a devotion originally established by Pope Pius X, who gave official approval to First Saturday devotions, granting a plenary indulgence to all "who, on the first Saturday or first Sunday of twelve consecutive months, devote some time to vocal or mental prayer in honor of the Immaculate Virgin in Her conception ..."[4] On June 13, 1912, Pius had encouraged confession and communion on First Saturdays, and "pious practices in the spirit of reparation in honor of the Immaculate Virgin." Where Pius offered plenary indulgences for observance of First Saturdays, the Blessed Virgin's reward for observance of five First Saturdays was "to assist at the moment of death, with all the graces necessary for salvation ..."

Later Lucy's confessor asked her: why five First Saturdays? While pondering this question in front of the Blessed Sacrament, Lucy felt herself "more intimately possessed by the Divine Presence and, if I am not mistaken, this is what was revealed to me":

"My daughter (said Our Lord), the reason is simple. There are five types of offenses and blasphemies committed against the Immaculate Heart of Mary:

1. Blasphemies against the Immaculate Conception;

2. Blasphemies against Her Perpetual Virginity;

3. Blasphemies against Her Divine Maternity, in refusing at the same time to recognize Her as the Mother of men;

4. The blasphemies of those who publicly seek to sow in the hearts of children indifference or scorn, or even hatred of this Immaculate Mother;

5. The offenses of those who outrage Her directly in Her holy images.

"Here, My daughter, is the reason why the Immaculate Heart of Mary inspired Me to ask for this little act of reparation ..."[5]

It was a Communion of Reparation that Lucy, Francisco, and Jacinta received from the Angel of Peace, who in 1916 instructed them to "make reparation" to God for the offenses of "ungrateful men." A year later the Blessed Virgin revealed that God's will was to establish devotion to Her Immaculate Heart. Eight years later She returned, as She had said She would,[6] and asked for the Communion of Reparation to Her Immaculate

Heart, a development of a devotion already officially approved by the Church. Although the Fatima Message occurred over a period of years, and in different locations, the Message retains a remarkable coherence and consistency.

Also noteworthy are the number of enemies of Heaven, as they are revealed by their blasphemies against the Immaculate. In addition to the millions of atheists, agnostics, unchurched, and assorted infidels and pagans, Our Lord includes Orthodox schismatics and the various Protestant sects who deny the Immaculate Conception. To be honest, one must also include a large number of Catholics, particularly since the Second Vatican Council, where Mary was explicitly denied Her proper title, "Mediatrix of All Graces", so as not to offend all the other blasphemers.[7]

Tuy

Four years after appearing to Lucy at Pontevedra, the Blessed Virgin returned again, as She had prophesied at Fatima in 1917, "to ask for the consecration of Russia to My Immaculate Heart ..."[8]

Lucy had been transferred to the Dorothean novitiate at Tuy, a town on the northernmost border of Portugal and Spain, in 1926. Two years later she made her first vows. The following summer, Thursday, June 13, 1929, to be exact, Lucy was observing a holy hour in the chapel. Sometime between 11 p.m. and midnight she knelt prostrate by the communion rails, and repeated the prayers the Angel of Peace taught her. She recalls:

"Suddenly, the whole chapel was illumined by a supernatural light, and above the altar appeared a cross of light, reaching to the ceiling. In a brighter light on the upper part of the cross, could be seen the face of a man and His body as far as the waist. Upon His breast was a dove of light.

"Nailed to the cross was the body of another man. A little below the waist I could see a Chalice and a large Host suspended in the air, onto which drops of Blood were falling from the face of Jesus crucified and from the wound in His side. These drops ran down onto the Host and fell into the Chalice.

"Beneath the right arm of the cross was Our Lady, and in Her hand was Her Immaculate Heart. It was Our Lady of Fatima, with Her Immaculate Heart in Her left hand, without sword or roses, but with a crown of thorns and flames. Under the left arm of the cross, large letters, as if of crystal clear water which ran down upon the altar, formed these words: 'Grace and Mercy.'"[9]

Lucy beheld the vision in silence. "I understood that it was the mystery of the Most Holy Trinity that was shown to me and I received lights about this mystery," she said later, "which I am not permitted to reveal." According to Lucy, the Blessed Virgin said:

"The moment has come in which God asks the Holy Father, in union with all the bishops of the world, to make the consecration of Russia to My Immaculate Heart, promising to save it by this means. There are so many souls whom the Justice of God condemns for sins committed against Me, that I have come to ask reparation: sacrifice yourself for this intention and pray."[10]

Lucy summed up the messages of Pontevedra and Tuy to Jesuit Father Goncalves, who was Lucy's spiritual director: "The Good Lord promises to end the persecution in Russia (the Bolshevik revolution) if the Holy Father will himself make a solemn act of reparation and consecration of Russia to the Sacred Hearts of Jesus and Mary, as well as ordering all the bishops of the Catholic world to do the same, and if the Holy Father promises that upon the ending of this persecution he will approve and recommend the practise of the reparatory devotion already described."[11]

The Fatima Message

The messages Lucy received at Tuy and Pontevedra complete the cycle of the Fatima Messages. The original apparitions (May 13 to October 13, 1917) stressed penance, conversion, and reparation, and revealed devotion to the Immaculate Heart of Mary to be the remedy willed by God for the Twentieth Century. In addition to many miracles, the Blessed Mother showed the children a terrifying vision of hell, and told them a Secret that predicted the end of one world war, the beginning of another, the designation of Russia as a scourge of the Church and the world, and the promise: "In the end My Immaculate Heart will triumph ..."

At Pontevedra the Blessed Virgin instructed Lucy to make known the Five First Saturdays devotion. At Tuy She requested, in God's Name, the consecration of Russia to the Immaculate Heart of Mary by the Holy Father, in union with Catholic bishops around the world. Both remedies were — and are — designed to appease the anger of God, especially His anger at the dishonoring of the Blessed Virgin Mary, and to save souls from hell.

The theology of the messages is profoundly Catholic. The Blessed Virgin Mary, Mother of God, is revealed as the Mediatrix of all graces. So prominent is She in Heaven's designs that "the justice of God condemns" those who commit sins against Her. Moreover, She is authorized to promise salvation to those who practice the Five First Saturdays reparatory devotion. Devotion to Her Immaculate Heart is given as the signal remedy to reduce the number of souls who are damning themselves to hell.

In the vision at Tuy Mary stands at the foot of the cross, Her Immaculate Heart crowned with thorns and bursting with flames. The striking image emphasizes Mary's role as Co-redemptrix of mankind. Above the

Blessed Virgin, blood flows from the crown of thorns and from the Sacred Heart of the God-Man. It flows onto a Host and into a Chalice, symbolizing what the Church has always taught about the Last Supper: "This is My Body, which will be given up for you ... this is My Blood, shed for you and for many unto the remission of sins ..."

The Eucharist is inseparable from the Cross, and the grace and mercy that continue to flow from the eternal sacrifice appear word for word in the vision of Tuy as crystal clear water falling from Christ's wounded left hand, spiked to the cross.

The vision also symbolizes the union between the Hearts of Jesus and Mary. Lucy received the vision at Tuy while performing a holy hour of adoration and reparation to the Sacred Heart — a devotion Our Lord suggested to Margaret Mary. In the vision shown to Lucy, Mary's heart is very similar to the Sacred Heart of Jesus as seen by Sister Margaret Mary — crowned with thorns and bursting with flames.

The union of the Sacred Heart of Jesus and the Immaculate Heart of Mary is hinted at by Lucy, who on occasion would refer to "the consecration of Russia to the most Holy Hearts of Jesus and Mary." Was Lucy contradicting herself? Why didn't she specify that Russia was to be consecrated to the Immaculate Heart, as the Blessed Virgin had told her? Given that Lucy has a decades-long record of not contradicting herself, two other solutions seem more likely. The first is that Lucy spoke imprecisely shortly after the vision of Tuy, due to the imagery of the Immaculate Heart, which appeared as almost identical to the Sacred Heart as seen by Margaret Mary. The supernatural union of the two Hearts, as symbolized by their virtually identical appearance, may have caused Lucy to initially blend them together in her thinking.

The second possible solution is that Lucy was not being imprecise at all, but dropping a hint concerning the supernatural lights she saw during the Tuy vision that she "was not allowed to reveal." Perhaps the mysteries Lucy was privileged to behold concerned the supernatural relationship between the Blessed Trinity, the Sacred Heart, and the Immaculate Heart. The union of the Hearts of Jesus and Mary is also implied in the words of Our Lord to Lucy. He told her He wished to "place devotion to this Immaculate Heart beside the devotion to My Divine Heart ..."[12]

The Holy Father Learns of Fatima

Obeying the Blessed Virgin's instruction "to announce in My name" the Five First Saturdays reparatory devotion, Lucy told her confessor and Mother Superior. The news spread beyond this small circle to Lucy's early defender, Canon Formigao, who immediately grasped the supernatural significance of Heaven's message:

"Our Lord is profoundly displeased with the offenses made against His Most Holy Mother. Because of these sins ... many souls have fallen into hell and many others are in danger of being lost. Our Lord promises to save them to the degree this devotion is practiced ..."[13]

He began broadcasting "the devotion of reparation to the Immaculate Heart of Mary" with great enthusiasm, asserting: "As Father Mateo came to intensify the devotion to the Sacred Heart of Jesus, now Lucy comes to intensify the devotion to the Immaculate Heart of Mary ... by these two devotions of reparation, the offenses against the Son and the Mother are atoned for, as is absolutely just."[14]

Dr. Formigao brought a letter from Lucy to Bishop da Silva, in which Lucy, with the consent of her superiors, humbly asked the bishop to formally approve the Five First Saturdays devotion of reparation to the Immaculate Heart. Da Silva cautiously approved the spread of a private devotion, but did not formally commit himself to the message of Pontevedra.

Nevertheless, for the very first time Lucy had — at Heaven's request — revealed a central feature of the Fatima Secret: devotion to the Immaculate Heart. In 1929 more veils were lifted when Lucy witnessed the spectacular vision at Tuy, and was told: "The moment has come when God asks the Holy Father to make ... the consecration of Russia to My Immaculate Heart ..."

Lucy's Jesuit confessor, Father Jose Bernardo Goncalves, instructed her to write down the answers to certain questions he asked her about the messages of Pontevedra and Tuy. Lucy did so with precision. Father Goncalves wrote Bishop da Silva, and sent him Lucy's responses. Da Silva acknowledged receipt of the letter, but did nothing more. Dissatisfied, Father Goncalves sent Lucy's messages to the Holy Father, Pope Pius XI. More than once Lucy has stated that Pius XI received this communication between July 1930, and August 1931. Her confessor, Father Goncalves, told Lucy Pius XI "had heard the message graciously and had promised to consider it."[15]

In fact Pius XI was already aware of the Fatima apparitions, having on a number of occasions shown his unofficial approval of the Fatima cult. Bishop da Silva had sent Pius a thick dossier on the apparitions and asked his advice. Pius reviewed it and encouraged da Silva to formally approve the apparitions. On October 13, 1930, Bishop da Silva published his solemn decision in a pastoral letter (*A divina Providencia*), which read in pertinent part:

"We judge it good:

1) To declare worthy of faith the visions of the children at the Cova da Iria, (in the) parish of Fatima in our diocese, which took place from May 13 to October 13, 1917;

2) To officially permit the cult of Our Lady of Fatima."[16]

At the time the apparitions were formally approved, the Fatima Secret (as expressed in 1917) had not been explicitly revealed. At Pontevedra Heaven had instructed Lucy to make known the First Saturday Communion of reparation to the Immaculate Heart of Mary, and at Tuy she was told to ask the Holy Father to consecrate Russia to the Immaculate Heart. The veils were lifted oh-so-slowly in the period between the world wars, as if a certain sense of timing was being followed. During these years many things were becoming obvious, for instance, the vastly different fates of Portugal and Russia: the land of holy Mary and the land that, unless consecrated to the Immaculate Heart, would "spread her errors throughout the world, causing wars and persecutions of the Church. The good will be martyred, the Holy Father will have much to suffer, various nations will be annihilated ..."

Note on First Saturday Reparatory Devotion

In 1927 Lucy, in a letter, explained the First Saturday devotion as follows: "During five months on the first Saturday, to receive Jesus in Communion, recite a Rosary, keep Our Lady company for fifteen minutes while mediating on the mysteries of the Rosary, and make a confession. This confession can be made a few days earlier, and if in the previous confession you have forgotten the (required) intention, the following intention can be offered, provided that on the first Saturday one receives Holy Communion in the state of grace, with the intention of repairing for offenses against the Most Holy Virgin, and which afflict Her Immaculate Heart."[17]

It is clear from other correspondence of Sister Lucy that she kept every first Saturday. Her meditation time involved thinking of one particular mystery of the Rosary (this was her preference, it is not a requirement). The meditation is in addition to recitation of the Rosary.

In 1930 Lucy was asked about the situation of rural people whose parish church did not have Saturday Mass. According to Sister Lucy, Our Lord told her, "The practice of this devotion will be equally acceptable on the Sunday following the first Saturday when My priests, for a just cause, allow it to souls."[18]

It would seem that "just cause" may exist in other situations as well, but this would be left to the priest's discretion. Frère Michel has added other precisions: there is no need to express the reparatory intention to the confessor, and a Saturday evening Mass (even an anticipated Mass, according to Frère Michel) will fulfill the Mass requirement.[19] Finally, according to Canon Barthas, "Confession may be made eight days before or after that Communion, provided Communion is received in the state of grace." In his book *Our Lady of Light* (published in 1947), Barthas also notes:

"On June 13, 1912, the Holy Office had already granted a plenary indulgence, under the usual conditions, to those who will accomplish, on the first Saturday of any month, the special exercises of devotion in honor of the Immaculate Virgin Mary, in reparation for the blasphemies of which Her name and prerogatives are the object. (See No. 335 of the official record: *Preces et Pia Opera*, 1938.)

"Mary's request of Sister Lucy only approves and sanctions a devotion already existing and encouraged by the Church. Those who practice the devotion of the Five First Saturdays will thus fulfill the conditions required to gain the plenary indulgence granted by the Holy Office."[20]

NOTES

1. De Marchi, op. cit., pp. 238-239.
2. Kondor, op. cit., p. 231, First Appendix to Sister Lucy's Fifth Memoir.
3. Ibid., p. 231.
4. As quoted in Frère Michel de la Sainte Trinité, *The Whole Truth About Fatima*, (*TWTAF*) published by Immaculate Heart Publications, Volume II, p. 257.
5. Ibid., pp. 265-266.
6. Kondor, op. cit., p. 162. In Lucy's Fourth Memoir, she states that during the July 13 apparition at Fatima, the Blessed Virgin said: "I shall come to ask for the consecration of Russia to My Immaculate Heart, and the Communion of Reparation on the First Saturdays."
7. Among many sources, see Thomas Bokenkotter, *A Concise History of the Catholic Church*, Revised and Expanded Edition, Image Books, 1990, pp. 383-386. The author notes with some surprise that even though the Council's "new approach" to Mary did "much to meet traditional Protestant objections to the Catholic position on Mary", Protestants have yet to engage Catholics in dialogue about Mary (p. 383).
8. Kondor, op. cit., p. 162, Lucy's Fourth Memoir.
9. This account appears in Appendix II after Sister Lucy's Fifth Memoir, pp. 234-5. The introduction to the Appendix states that this account was not written in Lucy's own hand, but was recorded by Sister Lucy's spiritual director at the time, Rev. Fr. Jose Bernardo Goncalves, S.J., "who transcribed it directly and literally from the Seer's notes."
10. Ibid, p. 235.
11. Part of a letter Sister Lucy wrote to Father Goncalves in May 1930, approximately one year after the apparition at Tuy. In June, 1930, Lucy wrote Father Goncalves again on the same topic, which again "indissociably unites the Holy Hearts of Jesus and Mary." *TWTAF*, Volume II, p. 465, fn 6 on p. 504.
12. Sister Lucy is not the only one to ever speak as she does of the Holy Hearts of Jesus and Mary. St. John Eudes sometimes referred to the Holy Hearts as one heart. Obviously, this is a physical impossibility; the signification is a theological one.
13. *TWTAF*, Volume II, p. 520.
14. Ibid., p. 519.
15. It is evident that Pius XI was aware of the Fatima apparitions, and the requests of the Blessed Virgin for the Communion of Reparation and the Consecration of Russis to Her Immaculate Heart during the years 1930-1931. See *TWTAF*, Volume II, pp. 530-546. See also De Marchi, op. cit., p. 253, for an anecdote about Pius XI handing out pictures of Our Lady of Fatima to students of the Portuguese College.
16. De Marchi, op. cit., p. 253.
17. *TWTAF*, Volume II, p. 820.
18. Ibid., p. 260.
19. Ibid., p. 821.
20. Barthas, op. cit., p. 224.

Chapter Five

Russia

Like most nations, Russia has committed her share of errors. Her most enduring error was a religious one – rejecting the primacy of the Roman Catholic Pope. The Russian Orthodox Church ended up deferring to the State instead, and paid dearly for this when the Russian monarchy was overthrown.

Until that time, however, Church and State in Russia co-existed relatively peacefully. When czarist Russia partitioned Poland near the end of the Eighteenth Century, the Orthodox Church persecuted millions of Polish Catholics, and attempted the forced conversions of thousands more. The Russian government herded millions of Polish (now Russian) Jews into the Pale of Settlement, an immense fermenting vat for the ideologies of Communism and Zionism. Both movements, which played major roles in Twentieth Century history, originated primarily in Russia.[1]

Another Russian error was Anarchism. Although the French Freemason Proudhon is often called the Father of Anarchy, it took a Russian by the name of by Michel Bakunin[2] to apply theory to real life. Born to aristocratic parents, Bakunin became a disciple of Adam Weishaupt, the founder of the Illuminati. By 1847 Bakunin and Proudhon were discussing "the universal revolution."[3] The anarchists (or nihilists) sought to completely destroy all religion and government everywhere. This credo — enthusiastically practiced throughout once Christian and now Masonic Europe — was a particularly dangerous idea in Russia, where loyalty to God and the Tsar were the only checks on a national personality that, despite a veneer of Christian culture, remained at root mystical, impulsive, given to heavy drinking, casual brutality, and random violence.

It was Russian Anarchists and radical Jews who repeatedly attempted to assassinate Alexander II — *after* the Tsar had instituted liberal reforms. He may as well have thrown red meat at a shark, and in 1881 he was killed by a bomb on the day he was going to grant Russia a constitution. The collaboration between Russian anarchists and radical Jews was unusual for the time (latter part of the Nineteenth Century). Revolutionary Jews tended to follow the man they called "the modern Moses", Karl Marx. Marx and Bakunin became enemies who wrestled for control of the international revolution. After a contest in which neither man fought fairly — they were, after all, revolutionaries — Marx won.

A disillusioned Bakunin expressed disgust at the "German-Jew company",[4] as he referred to international socialism. While it wasn't clear whether the Germans or the Jews upset Bakunin the most, Russian novelist Feodor Dostoyevsky was more specific: "Europe is on the eve of collapse, a universal, terrible, and general collapse ... Judaism and the banks now reign over all, as much over Europe as over education, the whole of civilization, and socialism, especially over socialism, for with its help Judaism will root out Christianity and destroy Christian culture."[5]

While Dostoyevsky hated the revolution as much as he hated the Roman Catholic Church, Bakunin's hatred of religion was as universal as his love for the revolution was particular. He saw, rising phoenix-like from the smoke and charred ash of worldwide destruction, the rule of "Pan-Slavism", with Russia as the leader of the "lesser" Slavs. His real problem with the Germans and Jews, then, may have been that they were not Slavs. By 1875 Bakunin realized he would not live to see the world writhe under his torch of progress. He died sick, old, and poor — poor not by choice, but because Michel Bakunin, a self-styled champion of the working class, never worked a day in his life.[6]

The Prophets

Much the same could be said for Grigorii Efimovich (better known as Rasputin), particularly after he became "employed" by Russia's last monarchs, Tsar Nicholas II and his wife, Tsarina Alexandra. Alexandra bore Nicholas one son, Aleksey, who was sickly and a hemophiliac. When Rasputin's prayers at Aleksey's bedside coincided with an improvement in the boy's condition, Alexandra was beside herself with gratitude. When Grigorii — better known by the diminutive "Grishka" — proved himself a soothing counselor to Nicholas and Alexandra, he became part of the royal family.

The Tsar and Tsarina were perhaps the only couple in Russia to esteem Rasputin. He was widely despised, partly because he was of mere peasant stock,[7] but mostly because he was an incorrigible wine-guzzling lecher who did not always remain fully dressed in public; his very name, Rasputin, is a play on the Russian *rasputnik* (or *rasputstvo)*, which means sexually debauched.[8] The royal family's chronic infatuation with such an individual was a source of keen national embarrassment.

It may have been this resentment that gave rise to rumors that Rasputin was a German spy. While he did try to talk Czar Nicholas II out of involving Russia in the Great War against Germany and Austria, Rasputin's motives were probably not treasonous. Not even years of drunken orgies could erase a certain peasant patriotism. This trait, which seemed instinctive, was coupled with what appears to be one of Grishka's legitimate gifts — a mystical sixth-sense about his homeland that was the real origin of his attempts to keep Russia out of the war. He told Nicholas that war with Germany would bring "disaster, grief, murky darkness and no light. A whole ocean of tears ... and so much blood ... We all drown in blood. The disaster is great, the misery infinite."[9]

One could say that about any war, of course, but to give him his due, Grishka's prophecy was not exaggerated. He had more of a hold on Nicholas' wife, however, and the Czar went to war despite Rasputin's warnings. The Russian army was known as *velikaya molchal'nitsa*, "the great silent one", a curiously appropriate name for an army that ran out of ammunition fifteen months into the war. Russian soldiers died so often and in such great numbers it was nearly impossible to keep track of the losses. Four million Russian men died in the first ten months of the Great War. Perhaps eight million perished in less than three years. A German commander was heard to remark on the great mounds of Russian corpses his entrenched army had to move in order to sight the enemy. As there were very few victories to report, Russian newspapers carried feature articles that began "How they die when they have to! ..."[10]

Morale in the great nation was very low. Alcohol consumption, already high, increased. Venereal diseases were as rampant as pagan superstitions. A prominent Russian lamented "the degeneration of the official Orthodox Church", stating:

> "Without religion the masses turn into herds of beasts, but beasts of a particularly evil type, for these beasts possess a greater intelligence than animals. Our church has unfortunately long since become a dead, bureaucratic institution; our priests serve not the high God, but earthly gods; Orthodoxy has become Orthodox paganism ..."[11]

Despite it all it is likely Russia would have survived, monarchical and decadently Christian, but for a sealed train of German agents secretly injected into Russia to torpedo the monarchy and knock Russia out of the war.

The train entered the Finland Station at Petrograd on Easter Sunday, 1916. The lead German agent was the Russian-Jewish son of a schoolteacher, the expatriate Vladimir Ulyanov, code name Lenin. He was accompanied by an international group of revolutionaries, none of whom were Russian. On arriving in Russia Lenin declared: "The worldwide Socialist revolution has already dawned ... Long live the worldwide Socialist revolution!"[12]

Nicknamed "Starik" ("the old man")[13], Lenin was calm and unflappable in public. Privately he could be maniacal, and as prophetic as Grishka Rasputin, as evidenced by a conversation with an old school friend, in which Lenin declared:

> "I spit on Russia! That's only one stage we have to pass through on our way to world revolution! ... We are going to tear the whole thing down! We shall destroy and smash everything, ha-ha-ha, with the result that everything will be smashed to smithereens and fly off in all directions, and nothing will remain standing!

"Yes, we are going to destroy everything, and on the ruins we will build our temple! It will be a temple for the happiness of all! But we shall destroy the entire bourgeoisie, and grind them to powder, ha-ha-ha, to powder. Remember that! ..."[14]

These are surprising sentiments, given that Lenin's upbringing was bourgeoisie. He idolized his brother Alexander, who was hung for the conspiratorial role he played in the assassination of Tsar Alexander II. It is often said this family tragedy made Lenin a revolutionary. Even if this is true it fails to explain the depth and intensity of Lenin's demonic fury. Rasputin didn't have Lenin's baggage, and lurid tales to the contrary, he was not nearly the devil incarnate that "the old man" was.[15] Grishka's prophecy was penned in 1916, when he wrote, "My hour will soon come." Not a particularly modest man, he also predicted Russia would die when he did, and that:

"People without number will be destroyed. Many martyrs will die. Brother will die at the hand of brother. There will be a great misfortune. The earth will tremble. Hunger, famine, and drought will come, and there will be signs seen all over the world ..."[16]

Rasputin never met Lenin, but he was not the only one to prophesy the horrors of the coming revolution. While Rasputin linked Russia's doom with his own, most of his countrymen either blamed Grishka for the storm, or viewed him as part of the problem. A pervasive sense of doom hung over the vast land. As one Russian put it: "There's going to be a revolution and we are all going to hang. Who cares which lamppost we dangle from?"[17]

Grishka never made it to the lamppost. He had become a national obsession, and the patience of a long line of would-be assassins finally expired. Shortly after foretelling his own end Rasputin was poisoned with cyanide. Refusing to die, he was shot. Thought dead, he revived to attack his would-be assassin. He was shot again, and then again. Still alive, a colossal kick to the left temple finally finished him.

His unusual life and death have caused sensational dark legends about Rasputin the evil genius. He probably was not as diabolical as he has been portrayed, which is not intended as a compliment. Rasputin cast no evil spell on Nicholas and Alexandra. He was able to help their son, and had a gift for soothing their anxieties as well. He is usually either demonized or dismissed as a charlatan, but at some point in his life he may have had some legitimate healing abilities. Perhaps this attracted him to the Tsar and Tsarina, who were remarkably lonely and isolated people. They were spiritually starved as well, it would seem, to entrust their religious welfare to a layman of dubious character like Rasputin.

Once inside the royal circle, Rasputin allowed personal ambition to dominate his natural talents. His religious instinct was smothered by continual drunkenness and adulteries (yes, he was married) until his "religion" was little more than personal magnetism and opportunistic sensuality. He taught his disciples that "without sin there can be no repentance; repentance is pleasing unto God; in order to repent you must sin in the first place." This bad advice recalled the confusions of an heretical Augustinian monk — also prey to sins of the flesh — who exhorted his followers to sin mightily.

Yet if Rasputin was at times more Lutheran than Christian, he was also more cynical than deluded. He called his followers "fools" even as he encouraged their adulation. Yet Rasputin's vision was as narrow as his peasant upbringing. His primary ambition was satisfying his own lusts, not espionage. Too busy fouling his own nest to plan or participate in intrigues against the monarchy, the last thing Grishka would have wanted was a change in the status quo. As a bewildered monarchy and apathetic church lurched toward their awful fates, Rasputin loomed, a mocking specter, an unintentionally blasphemous caricature of a priest, and a sign and symbol of the state of the Church and religion in Russia at the beginning of the Twentieth Century. A Church weakened by centuries of schism produced its own reward who, instead of enlightening the nobility with vital Christianity, only made them a laughingstock. The life of Grishka Rasputin is a parable of "Russia's errors" not normally associated with the Secret of Fatima.[18]

The Bolsheviks

Nicholas abdicated two months after Rasputin was murdered, and was imprisoned with his family. In February, 1917, a provisional government was installed. The new leader of Russia was a Freemason of Jewish descent called Alexander Kerensky. In April Lenin and the Bolsheviks arrived in Russia. In May the Blessed Virgin appeared to Lucy, Francisco, and Jacinta for the first time.

Shortly after the Miracle of the Sun and the Blessed Virgin's last appearance to the three children, Lenin "overthrew" Kerensky's provisional government. It was a surprisingly peaceful transition, and the most reasonable explanation is that Kerensky was holding the government for Lenin's arrival. Lenin came and Kerensky left with all the money and securities he could plunder. Some Cossacks and cadets considered offering resistance, then changed their minds and joined the Bolsheviks. Upon so doing a lieutenant blurted out an obvious fact: "Lenin's whole gang are Jews ..."[19]

Well, not all of them. According to the London Times, "of the Bolshevist movement not less than 75 per cent are Jews."[20] Two British journalists, Victor Marsden and Robert Wilton, observed the revolution first-hand and gave even higher percentages of Jewish involvement in the Bolshevik hierarchy.[21] Lenin himself agreed: "The Jews provided a particularly high percentage of leaders of the revolutionary movement."[22] So did Winston Churchill, who spoke of Bolshevism as "this worldwide conspiracy for the overthrow of civilization and for the reconstitution of society on the basis of arrested development, of envious malevolence and impossible equality, has been steadily growing ...

"There is no need to exaggerate (Churchill continued) the part played in the creation of Bolshevism and in the actual bringing about of the Russian Revolution by these international and for the most part atheistical Jews. It is certainly a very great one; it probably outweighs all others. With the notable exception of Lenin the majority of the leading figures are Jews. Moreover, the principal inspiration and driving power comes from the Jewish leaders."[23]

The American Ambassador to Russia, David R. Francis, reported: "The Bolshevik leaders here, most of whom are Jews and 90 percent of whom are returned exiles, care little for Russia or any other country, but are internationalists trying to start a worldwide social revolution."[24]

British military intelligence reported that the Bolshevik revolution "is organized and worked by Jews who have no nationality, and whose one object is to destroy for their own ends the existing order of things ..."[25] A report by American intelligence detailed the Jewish identities of the lead Bolsheviks, along with their Russian code names. The American report also identified several wealthy Americans of Jewish descent who purportedly bankrolled the revolution.[26]

Much of the information in the American report was confirmed during Senate hearings on Bolshevik propaganda, issued in 1919 as the Overman Report (for Senator Lee Overman, presiding).[27] It should be noted that several Jewish sources happily conceded the evidence — at first. The Jewish *Chronicle* noted that "so many Jews are Bolsheviks", then stated, "the ideals of Bolshevism at many points are consonant with the finest ideals of Judaism."[28] The American *Hebrew* declared the revolution to be "largely the outcome of Jewish thinking, of Jewish discontent, of Jewish effort to reconstruct..." A Russian newspaper, *The Communist,* carried an article (April 12, 1919) by one M. Cohan which stated:

> "... without exaggeration it may be said that the great Russian social revolution was indeed accomplished by the hands of the Jews ... The symbol of Jewry, which for centuries has struggled against capitalism, has become also the symbol of the Russian proletariat, which can be seen even in the fact of the adoption of the Red five-pointed star, which in former times, as it is well known, was the symbol of Zionism and Jewry."[29]

Jewish historian Leonard Schapiro wrote that "It was the Jews ... (who) kept the wheels of the whole (revolutionary) organization running."[30] Another Jewish historian, Louis Rappoport, notes: "Immediately after the Revolution, many Jews were euphoric over their high representation in the new government. Lenin's first Politburo was dominated by men of Jewish origins ..."[31]

More recently, Chicago University professor of History, Sheila Fitzpatrick, wrote that "In both parties (Bolsheviks and Mensheviks), Jews and other non-Russians were prominent in the intelligentsia-dominated leadership."[32] And very recently, Alexandr Solzhenitsyn, in his just completed two volume history on Russian-Jewish relations, has referred to the Jews as "the yeast of the Revolution," and stated, "The Jews were installed throughout the revolutionary apparatus of the Bolshevik Revolution."[33] Small wonder, then, that an American eyewitness to the Revolution, Frank Golder, wrote in his journal that "Many people object to the Revolution and the Republic because of the Jews."[34] This objection led to an outbreak of "anti-Semitism" by the Slavic masses. The new rulers quickly enacted a law against anti-Semitism, Lenin himself ordering "all Soviet deputies to take uncompromising measures to tear the anti-Semitic movement out by the roots. Pogromists and pogrom-agitators are to be placed outside the law."[35]

The royal family was also "outside the law". The Romanovs: Nicholas, Alexandra, their four daughters and young son, their servants, and even a pet dog were shot and bayoneted to death. Their corpses were chopped up, burned, soaked with acid, and dumped in an abandoned well.

After abolishing all private property (resulting in the greatest theft of land in the history of the world), Lenin "immediately unleashed a nation-wide antireligious persecution":

> "With the law of January 23, 1918, religion was ousted from the schools, State subsidies were withdrawn, and the Lenin Constitution of February 5, 1918, formally sanctioned the separation of Church from State and from the schools. By 1922 the entire organization of the Russian Orthodox Church, which was by far the strongest religious body, had been destroyed; thousands of priests had been shot or jailed or had died in the icy Siberian labor camps."[36]

The terror extended to the luckless proletariat. The poor wretches the Bolsheviks expressed such empathy for, and made so many promises to, fled from their benefactors by the tens of thousands. Those unfortunate enough to be captured by the pursuing Red Army either killed themselves or were slaughtered by the army or the Cheka (forerunner of the KGB). In one case fifty to one hundred and fifty thousand refugees were butchered en masse by the Bolsheviks.

The massacres were repeated all over Russia. By 1923 it is estimated that 28 bishops, 1,219 priests, 6,000 professors and teachers, 9,000 doctors, 54,000 officers, 260,000 soldiers, 70,000 policemen, 12,950 property owners, 535,250 intellectuals, 193,290 workmen, and 618,000 peasants had been murdered.[37] It is likely these are conservative estimates.

Fatima and Fascism

It was Trotsky who believed in "permanent revolution" on a world-wide basis. He was realistic enough to realize that not even the Bolsheviks could murder fast enough to avoid a reaction from the Russian masses. His remedy was not to stop murdering innocent Russians, but to attack the rest of the world just as ferociously, if only to establish another landing strip if the tide turned in Soviet Russia. Accordingly, Bolshevik operatives, mostly Jewish, began agitation in Poland, Hungary, Bavaria, and Germany. By Lenin's death in 1924 the tentacles embraced all of Europe.

Lenin's replacement was his possible assassin, Josef Stalin. It was Stalin who expanded the gulags, those slave labor camps wherein bishops, priests, intellectuals, "anti-Semites", counter-revolutionaries, and the proletariat — remember Bolshevism's shimmering promises of a better life for the working classes? — by the thousands, tens of thousands, and eventually the millions, were murdered through over-work, starvation, beatings, torture, and sub-zero Siberian winters.

It was Stalin who boasted openly of starving 10,000,000 peasants in the Ukraine between 1929 and 1934. The actual number of deaths was probably closer to 15,000,000, and may have even exceeded this amount. The horror stories of cannibalism, of starving families crawling to towns to beg for food only to be machine gunned by Red Army troops were suppressed by the Western media. *New York Times* reporter Walter Duranty privately admitted that Stalin inflicted genocide on his own country. Publicly he denied this, and was rewarded with a Pulitzer Prize for his "dispassionate, interpretive reporting of the news from Russia."[38]

The Bolshevik Revolution was a hideous monstrosity composed of equal parts lies and murders, which made its diabolical origin obvious. Perhaps it was an attempt to disguise this that led the Bolsheviks to demand to be called Communists. They were dutifully obeyed. A devil by either name, Communism and its violence did not originate with revolutionary Jews. Some effort has been made here to document the historical facts of the situation, but this is done for the sake of truth, not to vilify the Jews or the Russians — or anyone else, for that matter. The men responsible for the violence and death were not original; they were in fact witting or unwitting agents of the prince of this world, the "Father of Lies" whom Our Lord tells us was "a murderer from the beginning." Looking back on the Twentieth Century, it seems the homage paid there to his satanic majesty — the best and brightest minds of our age have spilled rivers of blood for his sake — has only whetted his appetite. It is also easy to see why the beautiful Lady at Cova da Iria said and did what She did. What appeal could be more attractive, more heartfelt, and more effective, than the appearance of the Blessed Mother? What could be more starkly opposed to satanic violence than Our Lady of Fatima asking for prayers and penance to save sinners from hell?

The Fatima apparitions, and its Secret, apply with acute precision to the vale of tears that was the Twentieth Century — the inevitable consequence of four hundred years of revolution (Luther in 1517, Freemasonry in 1717, and Bolshevism in 1917). What more logical result could occur when a worldwide secular state uproots religion from society than the members of that society losing their faith, offending God, and damning their souls? What better remedy for this crisis than the Rosary, devotion to the Immaculate Heart, and the consecration of Russia? What better remedy for the blaspheming, heretical spirit of modern man than She who is known as the destroyer of heresies, and revered as the one destined by Heaven to crush the serpent's head?

It was a measure of how de-Christianized Twentieth Century Europe already was that the main weapon wielded against Communist infiltration (the spread of Russia's errors) was not the Immaculate Heart, but the manmade remedy of fascism. First espoused in 1922 by an Italian socialist named Benito Mussolini, fascism was a circle-the-wagons brand of nationalism designed to violently combat Bolshevik agitation and promote patriotism and moral regeneration — not for their own sake, but as antibodies to Communism. The crucial point here is that, despite its occasional moral and even religious overtones, fascism was a purely secular response to the evil of Communism. The uneasy truce between Mussolini and the Vatican was routinely rocked by Pius XI's frequent criticisms of fascism on just that point.

Communism was offensive, fascism was defensive. Communism was an internationally coordinated revolution, fascism was isolated local reaction to that revolution. Because fascism was anti-Communist, its followers were often accused by Communists and the press of being "anti-Semitic". No doubt some were, especially if anti-Semitism is defined as disagreeing with the goals of Communism. But there was more to Bolshevism than the prominence in it of Jewish revolutionaries. The fact was that Communism was a murderous and evil creed that any sane nation with an ounce of strength would resist to the death, whether it was "anti-Semitic" or not.

It is generally believed that despite its major errors, fascism was the most effective remedy to creeping Communism in the years between the World Wars. This is incorrect. The most successful remedy to Communism was the successful Catholic counter-revolution waged by Portugal against "Russia and her errors".

NOTES

1. Chaim Weizmann, one of the founders of Zionism, was born in Motol, a small town in the Pale. It is his contention that this was where Zionism began (See his autobiography, *Trial and Error*, Harper & Brothers, 1949, First Edition, Chapter 1). Others argue that Zionism started in pre-partition Poland, or that it predated the Nineteenth Century. In either case, Zionism – and Communism, another popular ideology in the Pale – quickly spread well beyond their points of origin, splitting Jewish families apart as they spread – even though the two movements often cooperated with each other. While I am aware that Communism predated the Russian Revolution – Blessed Pius IX condemned it in 1846, for instance – the Communism referred to here is Twentieth Century Communism.

2. Also known as Michael Bakounine, and the "genius of destruction", born in 1814.

3. Nesta Webster, *World Revolution*, Veritas Publishing Company, 1994, reprinted by Omni Publications, p. 175.

4. Ibid., p. 278.

5. *The Journals of Feodor Dostoyevsky*, 1873-1876.

6. The general information about Bakunin is from Max Nomad, *Apostles of Revolution*, Little, Brown, and Company, 1939. The pseudonymous Nomad was favorably disposed to the revolution, and had an insider's knowledge of it.

7. He was born in Pokrovskoye, a small Siberian village in the province of Tobolsk. His father appears to have been a hard drinking horse thief; his son Grigorii was a semi-literate chip off the old block.

8. E.J. Dillon, *The Eclipse of Russia*, George H. Doran Company, 1918, p. 197. Dillon states that Rasputin was charged twice with rape, but not convicted.

9. Alex De Jonge, *The Life and Times of Grigorii Rasputin*, Carroll & Graf Publishers, Inc., 1989, p. 229. The misspellings – including the word Russia – are not included.

10. Ibid., p. 241. Solzhenitsyn's conclusion was "Russia must be governed by fools, there is no other way."

11. Ibid., p. 63.

12. Harrison E. Salisbury, *Black Night, White Snow: Russia's Revolutions, 1905-1917*, Doubleday & Company, Inc., 1977, p. 424. Actually, upon arriving at Petrograd's Finland Station, Lenin gave several speeches that were similar in content, including phrases like "shameful imperialist slaughter," "lies and frauds," and "capitalist pirates." Like Rasputin, Lenin was, at least publicly, against Russian involvement in the war. Unlike Rasputin, however, Lenin *was* a German agent.

13. Ibid, p. 249. "Old man" is also a nickname for Lucifer.

14. Robert Payne, *The Life And Death Of Lenin*, Simon And Schuster, 1964, pp. 418-419.

15. There are tales of Rasputin's supposedly demonic powers, and some fairly reputable historians have claimed he was possessed. For what it's worth, I think Lenin had the larger demon.

16. De Jonge, op. cit., pp. 308-309. In fact, after Rasputin's death Nicholas abdicated, the royal family were executed, and Communism brought martyrdom and famine, just as Rasputin had predicted.

17. Ibid., p. 283.

18. E.J. Dillon (op. cit., p. 220) knew Rasputin, disliked him, but acknowledged Grishka's uncanny knack for prophecy. Writing in 1918 Dillon noted that Rasputin "had told the Tsar and Tsaritsa, and repeated to many others as well at the time, that his destiny was entwined with the destinies of the Romanoffs and the Tsardom, and that his death would bring doom and disaster to them all. And hardly was his lifeless body thrust under the ice when the Empress was taken ill. Soon afterwards her son and two of her daughters were seized with illness and confined to bed. Then the sovereign was deposed, insulted, imprisoned, the army dissolved, the Empire abolished, and mighty Russia broken up ... What ancient oracle or prophet can point to so many fateful predictions accomplished?"

    Dillon concludes that had Rasputin been the sorcerer or cunning politician of his enemies' accusations, he would have exploited his relationships with the royal family far more than he actually did. "He (Rasputin) had no great purpose, good or evil, nothing but insatiable thirst for coarsest pleasures of sense. He reminded me of the Ukrainian of whom the story ran that he exclaimed, 'How I should love to be Tsar. I know what I then would do. I would steal a hundred roubles and from early morning until late at night I would gorge myself on bacon. Ah! If only I were Tsar!'"

19. Salisbury, op. cit., pp. 513-514. The Cossacks that the Cadets were arguing with are supposed to have also said, "The government is half full of Jews."

20. *London Times*, March 29, 1919, as quoted in *An Answer to Father Coughlin's Critics*, Published by the Radio League of the Little Flower, 1940, p. 150.

21. Victor Marsden was Russian correspondent for the *London Morning Post*. Present at the Bolshevik Revolution, Marsden compiled the list of 545 officials in the new Bolshevik government. He stated that 454 were Jews, 23 were Russian. His research has been disputed, but not contradicted. The same is true of Sir Robert Wilton, Russian correspondent for the *London Times*.

22. Vladimir Lenin, *Lenin On The Jewish Question*, International Publishers, New York, Second Printing, 1936, p. 16.

23. This was part of an essay Churchill wrote that was published in the February 8, 1930 issue of the *London Illustrated Sunday Herald*, as quoted in A.K. Chesterton, *The New Unhappy Lords*, Candour Publishing Company, 1972, Fourth Revised Edition, p. 16. Like most people, Churchill believed Lenin was not Jewish. For what it's worth, however, in 1991 a Moscow weekly reported that Lenin was of Jewish descent. Apparently his maternal grandfather, Israel (or Alexander) Blank, was a Ukrainian Jew. This news was also reported in the Jewish press.

24. From David R. Francis, *Russia from the American Embassy* (New York, 1921), p. 214, as quoted in the Introduction to Robert Wilton, *The Last Days of the Romanovs, How Tsar Nicholas II and Russias's Imperial Family Were Murdered,* Reprinted by the Institute for Historical Review, 1993.

25. The report was based in part on the testimony of the Dutch ambassador to Russia. His alarm at what he witnessed is evident: "The danger is now so great that I feel it my duty to call the attention of the British and all other Governments to the fact that, if an end is not put to Bolshevism at once, the civilization of the whole world will be threatened. This is not an exaggeration, but a sober matter of fact ... I consider that the immediate suppression of Bolshevism is the greatest issue now before the world, not even excluding the war that is raging, and unless, as above stated, Bolshevism is nipped in the bud immediately, it is bound to spread in one form or another over Europe and the whole world ... The only manner in which this danger can be averted would be collective action on the part of all the Powers." Quoted from Denis Fahey, *The Rulers of Russia*, Third Edition, 1986, p. 26. The ambassador's report was issued shortly after the beautiful Lady appeared at Fatima for the last time. She too would recommend "collective action" against Russia's errors, but by the Pope and his bishops, not the powers of Europe.

26. The document was drafted by the American Secret Service, and published in France. It is reproduced in Denis Fahey's *The Mystical Body of Christ In The Modern World*, Third Edition, republished in 1994 by the Christian Book Club, pp. 88-92.

27. There was corroborative testimony from independent witnesses on the predominantly Jewish leadership of the Bolsheviks. See *An Answer to Father Coughlin's Critics*, op. cit., Appendix VII, for extracts of testimony. The Overman Investigation Committee was a Senate sub-committee of the Committee on the Judiciary, United States Senate, 65th Congress, pursuant to *S. Res. 439 and 469.*

28. As quoted in Ibid., p. 61.

29. Webster, *World Revolution*, op. cit., pp. 286-287.

30. Leonard Schapiro, *Russian Studies*, Penguin Books, 1988, p. 271.

31. As quoted in Wilton, op. cit., "Introduction", p. ix.

32. Dr. Sheila Fitzpatrick, *The Russian Revolution*, Second Edition, Oxford University Press, 1994, p. 30.

33. These remarks were reported on June 20, 2001, by the *Times'* Moscow correspondent, Giles Whittell. According to Whittell, Solzhenitsyn's remarks, which were given in an interview with *Moskovskie Novosti*, "reflect a focus on the Jews as a separate nation with a particular role (as "catalysts") in the Russian Revolution" that informs much of Solzhenitsyn's recently completed history of Russian Jewish Relations, *Two Hundred Years Together,* the first volume of which reached Moscow bookstores in June, 2001.

34. T. Emmons and B. Pateraude, Editors, *War, Revolution, and Peace In Russia, The Passages of Frank Golder, 1914-1927,* Hoover Institution Press, 1992, p. 48.

35. From *Lenin and the Jewish Question*, op. cit.

36. Camille M. Cianfarra, *The Vatican and the Kremlin*, E. P. Dutton & Co., Inc., 1950, p. 52.

37. The standard numbers published at the time, as reproduced in Leon de Poncins, *The Secret Powers Behind Revolution*. Reprinted by Christian Book Club, 1996, p. 150.

38. Warren H. Carroll, *Seventy Years of the Communist Revolution*, Trinity Communications, 1989, Chapters 2-3 on Stalin and his manufactured famines.

Chapter Six

Portugal

The disintegration of the Portuguese monarchy was a centuries-long affair. In the view of historian Richard Pattee, "There seems to be little doubt that Freemasonry assumed the direction of much of the plotting against the monarchy ... its collaboration was of inestimable importance in furthering the atmosphere of disorder and growing anarchy."[1]

The climax came in 1908 when Portugal's King Carlos was assassinated. It is generally conceded that the plot was hatched by Magalhaes Lima, the grand master of Portuguese Masonry. The monarchy could not recover, in part because many of its ministers were already liberal enough to welcome the revolution. So it happened that on October 5, 1910, "the republic was proclaimed in Lisbon. The majority of the population accepted the new state of affairs with perfect indifference, while the wildest enthusiasm overcame the partisans of the movement."[2]

The back-slapping was understandable, as Freemasonry had been working for 150 years to overthrow the monarchy. Afterwards, at an international Masonic Congress, Magalhaes Lima would proclaim:

> "Here we are reunited ... sharing the same thought ... the same feeling and an identical desire. It is the thought, the idea, of a new morality, of a new religion."[3]

The new religion of Portugal's new rulers vigorously attacked Catholicism, the religion of virtually the entire population of Portugal. Like the Russian Bolsheviks, the Masons separated Church and State, confiscated all Church property, abolished religious education, and imprisoned or banished the clergy. They also suppressed the Jesuits, legalized divorce, forbade public religious processions, the public wearing of cassocks, and the public posting of religious notices.

Pope Pius X vigorously protested "the incredible series of excesses and crimes" of Portugal's new government, and observed:

> "When the Republican form of Government was adopted in that country there immediately began to be promulgated measures breathing the most implacable hatred of the Catholic religion ... an obstinate determination to secularize every civil organization and to leave no trace of religion in the acts of common life ..."[4]

What most inflamed the Holy Father was the "promulgation of a vicious and pernicious Decree for the Separation of Church and State," which Pius said "enacts in reality the reduction of the Church to utter want by the spoliation of her property, and to servitude to the State by oppression in all that touches her sacred power and spirit."[5] And as the Church went, so did the nation. The Masonic square and compass appeared on Portuguese currency, and Portugal descended into anarchy.

How anarchic was Portugal when the Blessed Virgin appeared to the three children in 1917? Mr. Pattee cites a Portuguese writer who documented twenty-two separate revolutions in Portugal between 1908 and 1921. This did not include "strikes, riots, attacks of political personalities, and persecutions of every kind." From 1911 to 1927, "occurrences of a violent nature, most of them politically inspired, reach the respectable figure of 208."[6]

As in Russia, Bolsheviks sought to replace the ruling Freemasons. Unlike Russia, however, in Portugal this dynamic led to a protracted power struggle. Violence, lies, and assassination became the politics of the day. The apparitions at Fatima coincided with the rise to power of Sidonio Pais, that unusual Freemason who tried to overturn Portugal's anti-Catholic policies. After he was assassinated by his Masonic colleagues anarchy ruled again.[7] It was the same old story — Freemasons were experts at destroying Christian government and culture, but were unable to equal either.

One would think the Masons, being intelligent men, might have noticed they were replacing palaces with dungheaps. Portugal was no exception — the nation became less religious, more violent, vulgar, and immoral, and its economy went into the tank. What Freemasonry did best was weaken a country so that it could be invaded by Bolshevism. This was the state Portugal was reduced to by 1926, when, according to Pattee, "the whole country had risen in arms and the central government in Lisbon capitulated."

It appeared that the Blessed Virgin's warning was coming to pass. Before she died little Jacinta told Canon Formigao about the Blessed Virgin's prophecy of "a civil war of an anarchist or communist character" that would erupt in Portugal unless "there were souls who would do penance and make reparation for the offenses done to God ..."[8] At this crucial point Portugal's President (and self-professed Freemason) Bernardino Machado resigned, and an unknown Catholic university professor named Antonio Oliveira Salazar began an unwilling rise to power.

The Counter-Revolution

Born in 1889 of peasant stock, Salazar attended seminary for eight years. He did not accept ordination and never married. A devout Catholic, his main ambition was to be a university professor at Coimbra. His reaction to the revolution was to become involved in Catholic Action. This led to his suspension from the university for "monarchical propaganda." In 1926 he was given perhaps the most difficult job in the Portuguese government — Finance Minister. As Antonio Salazar methodically unraveled Portugal's tortured finances, a priest who had been in residence with Salazar at Coimbra, Manuel Goncalves Cerejeira, was appointed to the Portuguese episcopate. On May 13, 1931 Cerejeira and his fellow bishops consecrated Portugal to the Immaculate Heart of Mary. The episcopal consecration was attended by hundreds of thousands of Portuguese, many of whom came on pilgrimage. The actual text of the consecration is worth quoting at length:

"The Shepherds chosen by Your Son to watch over and feed in His name the sheep He has acquired at the price of His blood — in this "Land of Holy Mary", whose name cannot be pronounced without pronouncing Your own — come today — as the official and consecrated representatives of their flocks, and in an act of filial "homage", (*vassalgem*) of faith, love and trust — to solemnly consecrate the Portuguese nation to Your Immaculate Heart. Take it from our fragile hands into Your own; defend it and guard it as Your own property; make Jesus reign, conquer and rule in it. Outside of Him there is no salvation.

"We, the pontiffs of Your people, feel a terrible storm raging around us, threatening to disperse and destroy the faithful flock of those who bless You because You are the Mother of Jesus. Afflicted, we stretch out our suppliant hands towards Your Son, as we cry out: 'Save us O Lord, for we perish!'…

"Intercede for Portugal, O Our Lady, in this grave hour when from the East blow furious winds, bringing cries of death against Your Son and against the civilization founded on His teachings, deceiving minds, perverting hearts, and lighting the fires of hatred and revolution in the world. Help of Christians, pray for us!

"Intercede for Portugal, Our Lady, in this troubled hour when the unclean waves of an open immorality, which has even lost the notion of sin, exalt the rehabilitation of the flesh in the face of the very Cross of Your Son, threatening to choke in this world the lily of virtue nourished by the Eucharistic Blood of Jesus. Virgin most Powerful, pray for us!

"Intercede for Portugal, Our Lady, in this hour of passions and doubts when even the good run the risk of being lost … Unite all the Portuguese people around Your Son, in the love of the Church and also in the cultivation of virtue, in respect for order and fraternal charity. Queen of Peace, pray for us!

"Remember, finally, Patroness of our country, that Portugal once taught so many lands to proclaim You blessed among all women. In remembrance of what it once did for Your glory, Our Lady of Fatima, save it, by giving it Jesus, in Whom it will find Truth, Life, and Peace!"[9]

The episcopal consecration of Portugal to the Immaculate Heart of Mary was the cornerstone of the Portuguese counter-revolution.

From it all things flowed, and against it Masonic and Bolshevik infiltration came to naught. In 1933 Antonio Salazar became the head of
the Portuguese government. An intensely private man who disliked
public speaking, Salazar was an unlikely leader of the counter-revolution. "If I am a revolutionary," he said, "it is only to the extent that I
am ... for truth against imposture, for order against disorder, to
which this country was only too accustomed."

He was not a nationalist, or a fascist like Hitler or Mussolini, with
whom he is usually, and incorrectly linked. He often appeared to despise
politics: "We are living in lies, hyperbole. Great, systematic attempts are
made to sow confusion in the soul of people ... This is not my goal. I wish
to normalize the nation":

> "We want to preserve at any price, from this wave that is fall-
> ing over the world, simplicity of life, purity of morals, gentleness
> of sentiments, the equilibrium of social relations, this modest but
> noble family atmosphere which is proper to Portuguese life."[10]

Salazar believed that Communism "is the 'great heresy' of our time ...
it tends to the subversion of everything", and "its destructive fury" and
"false conception of humanity" leads to "man's enslavement and his
worst subjection."

Democracy, on the other hand, "has resulted everywhere in instability and disorder." Liberal democracy "deprived us of some of the liber-
ties we possessed and has shown itself incapable of assuring us of those
we were able to obtain."[11]

These last remarks referred to the Masonic government that disfigured Portugal for sixteen years. In 1935 Salazar would ban Freemasonry, an act that almost cost him his life.[12] He owed his life, his political
career, and the successful counter-revolution in Portugal to the intercession of the Blessed Virgin, who deigned to respond to the Portuguese
episcopate's consecration of Portugal to Her Immaculate Heart by de-
feating Freemasonry and Bolshevism. Would She not do the same in
Russia, were She asked to do so by the Holy Father and the world episcopate?

"The Moment Has Come ..."

She had told Lucy that Russia would spread her errors until she was
consecrated to Her Immaculate Heart. Lucy's confessor, Father
Goncalves, transmitted this part of the Fatima Secret to the Holy Father in 1931. The apparitions at Cova da Iria were known to Pius XI; he
had advised Bishop da Silva to approve the apparitions. Pius was well
aware of the insane rampages in Bolshevik Russia. He was also aware of
the Catholic restoration of Portugal, and that country's consecration to
the Immaculate Heart of Mary. As the Blessed Virgin had told Lucy at
Tuy in 1929:

"The moment has come when God asks the Holy Father to make, in union with all the bishops of the world, the consecration of Russia to My Immaculate Heart, promising to save it by this means."[13]

But the consecration did not occur during the reign of Pius XI. In the summer of 1931 Our Lord told Lucy:

"They did not want to heed My request. Like the King of France, they will repent and do so, but it will be late. Russia will have already spread her errors throughout the world, causing wars and persecutions of the Church. The Holy Father will have much to suffer!"[14]

"They" refers either to Pius XI and his advisers, or to Pius XI and his successors as Pope. The reference to the King of France concerns Saint Margaret Mary's efforts to notify King Louis XIV of Heaven's will: that the King consecrate himself, and France, to the Sacred Heart of Jesus. This was not done by Louis XIV or his successors, and the result was the French Revolution.

The consequences of Pius XI's failure to consecrate Russia to the Immaculate Heart were the Spanish Civil War and the Second World War.

NOTES

1. Richard Pattee, *Portugal and the Portuguese World*, The Bruce Publishing Company, 1957, pp. 180-183.
2. Ibid., pp. 180-183.
3. The Cardinal of Chile, *Freemasonry Unveiled*, Christian Book Club of America, Fifth Printing, 1992, p. 80.
4. *Iamdudum* (On the Law of Separation in Portugal), Encyclical of Pope Pius X, May 24, 1911.
5. Ibid., the date of the encyclical, May 24, 1911, was the feast of Our Lady Help of Christians.
6. Pattee, op. cit., pp. 184-189.
7. Pais' assassin was released after a brief jail term, and never troubled again.
8. *TWTAF*, Volume II, p. 167. Our Lady reportedly told Jacinta that "Our Lord is very angry over the sins and crimes which are committed in Portugal. For this reason a terrible cataclysm of the social order menaces our country, especially the city of Lisbon. It seems that a civil war of an anarchist or communist character will break out, accompanied by plundering, killing, arson, and all sorts of devastation. The capital will become a real image of hell." Jacinta explained the prophecy was conditional, that is, the Blessed Virgin had told her that "if there were souls who would do penance and make reparation for the offenses done to God, and works of reparation were instituted to make satisfaction for crimes, the chastisement would be prevented."
9. As quoted in excerpts from *TWTAF*, Vol. II, pp. 391-393.
10. Ibid., pp. 413-419.
11. Ibid., pp. 413-419.
12. Untouched by a bomb detonated at close range, Salazar responded by going to Mass, and then, resuming his work day. (*TWTAF*, Vol. II, p. 425).
13. Kondor, op. cit., p. 235.
14. *TWTAF*, Vol. II, pp. 543-544. In an alternate version of this communication, Our Lord, according to Sister Lucy, told her: "Make it known to My ministers that given they follow the example of the King of France in delaying the execution of My request, that they will follow him into misfortune. It will never be too late to have recourse to Jesus and Mary."

Chapter Seven

The Spread of Errors and the Martyrdom of the Good

The Communists persecuted Russian Catholics as severely as the Orthodox. Catholicism was not even considered a religion. It was redefined as a religious "association", without the same rights, however, as other professional or cultural organizations. Worse, Church property was taken by the State, and in order to use the churches the faithful were taxed so oppressively many churches were unable to stay open.

A new Communist law, the separation of Church and State, was used to justify not only high taxes but the arrest, imprisonment, exile, and even execution of priests and bishops. By the end of 1923 all the episcopal sees were vacant. By 1926 more than half of the twelve hundred Catholic churches in Russia were either destroyed or closed. The number of priests dropped from nine hundred to four hundred. In 1917 there were 6,000,000 Catholics in Russia; by 1939 there were less than half a million.[1] Where did everyone go? Some escaped Russia. Others were murdered where they stood, died in prison, or disappeared into the gulags, never to be seen again.[2]

According to *The Red Book of the Persecuted Church*, "The years 1929-1932 saw the total liquidation of the Catholic hierarchy in the Soviet Union. Priests shared the fate of their bishops. Of the 66 priests in the diocese of Zytomir in 1918 there remained but one invalid priest in 1931. The roll of clergy imprisoned or deported during the period contains 114 names. In the whole of the USSR there were hardly 50 priests still at liberty."[3]

As churches burned and bishops and priests were martyred, Pope Pius XI followed the policy of his predecessor, Benedict XV. He protested the Communist persecution of the Church, but he did not condemn Communism, and he did not sever diplomatic relations between the Vatican and Moscow. The purpose of this policy was to aid Russian Catholics and, if possible, to lessen persecution. The Vatican policy also served Soviet purposes, however. Diplomatic relations with the Vatican gave the Soviet government an appearance of legitimacy, and communications with the Vatican facilitated Communist espionage and infiltration of the Church, in Russia and in Rome.

Pius XI created commissions to work with the Soviet government in supplying money and food for famine victims and refugees of the "people's government". Pius personally oversaw the raising of nearly one million pounds, but Russia's new rulers allowed precious little money or food to reach their starving subjects. In return for his earnest diplomacy, Pius "saw his priests murdered, churches destroyed, his commissions and his charitable advances repelled."[4] Through it all the Vatican appeared oblivious to the fact that the Soviet government had created the famine in order to deliberately starve to death millions of its own citizens.

It is likely that Pius' "Ostpolitik" ("opening to the East") was influenced not only by his predecessor Benedict, but also by the Western press, which downplayed the evil and violence of Communism, insisting the latter was a "democracy", and therefore superior to the previous Christian monarchy. The volume and consistency of this false message is remarkable for many reasons, not least of which being that Russia had been an ally of the Western powers in the World War against Germany and Austria. Since the original Bolsheviks were German agents who knocked Russia out of the war, why weren't Western opinion makers indignant over the treachery of its enemy? Why did it instead cheer the demise of its ally Russia?

Besides the Western press, Pius' Ostpolitik was influenced by his desire to be "the Pope of Reunion" between Rome and the Orthodox Church. Ratti developed this ambition in his contacts with Orthodox churchmen while he was papal nuncio in Warsaw. Now as Pope, he received intelligence reports that suggested the Communist revolution might prove providential for improving renewed relations between Catholic and Orthodox. The Soviets encouraged this hope by claiming to promote religious liberty in Russia. This pleasing lie would be used again and again by the Soviets, including Mikhail Gorbachev. In 1925 it served to reassure the Vatican that the Communist leaders were reasonable men, even though arrests, tortures, and murders continued.

"We had thought that the Russian government would be grateful for the Apostolic See's assistance in the famine, but this hope has deceived us," wrote Msgr. Constantine Budkiewicz to the papal nuncio in Warsaw. Despite Vatican diplomacy the Communists "persecuted our churches with the greatest severity, closing them, and desecrating the relics of the saint (Blessed Andrew Bobola)."[5] Budkiewicz was Pastor of St. Catherine's Church in Petrograd. Shortly after filing his report he was executed by the Bolsheviks. He was shot on Good Friday, 1923, for instructing young children in the Catholic Faith, and for refusing to cease his instruction.[6]

The Communists began rounding up all Church valuables, including the sacred vessels used in divine worship. The government claimed these materials would help the famine victims, an interesting claim since it was the Communist government who caused the famine. What the government roundup did was further impoverish the Church, and make it even more difficult to celebrate Mass. Pius XI offered to pay the Soviets an equivalent sum for the return of the vessels, not just for the Catholic but also for the Orthodox Church. The Vatican offer was turned down by the Soviet government.[7]

Publicly the Communists denied charges that they were persecuting religion. Privately the Communists frankly plotted strategy to destroy religion, as evidenced by this report of the 17th Conference of the Bolshevik Party, where it was declared: "The effort to bring about the death of religion during the Second Five Years' Plan will be no easy one ... We must, then, broaden and deepen the anti-religious struggle, ... observe the two maxims of Lenin, that the fight against the highly organized religions is more necessary, but more difficult than against the falsehoods of primitive religions, and that it cannot be separated from the fight against idealism, *for idealism ends in priestcraft*. Materialism, materialism, nothing but materialism."[8]

Pius XI certainly had his work cut out for him, and his refusal to condemn Communism did not make his diplomatic ventures more successful. It was not until 1933 that Pius abandoned his Ostpolitik – after discovering that his diplomatic commission to Russia was infiltrated by Communists. Worse than worthless, the commission had been feeding the Vatican disinformation — a Communist euphemism for lies — for years.[9]

Lucy and Jacinta

In all likelihood Pius XI learned of the Blessed Virgin's request for the consecration of Russia to Her Immaculate Heart by August 1931.[10] Although Pius had reviewed the Fatima dossier and given his approval for Bishop da Silva to approve the apparitions, it is evident that Pius was not as approving of the "Fatima Secret" as he was of the apparitions. Miracles and devotion on a Portuguese hillside was one thing; receiving unasked for advice on international diplomacy from a Portuguese peasant girl was quite another.

After receiving and making known Heaven's request for the consecration of Russia in 1929, Lucy remained in Tuy, Spain, until 1934. She made her perpetual vows on the Feast of St. Thérèse. Her mother was there and so was Bishop da Silva.[11] Afterwards Lucy returned to Pontevedra. The following year Jacinta's remains were transferred from Ourem to the cemetery at Fatima. Her casket was opened and it was discovered that her face was incorrupt, even though quick lime had been thrown on the corpse to hasten decomposition. Her casket was resealed and her remains were taken home to Fatima.

Bishop da Silva sent photographs of Jacinta's open casket to Lucy. Grateful, she wrote him of her "joy at seeing my childhood friend once more." Calling Jacinta "a child only in age", Lucy credited her company with helping "the preservation of my innocence," and concluded, "I have great esteem for her sanctity." Da Silva instructed Lucy to write Jacinta's biography. She completed it on Christmas Day, 1935. It became known as Lucy's first Memoir, and for a time served as a welcome distraction from the spread of Russia's errors into Spain.

"The Good Will Be Martyred"

Like Russia and Portugal, the revolution in Spain featured Freemasons and Bolsheviks, and the overthrow of a monarchy by a Masonic republic. Boasts of a "bloodless coup" were misleading, however, as Masonry's numerous assassination attempts against Spain's King Alfonso XIII had finally driven him into exile. Then there was the street violence instigated by the villainous Freemason and Anarchist Francisco Ferrer, who told his disciples: "against the police and the clergy there is only one means of action — bombs and poison."[12]

Nevertheless, the new republic was supported by many Catholics, including some clergy, who were enticed by promises that the Republicans would raise their salaries.[13] Other Spaniards were simply unaware that Spain's new rulers were violently anti-Catholic. Others, like Spain's Christian Democrats, a group of progressive Catholic intellectuals, were not upset to see the King flee.

Spain's new President was Alcala Zamora,[14] a lawyer and Freemason of Jewish descent who also claimed to be Catholic. The new government was dominated by Freemasons, as evidenced by the legislation it immediately enacted. As with Russia and Portugal, Church and State were separated, the Jesuits were banished, divorce was legalized and religious education was banned.[15] Then churches began burning.

Writes English historian Hugh Thomas, "Throughout Republican Spain, churches and convents were indiscriminately burned and despoiled ... Destruction rather than loot was the aim." He notes that "the breaking of images and of sacred objects, or the wearing by militia men of ecclesiastical robes, was often greeted with laughter." So, presumably, was the "firing squad" that opened fire on a large public statue of the Sacred Heart of Jesus.[16]

Thousands of churches were torched or sacked. The "Russian Kommintern" declared: "The flames ascending from the burning churches and monasteries of Spain have shown the true character of the Spanish revolution."[17] Portugal's President Salazar agreed: "This war is the fruit of Soviet influence in Spain." The Bishop of Tuy, Antonio Garcia, stated: "The present conflict is one of the most terrible wars waged by Anti-Christ, that is, by Judaism, against the Catholic Church and against Christ ... Jewry uses two formidable armies; one secret, namely that of Freemasonry; the other, open and avowed, with hands dripping with blood, that of the Communists ..."[18]

Garcia was not a lone voice. The entire Spanish episcopate declared that by February 1936, the Soviets "decreed the revolution in Spain and financed it with exorbitant sums."[19] The bishops also alleged that revolutionary militias were being trained and armed by the Soviets. Even worse was the establishment in Spain of the dreaded Soviet secret police, the *Cheka*. The institution of the *Cheka* made life in republican Spain a nightmare.

"It is estimated that some 225 of these instruments of terror existed in Madrid alone. That the government supported them is evidenced by the fact that the representatives serving on them were cloaked in the authority of public agents ... Cars labelled *CHEKA* and carrying red and black flags patrolled everywhere, loaded with armed men ... The number of victims will never be established, although it is estimated as 60,000 (dead) for Madrid, 30,000 for Valencia, and 50,000 for Barcelona, and these figures are taken as extremely conservative."[20]

Carlton Hayes, former American ambassador to Spain, spoke of the "early and extensive aid" Spain's Republican government received from Russia, and added: "Nor should there be doubt about the central purpose of this aid. It was not to safeguard, except temporarily and nominally, a liberal, democratic Republic. Rather, it was to make Spain a Communist country, a satellite of Moscow." This was confirmed by a British Republican volunteer, who recalled his arrival to Spain as follows: "The red flag was flying with the hammer and sickle of the Soviets, while the smallest children seemed to be able to sing the *Internationale* and give the clenched fist salute ... I began to think I had come to a Bolshevik state instead of a democratic one."[21]

In March 1936, Russian ships began delivering arms to Spanish ports. It was at this time that the Soviet Ambassador, Marcel (Moises) Rosenberg, and the bloody-handed Bela Kun[22] visited Spain as advisors to the new Spanish President, Manuel Azana. Under the benevolent gaze of the Mason Azana, the Bolsheviks made good on their pledge to, as one revolutionary put it, "create gigantic flames which can be seen all over the planet, and waves of blood which redden the seas."[23]

Between July 1 and September 1, 1936, approximately eight thousand religious were murdered: 12 bishops, over 5,000 priests, more than 2,000 monks, and hundreds of nuns and novices.[24] Hugh Thomas, while sympathetic to the Masonic republic, admits that "many of these crimes were accompanied by a partly frivolous, partly sadistic cruelty."[25]

For instance, one bishop was forced to scrub the deck of a prison ship, then was executed. Another, Bishop Asensio, was castrated, hit in the mouth with a brick ("Here, take Communion" he was told), and after somehow surviving a firing squad was left to die on a pile of corpses. "Do what you like", Asensio told his torturers, "I will pray for you in Heaven."[26] The fact that many of the bishops were elderly did not save them from revolutionary fury.[27]

A priest was beaten, scourged and crowned with thorns. A large beam of wood was placed on his back, and he was given vinegar to drink. The priest forgave his tormenters and blessed them. His torturers seemed bent on a ritual murder, but the less demonic ones ended up shooting the priest instead. According to Thomas, "His last request was to be shot facing his tormentors so that he might die blessing them."[28] Another priest, facing a firing squad, told his executioners: "I want to bless you. Please free my hands." The ropes were cut and his hands were chopped off. "Bless us now," he was told with a sneer, and bless them the priest did, moving his bloody stumps in the sign of the Cross until he died.[29]

Father Mariano Albas was murdered while giving last rites to a group of seminarians, who died with him. A *New York Times* reporter "saw the body of a priest, Father Jose de la Cora, crucified, head down," on the main door of his church.[30] Other priests were doused with gasoline and set on fire. Still others were buried alive. One was hung on a meat hook naked, with the sign "Pork meat for sale" on his stomach. Another priest was found, starved and half-mad, wandering the Spanish countryside. Really, what was there to do after your bishop had been executed, your church had been leveled, and all your parishioners had been murdered?

Even so, not many priests followed the unusual example of a young priest named Jose Maria Escriva, who avoided persecution by discarding his cassock and faking insanity at a psychiatric hospital in Madrid. Father Escriva must have put on a convincing act, for it was three months before the hospital staff got wise and told him to leave. He hid out until he found some of his followers, members of an embryonic religious group called Opus Dei, and escaped to safety.[31]

Many estimates place the deaths of Catholic laymen in Spain in the hundreds of thousands.[32] The majority were summarily murdered for being Catholic, a condition that apparently negated any right to a jury trial, due process, or any of the other rights of man the revolutionary government made so much of. Instead homicidal rage was the order of the day. Men were beaten to death, or hurled off cliffs.[33] Others were burned alive, or were forced to dig their own graves, in which they were then buried — alive.

Eight hundred more were thrown down a mine shaft. Still others were castrated. Women and children were not spared. The mother of two Jesuits had a crucifix forced down her mouth. A young man had his eyes gouged out. Another was tossed into the bull ring, "where he was gored to unconsciousness. Afterwards, one of his ears was cut off, in imitation of the amputation of the ear of a bull in honor of the matador ..." In all these inhuman scenarios, the revolutionaries greeted the moment of death with applause — "then there would be shouts of 'Liberty! Down with Fascism.'"[34]

American Communist sympathizer Cornelius Vanderbilt viewed a "howling mob" singing the *Internationale*, with oxen pulling a chained group of "three or four cowled monks, one of whom they had already beheaded." He also saw "two monks who had already been crucified. Their faces were twisted as if the pain had been unbearable. Large railroad spikes had been driven through their shriveled stomachs, and dried blood covered their legs."[35] Other monks had their eardrums perforated with Rosary beads.

Nuns were raped, mutilated, and lynched. Vanderbilt saw "nuns shackled to one another's ankles being dragged by lively mules through the cobblestone streets, the whole tops of their heads ablaze. I was told they had been dipped in kerosene and touched off with long, white church tapers."[36] Not content to merely bedevil the living, the Bolsheviks dug up the graves of nineteen Salesian nuns, and publicly profaned their corpses on the streets of Barcelona. Mr. Thomas writes that "in one month (July, 1936), close to one hundred thousand people were killed arbitrarily and without a trial." Masonic loyalties unshaken, the historian gamely patches up the ugliness where he can. Unfortunately the evidence is overwhelming, and he quietly admits, "At no time in the history of Europe or even perhaps the world has so passionate a hatred of religion and all its works been shown."[37]

In so dire a situation a group of exiled Spanish priests composed a prayer to the beloved Virgin of the Pilar:

"To You, O Mary, Queen of Peace, we always return, we the faithful sons of Your best-loved Spain, now vilified, outraged, befouled by criminal Bolshevism, deprived by Jewish Marxism, and scorned by savage Communism. We pray You, tears in our eyes, to come to our help, to accord final triumph to the glorious armies of the Liberator and Reconqueror of Spain, the new Pelayo, the *Caudillo*! *Viva* Christ the King!"[38]

The Caudillo was a small, rather nondescript Spanish army officer with an unremarkable military career. Fate and Providence made him the leader of the Spanish counter-revolution. Quietly, he turned to face the howling, implacable enemies of the faith, and engage them in a fight to the death.

NOTES

1. Cianfarra, op. cit., pp. 53-54.
2. But see Albert Galter, *The Red Book of the Persecuted Church*, The Newman Press, 1957, p. 39, where the author states that the 1921 Treaty of Riga, which changed the borders between Russia and Poland, was also responsible for the loss of many Catholics.
3. Ibid., p. 50.
4. Philip Hughes, *Pope Pius XI*, Sheed & Ward, 1937, p. 164.
5. An extract from an official Church document, as reproduced in James J. Zatko, *Descent Into Darkness, The Destruction of the Roman Catholic Church in Russia, 1917-1923*, University of Notre Dame Press, 1965. St. Andrew Bobola was a Polish Jesuit martyred in 1657. His body remained miraculously incorrupt, and was claimed to be the source of many miracles. The Bolsheviks stole the saint's body, desecrated it, and hid it in a museum. Pius XI persuaded the Communists to release the relic, and it was transferred to Rome. Pius XI canonized Bobola in

1938. Today his body, darkened yet still incorrupt, still bearing the disfiguring wounds of his martyrdom, rests in a reliquary beneath the main altar of the church bearing his name in Warsaw, Poland.

6. Galter, op. cit., p. 44. The Soviet Criminal Code forbade religious instruction.

7. Ibid., pp. 41-42.

8. Emphasis in original. Monsignor M. D'Herbigny (President of the Pontifical Commission for Russia) *Militant Atheism, The World-Wide Propaganda of Communism*, (Published by the Society for Promoting Christian Knowledge, London), 1933, pp. 76-77.

9. *TWTAF*, Volume II, Section 3, Chapter VIII.

10. Ibid., pp. 542-546. It is evident from Lucy's correspondence that she was satisfied Pius XI had received the Blessed Virgin's request for the consecration of Russia, and the promotion of First Saturday reparatory devotions.

11. In her sixth Memoir (p. 193) Lucy records a conversation she had with her mother after the ceremony. Lucy reminded Maria Rosa of her belief that when Lucy left Fatima "the whole story would come to an end." Lucy asked if this had happened during the ensuing thirteen years. Maria Rosa said, "Not a bit of it! It just gets worse and worse!" Lucy said, "So you see, I'm not there now to deceive people: it's God and Our Lady who are there!" Maria Rosa answered, "If I could be quite sure that it was Our Lady who appeared to you, than I would be only too glad to give Her Cova da Iria and everything else that I have. But I'm not sure!" It was the last time Lucy saw her mother alive.

12. Poncins, *The Secret Powers Behind Revolution*, op. cit., pp. 61-64.

13. Arnold Lunn, *Spanish Rehearsal*, Sheed & Ward, 1937, p. 204.

14. Evidence that Republican Presidents Zamora and Azana were Freemasons is provided by Denis Fahey, *Mystical Body of Christ in the Modern World,* op. cit., p. 325, 61, 95, and Appendix Four.

15. In his book *Militant Atheism, The World-Wide Propaganda of Communism*, Monsignor D'Herbigny (President of the Pontifical Commission for Russia) notes that Communist procedures seldom vary. They attack the Church first and foremost. They secularize education in order to indoctrinate the new generation. They attempt to "liberate" women by teaching them to, in the words of a Communist, "Fight against the law forbidding abortion. Abortion should be carried out gratuitously in hospitals by doctors every time that the parents are ill or cannot support their children. (Advocate for the) Sale of contraceptual means and of books explaining their use. It is also needful to insist on lectures, giving women instruction on the means for avoiding pregnancy. The fact must be grasped that present-day laws against these means proceed from the bourgeois, whose interest it is that the proletariat should be numerous in order that they may the better exploit it for their own ends." (p. 2).

16. The quotes are from Hugh Thomas, *The Spanish Civil War*, Etre & Spottiswoode Ltd., 1961. For better and worse, Thomas' book is the standard reference for the Spanish Civil War in English. Mr. Thomas was a respected establishment historian whose visceral distaste for Catholicism goaded him to reproduce any and all "facts" that reflected negatively on the Church, many of which are obviously propagandist in nature.

17. As quoted in Fahey, *The Mystical Body of Christ*, op. cit., p. 95.

18. As quoted in Fahey, *Mystical Body of Christ*, op. cit., p. 264.

19. See *TWTAF*, Vol. II, p. 628. Although the bishops were correct, there had been a Communist presence in Spain for decades. Spanish Marxists instigated a revolution in 1873, had a hand in 32 churches being burned in Barcelona in 1909, and orchestrated a general strike in 1917 that caused the Spanish government to declare a state of war. By 1932 membership in the Spanish Stalin party was 12,000. (Lunn, op. cit., pp. 125-129).

20. Richard Pattee, *This Is Spain*, The Bruce Publishing Company, 1951, pp. 259-260. According to Pattee's information, the Cheka were responsible for the death of at least one bishop (p. 267, fn 23.)

21. As quoted in Carlton J. H. Hayes, *The United States and Spain, An Interpretation*, Sheed & Ward, 1951, p. 118. The previous quotation from Hayes is on p. 121.

22. Real name Benjamin Cohen, Bolshevik dictator and architect of revolutionary terror in Hungary in 1919.

23. *TWTAF*, Volume II, p. 630.

24. Thomas, op. cit., p. 173.

25. Ibid., p. 173.

26. Robert Hutchison, *Their Kingdom Come, Inside the Secret World Of Opus Dei*, Doubleday, 1997, p. 75. Hutchison states that "in Madrid, three out of every ten priests were killed during the reign of terror. In Barbastro, nine out of every ten lost their lives. (p. 75).

27. Pattee (op. cit., p. 267) notes "The bishops who suffered martyrdom at the hands of the repub-

licans are: Eustaquio Nieto, Bishop of Siguenza, 72 years old, judged by street mob, executed July 27, 1936, and body burned. Silvio Ruiz, Bishop of Lerida, placed himself in government custody, and was turned over to militiamen. Shot before cemetery wall, Aug. 5, 1936. Cruz Laplana Laguna, Bishop of Cuenca, 71 years old, killed on a highway, Aug. 8, 1936. Florencio Aasensio Barroso, Titular Bishop of Urea and Apostolic Administrator of Barbastro, murdered, mutilated, and tossed into common grave, Aug. 9, 1936. Miguel Serra Succarrate, Bishop of Segorbe, 79 years old, killed on Aug. 9, 1936, by a band of Left republican supporters of President Azana. Manuel Basulto Jimenez, Bishop of Jaen, taken from a prison train on way to Madrid. Murdered at Vallecas on Aug. 12, 1936, together with 200 other prisoners. Manuel Borras, Auxiliary Bishop of Tarragona, executed Aug. 12, 1936. His body was examined by witnesses who reported mutilations and partial burning with gasoline. Narciso de Estenaga Echevarria, Bishop of Cuidad Real, taken from his house, escorted outside the city, and murdered on Aug. 22, 1936. Diego Vantaja Milan, Bishop of Almeria, murdered August 28, 1936, and body exposed to the profanations of the mob. Manuel Medina Olmos, Bishop of Guadizx, murdered with the Bishop of Almeria. Manuel Irurita Almandoz, Bishop of Barcelona, seized after flight from palace and taken before San Elias *Cheka*, murdered, Dec. 3, 1936. Anselmo Polanco y Fontecha, Bishop of Teruel, murdered near Figueras, Feb. 7, 1939, body left unburied. Juan de Dios Ponce, Apostolic Administrator of Orihuela."

28. Thomas, op. cit., 173.
29. Lunn, op. cit., p. 197. This story was told by the Bishop of Gibraltar
30. Ibid., p. 215. Father de la Cora may have been martyred while saying the Mass, as he died wearing ceremonial vestments. The reporter also witnessed "the body of his brother, Ramon de la Cora, was lying in front of the church door. He had been shot dead by the Communists." And the reporter goes on to detail other savageries committed against nuns.
31. Hutchison, op. cit., pp. 75-80, gives a less than flattering portrayal of Father Escriva.
32. Historian Arthur Bryant, after some examination, estimated at least 350,000 men, women and children to have been murdered. A leftist correspondent with the *Manchester Guardian* estimated that at least 40,000 were executed in Madrid alone. See Lunn op. cit., p. 219.
33. A visiting American novelist, Ernest Hemingway, wrote of this in *For Whom The Bell Tolls*.
34. Thomas, op. cit., pp. 174-5. Unless otherwise noted, most of the atrocities are recounted in Thomas' book.
35. Lunn, op. cit., pp. 214-215.
36. Ibid., p. 215.
37. Untouched by revolutionary violence was Spain's small Protestant population. None of their God-less churches were damaged either.
38. Thomas, op. cit., p. 451.

Chapter Eight

"The Epic of the Alcazar"

The incantations of "Liberty" evoked by the death rattles of the revolution's victims echoed throughout Spain, from Granada to Galicia, Spain's most northwestern province, which borders the Atlantic and sits on top of long, narrow Portugal like a cap. Galicia was the birthplace of Generalissimo Francisco Franco.[1]

When the revolution visited Galicia, "Lucy, with her community, spent hours of real fright, which is reflected in the house diaries and the correspondence of the time." According to Father Alonso, "At Pontevedra, the revolutionary militia first took hold of the city, and then they menacingly presented themselves before the artillery barracks ... At Tuy, on July 18, the revolutionaries captured the street and the episcopal palace was assailed."[2]

Lucy and her fellow Sisters may have owed their lives to the Nationalist troops that drove the revolution out of Pontevedra and Tuy one week later. After calm was restored, Lucy wrote her confessor, Father Goncalves: "In spite of the proximity of so many tempests and dangers, the good Lord watched over my Sisters, so that we can say that we passed through water and through fire, and that we came out safe and well. Thanks to God, up to the present, we still have had nothing more to suffer than a little fear.

"In truth I was not worried for a moment, partly because of the trust I had in the Holy Hearts of Jesus and Mary, and the joy I felt at going to be united with them in Heaven ... nothing would be more pleasing to me than to give my life for God, so as to repay Him in some way for giving His life for me; I recognize, however, that I am unworthy of so great a favor."[3]

Father Goncalves was less calm. He was convinced the revolution in Spain was the fulfillment of the Blessed Virgin's warning that "Russia will spread her errors" unless she was consecrated to the Immaculate Heart. Pius XI had been told of the consecration but apparently had decided on a different course of action. What should be done? Lucy responded that she had asked God "why He would not convert Russia without the Holy Father making that consecration."

According to Lucy, Our Lord told her: "Because I want My whole Church to acknowledge that consecration as a triumph of the Immaculate Heart of Mary, so that it may extend its cult later on, and put the devotion to this Immaculate Heart beside the devotion to My Sacred Heart."

Lucy then implored: "But my God, the Holy Father probably won't believe me, unless You Yourself move him with a special inspiration." She was told: "The Holy Father. Pray very much for the Holy Father. He will do it, but it will be late! Nevertheless, the Immaculate Heart of Mary will save Russia. It has been entrusted to Her."[4]

Lucy next worried to Father Goncalves: "Who will assure me that all this is not a mere illusion?" Maria Rosa had raised her daughter to hate lies. Consequently, Lucy was "afraid of deceiving myself and others, which I want to avoid at all costs": "When I speak intimately with God I feel His presence to be so real that there is no doubt in my mind, but when I have to communicate it, all I have is fear of illusion ... I leave everything in the hands of God and in the care of the Immaculate Heart of Mary, and I try to work in my field of action, which is sacrifice and prayer."[5]

Due to the insistence of Father Goncalves, and the demonic barbarism in neighboring Spain that threatened at any moment to spill into Portugal, Bishop da Silva finally wrote Pius XI and requested he consecrate Russia and institute the Five First Saturdays devotion. According to Father Alonso, "the document was received at Rome at the end of March, 1937. On April 8 the Holy See acknowledged receiving it."[6]

Pius XI

The Holy Father did not reply to Bishop da Silva's letter. He did not consecrate Russia or institute the Five First Saturdays devotion. He had adequate information and opportunity to do both. What happened?

Pope Ratti wrote several classic encyclicals concerning Communism, Socialism, and the Kingship of Christ that demonstrate his understanding of the natural and supernatural forces at play in the Twentieth Century. Pius' championing of the rights of Christ the King over the temporal affairs of men gave him the reputation of being the Pope of Catholic Action.[7] Paradoxically, however, Pius' tendency was to thwart attempts to put his principles into practice. This occurred in France, where Pius condemned *Action Francaise*, and more tragically, in the Mexican Revolution, where the Vatican ordered the victorious *Cristeros* to re-subject themselves to their Masonic/Communist rulers. The results were predictable. The Mexican Catholics were brutally suppressed, while a yawning Church in America looked the other way. It is said that Pius wept at the result, but it is safe to say that the *Cristeros* wept louder and longer.

Moreover, when it came to applying the principles of his encyclicals to concrete political situations, Pius tended to compromise; at times he behaved like a Wilsonian democrat. His failed diplomacy with the Bolsheviks is the most obvious example, but not the only one. Pius didn't seem a fan of monarchies, particularly the Spanish monarchy. Alphonse XIII visited Pius in Rome at the beginning of his pontificate, and dedicated Spain to "the cause of Christ." Consequently, seventy Masonic lodges in Spain were raided and closed down. Spain suffered a series of financial setbacks, engineered, it was alleged, by international finance.[8]

Increasing civil violence and assassination attempts drove Alphonse out of Spain. He thought his departure would avert civil war, but instead it hastened it. When the new Masonic republic began persecuting the Church, Pius' complaint was almost apologetic.

By 1936 red flags bearing the hammer and sickle waved over Spain, and shouts of "Viva Russia" filled the streets. Now over eighty years old, Pius abandoned his temporizing. He told journalists that Communism was "the primary peril" that "threatens everything, takes possession of everything, and infiltrates everywhere, overtly or secretly."[9]

Later the same year his Secretary of State, Cardinal Eugenio Pacelli, presented Spanish refugees to Pius. After consoling them Pius addressed another special group of Spaniards: "Our blessing goes out in a special manner to all those who have assumed the difficult and perilous task of defending and restoring the rights and honor of God and religion ..."[10]

At long last the Holy Father had blessed the Catholic counter-revolution, in the person of Spain's military leader, Generalissimo Francisco Franco.

Franco

There is little information in English that is favorable, or even objective, about Franco.[11] He is usually dismissed with one word epithets, the repeatable ones being "fascist" and "dictator". He was a dictator, though as much by default as by design. Strictly speaking, he was not a fascist. The persistent rumor that he was Jewish might be true; his Catholicism has never been disputed.

He was born in Galicia to middle class parents. Francisco's mother was a pious, long-suffering Catholic. His father was a naval officer, and reportedly was a heavy drinker and a womanizer. Their quiet, introverted son grew up to be an army careerist specializing in dangerous combat missions. He rose in rank quickly, becoming known as *comandantin* ("Little Major"), both for his height (five feet three inches tall) and his young age. At age 33 he became the youngest general in Europe since Napoleon. Politically, Franco was a conservative nationalist, in contrast to his younger brother Ramon, a committed leftist who joined the air force and led a conspiracy against the monarchy. When Francisco reproached his brother in a letter, Ramon attempted to humiliate his older brother by publishing his letter.

As anarchy under the new republic progressed, Franco repeatedly resisted attempts to enlist him in a coup d'etat. He was not blind to events, however, stating that Freemasonry "was the principal cause of Spain's ruin", and connecting Masonry and Communism as partners in crime.

This may have caused his banishment to the Canary Islands. Franco did not rebel at his exile, but he did write President Azana, warning him that the republic's military policies were eroding Army morale. Azana did not reply. The summer of terror in 1936 pushed Franco — and many others — to join what became known as the "Nationalist rebellion."[12]

"The Epic of Alcazar"

A consistent irony in nations where Communism has imposed itself is that the only true (as opposed to manufactured) "revolution of the proletariat" is the uprising *against* Communist rule. As Franco was being flown to Morocco to be reunited with his 32,0000 man army, the Spanish "proletariat" rose — convulsed is more accurate — to expel the intruders from Spanish soil.

If Franco and his battle-hardened troops were the brains and brawn of Spain's counter-revolution, the red-bereted Carlists were the counter-revolution's heart and soul. The Carlists (also known as the Traditionalist Communion) were derided as fascists, but in fact they were traditional Catholics of the Roman rite, who pinned Sacred Heart badges on their shirts and wore rosaries around their necks. The Carlists believed they were in a religious crusade, at grips with forces that issued from the very pit of hell. Said one: "This is a religious war and a war of Reconquest, for in Spain everything was conquered under the protection of the Cross and was preserved by the Cross."

Humanly speaking, the counter-revolution was no match for Russian machine guns, troops, and tanks. Russian ships patrolled the Gibraltar Strait to prevent Franco from entering Spain, while Russian arms strove to exterminate the determined, but isolated outbursts of counter-revolution. Until the Spanish Civil War the Western press had never met a revolution it didn't like. Now, suddenly, the Nationalist forces threatening the Spanish republic were viewed with collective horror by the press. The call was sounded for volunteers from around the world to save Spain's Masonic republic from the "fascist revolt". Thus were born the International Brigades.

An American publication, *Jewish Life*, reported on "the broad distribution of Jews in practically every International Brigade", and went on to assert that so many American volunteers were Jewish that Yiddish had become the common language.[13] The largest American battalion, The Abraham Lincoln Brigade,[14] was inspired by world press reports of the gallant, beleaguered Spanish democracy (that is, the violent Masonic/Communist anti-Christian revolution) struggling against the evils of "international fascism." Typical of this view was the *New York Times* report on the resolution of 200 American rabbis that the "conflict in Spain between the accredited legally elected government and the Fascist Rebels is of signal importance as foreshadowing the world struggle between democracy and the forces of oppression."[15]

Meanwhile, "the forces of oppression" were besieged at the Alcazar, a massive, towered castle in Toledo, that had once been the palace of the Holy Roman Emperor, King Charles V. It became a military college, and in July, 1936, the Alcazar became the residence of about 2000 Carlists: one thousand soldiers and their wives and families, who had retreated from the violent terror that had overwhelmed Toledo. Led by Colonel Jose Moscardo, a semi-retired soldier, the Alcazar was an island of reaction in a sea of republicanism. Toledo was just south of Madrid, and the whole area was controlled by the revolution; except the Alcazar.

For sixty-seven days Moscardo and the Alcazar were subjected to "unrelieved bombardment, shelling, mines, underground explosives, and constant attack."[16] At night huge floodlights were trained on the castle, an attempt at psychological warfare that failed, since most of the besieged were in the catacombs of the great castle. They knew their cause was hopeless when the siege began. Only later did they hear on their wireless radio that, to the great indignation of Soviet Russia and the Western media, Italian planes airlifted Franco and his troops over the Russian ships blocking the Strait of Gibraltar. The nationalist army began reclaiming cities and towns from the revolution, moving slowly and steadily northwards, in a straight line towards Toledo and Madrid.

It all seemed too little, too late, but Moscardo had no intention of surrendering. He made that clear enough when the besieging army captured his son, Luis. There was a telephone in the Alcazar, and Luis was made to call his father. "They say they will shoot me if the Alcazar does not surrender," Luis said. He asked his father what to do. "If it be true," Moscardo told Luis, "commend your soul to God, pray for us, shout *Viva Espana* and die like a hero." Luis said he would do just that. "Good-bye my son, a last kiss," Jose Moscardo said, "the Alcazar will never surrender."[17]

At this point Moscardo had lost about half his men, everyone was living in the cellars, living on hard bread and mule soup. In addition to continual bombardment by planes and artillery, the besieged, being mostly underground, could hear the enemy tunneling towards them, at times even feeling the vibrations of the pneumatic drills. Those inside knew early on exactly where the bombs would be placed which would detonate the Alcazar, and in all likelihood bury them under tons of rubble.

It was this likelihood that caused Moscardo to request a priest, in order to baptize the babies born during the siege, and have last Confessions. The only priest available, that is, alive and not in hiding,[18] was Canon Vasquez Camarassa. He was a friend of the Republicans, and entered the Alcazar in lay clothes. After performing his priestly duties, Camarassa made to leave – he had no intention of being around for the big explosion. Before he left, however, he exhorted all present to give up. He was ignored. Turning to the women, he asserted that they were being held against their will. "That's a lie!" Carmen Romero retorted. "I have talked with every woman in the Alcazar and all of them think as I do. Either we will leave here free, with our men and children, or else we will die with them in the ruins."[19]

One week later the drilling stopped. There was silence as everyone awaited the detonation. The entry in the log book of the Alcazar is underlined: "All possible having been done, we commend ourselves to God." The explosion was of tremendous force. The southwest tower was tossed into the air, and an entire wall disappeared. There were breaches on all sides of the Alcazar, which seemed little more than a pile of rubble. The Republican army advanced through the dust and smoke to look for survivors.

They were met with volleys of machine gun fire and beat a hasty retreat. Thin, dusty, bleeding and deafened, the defenders of the Alcazar emerged from the catacombs, clawed through the rubble, and somehow filled the breaches in the walls in time to repel the enemy. Waving red banners with the hammer and sickle, hundreds of Republicans hurled themselves at the dozens of defenders, who met them on the broken stones in desperate hand-to-hand combat. Again the Republicans retreated. There was another attack, and a tank lumbered up the rubble of the Alcazar, crushing stones as it came. The defenders filled bottles with gasoline, lit them, and heaved their homemade bombs at the tank. The red flags bearing the hammer and sickle retreated once again. A ragged cry went up from the "forces of oppression": *Viva Cristo Rey!*" — Long live Christ the King! The Alcazar had held.

A few days later nationalist planes began circling Toledo. Franco had made rapid progress, towards Madrid, it was assumed, in order to arrive there before the International Brigades arrived to reinforce the city against attack. In full knowledge of this, Franco unhesitatingly stopped in Toledo to relieve the Alcazar and its valiant defenders. "The epic of the Alcazar," writes Richard Pattee, "was unquestionably the culminating point of heroism in this war which was filled with instances of individual and collective valor. The Alcazar became the symbol of the nationalist spirit and to a very real degree of the spirit of Spain."[20]

Warren Carroll notes that on one of the stone walls of the Alcazar there is "a little mosaic picture of Our Lady set in the wall in blue and white tile, which was there at the time of the siege. All around the picture the stones are covered with bullet marks. But the face and form of the Blessed Virgin Mary in the mosaic is untouched. She and Her faithful people, in this terrible confrontation with Christ's enemies, had triumphed."[21]

The priestless defenders had erected an underground altar, at which they prayed and offered up their sacrifices to the Blessed Virgin.[22] It is not unreasonable to believe that some of these prayers were directed to Our Lady of Fatima. Later, one of the defenders summarized the Epic of the Alcazar (and unknowingly, the present state of the Faith in the world) as follows: "We are few, they are many. But numbers are not all. We believe, we have faith. They do not believe, they would destroy faith. They think; that is in the brain. We pray; that is in the heart. I myself, sometimes I cry. But I am not afraid. If I die, I die. But that is only myself. What I believe cannot die.

"We are filthy. We have not washed. Our clothes stench (sic). We have insects. All that is around us is reeking and disgusting. We live in filth. But we live half, away beyond it. We do not swear. We do not blaspheme. We do not allow ourselves carnal thoughts. Those who have wives within the Alcazar do not take them.

"The Reds think. Thinking is nothing. Presently they will give way. We believe. That endures for ever."[23]

NOTES

1. Catholic politician and martyr Calvo Sotelo hailed from the Galician border town of Tuy, where Lucy resided until 1934. Sotelo was a powerful political opponent of the Revolution until he was assassinated in 1936, an act that initiated the civil war.

2. As quoted in *TWTAF*, Vol. II, p. 641.

3. Ibid., p. 642.

4. Ibid., pp. 630-631.

5. Ibid., pp. 631-632.

6. Ibid., p. 645.

7. Even though in practice Pius did not always support Catholic Action, his encyclicals certainly gave lay efforts impetus and inspiration. Pius XI did not invent Catholic Action, however. In 1848 Blessed Pius IX gave his blessing to "Catholic Associations" organized by the laity all over Europe, in response to the Revolution. "These organizations expanded and continued through successive pontificates into the Twentieth Century when Pius XI emerged as special patron of this lay movement with the familiar title of 'the Pope of Catholic Action.' It was he who worded the classic definition of the work of Catholic Action: 'participation of the laity in the hierarchical apostleship.'" (Emmet John Hughes, *Report From Spain*, New York: Henry Holt And Company, 1947, p. 55). Needless to say, papal encouragement of lay apostolates did not begin with Vatican II.

8. Hughes, op. cit., p. 305. The Masonic lodges were closed under Primo de Rivera, while Alphonse was King.

9. *TWTAF*, Vol. II, p. 637.

10. Ibid., p. 639.

11. Most of the information about Franco presented here is from Stanley G. Payne, *Franco's Spain*, Thomas Y. Crowell Company, 1967.

12. The American Catholic press was split on the Spanish Civil War. One of the more powerful advocates for Franco's cause was American writer William Thomas Walsh (author of a book on Fatima, as well as many other noteworthy historical studies). Walsh made the obvious point that the cause of Franco was the cause of the Church, and he did this so well and so often that he earned the wrath of, among others, Emmett John Hughes, who slung mud with both hands when he claimed that Walsh's "exorbitant enthusiasm" for Franco "has kept alive the oratorical tradition of the most eloquent members of the Nazi party." (*Report From Spain*, Henry Holt And Company, 1947, pp. 132-133).

13. *An Answer to Father Coughlin's Critics*, op. cit., p. 112.

14. Each country named their brigade after a national hero. Italy's contribution, for example, was the Garibaldi Brigade.

15. Ibid., pp. 113-114.

16. Pattee, *Spain,* op. cit., p. 219.

17. Luis was executed. Moscardo's only other son, Pepe, was also executed that same summer. Jose Moscardo's last conversation with Luis is a composite of two accounts: Carroll, op. cit., p. 160, and Lunn, op. cit., p. 72.

18. Of all the priests in Toledo, only seven (besides Camarassa) were not massacred because they went into hiding (Lunn, op. cit., p. 750.)

19. Carroll, op. cit., p. 191. Richard Pattee recounts a slightly different version: "A republican officer proposed in parley that the women leave, but they themselves on consultation indicated they would not leave, nor surrender, and if the men capitulated they would fight on alone." (*Spain*, op. cit., p. 220).

20. *Spain*, op. cit., p. 218.

21. *Soul* Magazine, July August 1993.

22. Pattee, *Spain*, op. cit., p. 220.

23. A statement made to Major McNeill-Ross, as quoted in Lunn, op. cit., p. 163.

Chapter Nine

Fascism, Counter-Revolution, and Fatima

Franco's detour to Toledo to relieve the Alcazar allowed a massive infusion of arms and men from Russia, and the International Brigades, to beat the nationalists to Madrid. Consequently, the counter-revolution stalled outside the Spanish capital.

It was a temporary setback. In 1938 Franco personally led a series of crushing victories over the Communists. In 1939 Barcelona and Madrid fell. The revolution was defeated. The red-bereted Carlists marched through the streets of Madrid to wild applause. At a *Te Deum* Mass Franco laid his sword before the high altar. He swore never to draw it again except in self-defense, and prayed aloud: "Lord, benevolently accept the effort of this people, which was always Thine, which, with me and in Thy name, has vanquished with heroism the enemy of truth in this century."[1]

Pius XI didn't live long enough to see the fruit of his blessing of Franco's efforts, yet the crucial approval of the Holy Father secured victory for the counter-revolution in Spain. One can praise Pius XI for this, and wonder with regret what different outcomes Catholic Action in France and Mexico may have had if Pius had blessed their efforts as well. One can also wonder what results would have flowed from Pius' consecration of Russia to the Immaculate Heart.

His successor, Pope Pius XII, broadcast a message to the Spanish nation on April 16, 1939 (the Sunday after Easter), in which he spoke "with immense joy" of "heroic Spain", and offered his "fatherly congratulations for the gift of peace and victory" given to Spain by God. Pius XII asserted that "this providential peace" was "the fruit no doubt of that blessing" which Pius XI had bestowed upon the Spanish counter-revolution. He continued:

> "The nation chosen by God to be the principal instrument for the evangelization of the New World, and an impregnable bulwark of the Catholic Faith, has just given to the proselytizers of the materialistic Atheism of our age the highest proof that the eternal values of religion and of the spirit stand above all things."[2]

Aside from the Church and Spain, however, Franco's victory over

Communism disappointed and angered almost everyone. This was partly due to the consistent misrepresentation by the press of the revolutionary government in Spain as a well-meaning democracy. In fact the Popular Front, as the political Republic was called, was a coalition of Freemasons, Socialists, Bakunin Anarchists, and Communists, who pulled the strings of their more respectable liberal, moderate, and conservative puppets in the *Cortes* (Spanish parliament). This was the hidden face of the "amiable democracy" young men from Europe and America came to Spain to die for.

The Communist infiltration of the Spanish government was quite similar to the Bolshevik revolution. In both, the ruling Christian monarch was forced to abdicate, and was temporarily replaced by an interim republic. Spain had two "Kerenskys" — Presidents Zamora and Azana, both Freemasons (like Kerensky) and both more or less willing dupes for Communist machinations. The insane violence against the Church in Spain was vintage Bolshevism. So was the execution of citizenry, the bloody terrorism of the secret police, and the eventual domination of the revolutionary government by the Communists.

Soviet ambassador Rosenberg's repeated threats to withhold Russian military aid eventually persuaded the Spanish Socialists and their leader, the Freemason Largo Caballero (nicknamed "the Spanish Lenin") to fall in line with instructions from Moscow. The anarchists were another story. When Marx defeated the Russian anarchist (and Illuminati) Michel Bakunin for control of the International revolution, Spanish International members broke rank to follow Bakunin. Consequently Spain housed the largest group of Anarchists in Europe who, according to establishment historian Hugh Thomas, "formed a secret society whose numbers were never published, and whose task was to maintain the Anarchist ideals ... in all their purity." He adds that this society was "greatly feared".[3]

They were led by Durutti, assassin of the Cardinal Archbishop of Saragossa, attempted assassin of King Alphonse, and murderer of countless lesser-knowns. As the counter-revolution gained ground the Popular Front did as much finger pointing as fighting. In the Anarchist stronghold of Barcelona, for example, Communists attempted to shut down the Anarchist press. Anarchists bitterly denounced this as a "provocation" (they were probably right), and blamed the Communists for the revolution's defeats. Soon Communists and Anarchists were murdering each other in the streets.

As hapless police and Civic Guard patrols shot at both sides, a foreign Marxist writer named George Orwell recorded the defeat of the Anarchists for posterity, in *Homage to Catalonia*.[4] The Anarchists fled to France, Heaven's punishment for French assistance (200 planes) to the revolution in Spain. Communist dominance over the Spanish revolution was secured when the Anarchist leader Durutti was killed during the siege of Madrid — by one of his own men.[5]

After taking control of the revolution, however, Stalin abruptly ended support to Spain's Republic in the middle of 1938. This disillusioned more lefties than George Orwell.[6] A prominent Spanish Communist, Valentin Gonzalez, better known as *El Campesino*, spoke for many:

> "I sincerely believed that the Kremlin sent us its arms, its military and political advisors, and the International Brigades under its control, as a proof of its revolutionary solidarity ...

> "Only later did I realize that the Kremlin does not serve the interests of the peoples of the world, but makes them serve its own interests; that, with a treachery and hypocrisy without parallel, it makes use of the international working class as a mere pawn in its revolution, it consolidates its own totalitarian counter-revolution (sic) and prepares for world domination."[7]

A right-wing reactionary couldn't have put it better. It was a bitter swan song for the left's Popular Front, who, despite being portrayed as a "democratic coalition", ruled without ever being voted into office. Meanwhile, on the right there was the "Unpopular Front" of Franco, the Carlists, and the Fascists: the Falange (Spanish fascists), Mussolini, and Hitler.

It is a strange fact of history that many fascists were disillusioned socialists. The same can be said of the Falange. Some of them were religious, but most Spanish fascists were secularized ultra-nationalists eager to kill Communists. The left respected terror, if little else, and they learned to fear and hate the Spanish fascists. Proportionate to their small size, the Falange wreaked an exacting vengeance on the revolution, repaying atrocity for atrocity. It was a grim justice for the murderers on the left to be terrorized by their former comrades, now become their mirror opposites, the fascists. It must have been like being stalked by your own shadow.

Mussolini was another socialist turned fascist. Although much was made of the cooperation between Italy, Germany, and Spain, Fascism was never a coordinated international movement like the Revolution. Prior to the Spanish revolution Mussolini and Hitler criticized everyone: the "decadent democracies" of Europe, the Communists, and each other. Although after the revolution they became allies, Mussolini and Hitler aided Spain separately, for their own separate purposes. Mussolini's fear that a Communist or liberal (read: Masonic) government might control the Gibraltar Strait overcame his reluctance to help Franco. Having no more concern for Catholic Spain than he did for Catholic Italy, *Il Duce* sought increased Italian influence in Spain (and consequently Europe), and combat training for his army.

The other "former" socialist, Hitler, viewed Spain strategically as well. He wanted to open the Gibraltar Strait for his submarines, and to check Communist expansion in Europe. Yet he did not want the Communists *or* Franco to prevail in Spain, at least not for a long time. He aided Franco in order to extend the conflict, believing this would distract Russia and the democracies from Germany's massive rearmament efforts. Like Mussolini, Hitler cared not a bit for the Church in Spain; it is said he viewed its destruction "with relish." There is, therefore, more than a little irony involved in Mussolini and Hitler's assistance in what the Carlists and Franco called "a holy war."

Franco

How did Franco get mixed up with these mugs? Simple. He needed help, and Hitler and Mussolini were the only ones willing to talk to him. Russia and the democracies had already closed ranks against Spain, sending arms and men to prop up the Masonic republic. Germany and Italy became counterweights. The other ally Franco had was Portugal, who sent Spain 20,000 troops, mostly volunteers. It has already been shown that Salazar was no fascist, he was a Catholic counter-revolutionary like the Spanish Carlists. But what was Franco?

It appears Franco was a politically conservative military careerist who grew into the counter-revolution and the Catholic faith very slowly, through force of circumstance. He had been raised Catholic, but gave little evidence of this until his marriage to a pious Catholic in 1923 (he was thirty-one, she was seventeen). For years he remained docile to revolutionary leaders who seemed bent on destroying the Spanish military. The counter-revolution was begun by the Carlists; Franco refused persistent efforts to persuade him to join. Once in charge, however, he allowed the Carlists no more influence than the Spanish fascists; after the war Franco politically subordinated the Carlists to the Falange. Through it all Franco made his own decisions, including the courting of Mussolini and Hitler.

Yet while he was certainly anti-Communist, Franco was not quite a fascist either. He formed no lasting relationship with either Hitler or Mussolini, and kept the Falange firmly subordinate to his rule. Well then, was Franco really a counter-revolutionary? Yes, but by the press of circumstances as much as by intent. He was Spain's best general and best leader. He could win wars, command the obedience of his Spanish allies, and hold his own with Hitler and Mussolini. Although he publicly aligned himself with Spain's religious tradition, Franco was no Carlist. His conservative temperament was often mistaken for religious traditionalism, yet over time Franco's Catholicism became more profound. To his (perhaps eternal) credit he responded to the designs of Providence — he was the only man who could save Spain, and save her he did, by force of arms. He then proved himself an adroit politician by ruling Spain for over three decades.

Pius XI on Communism and Fascism

At issue in this brief study of Franco is the nature of Catholic counter-revolution. Fascism is not counter-revolution. It sought (and presumably still seeks) to defeat the revolution by purely natural means. Because the revolution is satanic as well as natural, fascism had little chance of prevailing. Moreover, fascists adopted the same "ends justify the means" approach as Liberalism, Freemasonry, Bolshevism, and Illuminism. This approach has no place in Catholic counter-revolution.

Pius XI said as much in his writings on the revolution and fascism. In *Divini Redemptoris* (On Atheistic Communism, 1937) Pius lamented "the sad consequences" of the revolution in Russia and Mexico, and "the horrors of Communism in Spain". According to Pius, three reasons explained the spread of Communism (what the Virgin called "Russia's errors"). First, Communism exploited "the religious and moral destitution in which wage earners had been left by liberal economics." It was no surprise, Pius said, "that the Communistic fallacy should be spreading in a world already to a large extent de-Christianized."

The second reason for the spread of "Russia's errors" was "a propaganda so truly diabolical that the world has perhaps never witnessed its like before." According to Pius, the diabolical propaganda was "directed from one common center." Through its "great financial resources, gigantic organizations, international congresses and countless trained workers", revolutionary propaganda penetrated "little by little" into "all classes of people."

Pius evidently did not feel it necessary to add that one of the "classes of people" included the clergy. There was international publicity when Franco executed several revolutionary Basque clerics who, according to the Spanish hierarchy, were such fervent Communists they involved themselves with politics and carried arms for the anti-Christian revolution in Spain. These *Chretiens Rouges* ("Red Christians") were publicly championed by French Catholic intellectual Jacques Maritain, who co-authored a "pro-Basque manifesto."[8] In addition to this public opposition from within the Church, Pope Ratti also had the painful knowledge that his Ostpolitik had been infiltrated and fatally compromised by Bolshevism. These were only two examples of how Russia's errors had already spread into the Church prior to the Second World War.[9]

The third reason Pius gave for the spread of Communism was "the conspiracy of silence on the part of a large section of the non-Catholic press of the world." The Pope explained:

> "We say conspiracy, because it is impossible otherwise to explain how a press usually so eager to exploit even the little daily incidents of life has been able to remain silent for so long about the horrors perpetrated in Russia, in Mexico, and even in a large part of Spain; and that it should have relatively so little to say

concerning a world organization as vast as Russian Communism. This silence is due in part to shortsighted political policy, and is favored by various occult forces which for a long time have been working for the overthrow of the Christian social order."

After noting that the atrocities in Russia, Spain, and Mexico were not "isolated excesses", but "the natural fruit of a system that lacks all inner restraint," the Holy Father declared, "For the first time in history we are witnessing a struggle, cold-blooded in purpose and mapped out to the least detail, between man and 'all that is called God'". He concluded with a well-known passage: "See to it, Venerable Brethren, that the Faithful do not allow themselves to be deceived! Communism is intrinsically perverse, and no one who would save Christian civilization may collaborate with it in any undertaking whatsoever ..."[10]

Twenty blood-soaked years had elapsed between the 1917 revolution in Russia and the issuance of *Divini Redemptoris*. The Fatima Message could not have coincided more closely with the pressing events of history. Yet Pius XI remained silent about the Blessed Virgin's warning of Russia "spreading her errors", and Heaven's remedy — the consecration of Russia to the Immaculate Heart of Mary.

He was not silent regarding the errors of Hitler's "fascism", however. In *Mit Brennender Sorje* ("With Deep Anxiety"), an encyclical written in German and directed to the German episcopate, Pius condemned the race-based "religion" of Hitler's National Socialism, his cynical violations of the Concordat signed with the Vatican, and the Socialist persecution of the Church in Germany. Circumstances dictated that Pius XI maintain more of a working relationship with the Italian ruler Mussolini, yet throughout his pontificate Pius constantly corrected Mussolini's errors, the main one being the urge to State totalitarianism. The Church always denounced fascism as error, but also realized that, for the most part, fascism was a much less murderous error than Communism.

The Iberian Counter-Revolutions

The success of the counter-revolution in Spain hinged on the Carlists and Pope Pius XI's blessing of Franco's *"Cruzada"* (Crusade). Without these two ingredients the war in Spain might have been the actual start of the Second World War, instead of a dress-rehearsal. Even with Catholic Action and the approval of Pius XI, there was no way for Franco to control his fascist allies. Hitler's bombers reduced the town of Guernica to rubble, killing or wounding 2,000 Spaniards. The Spanish painter Pablo Picasso re-created the violence in one of his better-known paintings, entitled "Guernica".[11]

Franco did not authorize the bombing of Guernica, or atrocities committed by his armies. Much of this violence was in retribution for the annihilation of hundreds of thousands of Catholic (religious and lay) Spaniards at the beginning of the revolution. Unlike the violence against the Church, violence against the revolution was widely publicized, and Franco was roundly condemned.

The Spanish bishops responded by issuing a letter that stated, in effect, that the revolution could dish it out but could not take it:

"Each war has its excesses; the national movement (Franco) will have some of its own; nobody can serenely defend himself against the attacks of a furious enemy." After recounting some of the bestial horrors committed against the Church, the bishops concluded:

> "We do not believe that in the whole history of Christianity ... there has been such an explosion of hatred against Jesus Christ and His holy religion ... the forms of profanation have been so incredible that they cannot be conceived of without presupposing a diabolical suggestion."[12]

The official version of history claims both sides were equally violent, and extols the Masonic "democracy" of "moderates" over Franco's "Fascist rebellion". Were Pius XI alive, he might term this "diabolical propaganda". No attempt is made here to exonerate fascist brutalities, but it cannot be honestly maintained that there was an equivalency of atrocities, for the simple fact that no merely natural force can match the satanic fury of the revolution. In the case of the Spanish civil war, there is an abundance of objective evidence confirming this assertion.

As for the revolution's complaint that the Spanish Republic was a legitimate government overthrown by Franco's "illegitimate" revolution, when one considers how many Christian monarchies the revolution has put to the torch, and the rivers of blood shed in toppling governments for the sake of "Liberty" and "Progress", the hypocrisy of this complaint is breathtaking. At least the revolution is consistent — they are ignoble in defeat as well as in victory. And to put things squarely in perspective, consider that Spanish Inquisition, in four centuries, killed at most 31,000 people. This number, which even a Protestant historian of the Inquisition calls an "extravagant guess," is about one third of the people killed by the Revolution *in the first three months* of the Spanish Civil War.[13]

Aftermath

The successful counter-revolutions on the Iberian peninsula are worth pondering, if only because there have been precious few victories by Christianity over the revolution. In our time victories are short lived, however, and true counter-revolution occurs far less frequently than its counterfeits. After Franco's victory Father Escriva stopped wearing his mother's wedding ring, put his cassock back on, had his long hair re-tonsured, and published a little book called *The Way*.[14] His fledgling lay organization, Opus Dei, soon had members holding key positions in Franco's new government. In less than ten years, Opus Dei had acquired a publishing house, numerous newspapers (three in Madrid), a large interest in a major Madrid bank, an appetite for international finance, and a marked inclination to secrecy.[15]

But that is another story, whose connections to the Fatima Secret are for the moment obscure. More obvious was the fulfillment of another one of the Blessed Virgin's prophecies. At Fatima She had told Lucy, "If people do not cease offending God a worse one (war) will break out during the reign of Pius XI. When you see a night illumined by an unknown light, know that this is the great sign given you by God that He is about to punish the world for its crimes ..."

The great sign was given in 1938. In the last year of Pius XI's life an unknown light illumined the night. It was viewed by even more people than the Miracle of the Sun. The world's punishment was the Second World War.

NOTES

1. *TWTAF*, Vol. II, pp. 652-653.
2. *The Pope Speaks: The Words of Pius XII*, Harcourt, Brace and Company, New York, 1940, pp. 134-136.
3. Thomas, op. cit., Chapter 5.
4. Orwell's *Catalonia* was an essay on left-wing infighting, and an unflattering critique of Communism. Spain disabused Orwell of his Marxist illusions. Ten years after *Catalonia* he wrote *1984*.
5. Hutchison, op. cit., p. 76.
6. The demise of the bickering Popular Front is the Left's version of modern tragedy. My main source is Hugh Thomas, who chronicles it pretty well, as do a lot of other sources on the left, who concede the truth of the arguments made by Father Denis Fahey and Count Leon Poncins, that is, that Communists assist revolutions in order to appropriate them. The left are left to argue among themselves about this, and the bickering has spilled over onto the Internet, where Anarchists blame "Stalinists and Trotskyites" for Franco's victory. See http://www.socialequality.com/public html/prioriss/iwb10-23/spcivilw.htm, as just one example. There is also some interesting art work on the Spanish Civil War pages on the Internet. One picture shows a muscular young Adam about to deal a death blow to a coiled serpent with the word "Fascism" on its belly.

   In addition to inspiring Hemingway, Orwell, and Picasso, the Spanish Civil War provided a backdrop for the 1940 play *Everyone Comes to Rick's*, which in 1942 became the film *Casablanca*. Humphrey Bogart's (fictional) character, the American Rick Blaine, had fought in the International Brigades of the Spanish Revolution. Unlike Orwell, Rick Blaine expressed no dismay about Communism. It would have been a different story if Bogart had played the Spanish Communist *El Campesino*, who fled Spain for Russia. Ten years later he escaped from Russia and, like George Orwell, wrote a book about his complete disillusionment with the revolution.
7. Burnett Bolloten, *The Grand Camouflage*, Hollis & Carter, 1961.
8. Thomas, op. cit., p. 449, 451. Maritain was also French ambassador to the Vatican.
9. It was interesting to find that not all anti-clericals in Spain were on the left, and not all those on the right were uncritical of the Pope. Said one distinguished Spaniard, "I'm a Catholic but I'm violently anti-clerical. All this trouble is due to the Church. The Church was so conciliatory to the Left, so anxious to work with the Republic, that it never gave Spain a clear lead against the Red peril ... The Pope (Pius XI), would you believe it, still recognizes the Madrid Government ... We have had Papal Nuncios here who were little better than Socialists." Lunn, op. cit., p. 204.
10. Source for *Divini Redemptoris* is *Five Great Encyclicals*, The Paulist Press, New York, 1939.
11. After years of maintaining that the bombing of Guernica was an inexcusable civilian massacre, prominent sources on the left – including Hugh Thomas – have admitted there were military reasons for bombing Guernica. The fable of fascist terrorism at Guernica belongs in the same category as the long debunked "massacre at Badajoz," and the Revolution's repulsive claims that the Church set fire to their own churches to turn people against the Masonic government.

12. *TWTAF*, Vol. II.

13. Lunn, op. cit., 219. The Protestant historian is Charles Lea, who was guilty of his own extravagances in his multi-volume work against the Inquisition. And of course, the Spanish Civil War did not afford any of its victims due process, as the Inquisition generally did.

14. Hutchinson, op. cit., pp. 73-83. According to the author, Escriva took off his cassock at the beginning of the civil war, and didn't put it on again until after Franco took Madrid.

15. Richard Herr, *Spain*, Prentice Hall Inc, 1971.

Chapter Ten

Signs in the Heavens

It was no ordinary aurora borealis that illumined the night sky over Europe on January 25, 1938. The sky became a brilliant blood-red sea, not only in Europe but in parts of North America and Africa as well. For hours night remained a crimson-soaked day as roosters crowed, dogs howled, and fire departments were mobilized. Scientists and journalists repeated the term "aurora borealis" like a calming mantra. Those less sophisticated reacted in jabbering terror, fearing the end of the world. Others, viewing the fiery night with eyes of faith, pondered the heavenly blaze in awe-filled silence.

In a limited sense the scientists were right: the remarkable night sky of January 25, 1938 displayed many of the characteristics of an aurora borealis. But that bare description denies its remarkable impact. A French newspaper said "the sky was ablaze" with "a very strong blood-red glow." A scientific bulletin spoke of "an aurora borealis of exceptional beauty", and recorded the statements of witnesses. For some the sky looked like "a giant conflagration ... there was a great red cloud; it was like a sheet of blood". Others "believed that it was the grim reflection of a vast inferno"; the "whole sky seemed to be on fire ... the sky seemed to be an ocean of flames."[1]

The blood-red sky lasted for many hours, and was seen around half the world at the same vivid intensity. Lucy and the Sisters watched the pulsating, violently hued inferno from Tuy. Of all the descriptions of that night, the most precise one had been prophesied over 20 years ago by the beautiful Lady at Cova da Iria. A "night illumined by an unknown light", the Virgin told Lucy, would be "the great sign given by God that He is about to punish the world for its crimes, by means of war, famine, and persecutions of the Church and the Holy Father."[2]

What more telling "sign of the times" could have been given to a blood-soaked century than a blood-filled sky? Faced with a reflection of the preceding three decades and a foreshadowing of future bloodshed, it is understandable that modern man sought to dismiss God's great sign as a "mere" aurora borealis. Lucy knew better. In her third Memoir, published in 1942, she wrote: "Your Excellency is not unaware that, a few years ago, God manifested that sign, which astronomers chose to call an aurora borealis. I don't know for certain, but I think if they investigated the matter, they would discover that, in the form in which it appeared, it could not possibly have been an aurora borealis. Be that as it may, God made use of this to make me understand that His justice was about to strike the guilty nations."[3]

Within two months of the great sign, Hitler's armies invaded Austria. As the Blessed Virgin had prophesied, the Second World War began "in the reign of Pius XI" (although later historians dated the war from Germany's invasion of Poland). In her third Memoir Lucy recounted a day she found Jacinta deep in thought. What about? Lucy asked.

"About the war that is coming", Jacinta answered. "So many people are going to die, and almost all of them are going to go to hell! Many homes will be destroyed, and many priests will be killed. Look, I am going to Heaven, and as for you, when you see the light which the Lady told us would come one night before the war, you run up there too."

"Don't you see that nobody can just run off to Heaven!"

"That's true, you cannot. But don't be afraid! In Heaven I'll be praying hard for you, for the Holy Father, for Portugal, so that the war will not come here, and for the priests."[4]

A New Pope

In 1938 Lucy's superiors had not yet authorized her to reveal the Secret, but she did what she could to make known the First Saturday Communion of Reparation and the consecration of Russia. "My intention was to obtain mercy and pardon, not only for the whole world, but for Europe in particular."[5] Since 1936 Pius XI had been offering his life for the same intention. As death approached, however, Pope Ratti began bargaining for days — he urgently desired to live to February 12, 1939. This was the scheduled day for an impassioned speech he would make against Mussolini, and Italian fascism's new slogan: "Nothing without the State, everything for the State." One account has Pius imploring his doctor, "Doctor, doctor, keep me alive until the twelfth! I have such imporant things to say on that day."[6] The blow remained undelivered, for the Holy Father's heart, which had been failing since 1936, gave out completely on February 10.

Secretary of State Eugenio Pacelli was Camerlengo (the one responsible for officially confirming the Pope's death). Following the time-honored ritual, Pacelli tapped Pius XI's forehead three times with the small silver hammer while calling out his baptismal name. Receiving no response, Pacelli turned to the witnesses and announced, "The Pope is truly dead."

The official cause of death was heart failure, although it may be truer to say that Pius XI simply wore himself out. As the Pope's body lay in state Mussolini made a point of not paying his last respects. Many Italians assumed Pius had been poisoned by Mussolini, via an injection by Pius' attending physician, Doctor Petacci, who happened to be the father of Mussolini's mistress. In fact, Il Duce did not assassinate Pius XI — although the thought may have crossed his mind.[7] As the last mourners left, the eighty-one-year-old body of Pius XI was placed in a triple coffin made of cypress, lead, and elm. The coffin was lowered into a vault in the basement of St. Peter's. There rests the mortal remains of Achille Ambrose Damian Ratti, near Pope Pius X, as he had requested. March 2, 1939 was Eugenio Pacelli's birthday. It was also the day he was elected Pope, in the fastest conclave on record (twenty-four hours). Pacelli chose the name Pius XII in part, he said, out of respect for Pius X (whom he would later beatify), but primarily to acknowledge his benefactor, Pius XI. And it was also "About March, 1939," according to Sister Lucy, "when Our Lord said to me once more":

> "'Ask, ask again insistently for the promulgation of the Communion of Reparation in honor of the Immaculate Heart of Mary on the First Saturdays. The time is coming when the rigor of My justice will punish the crimes of diverse nations. Some of them will be annihilated. At last the severity of My justice will fall severely on those who want to destroy My reign in souls.'"[8]

In June 1939, Lucy wrote to Father Aparicio, her former confessor, that "God in His anger will lift the arms of His mercy and let the world be ravaged by this chastisement. It will be a chastisement such as never before, *horrible, horrible.*"[9]

On September 1 Germany invaded Poland, and Europe formally declared war upon itself.

Pius XII and Lucy

Exactly one year later Lucy was ordered to write the new Pope. She did, telling Pius XII of the requests Jesus and Mary made at Pontevedra and Tuy, and requesting once more the consecration of Russia to the Immaculate Heart. Pius did not respond to Lucy directly, but was heard to remark: "We receive many requests from mystics, we shall examine the matter."[10]

In the fall of 1940 Lucy was ordered to write Pius XII again. This order came from Bishop Ferreira of Gurza, who knew both Lucy and Pius XII. Ferreira believed that Pius XII would be more receptive if Lucy would ask him to consecrate the world to the Immaculate Heart, with a special mention of Russia. This was not what the Blessed Virgin had requested, however, and Lucy was perplexed about how to proceed. To prepare herself to write she "spent two hours on my knees before Our Lord exposed in the Blessed Sacrament." According to Lucy she was told:

> "Pray for the Holy Father, sacrifice yourself so that his courage does not succumb under the bitterness that oppresses him. The tribulation will continue and augment. I will punish the nations for their crimes by war, famine, and persecution of My Church and this will weigh especially on My Vicar on earth. His Holiness will obtain an abbreviation of these days of tribulation if he takes heed of My wishes by promulgating the Act of Consecration of the whole world to the Immaculate Heart of Mary, with a special mention of Russia."[11]

It was clear that this was an interim promise related to the chastisement of the Second World War, not a revision of the promise that "in the end My Immaculate Heart will triumph ..." Lucy wrote a letter to Pius XII, and sent it to Bishop da Silva for his approval. Da Silva, who agreed with Ferreira that the Fatima Message had to be modified to gain Pius XII's approval, told Lucy to rewrite the letter. She did, and da Silva edited the rewrite and sent it on to Pius XII. What Pius XII read was a very watered down, incorrect version of the Fatima Message that asked for a consecration of the world, but did not even contain the promise of the triumph of the Immaculate Heart. In fairness to Bishop da Silva, he had already seen Pius XI refuse the consecration of Russia to the Immaculate Heart twice, and seen Pius XII refuse the same consecration once. Their refusals caused Bishops Ferreira and da Silva to change the message in an attempt to win papal approval.

The following summer Lucy was ordered by Bishop da Silva to provide Canon Galamba with additional information so he could revise a book he had written about Jacinta. "This order," Lucy remembered, "fell into my bosom like a ray of light making me know that the time had arrived to reveal the first two parts of the Secret and to add two chapters in the new edition of the book about Jacinta: one about hell and the second one about the Immaculate Heart of Mary." She finished her third Memoir – at twelve pages the shortest — in August, 1941.

Why Russia?

That same summer saw Hitler attack Russia, who in turn was befriended by the Allies. This fateful turning point in the war has caused the Message of Fatima to be scandalous to some. It is incorrect to consider Russia the ultimate evil of World War II, it is argued. Nazi Socialism and its race-based paganism was the true evil of the Second World War. After all, Hitler broke Germany's peace accord with Russia and nearly destroyed her. Russia's brave resistance to the Nazis turned the tide of the war, and her alignment with the Allies made the world "safe for democracy".

Consequently, branding Russia as evil while remaining silent about Germany destroys the credibility of Sister Lucy and the entire Fatima Message — according to critics.

This plausible objection fails to account for Josef Stalin, who murdered an estimated sixty million of his fellow Russians. In terms of body count, Stalin dwarfs Hitler. Furthermore, Stalin was a ruthlessly evil geo-political strategist whose goal was the goal of any good Communist: domination of the world. His plan was a continuation of Lenin's prophetic vision: "The World War (1914-1918) will see the establishment of Communism in Russia. A second world war will extend its control over Europe. And a third world war will be necessary to make it worldwide."[12]

Stalin strove to instigate a second world war in order to expand Communism into Europe. He spoke publicly of "exploiting the antagonisms between the capitalist states, to precipitate them into an armed conflict. The principal work of our Communist parties must be to facilitate such a conflict."[13] Consequently, Soviet Russia supported Germany's recovery from the First World War. When Hitler came to power Stalin delighted in pitting him against fretting European democracies. In 1935 Stalin signed a mutual assistance pact with France, and Communists around the world pressured the democracies to war against Hitler.

For the next few years Russia and Germany sparred in Spain. In 1938 Stalin abruptly ended aid to the Spanish Republic. Less than a year later Stalin and Hitler stunned Europe by signing the Germano-Soviet peace accord. This gave Hitler the green light to invade Poland, which he did. The Nazi invasion of Poland was in turn a direct provocation to the European democracies to declare war on Germany, which they did. When the smoke cleared atheistic Communism ruled Christian Eastern Europe, and the democracies were a shambles. Game, set, and match to the man the Western press affectionately dubbed "Uncle Joe."

None of this is intended to exonerate Hitler, who had already brutalized Austria before signing the peace accord with Stalin. Yet several historians have drawn some interesting conclusions about Hitler's 1941 invasion of Russia, believing it to be a preemptive strike rather than a betrayal of the Germano-Soviet accord.[14] According to this theory, Stalin planned to invade Europe after Germany weakened itself fighting its European neighbors. Anticipating this, Hitler stole a march by attacking Russia first. The Nazi offensive ("Operation Barbarossa") did not unduly startle Stalin, but Hitler's early successes in Russia thwarted Stalin's plan for a massive counter-offensive against the West. The irony here is that Hitler, seen with some justice as the bogey-man of World War II, may have saved Europe from Communism.

All this is terribly unfashionable, of course, as is Fatima. However, since the Fatima apparitions were approved by the Church as worthy of belief, it is reasonable to scrutinize the role of Russia in the Second World War. The point here is not to minimize Nazi evil, but to emphasize that Heaven's depiction of Russia as the scourge of humanity is factually and historically accurate. It cannot be disputed that Stalin was a greater mass-murderer than Hitler. A convincing case can be made that Soviet Russia planned a second World War, and that Stalin played a major role in instigating the war. It is therefore more than plausible to conclude that Our Lady of Fatima had it right when She warned that until Russia was consecrated to Her Immaculate Heart, "she will spread her errors throughout the world, causing wars ..."

This message was not well received among the Christian Democrats in the Church, who spoke of Lucy's "preoccupation" with Russia, implying she was emotionally unbalanced, or equally bad, a political "reactionary." She was neither. Lucy emphasized "Russia's errors" because the beautiful Lady emphasized Russia's errors. Lucy's only "preoccupation" has been to accurately transmit the Fatima Message. Time has vindicated the Fatima Message. Communist Russia continued its errors long after the defeat of fascist Germany because Communism is "diabolical" and "intrinsically evil", according to Pope Pius XI. History only confirms what is revealed by the supernatural light of Fatima: God's delegation of Russia as the temporal scourge of the world. There is only one remedy to the scourge, and one day it will be used.

The Great Secret

1942 was the twenty-five-year anniversary of the Fatima apparitions. Over 500,000 pilgrims observed the May 13 anniversary. On July 13 the Portuguese hierarchy published for the first time the prayers the Angel Guardian of Portugal (thought by most to be St. Michael) taught the three seers in 1916.

Three days later, on the feast of Our Lady of Mount Carmel, Maria Rosa dos Santos died in her home in Aljustrel.[15] On October 13 the third edition of *Jacinta* was published. It contained the exact rendition of the Fatima Secret that Lucy had written in her third Memoir. For the first time the public was made aware of the vision of hell, the prophecy of Russia's errors and the Second World War, and the role of the Immaculate Heart of Mary.

The obvious approval the Portuguese hierarchy gave these "new" Fatima themes was matched by Rome. Pius XII authorized the publication of two new books revealing the Fatima Message. The books received the imprimatur of the Vicar General of Vatican City. During the Jubilee year the Holy See granted Fatima pilgrims a plenary indulgence. At the close of the Jubilee Pope Pius XII delivered a radio message, in Portuguese, to the entire Portuguese nation, most of whom were listening. It was during this radio address that Pius consecrated the world to the Immaculate Heart of Mary with the following words:

> "To You, to Your Immaculate Heart in this tragic hour of human history, we confide, we consecrate, we deliver, not only Holy Church, the mystical body of Your Jesus which bleeds and suffers in so many parts and is in so much tribulation, but also the whole world, torn by mortal discord, burning in the fires of hate, victim of its own iniquity ...

> "Queen of Peace, pray for us and give peace to the world at war, that peace for which the peoples sigh, peace in the truth, the justice, the charity of Christ!"[16]

Pius went on to make a reference to Russia, which proved at least that the Pope read his mail, for his address complied with the request Lucy had sent him, edited and influenced as it was by Bishop Ferreira and Bishop da Silva. Interestingly, Pius XII did not consecrate Russia by name. Here are his exact words:

"Give peace to the peoples separated from Us by error or by schism, and especially to the one who professes such singular devotion to Thee and in whose homes an honored place was ever accorded Thy venerable icon (today perhaps often kept hidden to await better days); bring them back to the one fold of Christ under the one true Shepherd."[17]

It should be recalled that this request concerned shortening the war, not the triumph of Mary's Immaculate Heart. As Lucy expressed it to Bishop da Silva: "The Good Lord has already shown me His contentment with the act performed by the Holy Father and several bishops, although it was incomplete according to His desire. In return, He promises to end the war soon. The conversion of Russia is not for now."[18]

Lucy also wrote Bishop Ferreira, thanking him for his assistance, expressing joy in Pius XII's consecration of the world to the Immaculate Heart, but ending her letter somberly: "With anguish I await His Holiness' order to the bishops, and then the grace of peace for the poor world."[19] In her third Memoir Lucy said the Fatima Secret "is made up of three distinct parts, two of which I am going to reveal ..." In her fourth Memoir, completed near the end of 1941, Lucy for the first time divulged what is commonly thought to be part of the "third distinct part" of the Fatima Secret: "In Portugal the dogma of the faith shall always be preserved..."[20]

Normally in good health, for months she suffered from pneumonia, which turned into pleurisy — the illness that had taken Jacinta. In the summer of 1943 Lucy wrote Bishop da Silva: "Perhaps all this is the beginning of the end, and I am happy. It is good that as my mission on earth is being completed, the good Lord prepares for me the way to Heaven."[21] In July Lucy appeared to be recovering, but then an injection caused an infection. Then the same thing happened again. Fearing that Lucy might die without revealing the Secret, Bishop da Silva visited Lucy in September to discuss committing the Third Secret to writing. He told Lucy to write down the Third Secret "if she wished."

Lucy didn't quite know what to make of this request:

"It seems to me that to write it down is already in a way to disclose it, and I do not yet have Our Lord's permission for that. In any case, as I am used to seeing the will of God in the wishes of my superiors, I am thinking of obedience, and I don't know what to do. I prefer an express command which I can rely on before God, so that I can say in all security, 'They ordered me that, Lord.' But those words, 'if you wish,' disturb me and leave me perplexed."[22]

Lucy resolved not to write down the Secret unless expressly ordered to. Then she was taken to Pontevedra for an operation on her leg. The next month, October, found Lucy convalescing back at Tuy. Bishop da Silva wrote her and ordered Lucy to write down the Third Secret. This solved one dilemma but raised another, for "Heaven is now keeping silent. Is God wishing to test my obedience?" Lucy wondered to herself.

For the next two months Lucy was unable to commit the Secret to writing. Several times she tried to obey, but something prevented her. Her inability to comply with da Silva's order caused her no small anguish. In a letter written during this period, Lucy stated that her severe "writer's block" was "not due to natural causes."[23]

On January 2, 1944, the Blessed Virgin appeared to Lucy, who was in the infirmary at Tuy. After this appearance Lucy's anguish disappeared, and she wrote down the Third Secret in front of the Blessed Sacrament in the chapel at Tuy, where she had experienced the remarkable vision of the Blessed Trinity in 1929.[24] On January 9, 1944, Lucy wrote Bishop da Silva:

> "I have written what you asked me; God willed to try me a little, but finally, this was indeed His will: (the text) is sealed in an envelope and it is in the notebooks ..."[25]

She put the single piece of paper in an envelope and sealed it with wax. It was not until the summer of 1944 that Bishop da Silva actually received physical possession of the Secret, as Lucy refused to use the mail or normal messengers, entrusting the Secret only to a bishop.

The Third Secret is singular in that Lucy was not allowed to reveal its contents. Heaven willed that this decision be reserved to the hierarchy of the Catholic Church. Bishop da Silva could have opened the envelope and read it in 1944, but he refused to. He tried to send the Secret to the Vatican, but Roman officials recommended he keep the Secret in Leiria. Da Silva reluctantly agreed. He placed the envelope within another envelope, sealed the outer one with wax, and wrote upon it: "This envelope with its contents is to be given to His Eminence Don Manuel, Patriarch of Lisbon, after my death. Leiria, December 8, 1945. Jose, Bishop of Leiria."[26] The envelope remained in his safe until 1957.

Collaboration

Shortly after Pius XII consecrated the world to the Immaculate Heart of Mary in 1942 the battles began to turn against Germany. Had God joined forces with Stalin and the Allies? Or was He simply doing what He had promised to do — shorten the days of tribulation?

In spite of the eventual Allied victory over Germany and Italy, Europe would pay a heavy price for its collaboration with Soviet Russia. Against his better judgment, Pius XII had also cooperated with Soviet Russia, at least to the extent that he agreed to stop publicly criticizing Soviet Russia. Significant pressure had been placed on Pius by America's President Roosevelt. In an interesting letter to the Holy Father, Roosevelt informed Pius that "the churches in Russia are open," and that Communism was "less dangerous to the safety of other nations than is the German form of dictatorship."[27] As proof Roosevelt asserted that Russia hadn't invaded anybody like Germany had.

The historical Roosevelt faces an unflattering dilemma. Was he remarkably naive about Communism or a near treasonous Communist sympathizer? Surely he was aware that he was misrepresenting facts in his letter to Pius XII. Russia had invaded Poland, Finland, and the Baltic states, and prior to World War II had caused considerable mayhem in Hungary, Germany, and Spain. As for the "churches in Russia", official Soviet statistics disclosed that "the number of Orthodox churches had decreased from 40,407 in 1917 to 4,255 in 1941, and that of 130 bishops and 50,960 priests only 28 bishops and 5,665 priests remained."[28]

Mr. Roosevelt can be excused for not having these statistics available to him, but his factually inaccurate portrayal of Russia suggests partisanship. When Roosevelt wrote Pius the President's attempts to deliver aid to Soviet Russia were being stalled in Congress, due to the opposition of American Catholics who seemed to have actually read and believed Pius XI's *Divini Redemptoris*. To counteract this influence Roosevelt requested, through his envoy Myron Taylor, that Pius XII "reverse" *Divini Redemptoris*.

Pius refused, but he did allow the American hierarchy to issue a statement that "watered down" the implications of *Divini Redemptoris*. This provided Roosevelt enough of an opening to push his Russian aid package (the "lend-lease bill") through Congress. Pius also agreed, reluctantly, to stop publicly criticizing Soviet Russia. This was revealed in a letter Pius wrote to American ambassador Myron Taylor, in which the Holy Father stated:

> "At the request of President Roosevelt, the Vatican has refrained from all polemics against the Communist regime, but this silence which weighs on our consciences has not been understood by the Soviet leaders, who continue their persecutions against the Church and the faithful in the USSR and the countries occupied by Red Army troops. May God grant that the Free World may not have to regret my silence one day!"[29]

For the rest of the war Pius XII made it a point not to refer to *Divini Redemptoris'* solemn condemnation of Communism as "intrinsically evil", or Pius XI's admonition that "no one who would save Christian civilization may collaborate with it in any undertaking whatsoever." Indeed, how could he, now that he was in fact collaborating with Moscow, albeit indirectly and against his will?

Pius XII's policy was influenced not only by American diplomacy, but by the Pope's desire to maintain favorable relationships with the forces he believed would be the eventual victors of the Second World War. Another influence on Pius XII was his under-Secretary of State, Msgr. Giovanni Battista Montini. Montini's diplomatic skills made him well-regarded, at least among the Allies. The Italian government accused Montini of plotting against Mussolini's fascist state from the protection of the Vatican. It is likely the fascists were right about this, but by 1944 they were doomed anyway. A "red Christian" like Montini was far less dangerous than the Allied invasion of Italy.

Roosevelt also urged Stalin to try to act human. The hierarchy of the decimated Orthodox Church was filled with KGB agents. One such agent, Sergius, was made "Patriarch of all Russia". Stalin gave him a microphone to tell Roosevelt, Churchill, and the Vatican what they wanted to hear. Sergius told Russians that God had raised Stalin up to defeat Germany, and ordered them to pray for their ruler.

This illusion of religious freedom allowed Mr. Roosevelt to tell Pius XII that "the churches in Russia were open". The American President, a high ranking Freemason, preferred to wax enthusiastic over Stalin's supposed religious conversion than to criticize "the Marshall's" gruesome excesses — like the Katyn Forest massacre, where some 15,000 Polish officers, the elite of Poland's army, were murdered en masse, by the Red Army. The mass graves were uncovered in 1943. The corpses' hands were bound, and each had a bullet in the head.

The massacre occurred in 1940, when Germany and Russia were allies. By 1944 Stalin had had a religious conversion, and Russia and Poland were allies. As the Red Army approached Warsaw, Moscow Radio broadcast a message urging the Poles to revolt against the Nazis, who were beginning to evacuate Warsaw. Hearing Russian guns just outside Warsaw, the Poles rose against the Germans.

For the next two months 250,000 Poles in Warsaw — civilians and military — were systematically hunted down and murdered by the Nazis, while the Red Army patiently waited just outside Warsaw. After instigating the uprising, Moscow Radio called the Polish revolt a "conspiracy against the Soviet Union." Roosevelt and Churchill tried to send relief planes, but Stalin refused to let the planes land on the territory held by the Red Army. The betrayed Poles refused to surrender, and were massacred house by house. When the grim business was finally over, the Nazis expertly dynamited to the ground all that was left of Warsaw, the eighth largest city in Europe.[30]

Once more, Stalin had maneuvered the Germans into doing his dirty work for him. Over a period of years he had systematically destroyed — or had destroyed — hundreds of thousands of Poles who would have resisted the Communist dictatorship he was intent on imposing on them after the capitalists finished destroying each other. Clearly, the granting of religious liberty in Russia had made Stalin a new man.

To their great discredit, Roosevelt and Churchill gave Stalin Catholic Poland, ignoring the protests of Poland's government in exile. Stalin got the rest of eastern Europe too. Lenin's prophecy had been largely fulfilled: a second world war would deliver Europe into Communist hands. Not even the Moslems had been able to seize and retain such a large chunk of Christian land. This was the fruit of the collaboration between the Allies, Russia, and the Vatican. It made a prophet out of Pius XI, who had warned that Christian civilization would not be saved by collaboration with Communism.

The Church's voice was strangely muted regarding this tragedy. That this silence continued during the pontificate of a Polish Pope was certainly one of the more unexpected surprises of a very surprising century.

Soviet Expansion

By the end of the war Pius XII, like Stalin and Roosevelt, began extolling democracy. According to the Pope, the war was not God's chastisement, it was the fault of "dictatorships" — code for fascism. The cure was not the consecration of Russia, but the replacement of dictatorships with democracies. This was the essence of a radio address he gave near the end of the war.[31]

It is unlikely Pacelli believed a word of it. He was playing politics, no doubt under the encouragement of Msgr. Montini, his under-Secretary of State, who, if he didn't draft Pius' radio address, fervently believed its message.

Just what "democracy" was remained ill-defined. It was generally assumed that the United States was a democracy; yet Stalin claimed Soviet Russia was a democracy too. Since the Allies, both during and after the war, proved just as likely to prey on civilian populations and engage in other wretched conduct as their opponents, it seemed that what distinguished democracies from fascist governments was the ease with which democracies were infiltrated and corrupted by Freemasons and Communists. Whether or not this was desirable depended on your point of view, of course. The Church had been skeptical of democracy precisely because it was so easily utilized by the anti-Christian Revolution.

Msgr. Montini did not share the Church's traditional reserve. Son of a liberal Catholic newspaper editor, Montini served under Pius XII when he was Eugenio Pacelli, Secretary of State to Pius XI. Capable enough to handle double duty, Montini was also appointed national chaplain of an organization of Catholic students. He was their intellectual advisor as well, writing articles for the organization's journals, and plotting political strategy with student leaders. Gradually Montini came to spend more time pitting Christian Democrats against Italy's fascist government than attending his duties at the Secretariat of State.

The last straw for Montini's superiors was a memo the chaplain sent his spiritual charges for Lent. He advised them not to recite the Rosary, and to avoid churches with "too many" statues and candles. The gospel readings chaplain Montini recommended were accompanied by the warning that "they should not be read moralistically or uncritically." Montini was dismissed from this post, according to his (liberal) biographer Peter Hebblethwaite, for being "a dangerous liberal".[32]

He returned to the Secretariat of State with no serious consequences, however. When his boss, Eugenio Pacelli, became Pius XII, Montini was elevated as well, albeit to an unusual position: he became a "joint under-secretary of state" to Pius XII along with Msgr. Domenico Tardini. In any event, the main post-war activities involved a dreary repetition: Russia's errors were matched by the errors of the West. At Yalta in 1945, eastern and central Europe were handed over to Stalin, in consideration for his promise to establish democratic governments. He enforced totalitarian rule instead. To compound the misery, Allied troops forced almost 3 million Russian refugees back to Stalin at bayonet point. One third were executed; the rest died quickly or slowly in gulags.

In return for a promise to aid America against Japan, Roosevelt gave Stalin Manchuria, Mongolia, and North Korea, along with thousands of tanks and planes, which were used to advance Communist interests in China, which soon fell to the Marxists. Next fell Albania, Hungary, Yugoslavia, Czechoslovakia, Romania, Bulgaria, and East Germany. Communist agitation in North Vietnam began, eventually causing hundreds of thousands of Vietnamese Catholics to head south. The only rain on the Soviet parade occurred in Austria. Occupied by the Soviets at the end of the war, Austrian Catholics pledged to pray the Rosary and other devotions to Our Lady of Fatima. The Communists suffered a surprising defeat in Austria's national elections and unexpectedly left the country.

Austria was a blip on the radar screen, for the pattern for the spread of Russia's errors had been established. Allies during the war, Western governments remained allies with Soviet Russia afterwards. In spite of the Cold War Western governments assisted the expansion of Communism, which, of course, required more military contracts, either for offense or defense.

Through it all the Western press continued to whitewash the brutalities necessary to subjugate European Christians to the ever expanding Communist empire. Inside and outside the Church, Christian Democrats proved effective apologists of Communism, by bolstering the Communist claim of "religious liberty in Russia." This remarkable assertion was reported by the Western press with a straight face. French philosopher Jean Paul Sartre toured Russia and declared "There is total freedom of criticism in the USSR."

Sartre's tour bus must not have stopped in the Ukraine. Re-occupied by the Soviets after the war, the land that witnessed the awful famine now witnessed priests being hung and burned alive. In one instance a priest was immolated in his church, with his parishioners forced to watch. Over 2,000 priests, religious, and bishops were martyred, along with thousands of lay Catholics.

Perhaps the most effective rebuttal to Soviet claims of religious liberty was made by Russian citizens. Requesting that Pope Pius consecrate Russia they stated:

"The struggle undertaken against God and the Holy Church by the Bolsheviks is not led by mere human powers ... Money and weapons are powerless against the direct action of Satan ... We need a heavenly force, a supernatural force. This force, this support we have in the Most Holy Virgin ...

"Going parallel to the increasing strength of atheistic materialism is a profound submission to the Most Holy Virgin. Does not this tell us where the evil is and where the force capable of overcoming it is? The evil is Satan, who has assembled the appearance of Marxist-Bolshevik atheism, and the force capable of overcoming it is our Holy Queen and protectress the Mother of God ..."[33]

Lucy

In May 1946, Lucy returned to Fatima for the first time since her departure in 1921. She was thirty-nine years old.

Canon Galamba accompanied Lucy to the places where the Virgin and the Angel of Peace had visited her. She showed Father Galamba where the Angel had given the children Communion, telling him, "I felt the physical contact of the Sacred Host on my mouth and on my tongue." Father Galamba wrote:

"The unspeakable memories of that day long ago ... give her countenance an unexpected grace. Her soul reflected onto her face a resplendent and transforming light. In her glance there was reflected something indescribably mysterious, luminous, joyous, anxious, an expression of hope and certitude, Heaven and earth mingling and joined together so well that I never saw the like, nor shall I see it again. Lucy was different."

Spring on the Cova da Iria meant wild flowers, and Sister Lucy descended upon them as if she were still ten. "Sister Lucy loves flowers a great deal," Father Galamba noted, "and now, led here by Divine Providence to the places of her childhood, she feels like a little girl once more; she begins gathering flowers and making bouquets with the same avidity as of old."[34]

Surely Lucy made a bouqet to bring back to the Fatima cemetery, where after lingering long over the resting places of her two cousins, she placed spring flowers on Jacinta's grave.

Sister Lucy only stayed in Fatima two days, but this was long enough to rekindle her old longing for Carmel. She requested a transfer from the Dorotheans to the Carmelites. Pope Pius XII personally intervened on Lucy's behalf. In 1948 she received written approval of her request, signed by under-Secretary Montini. Lucy entered the Carmelite convent in Coimbra, Portugal, on March 25, 1948, the day of the Annunciation, and Holy Thursday.

"The Pope of Fatima"

It was around this time that Pius XII was considering convening a Council, or to put it precisely, reconvening the Vatican Council which was unwillingly terminated when Rome was besieged and captured by the revolution in 1870. Pius formed confidential commissions to explore the feasibility of resuming the Vatican Council, and to determine the orientation of the Council. The preliminary consensus was that the Council could be reconvened, and the orientation would be classic: errors outside the Church, like Communism, and errors inside the Church, like neo-modernism, would be condemned, and the Faith would be confirmed.

During these deliberations devotion to the Immaculate Heart of Mary grew on an international basis. The statue of Our Lady of Fatima that resided at the Cova da Iria made a triumphant pilgrimage through Europe, Africa, and Asia. When the Pilgrim Virgin visited Spain Franco was moved to consecrate his nation to the Immaculate Heart of Mary. White doves accompanied the statue through the streets of Madrid, braving huge, noisy crowds. Numerous reports of miracles and healings accompanied the Pilgrim Virgin. The high point was a solemn Mass in which Portuguese Cardinal Cerejeira said of Our Lady of Fatima:

> "Her voice is the haunting cry of a mother, who sees unfathomable abysses of misery opening up before her poor, terrified children. It is an appeal, it is a hope, it is salvation in this apocalyptic hour. Fatima has become the hope of nations ... it is the revelation of the Immaculate Heart of Mary to the present world ...

> "I repeat what I have often said: Fatima will be for the cult of the Immaculate Heart of Mary what Paray-le-Monial was for the cult of the Sacred Heart of Jesus. Fatima, in a certain way, is the continuation, or better, the conclusion of Paray-le-Monial. Fatima reunites these two Hearts which God Himself united in the divine work of Redemption."[35]

Communist-ruled Hungary was a sharp contrast to the counter-revolution in Spain and Portugal. When Hungarian Primate Cardinal Jozsef Mindszenty denounced the closing of Catholic schools he was arrested, subjected to a "show-trial" (Pius XII called it a "mock trial"), and imprisoned. After beatings, drug injections, and torture he finally signed a "confession" that he had tried to subvert Hungary's "people's democracy."

Unlike the Christian Democrats, Pius did not forsake Mindszenty. In a 1949 pronouncement he called Mindszenty a "worthy prince of the Church" who had "struggled so nobly to restore the Christian faith and Christian morals to the land of Hungary." Pius angrily denounced the charade of a trial, observing that prior to the trial "Cardinal Mindszenty had an iron constitution and was in the prime of his life. Yet suddenly he appears so weak that he can hardly stand. His weakness during the trial does not result from a sense of guilt, but rather constitutes an accusation against his accusers ... They are pursuing the policy described in Holy Scripture, "I will strike the shepherd, and the sheep of the flock shall be dispersed" (Mt 26:31).[36]

In Croatia Archbishop Stepinac would also be subjected to a show-trial, found "guilty", and imprisoned (where he eventually died). In other Communist-occupied lands, the Uniates (i.e., Catholics of Oriental rite) were fearfully persecuted. Hundreds of priests were deported, imprisoned, or murdered. The entire hierarchy was imprisoned, a fate two prelates could not survive. The brutal suppression was engineered by the Soviet government through the KGB-ruled Orthodox Church.

It all led Pius XII to coin the phrase "Church of Silence," to signify those Christian communities in Russia and eastern Europe "whose hands are bound and whose lips are closed."[37] The battle lines in eastern Europe being so drawn, it was fairly scandalous when the Church in Poland developed a working relationship with their Communist government. A mere twelve years had passed since Pius XI declared Communism to be "intrinsically evil" and warned that "no one who would save Christian civilization may collaborate with it in any undertaking whatsoever." Pius XII discouraged "dialoguing" with Communists "out of respect for the name of Christian." The Pope said "such tactics should cease, for, as the Apostle warns, it is inconsistent to sit both at the table of God and at that of His enemies." Consequently, Polish Primate Cardinal Wyszynski was viewed with suspicion. Why hadn't he been martyred like Mindszenty and Stepinac? Even his later (relatively brief) imprisonment left him, and the Church in Poland, suspect in the eyes of the Vatican.

Except in Poland, the distinction between the Communist revolution and the Catholic counter-revolution was stark. The former offered a brutal materialism which featured atrocities and atheism. The latter offered penance, conversion, miracles, and a remedy to the lies, homicides, and soul destroying ideology of Communism. In 1949, for instance, while Christians in eastern Europe were being murdered, tortured, and morally barbarized, 120,000 people converted to Catholicism. One of the converts was a former Communist named Hamish Fraser. He attributed his conversion to Our Lady of Fatima.

Further proof was the national and episcopal veneration of Our Lady of Fatima by Portugal and Spain. Devotion to Fatima explains the relative peace enjoyed by these two countries after the Second World War, a peace that is properly attributed to the intervention of the beautiful Lady of Cova da Iria, who was now recognized to be at the forefront of the counter-revolution. Opposition to Her began to focus, within the Church as well as without.

During the first half of his reign Pius XII, the self-described "Pope of

Fatima" (he was consecrated a bishop on May 13, 1917), was energetic in encouraging devotion to Our Lady of Fatima. In 1949 Pius XII approved the appointment by Bishop da Silva of a diocesan tribunal to investigate the heroic virtues of Francisco and Jacinta Marto. A new Fatima apostolate, the Blue Army, began publishing *Soul* magazine. Their efforts were blessed by Pius, who said "the time for doubting Fatima has passed. The hour for action has arrived."[38]

The following year Pius XII issued *Humani Generis* (August 12, 1950), wherein he censured many of the errors of the "New Theology" that would be encoded into documents of the Second Vatican Council fifteen years later. The Pope did not name the neo-modernists responsible for the novelties, but theologians seen heading for the high grass included Fathers Congar, de Lubac, Danielou, Chenu, and Rahner. After Pius' death they would resurface as *periti* at Vatican II — three of them would be made Cardinals by conciliar Popes.

The Assumption

That fall (October 30) in Rome Pius XII told thirty-five Cardinals and over four hundred and fifty bishops that he intended to define as dogma the Assumption into Heaven of the Blessed Virgin Mary. The Pope's intention was met with unanimous agreement. Later that afternoon Pius was walking in the Vatican gardens when he "saw a prodigy which profoundly impressed me." He wrote:

> "I was struck by a phenomenon I had never seen before. The sun, which was fairly high, looked like a pale yellow opaque globe completely surrounded by a luminous halo, which nevertheless did not prevent me at all from staring attentively at the sun without the slightest discomfort ... The opaque globe began moving outwards, slowly turning over upon itself, and going from left to right and vice versa. But within the globe very strong movements could be seen in all clarity and without interruption."[39]

Pope Pius XII had witnessed the dance of the sun.

He saw it again the next day. The following day, November 1, 1950, in the presence of over one-half million cheering and crying Catholics, Pius XII infallibly proclaimed as dogma the bodily Assumption of the Blessed Virgin Mary into Heaven.

It was a remarkably warm day. The cloudless sky was a deep blue. The brightness of the sun failed to make invisible a crescent moon, fixed just above the cross atop St. Peter's Basilica. On this rare day when heaven and earth were of one accord the crowd ceremonially chanted from the Apocalypse: "A great sign appeared in heaven, a Woman clothed with the sun, and the moon beneath Her feet ..."

Later that noteworthy day Pius XII witnessed the dance of the sun yet again, and a final time on the octave day of November 8. "It appears," the Holy Father wrote later, "that the Blessed Virgin willed in some way to confirm by a prodigy the sentence which the Vicar of Her Divine Son had pronounced."[40] The prodigies may have also been intended as a directional arrow urging Pius on to consecrate Russia to the Immaculate Heart. That Papa Pacelli witnessed — repeatedly — the signature miracle of the Fatima apparitions could hardly have been a coincidence. The signs in the heavens — first the unknown light, then the dance of the sun — were unmistakable. Whether they would be heeded was another matter entirely.

NOTES

1. *TWTAF*, Vol. II, pp. 670-677.
2. Kondor, op. cit., Lucy's Fourth Memoir, p. 162.
3. Ibid., Third Memoir, p. 109. Lucy addressed her entire Memoir to Bishop da Silva, as it was under his orders that she wrote it.
4. Ibid., Third Memoir, p. 109.
5. Ibid., Third Memoir, p. 109.
6. Charles Pichon, *The Vatican And Its Role In World Affairs*, Translated from the French by Jean Misrahi, E. P. Dutton & Company, Inc., 1950, p. 149.
7. Ibid., pp. 148-151.
8. *TWTAF*, Volume II, p. 685.
9. Ibid., p. 686.
10. Ibid., p. 758, fn. 18.
11. Ibid., p. 732.
12. From Lenin's Collected Works, as quoted in Douglas Reed, *The Controversy of Zion*, Veritas Press, p. 353.
13. As quoted in an article by Frère Michel, "'The War of Hitler' or the War of Moscow?", published in *The Fatima Crusader,* Issue 34, October-November, 1990, pp. 16-17 (see also http://www.fatima.org/library/cr34pg16.html).
14. In addition to the historians quoted in Frère Michel's article (cited in the preceding footnote), see *Stalin's War*, by Ernst Topitsch, St. Martin's Press, who argues that not only did Stalin provoke Hitler into military action, he planned to capitalize by a surprise attack on a Europe weakened by Hitler.
15. Maria Rosa wrote Lucy, asking her to come to see her before she died. Lucy was not given permission to do so. Maria Rosa's response was: "So they won't let her return to Fatima even to be present at my death! If I had known that that's how it would be, I would never have let her go there! However, I'll offer this great sacrifice to God so that He will keep her in his care and help her always to be good." A few days later, on her deathbed, Lucy's sister Teresa helped Maria Rosa to the phone so she could say good-bye to Lucy. When they phoned the convent, however, they were refused permission to talk to Sister Lucy, even though it was explained that Maria Rosa was on her deathbed. According to Lucy, "when my mother heard this further refusal, she said between sobs: 'This is the last drop the Lord kept for me at the bottom of the chalice and which I had yet to drink on earth. I'll drink it for love of Him." Lucy was unaware that her mother had called until years later, when Teresa told her. See Sixth Memoir, pp. 193-196.
16. The entire address is reproduced in Chanoine C. Barthas and Père G. Da Fonseca, S.J., *Our Lady of Light*, The Bruce Publishing Company, Milwaukee, 1947, pp. 215-220.
17. Ibid., p. 220.
18. *TWTAF*, Volume III, p. 18. Earlier that same year, however, Lucy had written in more ominous terms to Msgr. Ferreira, the Bishop of Gurza: "On the night of 5 March 1942 (Lucy wrote), Our Lord seemed to make me feel more keenly that He was refusing to grant us peace on account of the crimes which continue to provoke His justice, and also because He is not obeyed in His demands, especially regarding the consecration to the Immaculate Heart of Mary, *even though He has moved the heart of His Holiness to accomplish this*. Whence the idea came to me of renewing my request. But, in accordance with the advice of Your Most Reverend Excellency, I find it good to keep silent." (my emphasis, CRC No. 335, Nov.-Dec. 2000, p. 8)
19. Ibid., p. 66.
20. Kondor, op. cit., Fourth Memoir, p. 162.

21. Joaquin Maria Alonso, C.M.F., *The Secret of Fatima, Fact and Legend*, English translation, The Ravengate Press, 1990, p. 36.

22. Ibid., pp. 37-38.

23. *TWTAF*, Volume III, p. 45.

24. Ibid., p. 48.

25. Ibid., p. 47.

26. Ibid., p. 53.

27. Oscar Halecki and James Murray, *Eugenio Pacelli, Pope of Peace*, Farrar, Straus, and Young, Inc., Revised Edition, 1954, pp. 166-168.

28. Cianfarra, op. cit., p 56.

29. As quoted in *TWTAF*, Vol. III, p. 149. It is interesting that Pius was worried about his silence towards Communism. Today he is vilified for his supposed silence towards Nazi Germany.

30. The information on Katyn and Warsaw is from Adam Zamoyski, *The Polish Way*, Hippocrene Books, Second Printing, 1995.

31. *TWTAF*, Vol. III, pp. 179-181.

32. The quotations in this paragraph are all from Peter Hebblethwaite, *Pope Paul VI, The First Modern Pope*, Paulist Press, 1993.

33. *TWTAF*, Volume III, pp. 325-326.

34. All the remarks by Galamba are from Ibid., pp. 225-227

35. Ibid., p. 247.

36. Pronouncement of Pius XII, February 14, 1949, reproduced as an Appendix to Jozsef Cardinal Mindszenty, *Memoirs*, Macmillan Publishing Co., Inc., 1974.

37. From Pius XII's Radio Message, Christmas, 1951, as quoted in *The Red Book of the Persecuted Church*, by Albert Galter, The Newman Press, 1957, p. 465.

38. *TWTAF*, Vol. III, p. 279.

39. Ibid., p. 284.

40. Ibid., p. 289.

Chapter Eleven

Fatima and the Grand Convergence

In May, 1952, the Blessed Virgin appeared to Sister Lucy. "Make it known to the Holy Father that I still await the consecration of Russia to My Immaculate Heart," she said. "Without this consecration Russia cannot be converted, nor can the world have peace."[1]

Russian Catholics, clergy and lay, had also requested the consecration during an audience with Pius XII in 1950. They presented Pius with a moving letter that noted the dual acceleration of Russia's errors, and devotion to the Immaculate Heart of Mary: "Thus, going parallel to the increasing strength of atheistic materialism is a profound submission to the Most Holy Virgin ... Does not this parallelism tell us where the evil is and where the force capable of overcoming it is? The evil is Satan, who has assumed the appearance of Marxist-Bolshevik atheism, and the force capable of overcoming it is our Holy Queen and Protectress, the Mother of our God ..."[2]

The letter went on to request that Pius consecrate Russia to the Immaculate Heart. He did so in a letter to all Russians (*Sacro vergente anno*), writing in pertinent part, "today we consecrate and in a most special manner we entrust all the peoples of Russia to this Immaculate Heart ..." Did this act fulfill the request made by the Blessed Virgin?

No, according to Sister Lucy's private correspondence, for although Russia was explicitly named for the first time, the world episcopate was not involved in the consecration.[3] Today, over forty years after the fact, it looks like Lucy was right. There is no evidence of significant supernatural fruit from Pius' letter. *Sacro vergente anno* was a half-measure, and Pius XII probably knew it.

The Worker Priests

Almost immediately after issuing *Sacro vergente anno* Pius fell gravely ill. He eventually recovered, but decided not to convene a Council, citing his age (seventy-five) and poor health. "I am too old," he told the Italian bishops, "it will be my successor who does it."[4]

It was a well-known secret that Pius favored the Cardinal-Archbishop of Genoa, Guisseppe Siri, to replace him. Ironically, Pope Pacelli fired his actual successor, Angelo Roncalli, only a few months after issuing *Sacro vergente anno*. According to Pope John XXIII's sympathetic biographer

Giancarlo Zizola, Roncalli, papal nuncio at Paris during the rise of the "worker priests" that so alarmed Rome, lost his post after "try(ing) to check pressure from Rome to block the worker priest movement."[5]

Originally meant to re-Christianize large portions of France which, in the aftermath of two world wars, appeared apathetic and even hostile towards the Church, the worker priests rubbed shoulders with the "pagan proletariat", loading trucks, and doing foundry and other industrial work. The idea, as tentatively approved by Pius XII, was for the clergy to bridge the distance between empty parishes and the working classes by participating in the lives of the people.

But the worker priests seemed more interested in class warfare than eternal salvation: "They were present in the peace processions, they protested against the atom bomb, they directed trade union action, they contributed to the striker's organizations, and they began to taste Marx. This galloping development went on, in a great variety of experiences and attempts, under the eyes of the nuncio Roncalli."[6]

If Roncalli's response to this "galloping development" was a nod and a wink, French bishop Pierre M. Theas hailed his diocesan worker priests as the vanguard of the revolution:

> "Urged on by unrestrainable forces, today's world asks for a revolution. This revolution must succeed, but it can succeed only if the Church enters the fray, bringing the Gospel. After being liberated from Nazi dictatorship, we want to liberate the working class from capitalist slavery."[7]

This boiler-plate rhetoric was straight out of the Marxism 101 handbook. Similar language would resurface when the worker priests appeared in central America under the guise of "liberation theology" after the Second Vatican Council. But they debuted under the French episcopate shortly after the Second World War, in the pontificate of Pope Pius XII. It was an unmistakable signal that Russia's errors had spread into the Church. Alarmed, the Roman Curia pressed nuncio Roncalli for reports on the activities of the worker priests. Roncalli continued to stall the Curia, even when French Catholics were complaining to him that "the priest-workers were Communists in all but name."[8] Roncalli was supported in his disobedience by under-Secretary of State Montini, who defended the worker priests by saying "we have to run certain risks in order not to reprimand ourselves for not having done everything to save the world."[9]

If Msgr. Montini's implication that a "Marxist-Christianity" would save the world was simply an example of careless or intemperate language, why did Montini also defend the worker priests with the remarkable statement: "nothing supernatural should be impeded"?[10]

Unlike Msgr. Montini, Pius XII found nothing supernatural in these circumstances, particularly outbursts like the speech made by

Abbé Boulier, who at a "Communist inspired 'peace meeting'", declared: "If we, who are engaged upon the struggle for peace, are asked 'Who are the Communists among us?' we will reply, 'All of us'."[11] Rome's reply was not long in coming. In a 1950 exhortation to the French hierarchy Pius XII pointedly said: "We are sure you are well aware that among certain priests, not distinguished for learning or austerity of life, there has been an alarming spread of revolutionary ideas."[12] This statement came shortly after a worker priest had been injured in a fight with police during a Communist inspired demonstration against the French government. A Communist organization called the World Peace Movement was responsible for the violence.

Being on the scene in Paris, Roncalli became more ambivalent than Montini about the ways worker priests were distorting and de-gracing the priesthood. But the heady company of French intellectuals distracted the nuncio from his prudential reservations. Roncalli had more than a passing acquaintance with France's ambassador to Pius XII, Jacques Maritain, who not only believed the worker priest movement to be a "fascinating experiment", but also thought that Teilhard de Chardin and Henri de Lubac (French Jesuits), and Fathers Congar and Chenu (French Dominicans) were essential to the "renewal" of the Church. As Professor Maritain modestly put it,

> "France is light-years ahead of other countries. Hence the ambivalence of the Holy See in its regard; if the Holy See slams on the brakes, this is not because France is in error, but because France is way ahead. But one knows that it is opening the ways of the Lord, and that the rest of Christendom will follow where France has gone."[13]

Unfortunately for the Church and the world, Maritain was unintentionally prophetic. What used to be called Christendom would, as Maritain declared, "follow where France has gone." The destination was not the utopian Christian democracy Maritain envisioned. Instead, as Christ Himself had told Sister Lucy, the Church would follow France into "misfortune" — or "missed fortune" — due to its neglect of the Fatima Message. Along the road to ruin the nuncio Roncalli began reading Teilhard de Chardin, and a new book by Father Congar, *True and False Reform of the Church*.[14]

According to Zizola, "Up to the end of his mission in Paris, Roncalli could hinder Roman intransigence from intervening with a condemnation"[15] of the worker priests, and he did just that. Behind Roncalli's occasional public reservations were the actions — and inaction — of an ally. For months he sat on the Roman curia's order for a complete report on the worker priests. Finally even the socialist French government complained to Rome about the worker priests,[16] and Pius XII fired Roncalli by promoting him to Cardinal and transferring him to Venice.[17]

The new Paris nuncio, Paolo Marella, followed Rome's will and quickly pulled the plug on the worker priest movement. Ordered to disband, many of the worker priests left the priesthood instead.

Father Dhanis

In addition to deciding not to convene a Council, Pius XII also resolved, rather abruptly, to stop championing Fatima. His reasons are not all known, but a primary one appears to be significant opposition to Fatima at high levels in the Vatican. This is attested to by Father Schweigl, an Austrian Jesuit who was the secret envoy between Pope Pius XII and Sister Lucy. Schweigl was one of the few men to have read the Third Secret. In recalling Pius XII's 1952 consecration of the Russian peoples to the Immaculate Heart of Mary, he notes that "many circles were against the opportuneness of such a consecration."[18] Who were the opponents of Fatima?

The first opponents were, of course, the mothers of the three seers. Hard on their heels was the parish priest and an assorted townfolk. Next came Freemasons, liberals, and the other "free-thinkers" — quoting each other in lockstep, as usual. All the aforementioned groups believed nothing supernatural happened on Cova da Iria; some of them changed their minds with the passage of time. Years later, after Lucy's memoirs were published, opposition came from different sources. The hot button was the Blessed Virgin's singling out of Russia as the source of wars in the world and persecutions of the Church. It is easy to understand the opposition to the Fatima Message by Communists, socialists, and other men of the left outside the Church. More surprising was the opposition of Christian Democrats and neo-modernist (or "progressive") theologians inside the Church. The Christian Democrats were scandalized that the Blessed Virgin did not decry fascism as the ultimate evil. The neo-modernists had different reasons for opposing Fatima: a dislike of Marian doctrine, a belief in universal salvation, a contempt of popular piety, and so on. The earliest and most effective critic of Fatima was a neo-modernist theologian, the Belgian Jesuit Edouard Dhanis.

Father Dhanis' critique of Fatima appeared in a book published in 1945, entitled *On the Apparitions and Secret of Fatima: A Critical Contribution.* His main objection is that "the secret of Fatima seems to have undergone considerable additions."[19] He spoke of the original apparitions in 1917 as "Fatima I", and the Fatima message published in Lucy's memoirs in the 1940's as "Fatima II". Father Dhanis accepted the authenticity of "Fatima I", albeit joylessly. In this he had little choice, since the Church had already declared the apparitions worthy of belief. But "Fatima II", at least for Fr. Dhanis, was a different story.

It has already been shown how the visions Lucy received at Pontevedra and Tuy ("Fatima II") not only completed the 1917 apparitions, but were in fact predicted in 1917 by the Blessed Virgin. Father

Dhanis either didn't have a thorough enough knowledge of Fatima to know this, or he knew it and chose to ignore it. Instead, he argued that "Fatima I" and "Fatima II" were contradictory, and Lucy was to blame.

Dhanis alleged that the original apparitions ("Fatima I") traumatized Lucy. Later, still in a weakened state, she had, in good faith, "unconsciously invented" the Fatima Secret ("Fatima II") which first appeared publicly in the 1940's. The part of the message about Russia being the scourge of humanity was, according to Father Dhanis, Lucy's unconscious reaction to the Spanish Civil War. With these and other arguments Dhanis concluded that "Fatima II" was a "faint echo" of the original Fatima Message, which must remain forever unknown due to Lucy's incapacities.

Father Dhanis put it more elegantly, of course. He was writing during the reign of Pius XII, so he had to be careful, and clever. Yet if Lucy really was inclined to "unconscious inventions", one wonders why this unfortunate trait was unnoticed by everyone who knew Lucy except for Father Dhanis — who had never met her. Surely the Masonic journalists and historians would have pounced upon such a personality defect. Yet it remained unmentioned until 1945, and for good reason. For it was not Lucy, but Father Dhanis who was inventing things.

He was unable to offer a single example of Lucy's "unconscious inventions" — at one point he called them "hallucinations" — other than the Fatima Message itself. Despite his sophistication, Dhanis' argumentation was a form of circular reasoning which proved nothing. His thesis was no more than an unfounded accusation that sounded like a veiled calumny. Moreover, none of the numerous testimonies on Lucy's character and personality — by friend and foe — supports Dhanis' contention that she had "certain psychological defects" that caused her to distort the original Fatima Message. What is evident instead is how steadfastly Lucy stuck to the facts of the Fatima Message, whether she was being beaten by her mother or being threatened with death by Freemasons.

In addition to not squaring with facts, Dhanis' theory of Lucy's "hallucinations" doesn't explain the undisputed miracles that accompanied the apparitions. Did God err by "wasting" stupendous miracles on a message that would never be reliably transmitted? Could He not have found a more reliable messenger than the sincere, but hopelessly befuddled Lucy?

Obviously, one need not doubt God's capacity to choose wisely. The truth bears out the wisdom of His choice of messenger. Lucy was blessed with a remarkable memory, a balanced personality absent of Twentieth Century neuroses, and a simple, direct manner of expression. There was nothing uncomplicated, mysterious, or deceptive about her. The same could not be said of Father Dhanis, who was quickly taken to task, in print, by Jesuit colleagues who had studied the apparitions more than he had. Their telling critique of his book caused Dhanis to backpedal hastily, but he never recanted his veiled accusation that "Fatima II" was a fabrication.

Yet if Lucy was as unstable as Father Dhanis alleged, how could "Fatima I" be trusted either? The logical answer was that it too must be unreliable. This may have been Dhanis' ultimate point, coiled quietly behind his claims of devotion for Our Lady of Fatima, and his repeated affirmations that Lucy was a pious girl acting in good faith. His imitators — and there would be many — picked up the thread where Dhanis left it, and became increasingly critical of Fatima. In 1948 Cardinal Journet of France praised Dhanis' book and attacked Fatima, its miracles, and even Portugal with a violence and contempt that will not be reproduced here. In addition to being a disciple of Jacques Maritain, Journet was also a friend of under-Secretary of State Montini. Montini himself was well acquainted with Father Dhanis; like Journet he was also an admirer of Professor Maritain.

Father Dhanis attacked Fatima again in 1952, when Pius XII was being petitioned to consecrate Russia. The Jesuit repeated his argument of 1945:

> "it was practically impossible to make such a consecration ... without this act taking on the air of a challenge, both in regard to the separated hierarchy, as well as the Union of Soviet Republics. This would make the consecration practically unrealizable ... could the Most Holy Virgin have requested a consecration which, taken according to the rigor of the terms, would be practically unrealizable? ... This question indeed seems to call for a negative response."

Pius XII begged to differ, and the issuance of *Sacro vergente anno* decided the question against Father Dhanis. Dhanis may have won the larger battle however, for this was the last significant action Pius performed on behalf of Fatima.

It is ironic Dhanis had such influence on the fate of the Fatima Message, as he had only a superficial understanding of it. The progressive and neo-modernist elements in the Church rallied behind him, however, and ensuing years saw Father Dhanis receive promotion after promotion. In 1962 he was a consultor to the Holy Office. In 1963 he was rector of Gregorian University. During Vatican II he was a peritus, and member of the Theological Commission of the Council. In 1967 the former Msgr. Montini, now Paul VI, appointed Dhanis special secretary of the first Synod of Bishops.

Paul also refused to condemn the infamous Dutch Catechism, of which Dhanis was an author. Even with the tacit support of the Pope, the "Catechism" was so misguided it could only be published with a sixty page supplement correcting the original text. Interestingly, one of the Dutch Catechism's many areas of insufficiency was its treatment on the personal existence of angels. This may be traced back to Dhanis, who had criticized the prayers given the Fatima seers by the Angel of Peace, concluding it was "difficult to grant it the heavenly origin Lucy attributes to it ..."

In fact the Fatima prayers were a little too Catholic for Dhanis' sensibilities. So was the vision of hell shown the children, which Dhanis complained was "exaggeratedly medieval", wondering aloud "how Our Lady could present it this way to the Twentieth Century." Just what — if anything — Dhanis did believe was unclear, but it is safe to assume he had all his doubts about Fatima, angels, and hell answered definitively in 1978, when he left this world. A eulogy in *L'Osservatore Romano* described Father Edouard Dhanis, S.J., as someone Pope Paul VI had complete trust in.

Miracle at Syracuse

As it turns out, for several crucial years Msgr. Montini was someone Pope Pius XII had complete trust in. This may account not only for Pius' declining interest in Fatima, but for the Miracle of Syracuse as well.

It happened in 1953, to Angelo and Antonina Iannuso, a young married couple living in a working class neighborhood in Syracuse, Italy. They had a plaster statue of the Blessed Virgin in their home. The statue depicted the Madonna's heart pierced with thorns with a flame rising from it — remarkably similar to Lucy's description of the Immaculate Heart of the Tuy apparition.

On August 29 the statue began weeping. The tears were first seen by Antonina, who was bedridden by a difficult pregnancy. Tears flowed from the eyes of the plaster Madonna at irregular intervals throughout the day. The tears continued for several days, and were witnessed by thousands. On September 1 the inevitable commission of experts arrived to examine the statue. The possibility of fraud was ruled out. It was scientifically proved that the tears were real tears, and that it was impossible for them to be flowing from the non-porous, varnished plaster statue. In other words, the weeping Madonna was a miracle.

On September 2 Archbishop Baranzini of Syracuse visited the poor home, prayed the Rosary, and announced:

"Darkness continues to cover the world because the rebellion of sin and apostasy continues and increases, and behold the Lord sends Mary to save a society wandering in error, and our souls which are being lost ...

"Mary's tears are not tears of joy, they are tears of affliction, of sorrow. They are a warning for me, for my clergy, for all you faithful, that we become better ... Immaculate Heart of Mary, have pity on us!"[20]

After the Archbishop's visit the tears stopped, and miraculous healings began. Over a million people visited the Madonna during the next two months. In December, after visiting Rome, the Italian bishops declared the events in Syracuse miraculous. One year later the city of Syracuse was consecrated to the Sorrowful and Immaculate Heart of Mary.

Remarking on the miracle Pius XII asked, "Will men understand the mysterious language of these tears?"[21]

It may be asked here, respectfully, whether the Holy Father himself understood the connection between the weeping Immaculate Heart statue, the sad, beautiful Lady at Cova da Iria, and his own flagging enthusiasm for the Message of Fatima. It is likely he did, but Pius' actions belied his knowledge. When the Portuguese bishops requested a feast in honor of "the Apparition of the Blessed Virgin of the Most Holy Rosary", Rome flatly refused. This was a shock, given Pius' earlier outspoken encouragement of Fatima devotions. Was the voice coming from Rome that of Pope Pacelli or that of his advisors?

Msgr. Montini

Eugenio Pacelli met Giovanni Battista Montini when they both served in the Secretariat of State for Pope Pius XI. When Pacelli succeeded Pius XI as Pope Pius XII Montini remained in the Secretariat of State. After Pius' original Secretary of State, Cardinal Maglione, died in 1944, he was replaced not by another Cardinal Secretary of State, but by two under-Secretaries of State — Msgr. Giovanni Battista Montini and Msgr. Domenico Tardini. Tardini, a "combative, blunt Roman", was named head of the Congregation of Extraordinary Ecclesial Affairs. Montini, an "aesthetic, tortured Brescian", was named head of the Congregation of Ordinary Affairs.[22]

As a practical matter, Tardini was involved with international affairs of state, Montini with Italian affairs. Both got on well with their boss, who Tardini described as "by temperament gentle and rather shy. He wasn't a fighter ... His great goodness led him to wish to please everyone, and to prefer the path of gentleness to that of severity, to persuade rather than to impose." An Austrian diplomat would describe Pacelli as "handicapped by a caution that was the result of anxiety, and also by a lack of drive."[23]

After the war Montini's influence over Catholic Action prolonged the "worker priest" novelty, and ensured the prominence of Christian Democrats, particularly in Italy, which, like much of Europe, was in collapse after the war. Half a million Italians were homeless, and armed bands of Marxists roamed town and country looking for priests. In less than two years they found and murdered fifty-two clergy. Soviet Russia, the big winner of the Second World War, was now threatening a "Mussolini-less" Italy.

Of course, the Communist press in Italy blamed the country's devastation on the Church. Less silly was the accusation that under-Secretary of State Montini was a "meddler in politics."[24] It was Montini who organized political opposition to the Italian Communist party. He arranged a large loan to the Christian Democrats from the Vatican Bank. He also secured additional funding from the United States, who was characteristically eager to promote democracy. While Pius XII steeled himself to be martyred in the Vatican if the Communists won, Montini's behind the scene maneuvering secured a ballot-box victory for the Christian Democrats, and prime minister positions in the new government for his proteges, Guilio Andreotti and Aldo Moro.[25]

The first order of business for Italy's new rulers was to form a coalition with Italian socialists and Communists in order to seal off any political threat from the right. Pius XII's irritation at the treachery of the Christian Democrats caused the Holy Office to issue a formal announcement:

> "Catholics who profess, and particularly those who defend and spread, the materialistic and anti-Christian doctrine of the Communists, *ipso facto*, as apostates from the Catholic Faith, incur excommunication."[26]

The targets of this message were progressive political activists in Italy, France, Germany, and Poland, whose collaborations with the left had turned them into socialists. This did not deter Christian Democrats from collaborating with Italian socialists and Communists against legitimate forms of Catholic Action that were deemed by the coalition to be too conservative. As usual, Italy's Christian Democrats received the secret and effective support of their long-time mentor, Msgr. Montini, who, contrary to Pius XII and the solemn declaration of the Holy Office, was of the private opinion that "It is possible to collaborate with the left, but not with the right."[27]

Montini, Escriva, and Maritain

It was during these years that Msgr. Montini first met Father Jose Maria Escriva, the founder of Opus Dei. Montini's intervention with Pius XII on Escriva's behalf resulted in the latter leaving Rome with two documents: one, signed by Pius XII, contained indulgences for Opus Dei members; the other was a general "letter of approval" of Opus Dei's international mission of "carrying the light and truth of Christ, especially to the minds of intellectuals."[28]

According to investigative journalist Robert Hutchison, "Escriva de Balaguer was able to convince Montini that Opus Dei's 'apostolate of penetration' could be useful in combating the spread of Marxism."[29] In exchange, Montini influenced Pius to grant juridical status to secular institutes like Opus Dei. This change in status caused Escriva to return to Rome, where Msgr. Montini facilitated Opus Dei's purchase of their new headquarters, Villa Tevere, in a fashionable district in Rome. Montini then arranged for Escriva to be made a domestic prelate of the papal household (Father Escriva became Msgr. Escriva), and introduced Escriva to influential Italian Christian Democrats like Giulio Andreotti.

Montini's lack of regard for Franco's Spain had not lessened over the years,[30] so his attentive mentoring of Jose Escriva, the supposedly conservative Spanish Catholic nationalist, seems curious. The contradiction is resolved by understanding what Msgrs. Montini and Escriva had in common. Neither man relied on Pius XI's declaration of the "intrinsically evil" nature of Communism, much less the now published accounts of the Blessed Virgin's messages about the necessity of consecrating Russia. Instead, Montini believed Communism was reformable, and saw Communists as potential allies of Christian Democrats.

As for Escriva, in spite of Opus Dei's contemporary image as ultra-orthodox, his organization remains basically what it was at its founding: a clandestine, priestless society of (mostly) wealthy, influential laymen who accepted Escriva's view that Genesis 2:15 meant man was sanctified primarily through work. According to an Opus Dei biographer of Escriva:

> "Professional work becomes the pivot on which the entire task
> of sanctification turns. This is what led the Founder of the Opus
> to sum up life on earth by saying that: 'it is necessary to sanctify
> work, to sanctify one's work, and to sanctify others through one's
> work.'"[31]

Not surprisingly, Escriva tended to neglect the importance of the priesthood and the Sacraments. At times he also let the social, political, or financial prominence of potential Opus Dei members outweigh their religious beliefs. "Some of these (members) are not Catholic," Escriva admitted, adding, "and a large number, a very large number, are not Christians."[32]

These "collaborators", as they were called, anticipated the ecumenism of Vatican II. "The houses of Opus Dei are interconfessional residences where students of all religions and ideologies live," declared Escriva. Elsewhere he stated, "Pluralism is not to be feared but loved as a legitimate consequence of personal freedom."[33]

Equally important, at least to those driving his canonization campaign, was Escriva's preoccupation with being in the world, and his surprising disregard for the priesthood.[34]

An Opus Dei author concedes that "the climate of secularism and of personal initiative" resulting from the principles of Opus Dei "resulted in the Founder (Escriva) having been accused of being a progressive, a heretic and crazy."[35] Yet he was no crazier than another gentleman Montini took an interest in: Paris' ambassador to the Holy See, lay philosopher Jacques Maritain.

A convert from Protestantism, Maritain began his Catholic career as a right-wing Thomist. When Pius XI condemned Catholic Action in France Maritain veered left, and stayed there. A brilliant philosopher with a bold and penetrating mind, his book *Integral Humanism*, became the gospel of Christian Democrat and neo-modernist alike.[36]

His posthumous works reveal that Maritain believed all the inhabitants of hell would be pardoned and escape eternal fire — even the devil.[37] Prudent enough to keep these views secret while alive, Maritain, not unlike Msgrs. Montini and Escriva, believed in a "new Christendom" described by Peter Hebblethwaite as "lay rather than clerical, democratic rather than authoritarian, and capable of inspiring a mass political party in which all who shared 'Christian values' could participate."[38]

Maritain's errors were old ones. In the Nineteenth Century a French priest, Father Felicite de Lammenais, founded liberal Catholicism in order to baptize the Masonic revolution. Instead it was Father Lammenais who was baptized into the revolution. Coming to believe that revelation resided not in God but in the masses, Lammenais left the Church and died unreconciled. His Twentieth Century counterpart was Frenchman Marc Sangnier, the founder of the "Sillon" (French for "furrow," an agricultural metaphor for dogged persevering work), a French Catholic organization that sought to elevate the human dignity of the working class. The Sillonists believed that:

> "Man will be a man truly worthy of the name only when he has acquired a strong, enlightened and independent consciousness, able to do without a master, obeying only himself, and able to assume the most demanding responsibilities without faltering."[39]

Presumably the working classes, after being properly educated by the Sillon, were to be re-invested with the same authority Lammenais envisioned them with.[40] While Msgr. Escriva's glorification of secular work was general, Sillon founder Marc Sangnier was more particular. The Sillon sought to establish equality of social conditions in order to usher in heaven on earth. Like Escriva, Sangnier was "ecumenical": "All of us, Catholics, Protestants, and Free-Thinkers will have at heart to arm young people, not in view of the fratricidal struggle, but in view of a disinterested emulation in the field of social and civic virtues."[41]

The pity was that initially the Sillon had been Catholic. Many of its members sincerely sought to emulate the Gospel example of aiding the poor. Marc Sangnier seemed earnest enough, so maybe he didn't realize that the God of the Sillon was not Christ crucified, but Man glorified. At any rate, the Sillon's reckless idealism turned the association into a volatile mixture of utopian humanism, class-leveling "democracy", and secular messianism.

By contrast, the Church had always taught that societies or civilizations could not endure unless their premises were explicitly Catholic. What was to come from these ecumenical collaborations? Pope St. Pius

X predicted:

> "a mere verbal and chimerical construction in which we see, glowing in a jumble, and in seductive confusion, the words of Liberty, Justice, Fraternity, Love, Equality, and human exaltation, all resting upon an ill-understood human dignity. It will be a tumultuous agitation, sterile for the end proposed, but which will benefit the less-Utopian exploiters of the people. Yes, we can truly say that the Sillon, its eyes fixed on a chimera, brings Socialism in its train."[42]

And not just Socialism, for according to the far-seeing Pope, the errors of the Sillon would result in:

> "A Democracy which will be neither Catholic, nor Protestant, nor Jewish. It will be a religion (for Sillonism, so the leaders have said, is a religion) more universal than the Catholic Church, uniting all men to become brothers and comrades at last in the 'Kingdom of God'. 'We do not work for the Church, we work for mankind.'"[43]

Pius appears to be describing Freemasonry here, or at the very least, a philosophy of humanism that elevates man over God (which amounts to the same thing). Enter Jacques Maritain, defender of the "Red Christian" Basque priests, who was enough of an historian to realize the condemned path he was trodding, but not Catholic enough to resist his vision.

The same may be said of Maritain's self-described "disciple", Msgr. Montini, and perhaps Msgr. Escriva as well. If one looks beyond words to deeds — and their fruits — it is apparent that the eyes of Montini, Escriva, and Maritain gazed less on Heaven than on earth, and less on God than on man and his potential, his accomplishments, his material successes. It was often difficult to distinguish the "Christian humanism" of Maritain, Montini, and the Christian Democrats from the naturalism of Freemasonry, or the materialism of Communism.

Escriva was not a Christian Democrat, much less a Communist, and one assumes he would have sharply disagreed with Maritain and Montini's views of the Spanish Civil War (that is, their resentment of Franco and their sympathy to the "red Christians"). The convergence between the three men was their essentially secular solutions to the problems of the Twentieth Century, solutions that did not seem to require the involvement of Christ's Church.[44]

Where the Blessed Virgin had warned of Russia's errors, and stressed the Rosary, penance, reparation, and the consecration of Russia to Her Immaculate Heart, a number of influential Churchmen either urged the Church to collaborate with Communism, or offered lukewarm alternatives (Christian Democracy and Christian Humanism) that, instead of being defenses against Russia's errors, only seemed to encourage them.

The practical realization of Jacques Maritain's integral humanism was as illusory as the "human exaltation" of the Sillon. The "progress" during the decades between the movements changed their outcomes, however. For as the Sillon ushered in Socialism in the early Twentieth Century, so would Maritain's integral humanism usher in Marxism, and an attempted convergence between Marxism and Christianity.

The Grand Convergence

The philosophy of Marxism (in contrast to the political system of Communism), also known as atheistic humanism, views history as an inevitable series of conflicts triggered by the dynamic actions of the proletariat, from which true progress springs. Theoretically, Communism aids human progress by provoking the proletariat to revolution. This view is not terribly unlike poor Lammenais' conviction that revelation resided with the masses. Nor is it dissimilar to the Sillon's radical democracy, which idealized the working classes, and sought to infuse them with authority. In all three examples the disorder stems from a rejection of the hierarchical nature of authority as ordained by God and taught by the Catholic Church. Maritain's integral humanism was similarly blighted.[45] He claimed that, unlike other humanisms, his was a "Christ-centered" humanism. Chances are he was as sincere about this as Lammenais and Marc Sangnier were. Yet with all due respect for Maritain's intellectual prowess, he was more of a Marxist than either of his precursors. His first mistake was one common to many Western intellectuals of the Twentieth Century. He believed Communists were genuinely concerned with the welfare and dignity of man. This was demonstrably false. His second error was his acceptance of the Marxist version of history and progress — a view that radically excluded God — and his focus on the proletariat – instead of the Incarnation — as the key to history and progress.

In hindsight, it is clear that Professor Maritain's "Christ-centered humanism" was anything but. Even if one ignores the inherent contradictions of a "Christ-centered humanism" — any humanism worthy of the name will have man, not God, at center stage — it was simply impossible to transplant the divinely revealed religion of Christianity onto the premises of the atheistic humanism of Karl Marx. Such an attempt is not merely impossible, it is sacrilegious. Not an intentionally sacrilegious man, Maritain's ambition was to unite Marxism and Christianity by the one thing he believed the two systems had in common: a genuine desire for the welfare and dignity of man, in a word — humanism.

As Lammenais attempted to infuse liberalism with Christianity in the Nineteenth Century, so did Maritain seek to infuse Marxism with Christianity in the Twentieth. His attempted synthesis of Christianity and atheistic humanism, and his demand that the Church open herself to the world, enthralled Msgr. Montini, just as the attempted fusion of

Communism and the priesthood in the failed "worker priest" experiment had. Later Montini would proclaim, "I am a disciple of Maritain, I will call him my teacher."[46] In Poland a young priest named Karol Wojtyla thought the worker priest movement so "enormously important" that he wrote an article about it.[47] Like Maritain, Wojtyla attempted to graft a man-centered philosophy onto Thomism.

The last decade of Pope Pius XII's pontificate, then, witnessed more than the end of the Second World War predicted by the beautiful Lady at Cova da Iria. It witnessed the acceleration of Russia's errors, and the spread of Communism into eastern Europe, China, Asia, and Africa. It witnessed the acceleration of devotion to Our Lady of Fatima, and urgent pleas to the Holy Father to consecrate Russia to the Immaculate Heart of Mary. And it witnessed what may be that portion of the Third Secret that remains unrevealed even after the announcement of June 26, 2000 — the beginning of a universal apostasy in the Church wherein man replaces God. If the Third Secret treats of such an apostasy — and most Fatima experts consider this likely — it is also likely that such an apostasy is intimately linked to the Grand Convergence between the Church and world that had been sought for so long by the enemies of the Church. It is interesting to note that just as Communism and devotion to the Blessed Virgin accelerated "neck and neck" through this century, the Grand Convergence between the Church and the world has been accelerating equally rapidly. It reached a temporary climax at Assisi in 1986, and another during the millenial apologies of the Jubilee 2000. Nothing signals the acceleration of the grand convergence more dramatically than the fact that the last two attempts at convergence were spearheaded by a Pope.

The tool of convergence was — and is — the philosophy of humanism, a plausible, if rather transparent pretext on which to base collaborations between Christians and infidels, pagans, atheists, and other deniers of the true God. The vehicle of convergence is the Second Vatican Council. Predicted by various occult forces as early as the beginning of this century,[48] the Council's success at introducing neo-modernism into the mainstream Church was possible only because of the steadfast determination of conciliar popes. The entire drama, however, would involve the ideas and personalities of the enigmatic Msgr. Montini, the "ultra-conservative" Msgr. Escriva, the monarchist turned democrat Jacques Maritain, the terminated papal nuncio, Angelo Roncalli, and an admirer of the worker priests, Father Wojtyla. None of them were (or are) deliberately evil men. Father Wojtyla, Msgr. Montini, and Professor Maritain sincerely wished to re-Christianize a dying, war-torn civilization, and they dearly wished to appear relevant to that civilization. Good intentions cannot improve bad ideas, however. The three aforementioned gentlemen responded to the crisis of a dying civilization by applying the very principles of liberalism which undermined it. It is hardest, perhaps, to excuse Professor Maritain for this error, because he appeared to have had, at least for a short time, a grasp of the true nature of the disease, and its remedy. From all appearances, Monsignor Montini and Father Wojtyla lacked even this momentary glimpse of the supernatural realities of our century. When Pope Montini proclaimed, at the close of Vatican II, that the Church had embraced the "cult of man", he was thrilled at the progress made by the Council. Like beauty, progress is in the eye of the beholder. An argument can be made that the Church's "cult of man" is not essentially different from the "nocturnal adoration" devotions made before the embalmed corpse of Lenin.[49]

Pius XI and Pius XII grasped enough to condemn Communism and forbid collaborations with Communists. Their reasons may be summed up in an old expression: "He who walks with a lame man learns how to limp." Yet it is an open question as to how seriously either Pope took the Message of Fatima. The beautiful Lady at Cova da Iria had warned that Russia would "spread its errors throughout the world, promoting wars and persecutions of the Church." She had promised to convert Russia if that nation were consecrated to Her Immaculate Heart by the Pope and the world episcopate. Pius XI did not do this. Neither did Pius XII. It will be seen how Msgr. Montini and Father Wojtyla (as well as the erstwhile nuncio Roncalli) responded to Fatima when they ascended to the papacy.

And we will see how a Carmelite nun in Coimbra, Portugal, the last living seer of the Fatima apparitions, who had taken solemn vows of obedience to her religious superiors, responded when her superiors, and the Church, at least in her human members, turned against her as if she were a mortal enemy.

NOTES

1. This apparition was reported in an Italian work, *Il pellegrinaggio delle meraviglie*, published under the auspices of the Italian bishops. This reported apparition was also mentioned by Canon Barthas. See *TWTAF*, Vol. III, p. 327 and fn 29, p. 351.

2. *TWTAF*, Vol. III p. 326.

3. Neither did Pius XII mention Our Lady's request for the First Saturday reparation devotions.

4. Peter Wiggington, *The Popes Of Vatican II*, The Franciscan Herald Press, 1983, pp. 69-73. Ironically, Pius' successor, John XXIII, was older than Pius XII when he convened Vatican II. For what it's worth, there is speculation that Pius had other reasons besides his age for not convening a Council. Father Caprile, a liberal, claims a Cardinal told him that Pius canceled the Council "because his character would not have adapted to being near an organization of that type with the powers and influence of the Council." What this means is far from clear, but it sounds unflattering. Less vague, but also unflattering, is Frère Michel's assertion that in preparing the Council Pius XII became aware of significant opposition from a surprisingly strong and well placed group of neo-modernists. Instead of contesting this influence Pius backed off. I don't know that there's enough information to decide this, but let it be noted that Frère Michel's opinion is supported by Pius' undersecretary of State – and friend – Msgr. Tardini, who characterized Pius as timid and overly concerned with hurting people's feelings. Let it also be noted that Pius' other undersecretary of State, Msgr. Montini, may well have influenced Pius' decision not to pursue a Council.

5. Giancarlo Zizola, *The Utopia of Pope John XXIII*, 2nd Edition, English translation, Orbis Books, 1978, Chapter Six.

6. Ibid., p. 91.

7. Ibid., p. 90.

8. Peter Hebblethwaite, *Pope John XXIII, Pope of the Council*, Geoffrey Chapman, London, 1984, p. 216. Hebblethwaite rather flippantly reports about the "alarmed bourgeoisie" who told Roncalli "shock/horror" stories about priests celebrating Mass in boiler suits, saying "*Salut, les copains*" ('Hi, pals') instead of *Dominus vobiscum*, and other irregularities.

9. Ibid., p. 217.

10. Zizola, op. cit., p. 93.

11. Hebblethwaite, *Pope John XXIII*, op. cit., p. 222.

12. Peter Nichols, *The Politics of the Vatican*, Frederick A. Praeger, Publishers, 1968, p. 257.

13. Peter Hebblethwaite, *Paul VI, The First Modern Pope*, Paulist Press, 1993, pp. 216-217.

14. He found Congar's book more digestible. Roncalli never had much time for de Chardin, once asking, "This Teilhard fellow ... why can't he be content with the catechism and the social doctrine of the Church, instead of bringing up all these problems?" (Hebblethwaite, *John XXIII*, op. cit., p. 219).

15. Zizola, op. cit., p. 93.

16. Also, according to Nichols, op. cit., p. 257, "Some of the French hierarchy became dismayed; by no means all of the pressure against the movement was generated in Rome." Nichols also notes that a French Catholic worker's association "was angry at the confusion caused by worker priests who held offices in left-wing unions."

17. Nichols and Zizola are both sympathetic to Roncalli, and both believe he was fired by Pius XII. According to Nichols (pp. 257-258), Roncalli's promotion "was interpreted as evidence of the Vatican's conviction that he was incapable of dealing firmly enough with the situation, and needed to be withdrawn from Paris."

18. *TWTAF*, Vol. III, p. 352, fn. 39.

19. Dhanis' entire thesis against Fatima is analyzed in *TWTAF*, Vol. I, Part II, Chapter 1. All quotations concerning his thesis are from this source.

20. As quoted in *TWTAF*, Vol. III, p. 345.

21. Ibid., p. 388.

22. The descriptions of Tardini and Montini are from Hebblethwaite, *Paul VI*, op. cit., pp. 105. The term "Brescian" refers to Montini's birthplace, Brescia, Italy.

23. Ibid., p. 134.

24. Hutchison, op. cit., p. 102.

25. During the reign of Pius XI Montini provided spiritual direction and political strategy for his students, Andreotti and Moro, who would prove to be durable politicians who had unfortunate relationships with, respectively, Freemasonry and the Mafia.

26. As quoted in Nazareno Padellaro, *Portrait of Pius XII*, English translation, J.M. Dent & Sons Ltd., 1956, p. 223.

27. *Si Si No No*, April 1994, English Language Article Reprint, p. 19.

28. Hutchison, op. cit., p. 103.

29. Ibid., p. 103.

30. A stance that would not soften when he became Pope; Paul VI derailed the canonizations of many Catholics who died in the Spanish Civil War, "because it seemed to him to glorify fascism." Interestingly, John Paul II, according to his biographer, Jonathan Kwitny, picked up the canonizations, not on their own merit, but as a retaliation against Spain's socialist government, which refused to heed the Pope's request to legislate against abortion. (Kwitny, op. cit., p. 617.)

31. As quoted in Nicholas Dehan, *Opus Dei, A Strange Pastoral Phenomenon*, translated into English by Suzanne Rini, p. 15.

32. As quoted in Ibid., p. 20.

33. Ibid., p. 17.

34. The popular view of Opus Dei is the liberal view, that is, that Opus is run by autocratic priests who strip members of all autonomy. In fact, as Escriva's biographer, Salvador Bernal, states: "For us, the priesthood is a circumstance, an accident, because at the heart of The Work (sic), the vocation of priests and that of the laity is the same ... (As to) the way that apostolic works are organized by the *Opus Dei* ..., these are planned and governed from a lay mentality; ... by so doing, they are *not confessional*". (As quoted in Dehan, op. cit., p. 14.)

35. Ana Sastre is the Opus Dei author cited in Dehan, op. cit., p. 14.

36. See Brooke Williams Smith, *Jacques Maritain: Antimodern or Ultramodern? An Historical Analysis of His Critics, His Thought, and His Life*, Elsevier, 1976.

37. See Amerio, op. cit., pp. 697-8.

38. *Paul VI*, op. cit., p. 122.

39. Pope Pius X, *Our Apostolic Mandate*, a Letter to the French Bishops and Archbishops on the

"Sillon," reproduced by Instauratio Press, 1990, Sec. 25.

40. It is worth noting here that both Lammenais' faith in the masses, and the Sillon's "Catholic" glorification of the "proletariat" were both "Catholic," and that both movements preceded Bolshevism.

41. *Our Apostolic Mandate*, Sec. 34. Pius X is quoting the words of Sillon founder Marc Sangnier, from a 1910 speech.

42. Ibid., Sec. 38.

43. Ibid., Sec. 39.

44. Opus Dei strategists saw themselves as a "Third Force" between the right wing and the Christian Democrats. See Hutchison, op. cit., p. 110.

45. For a critique of Maritain's Integral Humanism (by French intellectual Louis Salleron), see Appendix VI of Michael Davies, *Pope John's Council*, Angelus Press, 1977.

46. Smith, op. cit., p. 25.

47. George Weigel, *Witness To Hope, The Biography of Pope John Paul II*, Cliff Street Books, 1999. According to Weigel, "During the summer of 1947, Starowieyski and Wojtyla traveled around Europe with funds provided by Cardinal Sapieha. They met Parisian worker priests in the French capital and discussed their efforts to evangelize the post-Christian French proletariat – an experience that Wojtyla later remembered as "enormously important," and the occasion for his first article in *Tygodnik Powszechny*, some time later." See also Jonathan Kwitny, *Man of the Century: The Life and Times of Pope John Paul II*, Henry Holt and Company, Inc., 1997, pp. 114-115, 310.

48. For the predictions of Vatican II by Freemasons and other ne'er do wells, see Dr. Rudolf Graber (Bishop of Regensburg), *Athanasius and the Church of Our Time*, Van Buren C.P. Ltd., England, 1974, pp. 31-40.

49. Galter, op. cit., p. 33. The "devotions" were organized by Soviet leaders, who "took pains to establish the cult of Marx, Engels and Lenin among the masses." In the same paragraph Galter observes: "While Christianity was in process of liquidation, the Bolsheviks entrusted the Communist Party with the task of finding substitutes for religion. Party meetings were intended to act as substitutes for religious ceremonies, and were supposed to perform the same social function that religion had previously done in the collective life of the people. The theatre in particular underwent considerable development and became in some sort the temple of the new regime. Whereas in 1914 there were only 210 theatres in Russia, this number had reached 6,000 in 1920 and increased still more in the following years. It frequently happened that churches were transformed into theatres, where Russian ballet and other performances of less artistic value became vehicles of propaganda in favour of sensualism and of the new political order ..."

To give Paul VI his due, he did recognize that secular humanism was a religion. He didn't seem to consider it a threat to religion, however.

Chapter Twelve

Twilight Begins

What was needed, according to Msgr. Montini, was *"astuzia"* — that is, cunning. "We are going through difficult times," he confided to a sympathizer, "times in which prudence is not enough, but in which prudence must become cunning."[1]

"Difficult times" was an allusion to Vatican suspicions about Msgr. Montini's activities as Pope Pius XII's pro-Secretary of State. His frank admiration for men like Jacques Maritain and the new theologians caused the left-wing press to advertise Montini as Pius' successor, even though he was only a priest at the time. His biographer, ex-Jesuit Peter Hebblethwaite, assures his readers that Montini "was perfectly loyal to the Pope he served."[2] If this was true, however, why was "cunning" required? To what end was Msgr. Montini concentrating his considerable talents? Where did his loyalties lie?

The Rise and Fall of Msgr. Montini

In addition to his admiration for Jacques Maritain, his friendship with anti-Fatima neo-modernist Father Dhanis, his support for the worker priests, and his assistance to the leftist faction of Italy's Christian Democrat party, Montini initiated and encouraged collaboration between the Church and neo-modernism, and the Church and Soviet Communism — collaborations that were expressly *against* the will of Pope Pius XII.

For instance, in 1944 Montini's covert admiration for the French modernist Maurice Blondel took tangible form. In order to reach modern man with the Gospel, the layman Blondel believed it was necessary to abandon Thomism in favor of Immanentism, a philosophy that located the supernatural inside man instead of in a transcendental God. For Blondel, religion was no more than a natural need man had — albeit a noble and edifying need — and religious truth was located not in Revelation but in individual experience. Since man's experience was constantly changing, religious dogmas were of essence evolutionary. Blondel is responsible for the idea of "living tradition"[3] one hears so much of today, a catch-phrase which sounds nice but is often little more than a license to believe whatever you will.

After his philosophy of Immanentism had been condemned by Pope Pius X (in his encyclical *Pascendi Dominici Gregis*), Blondel survived the next few decades by continually revising his thought in ever more ambiguous formulations, blending his errors with orthodox statements, and accusing his opponents (e.g., Dominican Father Garrigou-Lagrange) of purposely misrepresenting his ideas.[4]

In fact Blondel was no stranger to misrepresentation, at least if his private correspondence is any indication. Dropping his public persona of injured innocence, in 1932 Blondel informed his pen pal, neo-modernist Jesuit Henri de Lubac, that "It is necessary to embrace traditional ways and views, so that they may be used as a point of departure or a spring-board for a 'renewal' ..."[5]

Towards the end of his life (he died in 1949) Blondel began the publishing of a trilogy entitled *Christian Spirit and Philosophy*. His continuing efforts to relocate the supernatural on the natural level were sharply contested by orthodox theologians. As arguments became heated, Mr. Blondel received a letter from Rome. The letter, dated December 2, 1944, written and signed by Msgr. Montini, gave the impression that Pius XII was not only familiar with Blondel's writings but approved of them, with the exception of "a few expressions which theological rigor would have wished to be couched in more precise terms." Aside from this mild admonition, the letter had nothing but praise for Blondel's work, and closed thusly:

> "And so, greatly delighted at the good news regarding your improving state of health, the Holy Father expresses his wishes that you may have the strength required to bring your important work to a successful conclusion, and most cordially gives you His Apostolic Blessing."[6]

The timing of Msgr. Montini's letter was impeccable. It neatly undercut the orthodox theologians disputing Blondel's modernist ideas, making them appear to oppose not just Blondel but the Pope himself. But did the letter to Blondel truly express the opinions of Pius XII?

Two years later, in a 1946 address to the Jesuits, Pius XII spoke disapprovingly of the "New Theology, which must evolve just as everything evolves, as it progresses without ever being fixed once and for all." Pius asked the Fathers, "if we were to embrace or share such opinions, what would become of the immutable or unchangeable Dogmas of the Catholic Church? What would become of the unity and stability of the Faith?"[7]

In 1950 Pius issued *Humani Generis*. Vatican II peritus Romano Amerio called this encyclical "the third Syllabus" (the first two were by Pius IX and Pius X, respectively). According to Amerio, *Humani Generis* and the documents of Vatican II "constitutes the Church's principal doctrinal pronouncement since Pius X."[8] *Humani Generis* was a broadside against the New Theology and the error-riddled philosophy that supports it, both of which, according to Pius, "threaten to undermine the foundations of Catholic doctrine." Without mentioning him by name, Pius denounced Blondel's idea that Catholic dogma could be made more palatable to modern man by expressing it in "the concepts of modern philosophy, whether of immanentism or idealism or existentialism or any other system."[9] The Pope went on to denounce another of Blondel's beliefs, that "any philosophy or belief ... can be reconciled with Catholic dogma. No Catholic can doubt that this is quite false, especially since it involves those fictions which they call 'immanence,' or 'idealism,' or 'materialism,' whether historic or dialectic, or even 'existentialism,' whether professing atheism, or at least rejecting the value of metaphysical reasoning."[10]

It is very difficult to reconcile these statements of Pius XII, and his statements to the Jesuits, with Msgr. Montini's statement that Pius XII desired Mr. Blondel "to bring your important work to a successful conclusion, and most cordially gives you His Apostolic Blessing."

As can be imagined, *Humani Generis* caused considerable consternation in the neo-modernist camp. Less than a month after it was issued Msgr. Montini spoke with French intellectual (and Opus Dei member) Jean Guitton. Guitton complained the encyclical was "harsh", and believed that "several of its passages, taken literally and out of context, would suggest that Rome holds the progress of thought suspect ..."[11]

If by "progress of thought" Guitton meant immanence, existentialism, and atheistic humanism, he is certainly correct. Pius XII held these philosophies as suspect because of their divergence from objective truth as expressed in Thomism. Msgr. Montini did not point this out, however. Instead, he replied:

> "You have doubtless yourself noted the shades of meaning written into this papal text. For example, the encyclical never speaks of *errors* (*errores*). It only speaks of *opinions* (*opiniones*). This indicates that the Holy See aims to condemn not errors, properly speaking, but modes of thought which could lead to errors, but which in themselves remain respectable."[12]

What is the difference, please, between errors and "modes of thought" that lead to errors? Since truth does not lead to error, mustn't modes of thought that do so be themselves erroneous? Moreover, Msgr. Montini's assertion that Pius considered modern philosophy essentially respectable is manifestly contradicted by *Humani Generis,* wherein Pius declared it was his "sacred Duty" to bind "most seriously in conscience" bishops and leaders of religious orders to see "that such (erroneous) opinions be not advanced in schools, in conferences or in writings of any kind, and that they be not taught in any manner whatsoever to the clergy or to the faithful."[13]

Instead of acknowledging this, however, Msgr. Montini continues:

> "The encyclical, you will note, does not speak of an evil which has taken root; it only speaks of predisposition. You will notice

that it is in quite a different tone from the encyclical *Pascendi* which was brought out by Pius X against modernist doctrines. One might say that the intention of the Holy Father is precisely to avoid the need for a new *Pascendi* encyclical. The Holy See would much prefer not to have to say anything, but it cannot put aside its duties."[14]

In fact, the encyclical speaks of errors inside the Church "which threaten to undermine the foundations of Catholic doctrine." This seems serious enough, whether one calls it by its proper name, evil, or "predisposition" — a word that does not appear in *Humani Generis*. Msgr. Montini's attempt to distinguish *Humani Generis* from *Pascendi* is an unintentional admission of the link between the two — the second and third Syllabi. As for the benevolence Montini attributes to the Holy See regarding neo-modernism, again, it is very difficult to detect this in the encyclical itself, or in Pius' other comments on neo-modernism. If Msgr. Montini was correct in his comments to Mr. Blondel and Mr. Guitton, then one may fairly conclude that Pius XII was a hypocrite who publicly denounced beliefs that privately he either applauded or was indifferent to. Aside from the veiled comments of Msgr. Montini, however, there is no evidence to justify such a conclusion. Now if Pius XII was not a hypocrite, what may one conclude regarding Msgr. Montini?

Well, one could say that his list of interesting friends was growing. In addition to Mr. Maritain, Msgr. Escriva, Father Dhanis, and various officials in Soviet government (including Stalin), there was now Mr. Blondel, Mr. Guitton, and another French intellectual, the Jesuit Father Henri de Lubac, who, like Montini, was an admirer of Blondel. De Lubac told Blondel that the latter's abandonment of Scholasticism made possible "a (new) theology of the supernatural". This was intended as a compliment.

As Blondel's new philosophy abandoned Thomism, so did Father de Lubac's "new theology" abandon Catholic theology. Using Blondel's ideas of immanence and "living tradition" as a base, de Lubac proceeded to deny the existence of "pure nature". Believing there was no strict division between the supernatural and the natural worlds, de Lubac in effect divinized the natural world. Another word for his "horizontal" theology is naturalism. Pius XII took careful aim at de Lubac in *Humani Generis*, when he spoke of theologians who "destroy the gratuity of the supernatural order, since God, they say, cannot create intellectual beings without ordering and calling them to the beatific vision."[15]

This was precisely the problem with de Lubac's theology.[16] It contradicted the basic Catholic doctrine that grace was gratuitous, that is, freely bestowed upon man by God. If pure nature did not exist, then grace was automatic, even compelled, certainly not a gift. If grace was inherent to human nature, as de Lubac believed, then everyone was a Christian — the only distinction is that some knew it and some, the so-called "anonymous Christians", didn't. Evangelization consisted of informing the ignorant that they were actually in a state of grace. The logical conclusion to de Lubac's ideas was universal salvation, the idea that everyone went to Heaven, be they Buddhists or axe murderers.

It is not being implied here that Msgr. Montini was an adherent of universal salvation; simply that, like Father Wojtyla, Montini greatly esteemed Father de Lubac and Maurice Blondel.[17] Directly contradicting Pius XII's censure of de Lubac in *Humani Generis*, Montini told Jean Guitton:

> "... you may be sure that Père de Lubac will do great things for the Church. We (the Vatican?) know all about his learning, his virtues and his influence. His thought is not in itself worthy of condemnation ..."[18]

Later, as Pope Paul VI, Montini would continue to speak highly of de Lubac. Jean Guitton, an intimate friend, recalls Montini speaking highly of de Lubac, praising his "spirit"[19], among other things.

It is unlikely Pius XII knew the full extent of his pro-Secretary of State's infatuation with the New Theology, or his undermining of *Humani Generis* (much less "Pius XII's letter" to Maurice Blondel). In 1954, however, Pius became aware (via Vatican Intelligence, the Swedish Secret Service, and a Protestant bishop) that Msgr. Montini was making unauthorized contacts with Soviet Russia. According to Msgr. Georges Roche, Pius XII's "grief and bitterness were such that his very health was severely shaken and so he resigned himself to the idea of governing alone the work of external affairs of the Vatican's Secretariat of State."[20]

Pius learned of this betrayal in late summer, 1954. In September the pro-Secretary of State signed his last official document. On November 1 Msgr. Montini, like the nuncio Roncalli, was fired by being promoted (*"Promoveatur ut amoveatur"*, the Romans call it) to the Archbishop seat in Milan. After Montini became Pope Paul VI these bare facts became inconvenient for conservative and liberal Catholics alike. Yet it is clear that, after having consistently risen in the Vatican Secretariat of State for over thirty years, Montini had abruptly fallen from grace. His friend Jean Guitton admitted that "Pius XII seemed to have lost the trust he had placed" in Montini. Another close friend, Cardinal Roncalli of Venice, commiserated with the crestfallen Archbishop of Milan. Although the leftist press continued to champion Montini as a future pope, Pius XII made sure Montini would not participate in the next conclave by refusing to make Montini a Cardinal (even though Milan was a cardinalate see). Moreover, after seeing Montini daily for over a decade, after he left Rome Montini was never received by Pius XII in private audience. Not only that, but before Montini could leave Rome for Milan his two moving vans (containing some 8,000 books) were searched by Vatican officials.[21]

So to answer the questions asked earlier in this section, pro-Secretary of State Montini's energies and loyalties were in the service not of Pius XII but of the Grand Convergence. He saw himself as an agent of reconciliation between the Church and the world, and perhaps even between Christ and anti-Christ. For what was the new theology in all its various forms but a system of pleasant sounding, murky ideas that dissolved Christ and deified man? Nothing could be further away from Catholicism or the Message of Fatima, with its emphasis on man's sinfulness, and the desperate need for prayer and reparation to God.

Montini was prudent enough — or cunning enough, to use his term — to get away with quite a bit of mischief as pro-Secretary of State. He overreached himself and was banished from Rome, but his fall from grace was only temporary. He would quickly be rehabilitated after Pius XII died, and return to Rome more confirmed in his ambitions, and with far less restrictions on his activities.

The Secret Goes to Rome

The year following Montini's exile to Milan saw Cardinal Ottaviani, the pro-Secretary of the Holy Office, come to Portugal. On May 13 at the Cova da Iria Ottaviani delivered a homily to thousands of pilgrims. Then he visited Sister Lucy at the Carmelite convent in Coimbra, Portugal. Lucy asked Ottaviani to request from the Holy Father that the beatification processes for Francisco and Jacinta be accelerated. Ottaviani asked Lucy about the Third Secret and when it would be disclosed. Lucy told him no later than 1960. Ottaviani asked why, and Lucy answered, "Because it will seem clearer."[22]

Lucy had given the written Third Secret to Bishop da Silva in 1944. The understanding between them was that da Silva could have read the Secret anytime he wanted to. He refused to do so, however, telling Canon Galamba, "It's not my duty to interfere in this matter. Heaven's secrets are not for me, nor do I need to burden myself with this responsibility."[23] Galamba, who knew Lucy and was da Silva's advisor, recalled that "When the bishop refused to open the letter, Lucy made him promise that it would definitely be opened and read to the world either at her death or in 1960, whichever would come first."[24] This agreement between Lucy and da Silva was reached after it became clear that da Silva would not read the Third Secret. Then, on December 8, 1945, da Silva took Lucy's sealed envelope that contained the Secret, and placed it in a larger envelope. This he also sealed with wax, and wrote on it, "This envelope with its contents will be given to His Eminence Cardinal Don Manuel, Patriarch of Lisbon, after my death. Leiria, December 8, 1945. Jose, Bishop of Leiria." It is clear from this that the Third Secret was not reserved exclusively for the Pope. It was for the Church, which is why Lucy gave the Secret to her bishop. Of course, it could have been read by the Holy Father, or Bishop da Silva or Cardinal Cerejeira, at any time between 1944 and 1960, the date the Blessed Virgin had designated the

Secret to be revealed by. This was well understood by all parties. As Cardinal Cerejeira put it:

> "From the two parts of the Secret already revealed, the third part has not been made known, but it has been written and placed in a sealed envelope and will be opened in 1960; we know enough to enable us to conclude that the salvation of the world, in this extraordinary movement of history, has been placed by God in the Immaculate Heart of Mary."[25]

In 1944 the Vatican had refused to receive the Third Secret. In 1955 Cardinal Ottaviani of the Holy Office expressed no desire to receive the Secret. At the beginning of 1957, however, the Holy Office requested — through the papal nuncio at Lisbon, Msgr. Cento — copies of all Lucy's writings, "Especially the Secret."[26]

Eighty-five-year-old Bishop da Silva entrusted the task to auxiliary Bishop Venancio. Twice Venancio proposed that da Silva read the Secret, telling him, "This is the last opportunity we have." Da Silva refused. Before placing copies of Lucy's writings, and the Third Secret, in the hands of the nuncio Cento, Bishop Venancio held the envelope containing the Secret up to the light:

> "In the bishop's large envelope he discerned a smaller envelope, that of Lucy, and inside this envelope an ordinary sheet of paper with margins on each side of three quarters of a centimeter. He took the trouble to note the size of everything. Thus the final Secret of Fatima was written on a small sheet of paper."[27]

In March Venancio personally delivered the secret and Lucy's other writings to the nuncio in Lisbon. They were received by the Vatican on April 16, 1957. Although the Holy Office (renamed The Sacred Congregation for the Doctrine of the Faith after Vatican II) had requested the Third Secret, it was delivered to Pope Pius XII. He put the sealed envelope in a small wooden safe on a table in his apartment. For the next year and a half the "Pope of Fatima" would have the opportunity to read the mysterious Third Secret at his leisure.

Later (in 1967) Cardinal Ottaviani would insist the Vatican's sudden interest in the Third Secret was "to prevent something of so delicate a nature, not destined for public consumption from falling, for any reason whatsoever, even accidentally, into alien hands."[28]

Most Fatima experts think this is nonsense, and insulting to the Portuguese episcopacy besides. After all, how could Rome know the contents of the Secret were "delicate" without having read it? Moreover, Ottaviani's assertion that the Secret was not for "public consumption" contradicts the agreement between Lucy and the Portuguese hierarchy to reveal the Secret in 1960. Last, there were no security problems in Portugal. No one had attempted to break into Bishop da Silva's safe to steal the Secret. Just whose "alien hands" were the Vatican concerned about?

It is more likely that Rome wanted to control disclosure of the Secret. Since 1955 Lucy's visitors and public statements — such as they were — had been controlled by her superiors, at the behest of Rome. It is likely that the muzzling of Sister Lucy and the requesting of the Third Secret were not isolated occurrences.

Lucy and Father Fuentes

It turned out that the Vatican's timing was excellent, for Bishop da Silva died several months after the Third Secret was sent to Rome. This prevented the Secret from being sent to the Patriarch of Lisbon, Cardinal Cerejeira, who had an active interest in the Message of Fatima and the Third Secret. On the day after Christmas, 1957, Lucy was visited at her convent by Father Augustine Fuentes, a Mexican priest preparing to become postulator of Francisco and Jacinta's causes for beatification. It was in this context that he was allowed to speak to Lucy. Months later (May 1958), after Father Fuentes had returned to Mexico, he gave a conference in which he revealed the content of his interview with Lucy. According to Fuentes, Sister Lucy "was very sad, very pale and emaciated." She told him:

> "Father, the Most Holy Virgin is very sad because no one has paid any attention to Her Message, neither the good nor the bad ... But believe me, Father, God will chastise the world and this will be in a terrible manner. The punishment from Heaven is imminent."

Lucy then asked, "Father, how much time is there before 1960 arrives? It will be very sad for everyone, not one person will rejoice at all if beforehand the world does not pray and do penance. I am not able to give any other details because it is still a secret ... This is the third part of the Message of Our Lady which will remain secret until 1960."

In the statements of Lucy that follow, she appears to speak of two chastisements. The first is Russia:

> "Tell them Father, that many times, the Most Holy Virgin told my cousins Francisco and Jacinta, as well as myself, that many nations will disappear from the face of the earth. She said that Russia will be the instrument of chastisement chosen by Heaven to punish the whole world if we do not beforehand obtain the conversion of that poor nation ..."

As woeful as this prophecy was, Lucy stressed that "my mission is not to indicate to the world the material punishments which are certain to come if the world does not pray and do penance beforehand. No! My mission is to indicate to everyone the imminent danger we are in of losing our souls for all eternity if we remain obstinate in sin."

This recalls the "first secret" of Fatima, the vision of hell. Then Lucy speaks of a second chastisement, the apostasy of consecrated religious.

She told Fuentes:

"Father, the devil is in the mood for engaging in a decisive battle against the Blessed Virgin. And the devil knows what it is that most offends God and which in a short space of time will gain for him the greatest number of souls. Thus the devil does everything to overcome souls consecrated to God because in this way the devil will succeed in leaving the souls of the faithful abandoned by their leaders, thereby the more easily will he seize them."

Lucy continued to describe what in all likelihood is intimately related to the Third Secret of Fatima:

"That which afflicts the Immaculate Heart of Mary and the Heart of Jesus is the fall of religious and priestly souls. The devil knows that religious and priests who fall away from their beautiful vocation drag numerous souls to hell ... The devil wishes to take possession of consecrated souls. He tries to corrupt them in order to lull to sleep the souls of laypeople and thereby lead them to final impenitence ..."

Lucy could not be more grave as she speaks of the "faithful abandoned by their leaders" and the corruption of religious lulling laypeople to "final impenitence". Her next words are equally chilling:

"Father, we should not wait for an appeal to the world to come from Rome on the part of the Holy Father, to do penance. Nor should we wait for the call to penance to come from our bishops in our diocese, nor from the religious congregations. No! ... Now, it is necessary for each one of us to begin to reform himself spiritually. Each person must not only save his own soul but also all the souls that God has placed on our path ..."

During the reign of Pope Pius XII, the "Pope of Fatima", leader of the impregnable "pre-Vatican II" Church, here was Sister Lucy — who scrupulously obeyed her religious superiors — advising Catholics not to look to the Holy Father or the bishops for guidance! If possible, her message becomes even more alarming:

"Father, the Most Holy Virgin did not tell me that we are in the last times of the world but She made me understand this for three reasons."

The first reason:

"She told me the devil is in the mood for engaging in a decisive battle against the Virgin. And a decisive battle is the final battle where one side will be victorious and the other side will suffer defeat. Hence from now on we must choose sides. Either we are for God or we are for the devil. There is no other possibility."

The second reason:

"She said to my cousins as well as to myself that God is giving two last remedies to the world. These are the Holy Rosary and Devotion to the Immaculate Heart of Mary. These are the last two remedies which signify that there will be no others."

The third reason:

"God always, before He is about to chastise the world, exhausts all other remedies. Now, when He sees that the world pays no attention whatsoever ... He offers us with a certain trepidation the last means of salvation, His Most Holy Mother ... if you despise and repulse this ultimate means we will not have any more forgiveness from Heaven because we will have committed a sin which the Gospel calls the sin against the Holy Spirit ...

"This sin consists of openly rejecting with full knowledge and consent, the salvation which He offers. Let us remember that Jesus Christ is a very good Son and that He does not permit that we offend and despise His Holy Mother ..."

Lucy's statements regarding souls being damned to hell, and the chastisement of Soviet Russia, are consistent with what we know of the Fatima Message. A development is her statements concerning the apostasy of consecrated religious. These themes may well represent the Fatima Secret in a nutshell. Not surprisingly, the remedy for the dire prophecies is also part of the Fatima Message. "Sister Lucy told me," Father Fuentes said, "the two means to save the world are prayer and sacrifice."

"Look Father," Lucy told Fuentes, "the Most Holy Virgin in these last times in which we live has given a new efficacy to the recitation of the Rosary, to such an extent that there is no problem, no matter how difficult it is ... even of the life of peoples and nations ... that we cannot resolve by the prayer of the Holy Rosary. With the Holy Rosary, we will save ourselves. We will sanctify ourselves. We will console Our Lord and obtain the salvation of many souls."

"Finally," Lucy concluded, "devotion to the Immaculate Heart of Mary, Our Most Holy Mother, consists in considering Her as the seat of mercy, of goodness and of pardon and as the certain door by which we are to enter Heaven."[29]

Lucy's interview with Father Fuentes contained hard sayings; who could hear them? Not the episcopal curia in Coimbra, where Lucy's Carmelite convent was located. They accused Fuentes of fabricating the interview, and declared that Lucy herself renounced the interview as a fake. Father Fuentes was stripped of his duties as postulator for the beatification causes of Francisco and Jacinta.

Anyone who follows Fatima knows two things. First, that Lucy's interview with Father Fuentes is a synthesis of the entire Fatima Message. What is new are some blunt statements concerning the apostasy of consecrated religious. These statements are almost certainly veiled references to the Third Secret.

The second thing known to followers of Fatima is that over the years many statements have been attributed to Sister Lucy that later have turned out not to have been uttered by her. Today Fatima historians, including the "official" Church historian of Fatima, Father Alonso, and Father Fuentes' replacement, Father Luis Kondor, believe that Fuentes did not fabricate, exaggerate, or misrepresent his interview with Lucy. The statements falsely attributed to Lucy were those made by Coimbra's episcopal curia who claimed Lucy renounced the interview.

In fact it appears Lucy made the most of her opportunity. In the forty years following her interview by Father Fuentes she would rarely have the opportunity to speak so freely, and to have her remarks made public.

Twilight Begins

During his last years Pius XII considered abdicating the papacy because of health problems, particularly an abdominal hernia which caused acute, often very painful attacks of hiccups. It was an unusual malady, and in 1954 it was only the assurances of his doctors that he would recover with his thinking capacities unimpaired that persuaded Pius to continue as Pope.[30]

In almost twenty years as pope, Pius gave 2,300 speeches — about one every three days. In the last years of his life this pace accelerated. The last full month of his life, September, 1958, saw Pius give 13 speeches at the traditional summer residence of popes, Castel Gandolfo. In the last week of his life the painful hiccups returned to plague him. As if in a rush to say everything he had to say before it was too late, he gave four more speeches in the first five days of October.

He gave an audience to America's Cardinal Spellman and his group of very wealthy New Yorkers. Pius talked to the sophisticated, impeccably dressed pilgrims about guardian angels. His last audience was to delegates to the Fifth International Congress of Latin Notaries. Ashen and weak, his remarks were interrupted by hiccups. A watch he was holding in his hands fell to the floor. The audience ended early, and the eighty-two-year-old Pope calmly told a fretting Monsignor, "We have come to the end."

The following morning, October 6, Pius said Mass in his private chapel. He went to his office about 8:30 A.M., and suffered a stroke. It is said that just before he went into a coma he cried out, "I can't see — Immaculate Madonna, help me!"

For the next three days Pius struggled, calmly and quietly, for his life. Following the time-honored policy, "A Pope is never ill until he's dead", *L'Osservatore Romano* published hopeful headlines about the Holy Father's recovery. Inside Castel Gandolfo Pius came in and out of consciousness. The hiccups stopped, but his temperature soared to 106. Msgr. Tardini attempted to comfort the dying Pope with the headlines in *L'Osservatore Romano*. Pius read the headlines, then informed Tardini, "This is my last day."[31]

The Roman press agreed. Four newspapers announced Pius' death on the morning of October 8, with interesting details of the Pope's last hours, and his farewell message to the Church and the world. It was all rubbish, but the nasty impatience of the press underscored the reality that, unlike 1954, the Pope's condition would not improve. For Pius suffered another stroke and never regained consciousness. After midnight Tardini said a Mass for the dying in a room adjacent to Pius XII, and wept as he said the words of consecration. At 3:52 in the morning of Thursday, October 9, 1958, Pius XII died.

The press gathered around Castel Gandolfo scrambled to position their bulky photographic equipment around the local hearse that came to remove the body. It was a small, battered old car. Mounted on its top, noted a reporter, was a "two foot tall gilded model of a papal tiara surmounted by a cross, surrounded by four bare-armed, bare-waisted and bare-legged four-foot gilded cherubs holding dangling cords and tassels."[32] Upon leaving Castel Gandolfo the garish hearse promptly blew a tire, but managed to get to Rome without further incident.

As Cardinals began arriving in Rome for the conclave that would elect his successor, Pope Pius XII was entombed in a three hour ceremony. A boy's choir chanted and a crowd of thousands looked on as red ropes lowered the body of Eugenio Pacelli into a 1,000 pound triple casket composed of lead, elm and cyprus wood. Cardinals incensed the casket and sprinkled it with holy water. Next came the loud noises of power drills and hammers as the casket was sealed. A rope and pulley lowered it beneath St. Peter's basilica to its final resting place. Although the silver hammer had been abandoned, it was clear that the pontificate of Pius XII was truly over.

He had been the first Roman pope in generations, and the first pope to die outside Rome in generations. Perhaps there is a hidden meaning to these facts that would provide a key to the significance of Pius XII's pontificate. In the absence of this secret knowledge, however, it can be observed that Papa Pacelli's finest achievements were getting the Church through the Second World War relatively intact, defining the dogma on the Assumption of the Blessed Virgin Mary, canonizing Pope St. Pius X, and writing *Humani Generis*. In the first half of his pontificate he was a zealous advocate of Fatima, and was chiefly responsible for popularizing the cult of the Immaculate Heart of Mary. In the later years of his pontificate he rarely mentioned Fatima. The Third Secret sat in a safe on his desk for the last year and a half of his life. It is very likely that he died without reading it.

One can only wonder what he was waiting for. Perhaps he had been persuaded or embarrassed out of his early fervor for Fatima by the plausibly intelligent arguments of Father Dhanis. Perhaps he never attached

that much significance to the humble Portuguese nun who kept requesting the Five First Saturdays devotion. But then why did he promote the
Fatima cult, and attempt to consecrate Russia to the Immaculate Heart?
Perhaps he became irritated when this same nun contradicted him by
stating that he had not perfomed the consecration of Russia to the Immaculate Heart of Mary correctly. But this doesn't explain why he kept
the Third Secret in a prominent place on his oft-used desk.

Perhaps Pius XII was, as Msgr. Montini seemed to suggest, an admirer of neo-modernism and left-wing causes. It is true that Pius was responsible for numerous innovations during his pontificate. He
encouraged decolonization of Africa, thus hastening the advance of
Communism in Africa. He allowed the worker priest experiment. He
lessened the fast requirement before receiving Holy Communion; this
elated progressives, as it paved the way for another novelty, evening
Masses.[33] He allowed what later would be known as "natural family
planning." He allowed married pastors to become priests. And he created a pontifical commission on the liturgy, appointing Father Annibale
Bugnini to begin reforming the liturgy. Later, in his autobiography,
Bugnini recalled:

> "We enjoyed the full confidence of Pius XII who was kept in-
> formed of our work by Msgr. Montini and even more by Father
> Bea, his confessor. Thanks to these intermediaries we could arrive
> at remarkable results even in periods when the Pope's illness pre-
> vented anyone else from seeing him."[34]

Although Pius is viewed today as a "traditionalist" pope, it cannot be denied that his closest advisors were men of the left: Bea and Montini. Yet
progressives overstate things by claiming a kinship to Pius XII. That
Pacelli saw fit to allow dialogue masses and the vernacular is a far cry from
the madness rampant in the Mass today. Recall that the post-war concern
was bringing people back into the Church. Pius was less an innovator than
a priest concerned with administering sacraments to the most people. It
was this impulse that generated *Mediator Dei* and allowed the worker
priest experiment.

Unfortunately, this holy desire was used as a pretext by unscrupulous
men who made up in arrogance what they lacked in faith: like the worker
priests, like Fathers Bugnini, Dhanis, de Lubac, and many of the other
Churchmen we have visited these last few chapters. When Sister Lucy
spoke in 1957 of the apostasy of consecrated religious she was not just
prophesying, she was describing the state of affairs in the pre-conciliar
Church. It is indisputable that the rot was not merely present but growing in the Church, before, during, and after the Second World War.
Humani Generis is proof of that.

Consequently, the blackest mark, the gravest reproach that can be
made against the memory of Pope Pius XII was not that he didn't do

enough to help the Jews, but that he didn't do enough to help Christ's Church. Had he followed the example of the Pope he canonized, his namesake Pope Pius X, Pacelli, in addition to issuing *Humani Generis*, would have cleaned house or died trying — and health problems be damned. Can it be imagined that Pope St. Pius X, had he been graced with seeing the Miracle of the Sun and fated to have been confronted with the written text of the Third Secret, would have refused to have even read it? Would he not have — like his predecessor Pope Pius IX when faced with the secret of La Sallette — seized the envelope, tore it open, read with a burning heart the prophecies of Heaven, and then preached them to the world?

Is it not a shame and disgrace for Christ's Vicar on Earth *not* to do so, whether in the 1950's or today?

NOTES

1. Hebblethwaite, Paul VI, op. cit., p. 255.
2. Ibid.
3. *Si Si No No*, October 1993, *The Angelus* English language article reprint, p. 3b. "Living Tradition," according to Blondel, was something far different than the mere development of doctrine, which is always in harmony with Tradition. Blondel's "erroneous notion of Tradition ('living tradition') ignores the Church's logical and indispensable link that must exist between what the Church teaches now and what the Church has always believed and taught. This is because, based on Blondel's false notion of truth, progress in dogma and understanding of truth is in a continual state of evolution or development ... there can be no fixed, definite, unchangeable truths. (3b-4b)"
4. Father Garrigou-Lagrange privately wrote Blondel, asking him to "retract his (false) definition of truth before dying – if he didn't want to spend too long in Purgatory" (*Si Si No No*, October 1993, p. 3b).
5. Ibid., p. 5b. De Lubac was impatient that Blondel publish more of his ideas, and Blondel said it was "necessary to take my time, in order to let my thought mature *and in order to tame the minds that rebelled against it.*" (my emphasis)
6. *Si Si No No*, April 1994, *Angelus* English Language Article Reprint, p. 18, where the entire letter is reproduced.
7. *Acta Apostolicae Sedis*, 38, S.,2,13, 1946, p. 385, as reproduced in *Si Si No No*, *The Angelus* English language article reprint, October 1993, p. 23.
8. He does not add that *Humani Generis* refutes many of the errors that have sprung up from the ambiguous phrases in Council documents. See Romano Amerio, *Iota Unum, A Study of Changes in the Catholic Church in the Twentieth Century,* Sarto House, 1998, pp. 41-44.
9. *Humani Generis*, published by St. Paul Books and Media, Par. 15.
10. Ibid., Par. 32.
11. Jean Guitton, *The Pope Speaks, Dialogues of Paul VI with Jean Guitton*, English translation, Meredith Press, New York, 1968, p. 9.
12. Ibid., p. 10. Emphasis in original.
13. *Humani Generis* also applied to teachers of Catholic institutes, who Pius said, "know that they cannot with tranquil conscience exercise the office of teaching entrusted to them, unless in the instruction of their students they religiously accept and exactly observe the norms which we have ordained."
14. Guitton, op. cit., p. 10.
15. *Humani Generis*, Par. 26.
16. See Joseph Cardinal Siri, *Gethsemane, Reflections on the Contemporary Theological Movement*, Franciscan Herald Press, 1981, pp. 55-69.
17. Wojtyla's admiration for Blondel was expressed in 1993, when as Pope John Paul II he declared: "We intend to honor Blondel, who in his thought and life was able to effect the coexistence of the most rigorous criticism and the most courageous philosophical research with the most authentic Catholicism ... (This) did not come without its cost in terms of incomprehension and suffering, at a time when the Church found itself confronting the Modernist crisis ...

It is this courage as a thinker ... that present-day philosophers and theologians who study Blondel's work ought to learn from this great master." (Quoted in *Our Sunday Visitor*, June 28, 1998, p. 18). Having lived his life under a cloud, in death the person and ideas of Maurice Blondel have become positively luminous. He is one of a handful of men (most lived just before and after the Second Vatican Council) to be denounced by one pope and exalted by another – *for identical reasons*.

18. Hebblethwaite, *Paul VI*, op. cit., p. 237.
19. *Si Si No No*, April 1994.
20. Msgr. Georges Roche, secretary to Cardinal Tisserant and no traditionalist, stated in his book, *Pius XII in the Eyes of History*, that Montini had unauthorized contacts with Stalin himself in 1942. See also *Si Si No No*, April, 1994, p. 219, and *TWTAF*, Vol. III, pp. 454-460.
21. Hebblethwaite, *Paul VI*, op. cit., p. 258.
22. *TWTAF*, Vol. III, p. 474.
23. Ibid., pp. 467-468.
24. Ibid., p. 470.
25. Ibid., p. 471.
26. Ibid., p. 480.
27. Ibid., pp. 480-481.
28. Ibid., p. 483.
29. All the quoted extracts from Sister Lucy's interview with Father Fuentes are from *TWTAF*, Volume III, Part III, Chapter 6.
30. Barrett McGurn, *A Reporter Looks at the Vatican*, Coward-McCann, Inc., 1962, pp. 99-100.
31. Vittorio Gorressio, *The New Mission of Pope John XXIII*, Funk & Wagnalls, New York, 1969, p. 13. The statements of Pius XII in the preceding paragraphs are found on pp. 12-13.
32. McGurn, op. cit., p. 19.
33. Hebblethwaite, *Paul VI*, op. cit., p. 249.
34. As quoted in Mary Ball Martinez, *The Undermining of the Catholic Church*, Mexico, 1991, p. 90. Mrs. Martinez believes Pius XII was a crypto-leftist (my term, not hers) who intentionally collaborated with Montini in the undermining of the Catholic Church, the culmination of which was Vatican II. A more common opinion is that Pius XII was a majestic guardian of orthodoxy. I don't think he was either; the definitive biography on Pius XII remains unwritten.

Chapter Thirteen

"The Two Pentecosts"

Perhaps the riddle concerning Pius XII's apparent refusal to read the Third Secret of Fatima has less to do with his supposed traditionalism or progressivism than with his personality. Is it possible he just couldn't decide whether or not to read the Third Secret?

It is not an irreverent question. According to Domenico Tardini, who knew him well, Pius XII's "keen intelligence and sense of detail brought to his mind, rapidly and clearly, all possible solutions" of a given problem. This sounds like a good thing, until Tardini elaborates:

> "He immediately saw ... the advantages and disadvantages, the possible consequences both favorable and unfavorable. And so he was perplexed, hesitating, as though he were not sure of himself. He needed time for reflection and for prayer. But he was not always given time. One would suggest this, and another that ... All this left him troubled."[1]

Whether Pius was overly analytical or simply indecisive, such a vulnerable disposition would instinctively shrink from the Fatima controversy. "Pius XII was by temperament mild and rather shy," according to Tardini: "He was not made to be a fighter ... (His) inclination to prefer solitude and tranquility naturally disposed him to avoid rather than to face the battles of life."[2]

So while Pius — who was consecrated a bishop on the day the beautiful Lady first appeared at Cova da Iria, May 13, 1917 — seemed to intuitively grasp the Fatima Message, the determined opposition of a well placed minority of Churchmen deterred him from following his instincts. The problem was compounded by Pope Pacelli's tendency to isolate himself from those who could have encouraged his instincts, and to associate instead with men like Montini and Bea, who had precious little sympathy for Fatima or traditional Catholicism.

A stammerer prior to becoming Pope, Pacelli's timidity was effectively camouflaged by an austere reserve, and an ethereal, almost wraithlike appearance — caused in part by a zeal for fasting that caused his weight to dip to 125 pounds during the war (he was almost six feet tall). Pius' pronounced unwillingness to hurt anyone's feelings begat many professional and personal trials, which he bore stoically. Towards the end he seemed most comfortable in the company of his Bavarian housekeeper, the notorious Mother Pasqualina Lehnert (who even Cardinals tiptoed around) and the six birds he kept as pets (one was a goldfinch he named Gretel).

Suitable arrangements were made for the orphaned birds, and Pasqualina, as the Cardinals drifted into Rome for the conclave. Some of them were given a small picture of Pius that contained a prayer for his canonization. There was also a campaign by Roman laity to affix the word "Great" to Pius' name. In contrast, the conservative Roman newspaper *Il Tempo* lambasted the deceased Pope for his reclusiveness and his failure to meet with priests, bishops, and Cardinals regarding the day-to-day governance of the Church.[3] The press thought Pope Pacelli arrogant; Tardini thought him simply shy and weak, at least in his last years.

After several days of balloting Venetian Cardinal Roncalli was elected successor to Pius XII. When asked what name he would choose, he replied, *"Vocabur Johannes"* - I would be called John. The last Pope named John had been the antipope John XXIII — a former pirate, lawyer, and curial Cardinal named Baldassare Cossa. For five hundred years the name John had been avoided by popes for just that reason. The Cardinals were shocked at Roncalli's choice. Appearing to have anticipated not only his election, but resistance to his name as well, the new Pope took out a piece of paper and read off his reasons for choosing the name of an antipope. His father's name was John. St. John's was the church of his baptism. It was the name of many cathedrals. It was the name taken by the most popes — there were "twenty-two supreme pontiffs of undoubted legitimacy with the name of John," Roncalli told the Cardinals.

"Virtually all of them had short pontificates. We have preferred to cover the smallness of our name behind the magnificent succession of Roman Pontiffs."[4]

Maybe you just had to be there, for in retrospect Roncalli's reasons for choosing the name and number of an anti-pope don't seem that compelling. The surprises were just beginning, however. After greeting and blessing the cheering throng in St. Peter's Square, the second Pope John XXIII ordered the Cardinals not to disperse. He wished to meet with them in secret. This was a burden on several of the Cardinals who were in their nineties and in failing health, but in deference to the new Pope they all stayed. It must have been a very sensitive meeting, for when Secretary of State Tardini tried to enter, mistakenly believing the conclave was over, he was promptly excommunicated by France's Cardinal Tisserant.

After moving into the Vatican the new Pope ran into another antipope. John found an ancient statue of Hippolytus, an antipope of the Third Century. He had the statue restored and placed at the entrance of the Vatican Library. Then he visited the Holy Office to see his personal file. It was marked: "Suspected of Modernism."[5]

The Inheritance of Angelo Roncalli

This was not a surprise, and a brief explanation of Roncalli's "pedigree" should explain matters. He was born (the third of thirteen chil-

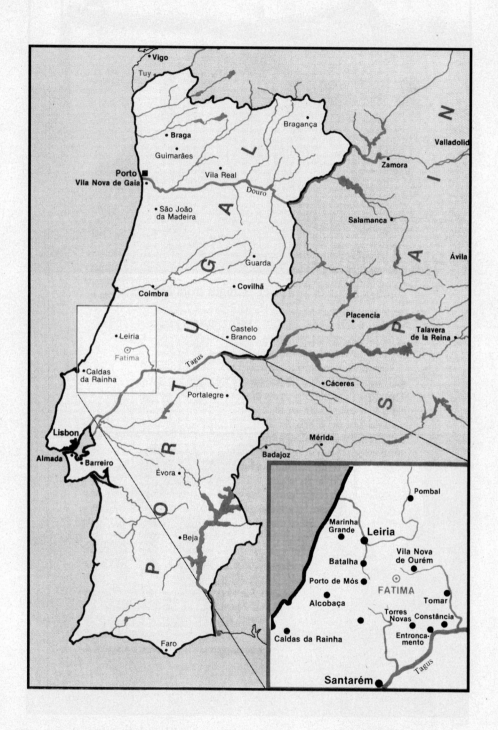

Lucy's home in Aljustrel, minutes from Fatima.

Francisco and Jacinta's home in Aljustrel, a small hamlet of less than two dozen houses, all lined along the same road.

Lucy, Francisco, and Jacinta in front of the Marto house, at the time of the Fatima apparitions.

After the apparition of July 13, 1917, when the children received the Fatima Secret, including the Vision of Hell.

October 13, 1917, the Cova da Iria before the final apparition.

Moments later, witnessing the Miracle of the Sun.

The Chapel of the Apparitions, next to the holm oak tree. In 1922 the chapel was blown up by Portuguese Freemasons, but was restored.

Another victim of Freemasonry, Portuguese President Major Sidonio Pais.

Lenin

Trotsky

Josef Stalin: from aspiring young Bolshevik to murderer of tens of millions, Western ally, and *Time* Magazine's Man of the Year (1942).

Undefeated: the garrison of the Alcazar.

Franco (L) relieves the Alcazar with Colonel Mascardo.

Reverend Dr. Luis Fischer examines the incorrupt face of Jacinta Marto at the first exhumation.

Jacinta's parents, Ti Marto and Olimpia, present at the exhumation of Jacinta's body, 1951.

Pope Pius XII welcoming the Pilgrim Virgin statue of Our Lady of Fatima to St. Peter's Basilica.

Forerunners of the Second Vatican Council, Jacques Maritain, the proponent of the Integral Humanism; and Opus Dei founder Jose Maria Escriva, declared a saint by Pope John Paul II in 2002.

Jacques Maritain

Jose Maria Escriva

Maurice Blondel

Fr. Yves Congar, O.P.

Henri de Lubac

Theologians condemned before the Second Vatican Council, and rehabilitated afterwards. Pope John Paul II made Congar and de Lubac Cardinals.

Pope John XXIII with his first creation, Cardinal Montini.

Sister Lucy in Dorothean habit, circa 1946.

Sister Lucy at Fatima, 1967.

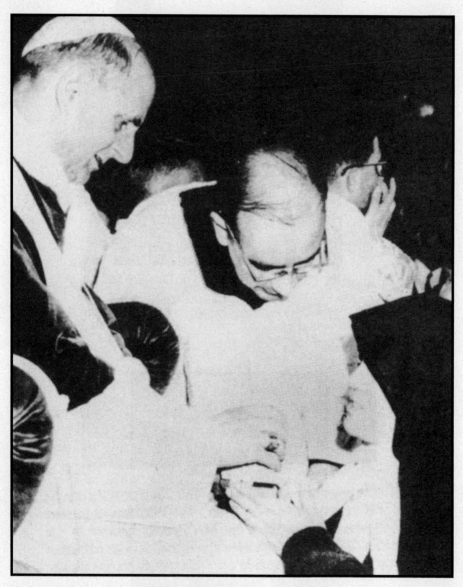

At the Fatima Jubilee, 1967, "I wish to speak to you alone," Lucy repeated.
Pope Paul VI told her to communicate to him through her bishop.

Portuguese President Dr. Antonio de Oliveira Salazar.

Father Joaquin Maria Alonso, the Church-appointed historian of Fatima.

Karl Rahner and Father Joseph Ratzinger at the Second Vatican Council.

Cardinal Karol Wojtyla and Pope Paul VI.

Pope John Paul II and Sister Lucy at Fatima, 1991.

dren) to sharecropper parents in Bergamo, Italy, a village on the foothills of the Alps, on November 25, 1881. Born three years into the pontificate of Pope Leo XIII, Angelo was the oldest boy in his family. He was one year away from finishing his seminary studies when Leo died in 1903.

In the ensuing conclave Leo's Secretary of State, Cardinal Mariano Rampolla del Tindaro (Rampolla), led after the first ballot. His election appeared certain when Cardinal Puzyna, Bishop of Cracow, announced a veto on Rampolla's election pursuant to a long neglected provision that allowed Austria, as the residual legatee of the Holy Roman Empire, to veto a papal election. The Cardinals were understandably indignant over the apparent trumping of the Holy Ghost by politics. Appearances deceived everyone, however, for the conclave ended up electing Giuseppe Cardinal Sarto, the Patriarch of Venice, who took the name Pius X.

There are several explanations of Austria's veto of Rampolla. Austrian Emperor Franz Josef was said to resent Rampolla's claims on Italian property still occupied by Austria. Others said Rampolla's pro-French sentiments irritated Austria. Yet these were longstanding political divisions that were not peculiar to Rampolla. The bombshell explanation is that the intrepid French priest and unmasker of Freemasons, Msgr. Jouin, presented indisputable evidence to Franz Josef that Rampolla was a Grand Master of the secret society *Ordo Templi Orientalis* (OTO). The story goes that Jouin first tried to warn Leo XIII, but was thwarted by Rampolla. Eventually he found a receptive audience in Austria, where Franz Josef's veto arose less from political intrigue than from a desire to protect the Church. Rampolla denied everything, but to no avail; he had lost his chance at the papacy. While there was disagreement over whether he was an occultist, everyone agreed Rampolla was very progressive.[6]

What does any of this have to do with Angelo Roncalli? Well, Rampolla was the mentor of another Churchman rumored to have occult associations, Bishop Giacomo Maria Radini Tedeschi.

Radini became the Bishop of Bergamo, and the mentor of the young Father Roncalli, who became Radini's secretary and protege. A close father-son relationship developed, Roncalli referring to Radini as "my spiritual father".[7] Pope Pius X, on the other hand, deemed Radini too progressive for the good of the Church. Since Radini and Roncalli appeared to be peas from the same pod, Roncalli was also "suspected of modernism", despite his seemingly sincere protestations of orthodoxy.

In 1914 Radini died. His biography was written by Father Roncalli, whose admiration for his mentor was as obvious as Pius X's significant distrust. That same year a Roman Cardinal warned Roncalli to "please be careful in teaching the Scriptures." Roncalli was upset and began a correspondence with the Cardinal. The letters have been preserved. Roncalli's sincerity and honesty appear above reproach, and eventually the Cardinal gave way.[8]

In spite of his convincing denials, the fact remains that Roncalli was formed by Churchmen of the left and owed his career to them. It was only natural then, that despite an apparently genuine admiration for Pope Pius X, Roncalli's general sympathies were — and would ever remain — with the progressives.

His next encounter with authority occurred in 1924. Roncalli was teaching part-time at the Lateran College in Rome. The subject was Patrology, the writings of Church Fathers. Roncalli was again accused of modernism, and dismissed after one term. Unlike the curial Cardinal's admonition, there is no "paper-trail" to inform the curious of the specifics of the charge against Roncalli. The resolution of the dispute was unambiguous: Roncalli was exiled to Bulgaria by personal order of Pope Pius XI.[9]

It may as well have been Siberia, although the eviction contained a promotion to Archbishop. He was kept in Bulgaria for ten years, then spent another ten years in Istanbul as Apostolic Delegate for Turkey and Greece. In 1944 Germany left France, and French General de Gaulle and his Communist sympathizers began purging the Vichy government and the French episcopate. Roncalli was sent as a mediator between de Gaulle's government and the Church in France.

This was a significant promotion. Pius chose Roncalli because the latter's politics were similar to de Gaulle's, and it was thought Roncalli would be the least offensive nuncio to the anti-clerical (and nominal Catholic) de Gaulle. Pius was right, although surely he winced when, as thousands of French Catholics were executed and imprisoned during "the Liberation", Roncalli praised de Gaulle: "Thanks to your clear-sighted policy and energy, this dear country has refound its freedom and faith in its own destiny."[10]

There was a time when France's faith and destiny were thought to involve her role as "eldest daughter of the Church", not the bloody purging of France's Catholic identity. This violent policy may have been hatched during de Gaulle's visit to Moscow, at the invitation of Josef Stalin. The result was, as one deluded Christian Democrat put it, "a marriage of love";[11] that is, a treaty of alliance and mutual assistance between France and Soviet Russia. Russia's errors spread to France, martyring the good, as the beautiful Lady had foretold.

In addition to complimenting de Gaulle, Roncalli also praised France's Christian Democrats, who handily avoided martyrdom by becoming members of the anti-Catholic government of "new France." And Roncalli waxed poetic on the memory of Marc Sangnier, founder of the *Sillon*. In a letter he knew would be circulated on the left, the nuncio Roncalli wrote:

"The powerful fascination of his (Sangnier's) words, of his soul, had thrilled me, and the liveliest memories of my entire priestly youth are for his person and his political and social activity ... During my service for the Holy See in Paris I rarely had any contact with him: but all our mutual relations were inspired by our common understanding of human difficulties ... my spirit was very comforted to see that the most authoritative voices ... of France came together, unanimously, to wrap Marc Sangnier in the honorable cloak of the Sermon of the Mount."[12]

Sangnier and his organization, the *Sillon*, had been forcefully and definitively condemned by Pope Pius X, which apparently made him a folk hero not only to Roncalli, but to the "Church of the left".

Two years after his eulogy of Sangnier, Roncalli was fired again. This time it was for his inability — or unwillingness — to intervene in the worker priest fiasco. It was standard to elevate Paris nuncios to Cardinals whether they were sacked or not, however, and pro-Secretary of State Msgr. Montini had the pleasure of announcing Roncalli's "promotion" to him. The two men had maintained a comfortable friendship since meeting during Roncalli's tutorship under Radini in Bergamo.

Things being what they were in post-war "new France", it was decided Roncalli would receive the red biretta from Pius in Rome. The President of France, Vincent Auriol, a Socialist and an atheist, intervened to assert the ancient privilege of French kings to present the Hat to Roncalli, who agreed to the idea. At a large, formal ceremony Roncalli knelt before Auriol and received his Cardinal hat from an unbelieving Socialist.

For Roncalli's brothers, who left Italy for the first time to see the crowning of Angelo's career (so they thought), the ceremony was probably thrilling and emotional. Diplomats on both sides viewed the ceremony as a political success and vied for credit. For anyone with the notion that princes of the Church should not kneel before atheistic heads of state, much less receive a Cardinal's hat from them, however, the whole affair was, at the very least, an exercise in extremely bad taste.

And perhaps it was something far worse.

The "Other School"

At seventy-two, Roncalli went to Venice to retire. Here he was under the watchful eye of Pius XII. Although there is no evidence of ill will by either man toward the other, establishment historian Paul Johnson notes that in matters concerning Venice, Pius "never hesitated to interfere in detail, invariably in a conservative direction ... Roncalli came (as he put it himself) from the "other school": he was part of a progressive tradition, the tradition of Rampolla, Radini and Benedict XV, in exactly the same way that Pius was the current head of the conservative tradition.

"Therefore, Roncalli was not to be trusted, and there are indications that Pius supervised Venice more closely than he did certain other cities which he had confided to more dependable members of his 'school.' We have Roncalli's own word that he was not even consulted by Pius in the appointment of his assistant-bishop, Msgr. Augusto Gianfranceschi."[13]

It was clear to anyone paying attention, however, that there was more to it than "political" differences of opinion between the "conservative" Pius and the "progressive" Roncalli. There was no equivalency between the two "schools", except perhaps for establishment historians. Moreover, neither Pius nor Roncalli were that easily pigeonholed. Pius seemed surprisingly liberal in some of his policies (e.g., decolonization and the promotion of democracy) and initiatives (appointing Father Annibale Bugnini to reform the liturgy), and Roncalli often appeared to be conservative, particularly in his disapproval of the ideas of Teilhard de Chardin, and his mistrust of modern inventions like the television, the radio, and even the telephone. Although not every entry in Roncalli's published diary, *Journal of A Soul*, can be taken at face value,[14] there is sufficient evidence that in many respects he was a traditional, "garden of the soul" Catholic. However ...

What Roncalli shared with Milan Archbishop Montini, and where both men diverged not only from Pope Pacelli but from the mind of the Church, was the "social question". Social progressives like Roncalli and Montini had no quarrel with the ecumenical, secularized political activism of the *Sillon* which, by seeking the equality and dignity of man as the highest good, hastened the advent of Socialism. Piux X condemned the *Sillon* for this very reason, and by implication, most of the left-leaning Christian Democrats who (quite rightly) shouted themselves hoarse about the evils of fascism, but were (quite wrongly) silent as a tomb regarding the monstrous, rapidly spreading evil of Communism. Later Pius XI would remind these folks that it was impossible to be simultaneously a good Christian and a Socialist. Much later he would finally condemn Communism as intrinsically perverse and irreformable. This was not a political decision of the "conservative school". It was the authoritative voice of Peter.

In 1950 Pius XII, in deference to the martyred "Silent Church" in Communist occupied Eastern Europe, forbade any collaboration with Communists under pain of excommunication. Therefore, Christian Democrats and social progressives who collaborated with Communists or socialists were not merely from "another school". They were acting against the mind of the Church as clearly expressed by her popes.

The men of the left appeared insensible to this teaching, however. Publicly respectful, they privately complained that such teaching was needlessly reactionary and counter-productive. Communism was reformable, and collaboration with non-Catholics — or even non-Christians — was not only permissible but a good in itself, as it was an opportunity to fight against social injustice. Presumably, this is why Cardinal Roncalli "exhorted the faithful to welcome the Socialists of all

Italy, who were holding their thirty-second party" in Venice.[15] For men of Roncalli's school, there was no need to antagonize the world. It was scandalous that Catholics absented themselves from political action. It was imperative for the Church to orient herself towards modern society.

It was ironic that the progressives used such outdated arguments to portray the Church as out-of-date. The idea that the Church should and ought to reconcile herself with modern society had been condemned by Pope Pius IX in the Nineteenth Century, even as liberalism and Freemasonry were uprooting the Church from the Christian civilization she had created. The apostasy was universal, and gained momentum by the decade. The Church replied through her popes, condemning the revolution in all its guises: Freemasonry, liberalism, Socialism, Communism, and modernism.

To affirm and even expand the teachings of popes there was Fatima, a Church-approved apparition that warned of the eternal pains of hell, predicted that the world would be chastised for its sins by the Second World War, and that Russia would spread her errors with dire consequences for the Church and the world. The only remedies were conversion and repentance, the Rosary, and devotion to the Immaculate Heart of the Mother of the Son of God.

If that wasn't bad enough for the social progressives and Christian Democrats, the implications of Fatima were even worse: no glorious utopia, no man-made Eden, no reconciliation between the Church and the revolution-corrupted world.[16] One had to choose, and eternal salvation hung in the balance. The choice was between Heaven and hell, between the Virgin and the prince of this world. There were no other choices and no other chances, for Angelo Roncalli or anyone else.

A Council is Announced

On January 20, 1959, about three months after John's election, the new Pope was expounding on the state of the Church and the world to his new Secretary of State, Domenico Tardini. Pope John recalled:

> "My listener (Tardini) followed in an attitude of reverent respect and expectation. Suddenly my soul was illumined with a great idea, come to the fore just in that instant and taken up with indescribable faith in the Divine Leader, and there came to my lips a solemn and committed word. My voice uttered it for the first time: a Council!"[17]

John would later record this conversation in *Journal Of A Soul*, writing that the idea of a Council occurred to him "without any forethought", and that "I was the first to be surprised at my proposal, which was entirely my own idea." According to John, Tardini's response was immediate and enthusiastic: *"Si, si, un concilio!"*

There are some problems with John's version of things. First, Tardini's supposed "attitude of reverent respect and expectation" is probably a polite falsehood. He had tried to resign after John became Pope, but John refused his resignation, saying, "You don't have much esteem for me, and you're perfectly right, but I esteem you." Tardini's status as a conservative curial insider was much needed by the new Pope, so practical politics overrode John's preferences. For his part, disobeying a Pope's request went too much against Tardini's grain, even when the Pope was Roncalli, who, when appointed nuncio to Paris, said to Tardini, "I presume you chose me for Paris." Shot back Tardini, "You're the last one I'd choose."[18]

Second, it is difficult to picture Domenico Tardini capering at the idea of a Council being announced for the vaguest of reasons by a transitional Pope with progressive tendencies. Tardini had proved himself more of a hard-headed realist as Pope Pius XII's Secretary of State. Another version of his reaction to John's idea of a Council seems more characteristic — Tardini seriously believed Pope John had gone temporarily insane.[19]

The larger problem with the Pope's now legendary version of events is that everyone — including John's friends — admits his story is untrue. For instance, Pope John had already written the speech announcing the Council before he met Tardini and had his "great idea" of a Council.[20] Moreover, Tardini was not the first person John spoke to about a Council. Far from it. On January 9 John told his friend Don Giovanni Rossi: "Last night I had the great idea of calling a Council!" Rossi was suitably impressed; how could he have known that this wasn't true either? For John had spoken of the Council to several people before telling Rossi.

Around Christmas, 1958, John told Giacomo Testa, the Bishop of Bergamo. In November of 1958 John spoke with Cardinal Ruffini about a Council. Prior to that, John told his private secretary, Msgr. Loris Capovilla, "There should be a Council." This occurred on November 2, 1958, before John had even taken the papal coronation oath. And according to Capovilla, John mentioned "the necessity of holding a Council" on October 30, 1958 — just two days after his election.[21]

So contrary to John's diary version of the idea of a Council coming to him in a mystical flash during his conversation with Tardini in January, 1959, the truth is that John had been chattering about the Council for months. Given these circumstances, it seems reasonable to ask whether the secret meeting John requested with the conclave Cardinals right after his election also concerned his idea of a Council. In fact, one could also ask: did Angelo Roncalli mention convening a Council before he was elected Pope? The answer, surprisingly, is yes. According to Desmond O'Grady, the former Vatican correspondent for the *Washington Post*, while stationed in Istanbul in 1944 Roncalli "gave a sermon on a council to be held in the postwar period."[22]

Well then, are Pope John's statements —that the idea of a Council came to him "without any forethought", and that he uttered the words "A Council!" under divine inspiration, "for the first time" in his conversation with Cardinal Tardini — merely so much pious gloss? No, if one can penetrate the ideas John was conveying in his diary. First, that the idea of a Council was his and his alone. In his diary he emphasizes his surprise "at my own proposal, which was entirely my own idea." He takes pains that everyone knows the Council was his idea and his alone. Why? If vanity is ruled out, what are the alternatives? Roncalli may have been attempting to distinguish his idea of a Council from Pius XII's idea of a Council, but his motives for doing so are obscure.

Is it possible that the proposal of a Council was not Roncalli's "own proposal", was not "entirely my own idea" at all, but was really the idea of another person or persons who preferred to remain anonymous as Roncalli implemented their idea?

Admittedly, the evidence for this is circumstantial. We have Roncalli over-emphasizing "his" brainstorm. We have a long ecclesiastical career where Roncalli did not distinguish himself as an "idea man", and rarely took on daring projects, facts that make his sudden inspiration of a Council improbable. And we have his unusual sermon in Istanbul in 1944, where he spoke of a Council that would happen after the war. Roncalli was not known as a prophet, so the question becomes — where, or from who, did he get his information?

None of this speculation — and that is what it is — is intended to disparage Pope John. That he was a goodhearted man is beyond dispute. His wit and sense of humor were often delightful, and instructive. Although his charm, kindness, and love of people lent a sense of spontaneity to his personality, in reality he was prudent rather than impulsive, a fact attested to by his long and mostly unremarkable religious career. He tended to be a role player, to await orders and then carry them out. If the Council was in fact John's idea, it would be characteristic for him to have thought the idea through fairly thoroughly. Of course, this would have had to have occurred prior to Roncalli's election to the papacy.

Also of note is John's insistence that the idea of a Council was a flash of divine inspiration. Unlike Vatican I (and other Councils), prior to Vatican II there was no formal consultation between Pope, Cardinals, and bishops. To all appearances it came from nowhere except the imagination of a newly elected "transitional" Pope that many in the Roman Curia had little respect for. By his claim of divine inspiration was Pope John attempting to enlist the infallible magisterium in support of his idea of a Council?[23]

In any event, not only did Pope John claim divine inspiration for an Ecumenical Council, he also appeared to have known he would be elected to the papacy. All he would say about this apparent foreknowledge was, "From certain indications I already knew that I would be elected."[24] This at least explains his prepared speech on his decision to use the name of an anti-pope. John's presentiment was shared by England's Cardinal Heenan. Present at the conclave that elected Roncalli,

Heenan later explained:

> "There was no great mystery about Pope John's election. He was chosen because he was a very old man. His chief duty was to make Msgr. Montini, the Archbishop of Milan, a Cardinal so that he could be elected in the next conclave. That was the policy and it was carried out precisely."[25]

Indeed. Less than two months after his election Pope John held a consistory where he created twenty-three new Cardinals (for a total of seventy-five), abolishing the limit of seventy Cardinals set by Pope Sixtus V in 1586. According to Pope John's biographer Alden Hatch:

> "The Pope paid special honor to Archbishop Montini by placing his name at the head of the list of new Cardinals, thus making him his *prima creatura* (first creation). Although a Pontiff may not name his successor, it is said that Pope John would like to be followed by Montini."[26]

Unlike the Curia and many Cardinals who reacted negatively to Pope John's idea of a Council, Montini was thrilled with the idea, proclaiming:

> "The Council will make Rome the spiritual capital of the world from whence the light will spread upon those places and institutions where men are working for the union of peoples, for the welfare of the poor, for progress, for justice, and for liberty."[27]

Cardinal Montini apparently hadn't noticed that Rome had already been "the spiritual capital of the world" for quite some time. Yet if his prediction for the Council sounded more like the Great Socialist Dream than restoring all things in Christ, he was not alone. Montini's enthusiasm for the Council was shared by his colleagues on the left, from Jacques Maritain to the new theologians. His exile from Rome ended, Montini began consulting with Pope John. Work on the Council had begun at once.

John Reads the Third Secret

One of the men Pope John made a Cardinal was Msgr. Ferdinand Cento, the papal nuncio to Lisbon who had personally transferred the Third Secret to Rome in 1957. John had been told of the existence of the Third Secret shortly after his election. After the consistory that made him a Cardinal, Cento told John:

> "It would be wise for you to find out what is in it. Sister Lucy has contacted me. She could issue a message to the world. I do not know if that would be opportune ..."

John was then asked if he wanted the envelope containing the Secret. He declined. The following month, January, 1959, John officially announced his plans for a Council. That summer (June and July) witnessed the publicity over Father Fuentes' interview with Sister Lucy, the Coimbra chancery publicly accusing Father Fuentes of being a liar, and Father Fuentes being stripped of his faculties as postulator for the beatifications of Francisco and Jacinta.

One month later Pope John was relaxing at Castel Gandolfo. He asked for the Secret, and on August 17, 1959, a Monday, Msgr. Paul Philippe handed John the envelope. The next day John opened the letter in the presence of his confessor, Msgr. Alfredo Cavagna. Then John called his private secretary, Msgr. Capovilla, who recalls, "(Pope John) gave me the text. It was written in Portuguese and several of its expressions were in dialect. We were not able to understand it all ..."

Yet another Monsignor, Paolo Tavares, was summoned to translate the text. After John had read the Secret with his confessor, it appears that he spoke about the Secret in general terms to several unspecified advisors. Afterwards Msgr. Capovilla claims that "John XXIII said to me, 'Write.' And I wrote what he dictated":

> "The Holy Father received this document from the hands of Msgr. Philippe. He decided to read it on Tuesday, in the presence of his confessor. Having taken note of the presence of obscure idioms, he summoned Mgr. Tavares, who translated. He had his closest colleagues read it also. Finally he decided to put it back in the envelope, saying, 'I make no judgment on this.' He maintained silence in the face of what might be a manifestation of the divine or might not be."[28]

In other words, Pope John doubted the authenticity of the Third Secret. This conclusion is compatible with another statement attributed to Pope John about the Third Secret: "This does not concern my pontificate."[29] The note he dictated to Capovilla was placed in the envelope with the Secret, where it probably remains to this day. The envelope was kept at John's work desk until his death in 1963.

The "Two Pentecosts"

In Italy in 1959 Fatima was more popular than Pope John. The Pilgrim Virgin statue had toured Italy that summer. The crowds were large and fervent. There was much anticipation about the reading of the Third Secret in 1960 — now just months away. Lisbon Primate Cardinal Cerejeira was prophetic when he declared:

> "It is an apocalyptic hour for the world. These are frightening winds from hell which are blowing, and the elect themselves are allowing themselves to be carried away ...

> "Our Lady of Fatima came to the Cova da Iria to remind men of the way of salvation: prayer and penance. It is the echo of what Jesus told His Apostles in the Garden of Olives: 'Watch and pray, that you may not enter into temptation ... Now behold Her on the road to Italy. It is the Woman "full of grace" who is passing through. With Her is always found Her Divine Son, in Whom

alone is salvation. And He brings with Him the Holy Spirit. This pilgrimage is like a Pentecost; it will be a shower of blessings."[30]

Yes, Cardinals really used to talk like that. The highlight of the Italian tour was the consecration of Italy to the Immaculate Heart, which was to be performed by Italian Cardinal Mimmi on September 13, the anniversary of the fifth apparition. Over 300,000 pilgrims gathered to witness the consecration, and to listen to a radio address by Pope John that was to precede the consecration.

The crowd did not know Pope John had read the Third Secret less than a month prior. Everyone assumed his radio address would concern the Immaculate Heart of Mary, the highly successful tour of the Pilgrim Virgin statue, the consecration about to take place, and perhaps even a word about the Third Secret. Instead, the Pope's lengthy radio address focused on the Eucharist. He barely mentioned Fatima, and did not mention the Third Secret at all. Later, when the Italian tour ended in Rome, Pope John was completely silent.[31]

At the end of this unusual month, on September 26, 1959, to be exact, John issued the encyclical *Grata Recordatio* (On The Rosary). In this brief encyclical John recalled Pope Leo XIII's exhortations for the faithful to pray the Rosary in October. He also quoted a passage from Pius XII's encyclical, *Ingruentium malorum*: "Turn in spirit with ever greater confidence to the Virgin Mother of God, the constant refuge of Christians in adversity, since She 'has been made a source of salvation for the human race.'"

The true purpose of the encyclical became apparent in its final paragraphs. John requested the recitation of "Mary's rosary (sic) through the month of October with particular devotion, and to entreat the Virgin Mother of God in suppliant prayer", for an "intention which is dear to Our heart ...

"... that the forthcoming Ecumenical Council, in which you will participate by your presence and your advice, will add wondrous growth to the universal Church; and that the renewed vigor of all the Christian virtues which We hope this Council will produce will also serve as an invitation and incentive to reunion for Our Brethren and children who are separated from this Apostolic See."[32]

In every visit She made to Cova da Iria the beautiful Lady — who called Herself "Our Lady of the Rosary" — had requested the Rosary be prayed every day, to obtain graces for conversion, healing, and world peace. John's request for Rosary prayers and his desire that the separated "Brethren and children" return to "this Apostolic See" seems reasonably consistent with the Blessed Virgin's requests at Fatima, until one realizes that John is anticipating that his Council, not the Rosary, will convert heretics, schismatics, and other sinners.

In contrast, the Blessed Virgin insisted that sinners would be converted by the Rosary and saved by devotion to Her Immaculate Heart.

In his encyclical on praying the Rosary in the month of October, Pope John not only omitted any reference to Fatima or the October miracle of the dance of the sun, he also put praying the Rosary in the service of the upcoming Second Vatican Council.

Well, of course he did, it can be argued; so would any holy Pope. What could possibly be wrong with praying the Rosary for the Holy Father's intentions, particularly when the intention is an Ecumenical Council?

Now it may not seem fair to ask this question thirty-five years after the Council, when the sorry — horrid is more accurate — fallout from Pope John's "new Pentecost" is everywhere to be seen and lamented. But before answering the question anyway, another question must first be asked. Just what were Pope John's intentions for the Second Vatican Council? They appear to involve the consummation of a particular vision which may or may not have originated with Pope Roncalli, but was alluded to in his encyclical on the Rosary:

> "Our thoughts (John wrote) turn to all the lands of this earth. We see all mankind striving for a better future; We see the *awakening of a mysterious force,* and this permits Us to hope that men will be drawn ... to advance the real interests of human society. That this goal may be realized in the fullest sense — that is, with the triumph of the kingdom of truth, justice, peace, and charity — We exhort all Our children in Christ to be 'of one heart and one soul' and to pour out ardent prayers in October to our Queen in Heaven and our loving Mother ..."[33]

This is a revealing paragraph. It seems unlikely the "mysterious force" John "saw awakening" was the Blessed Virgin — had it been, surely he would have named Her. Why did he not name this other, different mysterious force? And just what were the "real interests of human society" this mysterious force was thought to draw men to advance? Once upon a time it was taught that "the real interests of human society" were identical with the interests of the Church — helping souls orient their earthly pilgrimage towards the true reality — an eternal afterlife and the beatific vision. No doubt John still believed this, but it appears he believed something else besides.

This "something else" will herein be called the papal vision. Pope John was the first (but not the last) Pope to publicly subordinate not just the Fatima Message, but the Church and the Mother of God as well to the papal vision, which after his death became more recognizable, more defined. The vision of John and the other conciliar Popes appears to be rooted not in tradition or scripture, but in the future. The papal vision is in essence a gnostic, Masonic, and ultimately Godless earthly utopia. It is presently called the "new advent of humanity". It is likely the Second Vatican Council was convoked in order to consummate the papal vision, and to establish the new religion necessary for it to thrive (this will be elaborated in future chapters).

How much of this gnosis was penetrated by Pope John is debatable; a reasonable speculation is some, but not all. Prior to entering the conclave he knew would make him Pope, Angelo Cardinal Roncalli wrote to Bishop Piazza of Bergamo:

> "... My soul finds comfort in the confidence that a new Pentecost can blow through the Church, renewing its head, leading to a new ordering of the ecclesiastical body and bringing fresh vigor in progress towards the victory of truth, goodness and peace. It little matters whether the next pope is from Bergamo or not. Our common prayers will ensure that he will be a prudent and gentle administrator, a saint and a sanctifier. You follow me, Your Excellency?"[34]

Two of Pope John's fans, Peter Hebblethwaite and Msgr. Capovilla, interpret John's veiled references ("You follow me, Your Excellency?") as a message to Piazza that he was about to become Pope.[35] If this is so, it is interesting that the future Pope John refers to himself as "a saint and a sanctifier." But Roncalli could also have been referring to the Council he would shortly announce, or the "mysterious force" he saw animating mankind "in progress towards the victory of truth, goodness and peace." In any case, it is clear that John's optimistic vision of a "new Pentecost" predated his election as Pope.

There was another "Pentecost" to account for in 1959. Unlike Pope John's appealing vision of universal brotherhood, the Fatima Message was stark and frightening. The "first Secret", a terrifying vision of hell and the numberless souls falling there, and the somber, urgent warnings of Christ's Mother "not to offend Our Lord anymore, for He is already too much offended!" The "second Secret", the designation of Russia and the Second World War as God's scourge on an apostate, heedless humanity, and Heaven's remedy: devotion to the Immaculate Heart, the consecration of Russia, the Rosary, and the Five First Saturdays devotion. Then the Third Secret, which began by promising that Portugal would always keep the faith, and ended with the blessed assurance that "in the end My Immaculate Heart will triumph, the Holy Father will consecrate Russia to Me, and she will be converted, and a certain period of peace will be granted to the world."

Only one of the two Pentecosts could be true. Only one would triumph — the Immaculate Heart, or the man-made "kingdom of truth, justice, peace, and charity." The battle was joined, remarkably enough, by a Pope. For the next forty years a fascinating inversion would take place. The Message of Fatima would appear to be eclipsed by the papal vision of the conciliar popes, who attempted alternately to silence, distort, and subvert the Fatima Message. One would expect such papal discrediting to cause Fatima to languish in a twilight reserved for forgotten and unmourned religious imaginings.

What happened instead was that the prophecies of conciliar Popes that Vatican II was a "new Pentecost" broke on the rocks of reality. The often successful efforts of the "post-conciliar Church" to obliterate all memories of the "pre-conciliar Church" is only one more proof that the worldwide apostasy from the faith has not only entered the Church, but bids fair to command it. As will be seen, it is quite likely that the loss of faith among the Church hierarchy is the Third Secret of Fatima. This present-day reality continues to overshadow all, even the supposed revealing of the Third Secret on June 26, 2000. What is the fruit of this revelation? Instead of the wonderful promises of the Immaculate Heart – the conversion of Russia and a period of peace — we taste the ashes of the Pope's refusal to reveal the entire Third Secret. Alas, they no longer need to, for the supernatural rays of Fatima in twilight silently reveal where the real darkness lies.

NOTES

1. Domenico Tardini, *Memories of Pius XII*, translated into English by Rosemary Goldie, The Newman Press, 1961, pp. 41, 73-77, 98-101. Although Tardini's negative assessments of Pius XII are noted here, he was not an enemy; most of his book is laudatory towards Pope Pacelli.
2. Ibid.
3. Goressio, op. cit., pp. 20-22.
4. Alden Hatch, *A Man Named John, The Life of Pope John XXIII*, Hawthorn Books, Inc., 1963, pp. 175-176.
5. The anecdotes about Tardini's excommunication, Hippolytus, and Roncalli's personal file are from Paul Johnson, *Pope John XXIII*, Little, Brown, and Company, 1974, p. 37, 114-115, 130. After being a schismatic and an anti-pope, Hippolytus was reconciled to the Church, died a martyr, and was canonized.
6. The accounts of Rampolla and Radini Tedeschi are from Paul Johnson, *Pope John XXIII*, op. cit., pp. 27-35; and Mary Ball Martinez, op. cit., pp. 32-34. I have heard the story of Msgr. Jouin and Rampolla from several sources; none of which cite an authority for this contention.
7. Hatch, op. cit., p. 47
8. See Zizola, op. cit., Chapter 21, Roncalli and Modernism, for the correspondence between Rome and Roncalli regarding his alleged modernism.
9. The source for the second charge of modernism against Roncalli is Paul Johnson, op. cit., pp. 42-43. In his biography of Pope John XXIII, Peter Hebblethwaite glosses over the second charge, blaming the big, bad Italian fascists for Roncalli's exile. Mrs. Martinez, on the other hand, makes an unsourced claim that Roncalli's termination resulted from his infatuation with the theosophic themes of former OTO member Rudolf Steiner; Roncalli was suspected of spiking his lectures with Steiner's ideas.
10. Zizola, op. cit., pp. 83-85.
11. See *TWTAF*, Vol. III, pp. 171-175, for de Gaulle's trip to Moscow and the Red Christians in France.
12. Don Loris Capovilla, Editor, *Angelo Giuseppe Roncalli, Pope John XXIII, Mission To France, 1944-1953*, McGraw-Hill Book Company, 1966, pp. 124-125. See also *TWTAF*, Volume III, pp. 353-355.
13. Johnson, op. cit., p. 82.
14. It is there we find the fiction that the idea for a Council came to him by sudden (divine) insight.
15. Gorresio, op. cit., p. 113.
16. It is unfortunate that well-meaning social-justice Catholics do not seem to realize that their sincere efforts to alleviate suffering, poverty and war would be so much more effective if these efforts were performed in union with Our Lady's Message of Fatima, wherein hope for peace can be truly realized.
17. Hebblethwaite, *John XXIII*, op. cit., pp. 316-317.
18. Desmond O'Grady, "Almost A Saint", an article published in *St. Anthony's Messenger*, November, 1996. Another version of this story has Tardini telling Roncalli, "You're not the only one who's astonished," and then gesturing to Pius XII's office, Tardini snapped: "It was all *his* idea." (Lawrence Elliott, *I Will Be Called John, A Biography of Pope John XXIII*, E.P. Dutton

& Co., Inc., 1973, p. 174.

19. E.E.Y. Hales, *Pope John And His Revolution*, Eyre & Spottiswoode, 1965, p. 100.

20. Goressio, op. cit., p. 232.

21. There are many sources for this information. See Peter Hebblethwaite, *Pope John XXIII*, op. cit., Chapter 14 ("The Inspiration of a Council"); Johnson, op. cit., pp. 170-174; Gorresio, op. cit., pp. 231-235; Zizola, op. cit., Chapter 17, "The Idea of the Council".

22. *St. Anthony's Messenger*, November, 1996.

23. See Amerio, op. cit., p. 48, on the significance of John's claim of divine inspiration; it has been used to bolster the authority of Vatican II by Pope John Paul II, among others.

24. Goressio, op. cit., p. 77.

25. From Cardinal Heenan's biography, *Crown of Thorns*.

26. Alden Hatch, *A Man Named John, The life of Pope John XXIII*, Hawthorn Books, Inc., 1965, p. 209-210.

27. Johnson, op. cit., p. 174.

28. This account of Pope John requesting and reading the Third Secret is from an interview with John's private secretary, Msgr. Loris Capovilla, as reproduced in *CRC* December 1997.

29. This remark is attributed to Pope John by Father Alonso.

30. *TWTAF*, Volume III, p. 535.

31. Ibid., pp. 559-564.

32. *Grata Recordatio* (On the Rosary), par. 20.

33. Ibid., par. 19. Emphasis supplied.

34. Hebblethwaite, *Pope John XXIII*, op. cit., p. 278.

35. Ibid., pp. 278-279.

Chapter Fourteen

Pope John's Secrets

On November 19, 1959, Pope John granted an audience to the new Bishop of Fatima-Leiria, Bishop Venancio. Later he noted in his journal, "We talked at length about the seer of Fatima, today a good religious at Coimbra. The Holy Office will take care of everything and keep it on the right lines."[1]

John's allusion to the Holy Office "taking care of everything" was probably a reference to the silencing of Sister Lucy, and the restrictions on who could visit her.[2] It is likely John's audience with Bishop Venancio was also related to "security issues", for although Pope John spoke of the Secret with many advisors, the original "owners" of the Secret, the Portuguese episcopate, were never consulted.

It was an interesting situation. In 1944 Lucy had given the written text of the Third Secret not to Rome, but to the Portuguese hierarchy, namely, Bishop da Silva. The stipulation known to all — including Rome — was that the Secret was to be revealed by 1960 at the latest. According to Sister Lucy, this directive was from the Blessed Virgin Herself, who had told Lucy that by 1960 things would be "clearer".[3]

Bishop da Silva could have read the Secret in 1944, but chose not to. He tried to send it to Rome, but acceptance was withheld until 1957, when Rome asked for and received the Secret. Bishop da Silva died later the same year.[4] Had Rome not intervened the Secret would have passed to Portuguese Primate Cardinal Cerejeira, who was well disposed to Fatima. Instead, the Secret went to Pius XII, who, like Bishop da Silva, died without reading it. His successor, Pope John, was the first to read the Secret. John doubted its authenticity. Yet the world was expecting the Secret to be made public in 1960. What would the Pope do?

The Betrayal

1960 was similar in mood to that fateful, rain soaked day of October 13, 1917, when tens of thousands of people — some fervent believers, some merely curious, some scoffing atheists — descended on Cova da Iria full of violence, piety, hope, and fury. By 1960 the crowd encompassed the whole world, and so did the stakes.

On February 8, 1960, a Portuguese news agency received and published the following communique:

"It has just been stated, in very reliable Vatican circles, to the representatives of United Press International, that it is most likely that the letter will never be opened, in which Sister Lucy wrote down the words which Our Lady confided as a secret to the three little shepherds in the Cova da Iria.

"As indicated by Sister Lucy, the letter can only be opened during the year 1960.

"Faced with the pressure that has been placed on the Vatican, some wanting the letter to be opened and made known to the world, others, on the supposition that it may contain alarming prophecies, desiring that its publication be withheld, the same Vatican circles declare that the Vatican has decided not to make public Sister Lucy's letter, and to continue keeping it rigorously sealed.

"The decision of the Vatican is based on various reasons: 1. Sister Lucy is still living. 2. The Vatican already knows the contents of the letter. 3. Although the Church recognizes the Fatima apparitions, she does not pledge herself to guarantee the veracity of the words which the three little shepherds claim to have heard from Our Lady.

"In these circumstances, it is most probable that the Secret of Fatima will remain, forever, under absolute seal."[5]

The press release was not an official Church document, or an excerpt thereof. Its ultimate source was never revealed. The final decision not to reveal the Secret, however, had to have been Pope John's. The decision to disguise his decision in an anonymous press release must also have been his. Moreover, he must have desired his name not appear once in the press release, and he must have approved the dagger of doubt hurled at "the words which the three little shepherd children claim to have heard from Our Lady." Finally, he must have made the decision, remarkable for its arrogance and audacity, that the Third Secret would "never" be revealed — by anyone!

Pope John never spoke publicly of the Secret again. He never issued a text (anonymous or otherwise) clarifying the rather muddled and illogical press release. What did it matter, for instance, whether Sister Lucy was still living, or whether or not the Vatican knew the contents of the Third Secret? Yet these were advanced as "reasons" for not revealing the Third Secret.

The anonymous Vatican press release was the first of a series of papal blows against Fatima. It insinuated that the Third Secret contained "alarming prophecies" and that the Church could not "guarantee the veracity" of the seer's (that is, Lucy's) account. This discredited not just the Third Secret, but the entire Fatima Message. Curiously, this assessment was made without speaking to the Portuguese episcopate or Sister

Lucy — except through the newspapers. It is difficult to imagine the situation being handled in a worse way, particularly since there was a very plausible argument John could have used for not revealing the Third Secret. It was advanced in an article in *Civilta Cattolica*, published in June, 1960, which stated in pertinent part:

"... it belongs to the Church not only to watch over and interpret Revelation, which ended with the death of the Apostles, but also what is connected with it, precisely as are private revelations. Only the ecclesiastical authority, invested with this power, has the right, then, to judge whether or not it is opportune to stress a private and secret revelation ..."[6]

This is true up to a point. But it has also been argued that once the Church has recognized an apparition as genuine – that is, from Heaven – the content of that apparition imposes a duty on the Churchmen, including the Pope.[7] Let us apply this to Fatima.

Fatima has often been called a "private revelation", usually in an attempt to minimize its importance. It has seldom been called "a private and secret revelation", but the author of the *Civilta Cattolica* article had obviously been ordered to do some serious damage control. Anyway, to put the "private" revelations of Fatima in perspective, they occurred in front of thousands of people and were approved by the Church. The "private" messages transmitted to the seers were not merely personal admonitions, but serious warnings to mankind. Theologians have held that messages of this latter sort are of a far more serious matter, and must be treated accordingly.[8]

Moreover, two-thirds of the Fatima Secret was approved by Pope Pius XII in 1942, and published for the education and edification of the faithful. In addition to the obvious humility, sanity and balance of the pious Sister Lucy, there were the countless exhortations and references to Fatima by Pius XII and the world episcopate. The "ecclesiastical authority" had obviously judged it "opportune to stress" the Fatima Message, even though it was "a private and secret revelation".

So the real question is why, in 1960, did the Church so abruptly jettison a Church approved, papally promoted apparition she had spent decades urging devotion to. Certainly the message itself had not changed. What had happened to make Fatima "inopportune"? Was not the real problem that Fatima, especially the Third Secret, was "too opportune"? Too truthful about the perils of Communism and the temptation to the Church to join the worldwide apostasy that Communism heralded? What else can explain the sudden coldness of the Church to Fatima, after the Portuguese "ecclesiastical authority" had publicly agreed to reveal the Third Secret in 1960? As Frère Michel puts it:

"... for over fifteen years no authoritative declaration had come to deny these promises (of the Portuguese hierarchy to reveal the Secret) — the faithful were perfectly right to request this promised disclosure from the supreme authority (Pope John XXIII). Besides, the revelation of the first two Secrets in 1942, with the approval of Pope Pius XII, constituted a precedent. At least they had a right to an exact and honest explanation on the part of the Holy Father.

"This is why it was normal that the lies of the Vatican authorities on such a grave subject should be a cause of scandal for them ..."9

And this is why the most accurate word for Pope John's actions is — betrayal. Unfortunately for him, it was not merely the simple pious folk he was betraying ...

Communism and the Council

In his first encyclical, *Ad Petri Cathedram* (On Truth, Unity, and Peace) John linked his proposal of a Council to the idea of religious unity. After citing our Lord's prayer, "That all may be one, even as Thou, Father, in me and I in Thee; that they also may be one in Us" (John 17:21), Pope John wrote:

"Surely this prayer was heard and granted because of His reverent submission. This is a comforting hope; it assures us that someday all the sheep who are not of this fold will want to return to it. Then, in the words of God our Savior, 'there shall be one fold and one shepherd.'

"This fond hope compelled Us to make public Our intention to hold an Ecumenical Council ..."10

John also had a fond hope the Russian Orthodox Church would attend his Council as a tentative step toward unity. This would be difficult for two reasons. The first was Fatima, particularly its "anti-communism". As in the days of Czar Nicholas, the Orthodox hierarchy were "homers" — the only difference was that now they backed the Soviet government, and took umbrage at the thought of Russia converting.

So Lucy was silenced, the Third Secret was hidden, and the entire Fatima Message was discredited. Pope John's next step was to begin secret negotiations with the Russian Orthodox Church. France's Cardinal Tisserant, who spoke Russian, represented the Vatican. Representing the Orthodox was its Patriarch, the youthful KGB agent Bishop Nikodim. An agreement was reached.

Later the terms of the Vatican-Moscow Agreement were revealed. In exchange for the presence of Orthodox observers at the Second Vatican Council, Pope John agreed to prevent the Council from condemning Communism. As Cardinal Tisserant's secretary, Msgr. Georges Roche, put it, "the decision to invite the Russian Orthodox observers to the Second Vatican Council had been taken personally by His Holiness Pope John XXIII, with the obvious encouragement of Cardinal Montini, who had been adviser to the Patriarch of Venice when he himself (Montini) was Archbishop of Milan."[11]

Two things may be marveled at here. The first is Pope Roncalli's apparent belief that he could simply brush Communism under the rug as if it didn't exist, and as if ignoring the evils and perils of Communism would not taint an Ecumenical Council as morally suspect. The second thing to marvel at is the frequency and the ease at which Giovanni Battisti Montini gained access to the highest levels of authority in the Vatican.

"Cardinal Montini went often to Rome in the days before the opening of the Council," an observer noted, "flying in one hour from Milan and returning the same day when possible." It is likely that these trips involved Montini's drafting of Pope John's famous speech that opened the Council. This is the opinion of another Vatican watcher, who noted that:

"Cardinal Montini had worked closely with the Holy Father and knew his mind. Between them they knew the Church very well, on the diocese firing line and in the offices of the Curia. It was remarked by correspondents that Pope John's arresting address which opened the Council sounded much like Montini's *Discorsi*."[12]

Roncalli was the second Pope John XXIII to open an Ecumenical Council. According to the legend, when his predecessor, anti-pope John XXIII, invoked the Holy Spirit to open the Council of Constance in 1414, a screech owl landed on his head. Shortly after that the first John XXIII fled his own Council, only to be captured, dragged back, and deposed.

The opening of the Second Vatican Council was sedate by comparison; the drama was mainly rhetorical. To state that the opening speech was drafted by Montini does not imply that the Cardinal was putting words in the mouth of Pope John XXIII (as he did when "speaking for" Pius XII). For Montini and Roncalli were on the same wavelength — and it was an interesting frequency. Near the beginning of the speech John gave his "assessment of the happy circumstances under which the Ecumenical Council commences." His very next words verge on contemptuous:

"In the daily exercise of our pastoral office, we sometimes have to listen, much to our regret, to voices of persons who, though burning with zeal, are not endowed with too much sense of discretion or measure. In these modern times they can see nothing but prevarication and ruin. They say that our era, in comparison with past eras, is getting worse, and they behave as though they had learned nothing from history, which is, none the less, the teacher of life. They behave as though at the time of former Councils everything was a full triumph of the Christian idea and life and for proper religious liberty ..."[13]

It is interesting that Pope John believed the Church's teaching on religious liberty had not been "proper"; this at least was the implication of his words, and in hindsight, one can see how this seemingly "throw-away" remark was only the tip of the "new religious liberty" iceberg. Also of interest is the scornful caricature of traditional Catholics as wailing Cassandras. An historian himself, Pope Roncalli knew better than most that the history of mankind invites pessimism. He continued:

> "We feel we must disagree with those prophets of doom, who are always forecasting disaster, as though the end of the world were at hand. In the present order of things, Divine Providence is leading us to a new order of human relations which, by men's own efforts and even beyond their very expectations, are directed towards the fulfillment of God's superior and inscrutable designs."[14]

What a relief this must have been to John's listeners. Imagine, after a century that saw two World Wars, the spread of Communism over one quarter of the world, the martyrdom of (literally) tens of millions of Christians, the secularization of tens of millions more, and the complete uprooting of the Church from Western civilization — after all this the Pope informed everyone that, despite all appearances to the contrary, mankind was now in full harmony with Divine Providence, and that anyone who thought differently were "prophets of doom". Well, that was that. All that remained was to proceed in a calm and orderly fashion towards utopia.

In reality, the passages quoted above reveal the *gnosis* (secret knowledge) of the papal vision: a "new order" of humanity is emerging, and what's more, it is all part of God's plan. This was the "new Pentecost" of Pope John (it is now the "new advent of humanity" of Pope John Paul II).

Next came a coded reference to the Vatican-Moscow Agreement. Pope John informed the Council Fathers that the Church "considers that she meets the needs of the present-day by demonstrating the validity of her teaching rather than by condemnation."[15] While admitting the presence of "fallacious teaching" and "dangerous concepts to be guarded against and dissipated", Pope John nevertheless insisted that:

> "these are so obviously in contrast with the right norm of honesty, and have produced such lethal fruits, that by now it would seem that men of themselves are inclined to condemn them ... They are ever more deeply convinced of the paramount dignity of the human person and of his perfections ..."[16]

The translation is: Communism is reforming itself, it is evolving into something worthy of being blessed by God and the Church, and this process should be respected rather than condemned. No evidence was given for this surprising claim — just a bare assertion. No doubt John believed this as sincerely as Cardinal Montini and the other Churchmen of the left. This was contrary to the warnings of Pius XI and Pius XII, and the warning of the beautiful Lady that Russia would "spread her errors, causing wars and persecutions of the Church ..." until that nation was consecrated to Her Immaculate Heart. It was evident the Second Vatican Council was going to teach something entirely different, and anything contradicting the papal vision would be abruptly dismissed — including the warnings of the Bessed Mother of God at Fatima.

Pacem in Terris

Also dismissed were the warnings of three Twentieth Century Popes named Pius. In fact, only nine years before Pope John's speech, Pope Pius XII had denounced Communist expansion in the most ominous tones, as:

"... the realization of a terrifying plan seeking to radically wrest minds away from the faith of Christ, to a world domination by the enemy of men of God. And there are men — miserable men — who serve as the instruments for this destructive work. A struggle is in progress, which so to speak increases each day in its proportions and in violence; hence it is necessary that all Christians, but especially all Catholic militants, be on their toes and fight, even to the death if necessary, for their Mother the Church, with the weapons permitted to them."[17]

The consistent teaching of Popes had forbidden Catholics from collaborating with movements or political parties based on erroneous principles — like liberalism, Freemasonry, socialism, and Communism. It was thought that close contact with bad ideas could lead to the acceptance of those ideas by Catholics. A good example of this was the worker priest experiment, which self-destructed when the priests became Marxists and left the Church. Angelo Roncalli personally witnessed this debacle. Nevertheless, with the little time remaining him, Pope Roncalli set about to contradict his predecessors, and legitimize collaborations between Catholics and Communists.

In April, 1963, he issued the encyclical *Pacem in Terris* (Peace On Earth), a prescription for "Establishing Universal Peace in Truth, Justice, Charity, and Liberty."[18] As John saw it, Communism was an erroneous doctrine, but this fact was secondary to the importance of respecting the Communists as human beings:

"One must never confuse error and the person who errs ... The person who errs is always and above all a human being, and he retains in every case his dignity as a human person; and he must be always regarded and treated in accordance with that lofty dignity."[19]

Pope John is referring here to the same individuals Pius XII called "miserable men" who sought to "radically wrest minds away from the faith of Christ." As for Communism itself, Pope John distinguished between its false teachings and the actual movement of Communist organizations in the world. Regarding the latter, John asked:

"... who can deny that those (Communist) movements, in so far as they conform to the dictates of right reason and are interpreters of the lawful aspirations of the human person, contain elements that are positive and deserving of approval?"[20]

John is referring here to an ideology Pius XI called "intrinsically perverse", warning that "no one who would save Christian civilization may collaborate with it in any undertaking whatsoever." Without intending unkindness, the logic of Pope Roncalli's apologia for Communism (and socialism) is akin to declaring that a skunk could be a rose if it didn't stink so badly. Even a sympathizer of the Pope later called his attempt to foster Catholic-Marxist collaborations "blindly utopian".[21]

Predictably, Moscow praised *Pacem in Terris*, and for good reason. One month after its issuance the Italian Communist Party won a surprise landslide victory, which it happily attributed to "good Pope John's" blessing of their cause. Soviet Premier Nikita Khrushchev declared, "We applaud the taking of positions of Pope John XXIII in favor of peace."[22] Elated by this reaction, Pope John seemed not to realize that "peace" for Communists was not the universal love and brotherhood of the "new Pentecost"; peace for Moscow was the absence of opposition to Communist expansion. It was a significant difference.

One month after the victory of Italian Communism, Cardinal Suenens came to New York to explain *Pacem in Terris* to the United Nations. Asked if Pope John condemned Communism, Suenens replied from the encyclical: Communism was erroneous, but "people are always deserving of respect and have a value far above whatever views they may hold."[23] The answer appeared to be No, the Pope did not condemn Communism.

Equally significant was the logic of *Pacem in Terris*, which appeared to be an exaggeration of the age-old Church teaching, "Love the sinner, hate the sin." John's logic, that human beings are more important than what they believe, tended to dissolve distinctions between right and wrong. For the logical extension of the encyclical's assertion of people over ideas is that people are more important than doctrine. But doesn't this also mean that people are more important than Christian doctrine? If so, does it not also mean that, ultimately, people are more "valuable" than the Church? Could it also eventually mean that people are more important even than Christ, whom we must believe in order to be saved?[24]

Who Was Pope John?

Pope John certainly wouldn't have carried things that far. Yet friendly relations with the Communists were important enough to John for him to use loose logic. Friendly relations with the Communists also appeared to be worth lying for. On the occasion of his eightieth birthday John received a telegram from Khrushchev offering his "congratulations and sincere wishes for good health and success in his noble aspiration to contribute to ... peace on earth."

As with his idea for the Council, John claimed Khrushchev's telegram was "a sign of Divine Providence." He told Capovilla, "Something is moving in the world. The Lord is using the humble instrument that I am to move history." The impression given was that Russia had made the first friendly move in what could be a thaw in the Cold War relations between the Vatican and Moscow. Only much later was the truth discovered. John had requested Khrushchev to wire him in order to provide the Pope with a pretext for communicating with Moscow.[25] Not exactly Divine Providence.

Neither was an incident reported on by John's biographer, Peter Hebblethwaite. In order to further the liturgical reform Hebblethwaite claimed John "favored", the Pope "added to the Roman canon the name of St. Joseph — *beati Joseph, eiusdem Virginis Sponsi* — a pious ruse to show that the text was not immutable," according to Hebblethwaite.[26]

Granted, by today's standards this was a pretty tame innovation. The point is that on several occasions Pope John cloaked his motivations behind "pious ruses". The Council was not the "inspiration" John made it out to be. Khrushchev's telegram was not "Divine Providence" and John knew it. Likewise with the addition of St. Joseph to the Roman canon. It was impossible to scrape together a credible pious ruse concerning the burying of the Third Secret of Fatima, so John's dishonesty with the press release was more difficult to disguise. In this instance his refuge was silence and a manufactured anonymity.

These subterfuges are more in keeping with a career diplomat than a "country priest", which John is often likened to. That makes sense, however, because John was never a country priest. He was a career diplomat (and historian) who, for various reasons, acquired the persona of a pastoral "shepherd of souls", even though it was only for a brief few years near the end of his life that he acquired a flock. This was his appointment to Venice, which occurred after he was fired as papal nuncio to Paris.

Due to his charm and personal warmth, and a seemingly genuine concern for others, Roncalli may in all likelihood have been a genuine shepherd of souls, had he been given the opportunity. But as Pope he often appeared more pastoral to Communists and Socialists than to Catholics. While opening windows to the former he slammed doors shut in the faces of the latter — particularly with his regrettable handling of the Fatima Secret.

After issuing *Pacem in Terris*, John's final days concerned the progress of the Council. Contrary to the statements of well meaning defenders, there is no credible evidence that John was distraught over the direction the Council was taking.[27] His main anguish was that things were moving too slowly. His involvement with the Council invariably favored the progressive faction, which was part of a moderate to liberal majority of Council Fathers. The "conservative" minority was caught off guard by the Pope's allegiances, and never recovered.

After suffering a stomach hemorrhage, Pope John never recovered either. In the last six months of his life he underwent what for him was a novelty — physical pain. By all accounts Pope John accepted his suffering peacefully, offering it, and his life, for the success of the Council. The phrase most often on his lips was *"Ut Unam Sint"* — That They May Be One, Our Lord's prayer to the Father. By the feast of Pentecost, 1963, he had lost more than fifty pounds. The hemorrhaging increased, and John developed peritonitis. His temperature soared, and relatives gathered at his bedside. So did Cardinal Montini, who John predicted would succeed him as Pope.

He became resigned to dying before his Council finished. "I shall watch its joyful conclusion from Heaven, where I hope — rather, where I am certain the Divine Mercy will draw me,"[28] he told his visitors. On June 3, 1963, the Monday after Pentecost, he lapsed in and out of consciousness. At 7:49 that night he died. His final words, "At least as far as the bronze gates ..."[29] remain a mystery.

Less mysterious was the obituary of Cardinal Siri, delivered shortly after John's death: "It will take forty years to repair the damage this Pope inflicted in four years."[30] Siri was one of those "prophets of doom" Pope John shook his head over. In hindsight, however, Siri sounds like a raving optimist, for as of this writing the damage caused by his Council continues to metastasize, and figments of restoration are as chimerical as John's "new Pentecost".

The inevitable question of Angelo Roncalli's Masonic affiliations is even more sensitive than usual after his recent beatification. Whatever he was, it can fairly be said that John's vision of unity and peace was at least as Masonic as it was Christian.[31] While it is certainly true that Christ prayed "that they may be one", no Pope before John ever considered those words to be a promise of future unity, at least not on the grand scale Pope John envisioned things, and certainly not between atheists and Christians.

On the other hand, the centuries-long preoccupation of Freemasonry and the other occult societies has been initiating the reign of universal brotherhood, and their infiltration of the Church to achieve this end is too persistent and well documented to ignore without comment. The occultist Rudolph Steiner, who some have claimed Angelo Roncalli was sympathetic to, proclaimed "We need a Council and a Pope to proclaim it" at the beginning of this century. An apostate priest named Roca (1830-1893), after being excommunicated, bespoke this chilling vision:

> "There is a sacrifice in the offing which represents a solemn act of expiation ... The papacy will fall; it will die under the hallowed knife which the fathers of the last council will forge. The papal Caesar is a host crowned for sacrifice."[32]

The sacrifice spoken of here may quite literally be a deal with the devil, involving the surrender of the keys of Peter to the prince of this world. Does it not also seem that Roca implies the death of the papacy will be a voluntary act of homage to the prince of this world, and that the "sacrifice" will be prepared by an Ecumenical Council?[33]

Perhaps this is taking the ravings of an occultist too seriously. Yet this Luciferian strategy fits into the grand convergence spoken of earlier. The revolution burrowed into the Church in the Nineteenth Century, in the guise of liberal Catholicism. This infiltration begat the modernism, social progressivism, and Christian Democracy movements of the early Twentieth Century. This is the "other school" which formed Angelo Roncalli, the school he quite frankly pledged his allegiance to.

This allegiance may have caused his election to the papacy. A career diplomat accustomed to making public acts and private deals, he predicted his election, and was speaking of convoking a Council even before taking the papal coronation oath. He spoke of an Ecumenical Council in the 1940's. How much else Pope Roncalli knew is veiled. In addition to getting the Council off the ground, Pope John displayed the sort of integral humanism that would prove to be the mortar for the grand convergence of Communism, Masonry, and a host of noxious "isms" into the Luciferian world republic which has been prophesied for so long by Christians and occultists alike. Proceeding as issue from the Luciferian world order would be the new religion of "man made God." The only stumbling stone was the true religion of "God made man", and the insistence of the Roman Catholic Church that this was the one true religion, and that one must either convert to the true religion as taught by the Church or die the eternal death.

Fatima underlined this constant teaching and specified that one nation in particular must be converted to Catholicism, and that this could only be done by the Roman Pontiff consecrating that nation, Russia, to the Immaculate Heart of the Blessed Virgin Mary. It is interesting to note that Pope John XXIII, although he hid the Third Secret and did not even attempt to consecrate Russia, still desired what he called "the conversion of Russia to the Catholic Church."[34]

This desire of Pope John was seen as an "enigma" by his sympathetic biographer, Giancarlo Zizola, since "during the Council" the word "conversion" had "taken on a meaning quite different from that of a proselytized incorporation of heretics into the Roman Church." Zizola believed that "What John hoped for was the rebirth of the sense of transcendence within Soviet Marxism," but was impoverished by his traditional vocabulary into calling this "the conversion of Russia to the Catholic Church."[35]

While Zizola, a progressive, may be putting words in Roncalli's mouth here, John's retention of some traditional forms of piety is a fact that is, unfortunately, marginal to his papacy. Whatever "transcendent" hopes he had, it seems true enough that John's aspirations for Russia did not involve Fatima.[36] John's solution to Communism was not the consecration of Russia, but the agreement not to condemn Communism at Vatican II, in exchange for the participation of Orthodox clergy, many of whom were KGB agents. This proved to be no solution at all.

The Soviets took what John gave them, praised him, and continued to persecute the Church in Russia. In his desire to inflict a "new Pentecost" on the Communists, Pope John seemed oblivious of the fact that grace must also be received by an act of the will. Pope John was the Pope who single-handedly rehabilitated Communism, discredited Fatima, and used deceitful methods to bury the Third Secret.

Like John the Baptist, John XXIII was a precursor. He proclaimed the coming of a "new order" (his words) of humanity that was mandated by Divine Providence. By treating mankind as if we had actually evolved beyond original sin, John proved that we haven't. He convoked a Council in order to further the causes of unity and peace, and only accelerated the slide of the Church into the worldwide apostasy She had defended Herself against for centuries.

If, as most Fatima scholars believe, the Third Secret concerns the apostasy in the Church, in better days it may be possible to locate the origins of this lamentable period in Pope John's refusal to reveal — or heed — the Third Secret. His enchanting vision of a 20th Century Pentecost was so brilliant it forced into twilight anything to the contrary, including Church dogma about hell, original sin, and the devil, and the intimate relationship of these dogmas to the Fatima Message.

It appears the merciful blessing of Fatima, when spurned, rebounded into a curse, leaving Pope John and his successors to the fruits of their grace-deprived labors. Did the chastisement of apostasy enter the Church because the successor of Peter defied the Fatima Secret? If this is so, it explains Jacinta's anguished preoccupation with the Holy Father, and her pleas for all to "pray, pray very much for the Holy Father."

For who Pope Roncalli was, is, finally, not really that much of a mystery. In the light of Fatima, he was the Pope of the Apostasy.[37]

NOTES

1. *CRC* No. 304, December, 1997, p. 8.
2. The short list did not include her former confessor.
3. *TWTAF*, Vol. III, p. 474.
4. Da Silva died on December 4, 1957. The Third Secret arrived in Rome on April 16, 1957. See *TWTAF*, Vol. III, pp. 481, 498.
5. *TWTAF*, Vol. III, pp. 578-579. See also Frère Michel's (withering) critique of the unfortunate communique on pp. 579-589.
6. As quoted in ibid., p. 597.
7. See Father Joseph de Sainte Marie, O.C.D., "The Church's Duty in the Face of the Fatima Message," *Catholic Family News*, July 2000, p. 13. Father Sainte-Marie states, among other things, that "The Pontiff must discern – that is his duty – whether the words of the prophet are of God. But once he has judged and recognized that a given prophecy is indeed from God, then he must obey, not as obeying the prophet but as obeying God, whose instrument the prophet is."
8. See Bishop Rudolf Graber, "The Obligation to Believe the Message of Fatima", *CFN*, July 2000, p. 14.
9. *TWTAF*, Vol. III, pp. 597-598.
10. *Ad Petri Cathedram*, Par. 60, 61.
11. The remarks of Msgr. Roche were first published as a response to an article by Jean Madiran in the July-August 1984 issue of the French journal *Itineraires*, as reprinted in Father Nicholas Gruner, Editor, *World Enslavement or Peace: It's Up to the Pope,* Immaculate Heart Publications.
12. The two quotations on Council collaborations between Pope John and Montini are by Msgr. Clancy, and William Barrett, respectively. See Wiggington, op. cit., p. 111.
13. Walter M. Abbott, S.J., Editor, *The Documents of Vatican II*, Guild Press, 1966, pp. 710-719.
14. Ibid.
15. Ibid.
16. Ibid.
17. As quoted in *TWTAF*, Vol. III, p. 453.
18. So stated the introduction to the encyclical.
19. *Pacem In Terris*, Par. 158.
20. Ibid., Par. 159.
21. Dominican Father P. Innocenzo Colosio, in his article in *Si Si No No*, Angelus English Language Article Reprint, May 1997, p. 21.
22. As quoted in Frère François de Marie des Anges, *Fatima: Intimate Joy, World Event*, Vol. IV, Immaculate Heart Publications, p. 67.
23. As quoted in Hebblethwaite, *Paul VI*, op. cit., p. 316.
24. See John 6. The other problem with *Pacem In Terris* was this: it is a fact of history that some men, by acting on their bad ideas, have lost their dignity, or forfeited it; Judas Iscariot comes to mind, along with Stalin, Hitler, and others. *Pacem In Terris* does not acknowledge a limit to the bad ideas one can have, and more importantly, it makes no mention that the violations by Communists of God's laws damn them, and their vaunted dignity, to perdition.
25. Hebblethwaite, *John XXIII*, op. cit., p. 433.
26. Hebblethwaite, *Paul VI*, op. cit., p. 309.
27. Of the numerous biographies of Pope John, and accounts of the Council that I researched for this chapter, I found one account of John voicing concern over the radical direction of the Council. The author of *The Battle for the American Church* (Doubleday & Company, Inc., 1979), Msgr. George A. Kelly quotes Cardinal Heenan quoting Pope John asking after the first session, "How can we call this thing off gracefully without this thing going into more sessions? (p. 20)" John rarely spoke this clumsily, so this may be a poor translation. However, it is entirely possible John entertained momentary ambivalence about the direction of the Council. One would certainly hope he did. If this in fact happened, it may have been similar to John's verbal reservations about some aspects of the New Theology, which were merely rhetorical. It is perhaps more telling to look at John's *behavior* during the Council, e.g., his appointment of new theologians to important commissions, and his scrapping the orthodox schemas prepared for the Council, in order to give the new theologians more room to operate.
28. Ralph Wiltgen, S.V.D., *The Rhine Flows Into the Tiber*, Hawthorn Books, 1967, p. 73.
29. Goressio, op. cit., p. 316.
30. Ibid., p. 317.

31. This is descriptive, not pejorative.

32. The quotations by Steiner and Roca are found in Dr. Rudolf Graber (Bishop of Regensburg), *Athanasius And The Church of Our Time,* English translation by Susan Johnson, published by Van Duren C.P. Ltd., England, 1974, republished by Christian Book Club of America.

33. This all seems compatible with the progressive 'doctrine' of *kenosis,* the willful self-annihilation of the Church. See Atila Sinke Guimarães, *Animus Delendi (Desire to Destroy),* Volume IV of the Collection *Eli, Eli, Lamma Sabacthani?,* published by Tradition in Action, Chapter II. The best that can be said for this revolting 'doctrine' is that people who adhere to *kenosis* are educated far beyond their intelligence.

34. Zizola, op. cit., p. 145.

35. Ibid.

36. The 1984 edition of Hebblethwaite's *John XXIII* contains the following diary entry by Pope John, dated December 26, 1962: "I got out of bed and then, kneeling before the crucified Lord, I consecrated my life and the final sacrifice of my whole being for my part in this great undertaking, the conversion of Russia to the Catholic Church. I repeated it in the same spirit at Holy Mass. At noon during the general audience in the *Sala Clementina,* still under the same inspiration, I put great fervor of heart and lips into the words, *Domine, tu scis quia amo te* (Lord, you know that I love you. John 21:17)." With sentiments like these, how easy it would have been for Pope Roncalli to consecrate Russia to the Immaculate Heart during the Second Vatican Council. Why he didn't do it, and what exactly he meant by 'conversion', remain unclear. "This great undertaking" would seem to be the Vatican Council.

37. "Good Pope John" probably holds the record for the pope most often accused of membership in occult organizations. The Italian political and religious journal *30 Days,* influential enough to be published in six languages, published an article in December, 1993, about the Masonic affiliations of Pope John XXIII.

The French Freemason and author, Baron Yves Marsaudon, claims Archbishop Roncalli became a thirty-third degree Mason while a nuncio at France. Mary Ball Martinez writes of French Republican Guards who from their posts observed:

"... the Nuncio in civilian clothes leaving his residence to attend the Thursday evening meetings of the Grand Orient of France. Whereas exposure to such a dramatic conflict of loyalties would unnerve the average man, be he Catholic or Freemason, Angelo Roncalli seems to have taken it in his stride." (Martinez, op. cit., p. 117).

When Roncalli became Pope, Marsaudon declared, "With all our hearts we (his fellow Masons) wish for the success of John XXIII's Revolution." In 1976 *The Prophecies of Pope John XXIII* was published in Italy. It was a small book containing prophetic poetry and prose. The introduction declares that it is the writings of Pope John, and further declares that John was initiated into the Rosicrucians while working in Turkey in 1935. The book offered no evidence to support this claim. See Michael Baigent, Richard Leigh, and Henry Lincoln, *Holy Blood, Holy Grail,* Dell Publishing, 1982, pp. 159-161. Mary Ball Martinez attributes a similar version to Milanese journalist Pier Carpi, "who claims to have absolute proof" that Roncalli was an eighteenth degree Freemason in Istanbul. See Martinez, op. cit., p. 117.

In 1994 *30 Days* published "A John XXIII Update", in which the Grand Master of the Italian Grand Orient Order of Freemasonry repeated Baron Marsaudon's assertion that Roncalli was a Freemason in Paris in the 1940's.

One of the marks of the conciliar Church is the polarizing effect it has — on Catholics. The legacy of Pope John XXIII is a case in point. It should be remembered, however, that Freemasons are not reliable reporters, and may well have their own reasons for falsely claiming Masonic connections for Pope John XXIII. Moreover, whether or not Roncalli was a Mason has no bearing on assessing his responsibility for the present state of the Church. If there is an indictment to be brought against him, it does not depend on his alleged status as a Mason, or, for that matter, on his status as a *beati.*

Chapter Fifteen

Fatima Time

Nobody could say Pope John XXIII hadn't had chances to change his mind about Fatima and the Third Secret. In 1960 the future Cardinal Oddi asked him why he did not reveal the Secret. "Do not speak to me about it," the Pope replied. Oddi persisted: "If you wish, I won't speak to you about it anymore, but I cannot prevent the people from speaking about it ..." Again the Pope replied, "I told you not to talk to me about it."[1]

Bishop Venancio of Fatima-Leiria sent a letter to the world episcopate, asking them to initiate days of prayer and reparation in dioceses around the world. His hope was that Pope John would relent, and reveal the Third Secret on October 13, 1960, the anniversary of the Miracle of the Sun. This was also the prayer of the thousands who headed for Cova da Iria that October. Unlike 1917, there were far fewer curiosity seekers, skeptics, and journalists. It was a hope-against-hope pilgrimage by the true believers. Like 1917, much of the pilgrimage was made in the pouring rain. Many of the pilgrims walked, and spent the night exposed to the cold rain and a fierce wind that threatened to blow them off the Cova da Iria. Medical teams cared for those injured by the elements and others whose feet were bloody and bruised from the trek. The bishops repeated Pius XII's consecration of the world to the Immaculate Heart. Pope John was not in attendance. Nor did he follow custom by encouraging the pilgrims with a radio message. Instead, the Pope sent a short telegram that did not mention the Fatima apparitions or the Secret. That was all. The wind continued to howl, and on this October 13 the rain did not stop and the sun did not shine.

None of this was lost on Lucy. "Due to the present state of things, and the lamentable events," she wrote a fellow religious in 1961, "this year has been very sad for us."[2]

This remark encompassed more than the non-disclosure of the Third Secret and the discrediting of the Fatima Message by Pope John. Portugal's colonial settlements in Angola and Mozambique had become the focus of Communist terrorism. At home a determined propaganda campaign in the press and the universities railed against the "fascist" government of President Salazar.

Portuguese Christian Democrats were aligned with Communist and Socialist forces. Their strategy was a familiar one. Through propaganda and street violence they sought to discredit Salazar, and to replace him

with a temporary democratic republic, which would then give way to
"the dictatorship of the proletariat" — in plain language, a totalitarian
state. Although this was not the first time Russia's errors had spread to
Portugal, by the 1960's it did not appear that the small Catholic nation
would be able to resist Communist propaganda and terrorism. Sister
Lucy wrote of Portugal's plight:

> "God permits it thus in order to purify us, for the sins in which
> the world wallows are numerous, and it does not want to open its
> eyes to the truth of the good road. It would have been necessary
> (for Portugal) to execute an energetic and national campaign
> against the evil which is spreading and for the promotion of good,
> which is presently retreating awkwardly."[3]

According to Lucy, however, Portugal was not an innocent victim.
The Portuguese needed to "ban sin from the public life of the nation, as
well as everything which sustains and supports sin: divorce, immoral
houses, illicit unions ..." She continued:

> "... public sin always draws down on the people great
> chastisements and God's anger because public sin is visible and
> the rest of the people consent to it. These chastisements espe-
> cially happen when the number of just and reparatory souls is not
> sufficient to counter-balance the evil done by those public sins ...
> May God help us do what we can on our part."[4]

Her assessment could not have been more different than John
XXIII's. While Lucy saw even Catholic Portugal deserving of chastisement, Pope John believed that non-Catholic modern man had outgrown
error, and urged the Church and the world to respect the "lofty dignity"
Communists had by virtue of their status as "human persons."[5]

Unlike Pope John, Lucy believed that whether or not the Third Secret
was revealed in 1960, from that point on the Church — and the world —
were living on Fatima time. Not only would Russia continue to spread
her errors, "causing wars and persecutions of the Church", but the
Third Secret, which began with an ominous qualification, "In Portugal
the dogma of the faith will always be preserved ..." would reveal itself in
"the signs of the times" one heard so much of as Pope John's successor
opened the second session of the Second Vatican Council in September,
1963.

An "Occult" Council?

Characteristically, John had planned ahead for his successor. He
wished to prevent the conclave from being "a conclave against me, for
that would destroy all that I set out to achieve." This meant he had to be
prudent about signaling his preference for a successor. "Pope John was
far too shrewd to show his hand," observes Peter Hebblethwaite, who
believes John's desire was to have elected "someone who would con-

tinue his line, but prudently, so that neither the progressives nor the conservatives could claim utter victory."[6] The obvious man for the job was Cardinal Montini.

In an irony unremarked upon by liberals and conservatives for the obvious reasons, two men sacked by Pope Pius XII consecutively succeeded him as Pope. Both Montini and Roncalli endeavored to pull Pope Pacelli into their spiritual orbit, in order to lend credibility to the unusual emphasis given modern ideas at Vatican II. While it is true that Pacelli was more innovative than many Catholics generally realize, it is difficult to imagine Pius XII agreeing with Montini and Roncalli's dismissal of the "prophets of doom", much less the deference Popes John and Paul paid to Congar, de Lubac, and the other new theologians Pius XII had censured in *Humani Generis*.

In his address at the Requiem Mass for John XXIII, Cardinal Montini eulogized his good friend, and advertised his own position on the Council thusly:

"... John XXIII combined internal and external ecumenism ...
the effort to bring about the reunion of the so many separated
Christian fractions in the organic unity of the faith and charity of
the Mother Church ... and the effort to spread peace between nations ... Could we ever stray from the paths that Pope John has so
masterfully traced out, even for the future? I think not!"[7]

In fact, John was more ambitious than Cardinal Montini let on, at least according to his opening speech to the Council Fathers, where he informed the Council Fathers that "the aim of the ecumenical council Vatican II was to consolidate the path toward that unity of mankind which is required as a necessary foundation in order that the earthly city may be brought to resemble that heavenly city ..."[8]

It is clear from this speech (which Montini drafted) that the Council had far more ambitious goals than religious unity: it sought the unity of mankind, be they Christian, pagan, Jew, or infidel. It is likely that John's axiom, "What unites us is greater than what separates us", was code for the un-Catholic notion that our common humanity was to become the foundation for religious unity, instead of an often divisive Christian truth. The elevation of humanity to an almost sacred status was one of the distinguishing marks of the new religion that emerged during the implementation of Vatican II documents.

If one notices the carefully crafted ambiguities in Council documents that served as footholds for a surprising variety of novelties, it becomes apparent that each ambiguity tends to dissolve a doctrine unique to Catholicism by favoring an interpretation designed either to attract or flatter non-believers.[9] This recurring feature makes Vatican II unique among all Ecumenical Councils in the 2,000 year history of the Church. Consequently, Vatican II may properly be called an "occult" Council, in the sense that the documents contained "secret knowledge" implanted by initiates, that would be exploited after the Council.[10]

It is even possible that the un-Catholic conciliar novelties are part of the apostasy in the Church that almost certainly is mentioned in the Third Secret.

Fatima and Vatican II

Regarding Fatima, part of the secret knowledge handed to Pope Paul from Pope John was that the Council was forbidden to condemn Communism. Accordingly, Pope Paul ignored over 20 Council Fathers who requested a condemnation of "Marxism, socialism and Communism" at the end of the second session. This began a dispute, which intensified during discussion of Schema XIII (later, *Gaudium et spes*) in the third session, when repeated requests by the conservative minority to add a paragraph condemning Communism were ignored.[11]

Finally, an initiative supported by 435 Council Fathers to have Communism condemned in Schema XIII was formally presented to the General Secretariat of the Council by Archbishops Sigaud and Marcel Lefebvre. To their astonishment, the revised Schema did not contain the amendments, although this was required by Council rules of procedure. In the investigation that followed, the 435 Council Fathers were (incorrectly) blamed for not presenting their intervention within the time limit. Eventually the truth came out. French Archbishop Achille Glorieux deliberately suppressed the amendment from the Commission. Commission member Archbishop Garonne apologized, but justified the violation of Council rules by declaring: "It seemed to the Commission that this manner of proceeding agrees very well both with the pastoral ordination of the Council and the express will of Popes John and Paul."[12] Which was true enough, although to their discredit some progressives insisted that everything that happened during the Second Vatican Council, including open deceits, was the work of the Holy Spirit. Curiously, a number of conservative Catholics agreed. At any rate, the Communists seemed wise to the deal, even if Catholics weren't. A French Communist newspaper reported in 1963 that the Church "has even promised there will be no direct attack on the Communist system at the Council."[13]

Thus it appeared that Russia's errors had spread even to the Second Vatican Council, at least to the extent that the Church hierarchy protected Russia's errors by not condemning them. This led to the Council's disoriented exaltation of the Church's "freedom" while Catholics in Russia, eastern Europe, and around the world were being martyred by Communist governments — which the Council refused to condemn. Shouldn't progressive and conservative Catholics alike be more prudent about attributing this incoherence, this disorientation, to the Holy Ghost?

The conservative Council minority had no such delusion, at least on this point. "The Council will be blamed — and quite justly so — for its silence in regard to Communism, a silence that will be taken as a sign of cowardice and connivance,"[14] they declared. Chinese Cardinal Yu Pin, who likewise had no delusions about Communism, noted that "the schema puts a great emphasis on the signs of the times, but appears to ignore that Communism and Marxist materialism are the greatest and saddest characteristic signs of our times. A declaration about this point is necessary in order to defend the truth ..."[15]

Ducking Communism makes it harder to credit the moral authority proponents claim for Vatican II, unless one is willing to use the excuse of "a pastoral Council" to whitewash the secret political collaboration between Moscow and Rome. Here again, however, one verges on nonsense, since there is nothing pastoral about an immoral decision not to condemn a murderous anti-Christian doctrine responsible for shedding the life-blood of millions. Moreover, it seems clear this decision came from the papacy: Pope Paul VI was merely continuing Pope John XXIII's original agreement with the Orthodox not to condemn Communism in exchange for their attendance at the Council.

In addition to observing the slow strangling of attempts to condemn Communism, Paul also turned a deaf ear to petitions by Council Fathers to consecrate Russia to the Immaculate Heart. During his speech that closed the third session of the Council, Paul gave a reply of sorts. After first admonishing Catholics not to scandalize "separated brothers" by excessive devotion to the Virgin, Paul petitioned Mary to "bless the Ecumenical Council and the entire Church, hastening the hour of union of all Christians." He then "recalled" Pius XII's consecration of the world to the Immaculate Heart of Mary. The subtlety here involved "recalling" the consecration without actually renewing or repeating it. Such a minimal response probably cannot be considered an attempt to consecrate Russia to the Immaculate Heart in union with the Council Fathers. This was unfortunate, since the Council was the perfect occasion for performing the consecration, since the concentration of the world episcopate eliminated many logistical problems. Instead, Paul contented himself with declaring, "we intend to entrust to the care of this heavenly Mother the entire human family, with its problems and anxieties, with its legitimate aspirations and ardent hopes."[16]

It was unclear who Paul "intended to entrust" the *sins* of "the entire human family" to, but even the little he did say regarding the Blessed Virgin mortified the majority of Council Fathers, who felt betrayed by Paul. In fact his modest gesture towards the Blessed Virgin was a diplomatic gesture designed to keep the conservative minority signing documents, not a true act of devotion. It is a measure of the prominence of Council progressives that they contested even the bones Paul threw the traditional minority. The point to be remembered here is that the remedy for the ills of the world, according to the Second Vatican Council and the conciliar popes, was brotherhood, peace, and religious unity, not the elevation of the Immaculate Heart and the consecration of Russia.

A final point about the Council. The strategy used in the political world, of adopting democratic principles to dissolve monarchies and usher in socialist totalitarianism, worked equally well when applied to the hierarchy of the Roman Catholic Church during Vatican II. Non-Catholic "observers" were granted a surprising amount of authority. While the boast of an eastern European newspaper that the Council was completely infiltrated by Communists may have been an exaggeration, the comments of French journalist (and observer) Henri Fesquet seem accurate enough:

> "Thanks to the support of two popes ... The 'people of God' played an important role at the Council. Vatican II, an open house almost from the outset, welcomed the more or less prophetic aspirations of the unranked. Thanks to the mass media, information was easily passed from the bottom to the top. This is a just redress of the balance after centuries of authoritarianism. Vatican II, without any doubt, precipitated this evolution."[17]

The strategy used by Communists to topple Russian and European governments worked at the Council because of "the support of two popes". For if the support of Pope Paul prevented Mary from receiving Her traditional title "Mediatrix of all graces" at the Council, it was also his support, according to Mr. Fesquet, that was responsible for the Council rehabilitating the "worker priest" experiment Msgr. Montini championed in the 1940's. After exulting that, "Against all hope, this form of the apostolate was explicitly approved by the Council", Mr. Fesquet explained:

> "We are in a position to say that it was at the Pope's personal request that the Holy Office authorized the French episcopacy to take this decision before the end of the Council and thus in Rome itself, a circumstance that confers additional weight on this initiative."[18]

A student of Opus Dei member Jean Guitton, and the neo-modernist Dominican Yves Congar, Mr. Fesquet concludes:

> "This liberation of Catholic thought, too long imprisoned in the negative tide of the Counter-Reformation, in a way enables the Church to take up the standard of the French Revolution, which made the rounds of the secular world before coming to rest in Catholicism, whence it originated. Liberty, equality, fraternity: this glorious motto was the quintessence of Vatican II, as Hans Küng recently suggested."[19]

It was only proper then, that someone should rehabilitate the anti-Christian revolution. Pope Paul attempted to do so in 1963, stating:

"We are living in the era which succeeded the French Revolution, an era that reflects all its disasters and its chaotic and confused ideas, but also its thrill and confidence ... We became aware of something new: of living ideas, of parallels between the great principles of the Revolution (sic) which had, after all, only adopted certain Christian ideas — fraternity, equality, progress, the desire to raise up the humble classes. To this extent it was something Christian, but it had taken on also an anti-Christian, secular, anti-religious nature, which tended to pervert that share of the heritage of the Gospels which was calculated to increase man's nobility and dignity."[20]

In fact, what Paul called "the great principles of the Revolution", liberty, equality, and fraternity, did not originate in the Church. They emerged as a diabolical half-truth from the bowels of Masonic lodges in Paris as the Revolution spewed its violent hatred at the Church and Christian civilization. The "humble classes" preferred remaining Catholic to being "raised up", and were massacred for their disobedience. Until Paul VI every Pope (except perhaps for John XXIII) had thoroughly condemned the Revolution — which made its public debut in an ecumenical Council all the more remarkable. Also remarkable is that Paul's view of the Revolution could have been voiced comfortably by a Freemason.

Paul Goes to Fatima

That Pope Montini played favorites at the Council was no surprise to his friends, like Father de Lubac, Jacques Maritain, and Fatima foe Father Edouard Dhanis. Neither was it surprising that he strove to present an appearance of fairness in his dealings with the conservative minority and the liberal majority. No doubt the Pope sincerely wanted agreement for its own sake, but his occasional concessions to the conservative minority also served the larger purpose of Council unity, which was essential to enhance the authority of Council documents. The purpose served by the Pope's visit to Fatima in 1967 was less clear, at first. Paul VI read the Third Secret in 1963, shortly after being elected Pope. Early in 1967 he announced (through Cardinal Ottaviani) that the Third Secret would not be revealed. Afterwards Paul, like John XXIII, never spoke publicly about the Third Secret.[21]

Obviously Paul wasn't coming to Fatima to reveal the Third Secret. Moreover, it was apparent that Paul disliked an enduring trait of the Portuguese nation, its "colonialism". It was said that Portugal's faith could not be contained within its tiny borders, and so for centuries had leapt out across the seas to win nations for Christ. By the 1960's, however, such heroic leaps of faith were thought to be in extremely poor taste, if not downright evil.

Paul VI said nothing that contradicted these anti-Catholic sentiments, and did not lament Portugal's loosening grip on its African possessions, which were slowly being wrested away by Communism.[22] The international propaganda that provided cover for the agitation in Africa was quite intelligent. It pitted blacks against whites under the guise of restoring equal rights to blacks. Terrorism against blacks and whites sowed fear and hatred on both sides. The subsequent racial strife was used by the Communists as "evidence" to discredit Portuguese rule as fascist and racist. (Similar tactics were being used in the southern United States around the same time).

Paul's speeches, replete with references to religious liberty and the dignity of man, and unqualified praise for liberation and racial equality, encouraged violence against Portuguese colonies which, in spite of the failings inherent in all human endeavors, were legal governments who did a passable job of governing their subjects. Yet the very fact that the governments were European was taken as proof of racist intent. That the Portuguese government seemed not only to ignore Vatican II's teaching on religious liberty, but actively encouraged the missionary efforts of the Church, only deepened the scandal. When Paul VI made a point of greeting leaders of terrorism in the Portuguese possessions of Angola and Mozambique after a public audience in Rome, it was clear enough whose side he was on.[23] In contrast, when Paul landed in Portugal in 1967 he pointedly snubbed the "fascist dictator", Portuguese President Salazar. This flash of rudeness towards one of the few truly Catholic rulers in the world was cheered by progressives inside and outside the Church. Paul's trip to Fatima still alarmed them, however. As one progressive put it:

> "One must not forget that Fatima is a symbol, in Portugal even more than in other countries, of both religious and social 'integrism'. The help of Our Lady of Fatima is invoked for the armed forces defending Christian civilization in Africa. Some time before the Pope's visit a group of Portuguese Catholic women had subscribed to the cost of distributing medals of Our Lady of Fatima by plane over the rebel zones of Angola."[24]

The writer thought these were all bad things, particularly the "symbolism" (he could not bring himself to say reality) of Fatima. He nevertheless recognized Our Lady of Fatima as the "symbol" of religious and social counter-revolution. This is true, of course, and one must acknowledge the perceptiveness of the other side. Unlike Catholics, at least they realize who their enemies are.

Paul arrived at Fatima on May 13. It was a Jubilee year, the fiftieth anniversary of the first appearance of the beautiful Lady. Hundreds of thousands of pilgrims rejoiced at the sight of a Pope on the Cova da Iria. In his remarks, however, Pope Montini did not mention the apparitions that had occurred a stone's throw from where he stood. Nor did he allude to the known parts of the Fatima Secret. Instead, Paul revealed his reason for coming. It was to re-catechize a captive audience of traditional Catholics by "express(ing) in living terms the doctrine of Vatican II", and to speak not of God but of man:

> "Men, be men. Men, be good, be wise, be open to the consideration of the general good of the world. Men, be magnanimous ... Men, think of the gravity and importance of this hour which can be decisive for the world of today and tomorrow. And begin again to approach one another with the will to construct a new world ..."[25]

Then Paul VI celebrated Mass and gave Holy Communion to Sister Lucy. Afterwards the seer presented the Pope with a handmade gift. Kneeling before him she said repeatedly, "I wish to speak with you alone." Pope Paul replied, "You see, it is not the time," adding, "If you wish to communicate something to me, tell your bishop ..." Seeing the Pope and Sister Lucy together excited the crowd, who began to chant, "Lucia, Lucia ..." Lucy was taken to the front of the podium. She faced the crowd and wept.[26]

By nightfall the Pope was back at the Vatican. He announced that at Fatima the Blessed Virgin told him that worldwide peace "was a realizable goal."[27] Not only did Paul use the Fatima Jubilee to indoctrinate Fatima pilgrims with the pastoral dogmas of Vatican II, he also implied that the beautiful Lady at Cova da Iria gave Her stamp of approval to his policies. Even with Paul's snub of Salazar, the left remained mortified he even bothered to travel to Fatima. This was an attitude that, strangely enough, seemed to be shared by Sister Lucy. She had strongly desired not to attend the Jubilee, and came only because Paul ordered her to attend.[28] Having so insisted, the Pope then refused Lucy the courtesy of a private audience. More interesting than the pontiff's bad behavior, however, is Sister Lucy's reluctance. From girlhood Lucy had consecrated herself to the message given her by the sad, beautiful Lady at Cova da Iria. Lucy had not been to Fatima for twenty years. Francisco and Jacinta, and Lucy's family were entombed there. Yet Lucy strongly preferred to decline a Pope's request to attend the Fatima Jubilee.

It is likely that her resistance to Paul VI arose from the tension of being an obedient religious and a seer charged by Heaven to contradict those she had scrupulously willed herself to obey. One can only guess at the anguish Lucy experienced when, in order to fulfill her mission as Heaven's messenger, she was forced to refute Christ's Vicars on Earth. Judging from her unenthusiastic response to the overtures of John Paul II, it appears Sister Lucy's cross continues.

The Scandals

As for the "resistance" of the left to Paul VI, this was akin to a lover's quarrel, more a measure of their endless discontent than a reaction to an unsympathetic Pope. For a perceptive observer of the Pope at Fatima noted:

"Nothing that Paul VI said or did at Fatima could bother the most fastidious partisans of post-conciliar ecumenism. Nothing that Vatican II has decided has been compromised ... Paul VI went to Fatima for a very simple reason: on the occasion of the fiftieth anniversary of the apparitions of Our Lady to the three children from the small hamlet of Aljustrel, he was sure to find there one of the most extraordinary platforms in the world ..."[29]

The image of Paul VI as a careworn moderate with a Hamlet complex doesn't begin to approach the intricacies Pope Montini brought to the papacy. He had remained a "man of the left" after Pius XII banished him to Milan and removed the possibility of Msgr. Montini being his successor. One of Pope John's first acts was to make Montini a Cardinal, and involve him in planning the Second Vatican Council. Montini quickly proved so indispensable that he was given the singular privilege of a Vatican apartment, where he could consult freely with Pope John, unhindered by his duties as Archbishop of Milan. And if "good Pope John" unleashed a whirlwind by suppressing Fatima and morally compromising the Second Vatican Council by barring a condemnation of Communism, Pope Montini's hammer blows seemed designed to seal forever the coffin of the "pre-Conciliar Church."

For instance, on November 13, 1964, during the third session of Vatican II, Archbishop Felici announced:

"Listen, all you here present. It is as though Christ's words were echoing to us from Jerusalem: 'I have compassion on the multitude'. The Church is truly the mother of the poor, and the Pope has decided to bear new witness to this truth by giving his tiara for the benefit of the poor."[30]

Pope Paul approached the altar at St. Peter's, and placed on it the triple-decked tiara given him (and his predecessors) at his coronation, with the instruction:

"Receive the tiara adorned with three crowns and know thou art the father of princes and kings, to direct them on earth, the Vicar of our Saviour, Jesus Christ, Whom we honor and glory forever."[31]

The real significance of the tiara was not its monetary value, but the visible recognition of the temporal authority of the Pope over princes and kings. Was Paul renouncing wealth, or his authority — and obligation — to rule?

The progressive Henri Fesquet and the traditionalist Abbé de Nantes both agree that, to quote Fesquet, "By giving away his tiara, Paul VI at the same time irreversibly abandoned the specific sign of his temporal royalty which made him in some sense the equal of other heads of state."[32]

Poor Mr. Fesquet can't quite bring himself to blurt out the awful truth — the Pope is not just an equal, he is "the father of princes and kings". Paul's gesture verged on an act of abdication, a solemn refusal to assert the spiritual authority of the papacy against the spirit of the age. His act has been admired by no less a personage than Pope John Paul II, who declared, "My venerable predecessor, Paul VI, in giving up his tiara, made a gesture which has not stopped bearing fruit for the Church."[33]

Indeed, such subtlety seemed designed to bear a very specific sort of fruit. So did Paul's visit one year later to the United Nations headquarters in New York, where he told delegates:

> "We are conscious that you are the interpreters of all that is paramount in human wisdom. We would almost say: of its sacred character. For your concern is first and foremost with the life of man, and man's life is sacred: no one may dare to interfere with it."[34]

Presumably "no one" does not include God. Paul's performance at the United Nations, an organization long viewed with suspicion by the Church for the obvious reasons, sent many a Catholic reeling. So did another papal act just two months later, when Paul gave back to the Muslims the Standard of Lepanto. The history of the flag was venerable. It was taken from a Turkish admiral during a great naval battle in 1571. While Pope St. Pius V fasted and prayed the Rosary, an out-numbered Christian fleet defeated a much larger Moslem navy, thus saving Christendom from the infidel. In honor of the miraculous victory, Pius V instituted the Feast of Our Lady of the Most Holy Rosary to commemorate Her intercession.

In one dramatic act Paul renounced not only a remarkable Christian victory, but the prayers and sacrifices of a great Pope and saint. Worse, he appeared to be rejecting the intercession of Our Lady of the Most Holy Rosary — again. "The wars of religion are finished for good,"[35] Paul told the Turks by way of explanation. Their immediate response was not recorded, but the rise of militant Islam in the last three decades indicates that yet another of Pope Paul's prophecies has gone awry. The next giveaway involved Paul's Shepherd's Crook and fisherman's ring, which he gave to the Buddhist U Thant. Paul also abolished the anti-Modernist oath of St. Pius X, and the Profession of Faith of the Council of Trent. In 1966 the Index was abolished.[36] The Holy Office was reformed: its primary function was now research, not defending the faith.

There was much more activity by Paul in the early years of his pontificate. Some of it was orthodox. Much of it was either ambiguous or shocking, at least to a Catholic sensibility. The deadliest blow was the *Novus Ordo Missae*, and the Pope's simultaneous attempt to suppress the Mass. This brought thousands of Catholics to Rome, where they patiently waited outside St. Peter's for an audience with the Pope, to plead with him to reconsider. Paul refused to see them, and gradually, one by one, they faded away.

Paul claimed the New Mass was the fruit of Vatican II, although in

1967 the Synod of Bishops disagreed when they rejected the *Novus Ordo Missae*. Moreover, nothing in Council documents mentioned Paul's Mass. Given the cryptic nature of portions of the documents, however, Paul may have been right. His Mass was certainly in the spirit of the penetrating reform that was cracking the Church into fragments, and there were any number of Catholics ready to defend the Holy Father no matter what he did. It was even argued that Paul's liturgy was superior to the Mass of all time. There were other voices as well, many voices ... some confused, some angry, some strangely eager. The Church had become a babel of voices, loud enough to drown out not only the silence of worship, but another silence, a horror-filled silence at the murder that had just been committed.[37]

The new liturgy proclaimed that the months after Pentecost were now to be called "ordinary time". But after 1960 there was no more "ordinary time". The Church was now on Fatima time.

NOTES

1. Frère François de Marie des Anges, *Fatima: Intimate Joy, World Event*, Volume IV, Immaculate Heart Publications, p. 76. Hereinafter this volume will be referred to as "FIJWE, op. cit."
2. Ibid., p. 71.
3. Ibid.
4. Ibid., p. 72.
5. *Pacem In Terris*, Par. 158.
6. Hebblethwaite, *Paul VI*, op. cit., p. 316.
7. *John XXIII*, Pope Paul on his Predecessor, Herder and Herder New York, 1965, p. 13.
8. Ibid., p. 41.
9. For instance, the phrase that the Church of Christ "subsists" in the Catholic Church has been used to justify all sorts of indiscriminate ecumenism, and overshadow the Church dogma that "outside the Church there is no salvation."
10. Another meaning of occult is "Of or relating to supernatural influences, phenomena, or knowledge." The connotation most often attached to "occult" in this sense is that of an angelic intelligence not of Heaven. I am not using this meaning of occult.
11. For a relatively recent confirmation of the Vatican-Moscow Agreement, see Amerio, op. cit., p. 76.
12. The story of the suppressed amendment to Schema XIII, and the quote by Archbishop Garrone, are from Atila Sinke Guimarães, *In The Murky Waters of Vatican II*, Volume I, published by MAETA, 1997, Chapter VI, Sections 85-99. Msgr. Glorieux's accomplice was German theologian Father Bernard Haring, who recently declared: "I have no reason to deny that I did everything possible to avoid this condemnation (of Communism) ... I knew that John XXIII had promised the Moscow authorities that the Council would not condemn Communism in order to make possible the participation of observers from the Russian Orthodox Church." (Ibid., pp. 161-162).
13. Amerio, op. cit., p. 75
14. Guimarães, Volume I, op. cit., p. 159.
15. Ibid.
16. Xavier Rynne, *The Third Session, The Debates and Decrees of Vatican Council II, September 14 to November 21, 1964*, New York, Farrar, Straus & Giroux, 1965, pp. 388-389.
17. Henri Fesquet, *The Drama of Vatican II, The Ecumenical Council, June 1962 to December 1965*, English translation, Random House, New York, 1967, pp. 724, 812-815.
18. Ibid.
19. Ibid.
20. As quoted in the Abbé Georges de Nantes, *Liber Accusationis In Paulum Sextum*, published in 1973 by the Catholic Counter Reformation, p. 18.
21. *FIJWE*, op. cit., pp. 115-116.
22. The competing forces in Africa in the 1960's (and today) were international Communism, international capitalism, and the United Nations. All three had interesting relationships with

international finance. The force most hostile to the Church was Communism, of course, but international capitalism was no ally. After Communist terrorism "liberated" Africans from European rule, the capitalists fought over the spoils (i.e., the land and its resources) with the Communists. Ostensibly a peacekeeper, the U.N.'s basic role was to sanction certain forms of violence and frown on others. As for the Church, not even Her popes defended Her traditional missionary activities.

23. As recounted by the French newspaper *La Croix*, as quoted in the Abbé de Nantes, *Liber Accusationis In Paulum Sextum*, op. cit., pp. 58-59.

24. Francois Houtart and Andre Rousseau, *The Church And Revolution*, English translation by Violet Neville, Orbis Books, Maryknoll, New York, 1971, pp. 245-257, for an interesting history of Portuguese mission work in Africa.

25. *FIJWE*, op. cit., p. 126.

26. Ibid., pp. 121-123.

27. Ibid., pp. 126-127.

28. According to Canon Barthas, "Lucy had obstinately refused to obey the order which the Bishop of Coimbra had transmitted to leave her cloister on the 13th to go to Fatima. Finally she telephoned herself the Nuncio in Lisbon who informed her that she would gravely disobey the Holy Father if she didn't go there. If that had only been a wish of the Holy Father, and not a command, she would have preferred to stay in the convent." (As quoted in *FIJWE*, op. cit., p. 120).

29. Journalist Robert Serrou, as quoted in *FIJWE*, op. cit., pp. 124-125.

30. Fesquet, op. cit., p. 516.

31. Ibid., pp. 516-517.

32. Ibid.

33. As quoted by Abbé Daniel Le Roux, *Peter, Lovest Thou Me?*, Instauratio Press, 1990, p. 18.

34. Abbé de Nantes, *Liber Accusationis In Paulum Sextum*, op. cit., p. 7.

35. Ibid., pp. 55-56.

36. Ibid., pp. 7-9. A word about the Abbe de Nantes, who has been in chronic hot water with the Vatican for decades now, for, among other things, requesting Popes Paul and John Paul II invoke papal infallibility to judge the orthodoxy of the documents of Vatican II. This request has not been replied to in any fashion. Other non-Vatican sources have criticized the Abbe for allegedly teaching the pre-existence of the soul of the Blessed Virgin.

Is the Abbe a credible source? I believe that in matters concerning Fatima, and the Holy Shroud, that he is very credible. Hamish Fraser studied the Abbe's *Liber* against Paul VI and "did not dispute the factual basis of the Abbe's case. When the Abbe de Nantes claims that the Pope has said something or done something it will be found that he has said or done what the Abbe alleges. When the Abbe claims that these words or actions have harmed the Church or conflict with the words or actions of his predecessors it will generally be found that such judgments are correct. But the Abbe frequently weakens his case by putting it in language which is manifestly lacking in the filial respect toward the Sovereign Pontiff which he professes, and above all, when he speculates on the motives of Pope Paul...even to the point of suggesting that Pope Paul is maliciously attempting to destroy the Church, that he could be Antichrist upon the papal throne." (Michael Davies, *Pope John's Council*, Angelus Press, 1977, pp. 187-188). I too have read the *Liber*, and I don't disagree with Fraser's (or Davies') critique, as far as it goes, although I don't recall the Abbe suggesting Pope Paul was Antichrist. If he did, then I disagree with him, although other traditional Catholics have argued quite seriously that Paul VI indeed was Antichrist (If that were true, however, then who in the world is Pope John Paul II?) Credit the Abbe with this, anyway: for a very long time he was one of the few people publicly criticizing the Council. Time has proven the merit of these criticisms, some of which, in hindsight, verge on the prophetic.

37. Is my language – that "murder" was "committed" against the Mass – purple prose? Michael Davies, among others, has argued persuasively that the Mass could not legally be suppressed, much less "murdered". I agree with his arguments, and I'll stick by my language. Although the venerable rite of the Mass cannot "die", was not the intent behind its suppression murderous, at least on a spiritual level? Most Catholics living in 1969 when the New Mass was imposed did not have the perspective of Mr. Davies. When Paul imposed the change, the Mass disappeared. Such an abrupt, monumental change, and the often disgusting spirit that has hung over the New Mass from its inception justify, in my opinion anyway, calling the whole thing a murder.

Chapter Sixteen

Graces for Pope Paul

At the end of the last session of the Second Vatican Council Pope Paul VI embraced Jacques Maritain on the steps outside St. Peter's Basilica. A self-professed "disciple" of Maritain, Montini and his master publicly celebrated a hard-won victory.

Less than ten years later both men were distancing themselves from the consequences of their ideas. Maritain, who had insisted the Church collaborate with the world, particularly with the "prophetic" ideology of Marxism, and who had tended to subordinate revelation to the movement of man's ideas in the world, now spoke of a "crisis" in the Church. He rebuked Catholics for "kneeling before the world", and bemoaned "A complete temporalization of Christianity!"[1] It doesn't appear to have occurred to Maritain that his man-centered philosophy of Integral Humanism had anything to do with the post-conciliar confusion.

No doubt he was as sincere on this point as Pope Paul VI was bewildered about the implosion of the Church. In his hunt for culprits Pope Montini even censored modernism. In a 1972 discourse Paul affirmed the factual basis of Revelation, then declared:

> "In asserting that (Revelation), our doctrine detaches from errors which have circulated and which still now appear in the culture of our times, and which could totally ruin our Christian conception of life and history. Modernism represents the characteristic expression of these errors and under other designations it is still actual."[2]

Admittedly, this is not exactly *Pascendi*, but it helped conservative Catholics ignore Paul's (more typical) odes to mankind with a clearer conscience. Such backpedaling in the last years of Paul's life was more rhetorical than real, however. He had long been a devotee of neo-modernism, and there is no evidence this changed even after the emergence of that dreadful disaster known as the post-conciliar Church. For all his very public teeth-gnashing over the state of the Church, and the widespread opinion that he "turned conservative", Paul remained a relentless reformer. This is also the opinion of the neo-modernist Jesuit, Father Henri de Lubac, who wrote admiringly of Paul, "With a stubborn and methodical firmness ... he (Paul VI) steers the barque."[3]

De Lubac should know; Paul used the full authority of the papacy to rehabilitate the Jesuit and his theology. In 1974, two years after Paul's remarks about modernism cited above, his good friend Jean Guitton wrote: "The Pope, in my presence, praises today's theologians to the skies. He quotes Manaranche, de Lubac, whom he considers the very best, also citing Congar, Rahner ..."[4]

So much for Paul's campaign against modernism. Guitton doesn't specify what it was about de Lubac and Rahner that appealed to the Pope, but both blurred the distinction between the natural and supernatural worlds by their belief that grace was inherent to man's nature. It was a short step from this mistake to many others: the naturalism of Freemasonry, the secular messianism of Judaism and Marxism, the heresy of universal salvation, and so on.

And the natural (no pun intended) philosophical complement to the new theologies of de Lubac and Rahner was Maritain's integral humanism, which viewed man as intrinsically good, and movements like Marxism as God's hand moving in the world. Maritain and his disciples forgot that, to quote Council *peritus* Romano Amerio, the Holy Ghost "is the soul of the Church, but not of the human race as such."[5]

Ultimately, the "new" ideas in religion and philosophy tended to relieve man of his dependence on an objective, transcendent God for salvation. This was the aim of liberals and Freemasons as well, and the Nineteenth Century saw their credo implemented on a global scale. By the beginning of the Twentieth Century the worldwide apostasy was established everywhere but inside the Roman Church. That this century has witnessed a wholesale apostasy from divine revelation within the Roman Catholic Church is difficult to dispute, whether or not one believes that the Third Secret of Fatima concerns the apostasy of the hierarchy of the Church — or believes in Fatima at all, for that matter. It is quite unfashionable to speak of cause and effect, though, since the conciliar popes have so obviously embraced the "new" ideas in religion and philosophy that are so corrosive to Catholicism.

Whatever form it takes, however, the source of the temptation to "rid" oneself of the need of God is as obvious as it is old: the silvery assurances of the angel of light — "Ye shall be as gods ..."

"Diabolical Disorientation"

Since 1960 Lucy had been silenced and her visitors reduced. Her former confessor, Father Aparicio, remarked, "I have not been able to speak with Sister Lucy because the Archbishop could not give the permission to meet her. The conditions of isolation in which she finds herself have been imposed by the Holy See. Consequently, no one may speak with her without a license from Rome. The Archbishop has only a very limited number of these licenses."[6]

It appears that Lucy was also forbidden to speak of Fatima. It was not the first time. She had also been silenced by Bishop da Silva when, as a girl, she first left Fatima for boarding school with the Dorothean Sisters. As always, Lucy obeyed the orders of her religious superiors.

In 1973 excerpts from letters she had written (1969-1971) were published in book form, under the title *A Little Treatise On The Nature And Recitation Of The Rosary*. Lucy's letters were to three of her nephews who were also priests. They were written during a time when, in accordance with the "spirit of Vatican II", there were campaigns to suppress the Rosary. What these "disoriented souls have spread against the recitation of the Rosary is false," Lucy wrote. After comparing the Rosary to a "chain that lifts us right up to God and unites us to Him", Lucy warned her correspondent, "This disorientation is diabolical! Do not let yourself be deceived."

In a letter dated 1970 Lucy again wrote against the campaign to suppress the Rosary, advising another priest-nephew "not to be led by the doctrines of disoriented disputants." Repeating that "The campaign is diabolical," Lucy continued:

> "Now, more than ever, we must pray for us and for those who are against us! We must recite the Rosary every day. This is the prayer which Our Lady recommended the most, as if to arm us in advance, foreseeing these days of diabolical campaign!

> "The devil knows that we shall save ourselves through prayer. Hence he leads his campaign against it to destroy us ... It is easy to recognize here the ruse of the devil and his followers, who want to lead souls away from God by leading them away from prayer ... Do not let yourselves be deceived."[7]

Advising her priest-nephew to instruct his flock to "ask for peace for the Church, for our provinces beyond the sea, and for the world," Lucy concluded: "the sheep follow their pastor when he knows how to guide them and lead them on the good road."[8] To her third priest-nephew, Father Jose Valinho, Lucy wrote:

> "I see by your letter that you are preoccupied by the disorientation of our time. It is indeed sad that so many persons let themselves be dominated by the diabolical wave sweeping over the world, and that they are blinded to the point of being incapable of seeing error! Their principal fault is that they have abandoned prayer ...

> "The devil is very clever and looks for our weak points so as to attack us. If we are not diligent and attentive in obtaining strength from God we will fall, for our times are very evil and we are weak. Only the strength of God can keep us standing."[9]

Three themes emerged in Lucy's letters. First, praying the Rosary was crucial. It could not be neglected. Second, a "diabolical disorientation" was sweeping the Church and the world, preying in particular on those who did not pray. Third, the failure of religious leaders to uphold their responsibilities. In writing to a former co-religious, a Dorothean Sister, Lucy lamented:

"It is painful to see such a great disorientation and in so many persons who occupy places of responsibility ... the devil has succeeded in infiltrating evil under cover of good, and the blind are beginning to guide others, as the Lord tells us in His gospel, and souls are letting themselves be deceived.

"Gladly I sacrifice myself and offer my life to God for peace in His Church, for priests and for all consecrated souls, especially for those who are so deceived and misled ... he (the devil) has succeeded in leading into error and deceiving souls having a heavy responsibility through the place which they occupy ... They are blind men guiding other blind men ..."[10]

The difference between her warnings and the optimism of the Council is striking. Sister Lucy was clearly one of those "prophets of doom" Pope John and Cardinal Montini warned everyone about. Even worse, she seemed to have no inclination to embrace the cult of man. "I must remain in silence, in prayer, and in penance," she wrote a friend, adding:

"In this way I can and must help you the most ... such is the part the Lord has chosen for me: to pray and sacrifice myself for those who struggle and work in the Lord's vineyard and for the extension of His kingdom ..."[11]

Given her implicit estrangement from the spirit of the post-conciliar Church, it is surprising that Sister Lucy's concerns were echoed by Pope Paul himself. For instance, in 1968 Paul spoke of "the practical apostasy which is so widespread", adding:

"The Church has suffered and suffers still from a whirlwind of ideas and of facts which are certainly not inspired by the good spirit, and do not announce this renewal of life which the Council promised and promoted."[12]

Later that same year Paul said:

"The Church finds itself in a period of uneasiness, autocriticism, we would say even of autodestruction. It is like an interior confusion, sharp and complex, which no one would have expected after the Council ... We thought of a flowering, of a sane expansion of the ripened conceptions in the great assizes of the Council. That aspect exists likewise. But ... we come to notice above all its dolorous aspect. As if the Church was striking itself."[13]

One year later Paul, who had read the Third Secret, seemed to exactly echo Sister Lucy when he said, "A sentiment of confusion seems to be spreading among the children of the Church, even among the best ones, and sometimes also with the most qualified, who exercise the greatest authority."[14]

The reference to "confusion" among those "who exercise the greatest authority" is very similar to Lucy's references to a "disorientation" among "persons who occupy places of responsibility."

After declaring, "We are at a moment of crisis of the faith," in 1971, Paul VI uttered the following oft-quoted words:

> "Through some crack the smoke of Satan has entered into the temple of God: the doubt, uncertainty, the problematic, the inquietude, the dissatisfaction occur daily. We would have believed that the day after the Council would be a day of sun for the Church. But we have found new storms. We seek to dig new abysses in place of filling them up."[15]

Barely ten years previously Cardinal Montini helped Pope John draft the opening speech to the Second Vatican Council, in which "prophets of doom" were criticized for "always forecasting disaster, as if the end of the world were at hand." At the time it is unlikely Montini (as opposed to Pope John) knew the contents of the Third Secret. A decade later he knew, however, and as Pope may even have referred to parts of the Third Secret in his mournful discourses, which coincide so closely with Sister Lucy's expressions.

For instance, Frère Michel has speculated that the phrase "diabolical disorientation" appears in the text of the Third Secret, due to the number of times Sister Lucy used this phrase after 1960, the year the Third Secret was supposed to be revealed, and the fact that she had not used the phrase prior to 1960. One could also infer that if the words "diabolical disorientation" appear in the Third Secret, they could be describing the apostasy most Fatima experts believe the Third Secret concerns.

While Paul did not use the exact words "diabolical disorientation", the euphemisms he used to describe the state of the Church — "confusion", "apostasy", and "crisis in faith" correspond to Lucy's description of a "diabolical disorientation". Moreover, Paul and Lucy both refer to the grave failure of leadership in the Church. As for Paul's famous remark about "the smoke of Satan", no less a journalist than Vittorio Messori has suggested that Paul lifted these words from the Third Secret of Fatima.[16]

Whether this is true or not, it cannot credibly be denied that demonic forces had not only infiltrated the Church, but were doing much of the lever pulling. What else could account for the thorough divergence from orthodoxy that seized the entire Church after 1960, and particularly after the Second Vatican Council? Something that looked a lot like apostasy was winnowing the hierarchy of the Roman Catholic Church.

Paul's Ostpolitik

It is unclear whether the apostasy Paul referred to deeply affected him, or whether it was simply an embarrassing counterpoint to his optimistic prophecies. In either case he failed to take the necessary steps to mitigate the damage. The same was true with the "second Secret", the spread of Russia's errors.

The dialogue that Vatican II proposed as a solution to atheism (the Council's euphemism for Communism) succeeded primarily in converting Catholics to Marxism. Despite great expectations to the contrary, Soviet Russia continued to persecute the Church in eastern Europe. Cardinal Slipyi, who had been imprisoned and tortured by the Soviets for almost twenty years, blistered the ears of his complacent colleagues at the 1971 Bishops Synod in Rome:

"Out of fifty-four million Ukrainian Catholics, ten million have died as a result of the persecutions. The Soviet regime has suppressed all the dioceses. The bodies of the dead would build a mountain and yet there is nobody, even within the Church, who will so much as defend their memory. Thousands upon thousands of faithful remain imprisoned or deported.

"But the diplomacy of the Vatican desires that we should keep silent about them, for they interfere with its negotiations. We are back in the days of the catacombs. Thousands upon thousands of the Church's faithful have been deported to Siberia and as far as the Polar Circle, but the Vatican remains wilfully ignorant of this tragedy. Can it be that the martyrs have become an embarrassment to the Church?"[17]

Two years later another source of embarrassment was excised when Hungarian Primate Jozsef Mindszenty was officially removed from his post by Paul VI. Mindszenty had been imprisoned and tortured by the Communists, then spent fifteen years in asylum in the American embassy in Budapest. Paul had requested his abdication because he believed Mindszenty was an obstacle to better relations between the Church and the Communist government in Hungary.

Mindszenty believed his abdication would weaken the Church. He was induced to come to Rome with the promise that he would remain Primate. Once in Rome, however, Paul announced Mindszenty's abdication for him. This nasty bit of business occurred, as Mindszenty recalled in his memoirs, "exactly on the twenty-fifth anniversary of my arrest" by the Communists.[18]

Not only that, but the press release made it sound like Mindszenty voluntarily abdicated. The Cardinal issued a correction, stating he "has not abdicated his office as Archbishop nor his dignity as primate of Hungary. The decision was taken by the Holy See alone."[19] Mindszenty's replacement proved better at dialoguing with Hungarian Communists than Paul was at dialoguing with Cardinal Mindszenty.[20]

Mindszenty's exile from his homeland began. In October of 1972 he made a pilgrimage to Fatima for the fifty-fifth anniversary of the Miracle of the Sun. Although the papal nuncio in Lisbon censored Mindszenty's speech at the print shop[21], the long-suffering Cardinal participated in the torchlight procession on the evening of October 12, and in the Rosary procession the next morning. Later on October 13 he concelebrated Mass with members of the Portuguese episcopate. The next day he visited Sister Lucy in Coimbra. One and one half years later, April 25, 1974 to be exact, the Communists took control of the government of Portugal. Salazar had left office earlier, due to poor health. Filling the vacuum were plans to institute a "revolutionary workers' state." Banks were nationalized (that is, the Communists took everyone's money) and freedom of the press and radio were sharply curtailed. Just when it appeared that Catholic Portugal was about to become Socialist Portugal, however, the strangest things started happening to the Revolution.

"It cannot possibly have been mere coincidence," writes historian Warren Carroll, "that the open Catholic resistance to Communism in Portugal began precisely on July 13, 1975 — the anniversary of the Blessed Virgin's warning to Lucia against the errors to come out of Russia that would 'provoke wars and persecutions of the Church.'[22]

"It was a unique campaign of counter-revolution," he continues. "No historian has been able to identify any organization which planned, inspired, or led it; there does not seem to have been one." Dr. Carroll explains:

> "Its target in almost every case was buildings, not people. Fighting occurred and injuries were inflicted only when the Communists insisted on defending their buildings. Where they tried to do so, they almost never succeeded. Twenty-two Communist headquarters were destroyed in the first nine days ... Within thirty days almost every Communist headquarters in northern Portugal, except for a few in the larger cities, was reduced to rubble or ashes."[23]

Like the attempted Communist takeover in Spain, the fighting in Portugal became a religious crusade led by the Portuguese bishops. When the "Portuguese Lenin", Alvaro Cunhal, mysteriously collapsed during a battle in the Portuguese countryside, the handwriting was on the wall. By April, 1976, the Communists were defeated. "The historians are still not sure how Portugal was saved," Dr. Carroll concludes. "But cloistered in her convent, Sister Lucia of Fatima must have been sure she knew how and by whom it was done ..."[24]

Humble little Portugal chose to rely on the intervention of the Blessed Virgin and committed Catholic resistance instead of diplomacy and dialogue. The most effective resistance to Communism continued to be, not Fascism or Ostpolitik, but Catholic counter-revolution arrayed under the banner of Our Lady of Fatima.

Graces for Pope Paul

Portugal fared better against Communism than Italy. Despite (or perhaps because of) Paul VI's decades-long involvement with the Italian Christian Democrats, the Communists were perpetually on the verge of taking over the country. Seen as the remedy for Italian Communism, the Italian Christian Democrat party was frequently charged with corruption and collaboration, not only with Communists, but with the Mafia and Freemasonry, particularly Italy's "P-2 Masonry."

The "P" stands for Propaganda, the name of an Eighteenth Century masonic lodge. P-2 is often described as a conservative, anti-Communist branch of Freemasonry, a covert group of retired Italian military officials, wealthy businessmen, Italian bishops and other Vatican dignitaries. Lists of prelates who are supposedly members of P-2 or other branches of Masonry routinely show up in the Italian press. So do allegations that P-2 collaborates (in Italy and on an international level) with the Mafia, the CIA, and even Opus Dei. The common enemy, supposedly, is Communism. The common interest is murkier. Like other secret societies, it is difficult to know with certainty who belongs to P-2 or why.

The allegiances of Italy's Christian Democrat party straddled P-2 Masonry and Communism. The party's leader, Aldo Moro, was a long-time friend of Pope Montini. The two had organized anti-fascist protests during Mussolini's rule. In March of 1978 Aldo Moro was kidnapped by the Red Brigades, a Communist terrorist group who murdered the five men they found Moro with.

Moro was seized after having "taken the historic step of bringing the Communists into the Parliamentary Alliance to support a Christian Democratic government," according to investigative journalists Gordon Thomas and Max Morgan Witts.[25] Within the triangle of Communism, Christian Democracy, and P-2 Masonry (and its affiliates), it wasn't always clear who was betraying who. It was known that neither the Communists nor P-2 were happy with Moro. Predictably, the Red Brigades declared they would subject Moro and the Christian Democrat party to a Communist show-trial. Less obviously, the complete lack of progress or motivation in the police investigation of Moro's kidnapping suggested the influence of P-2.

Paul was in anguish during Moro's fifty-five-day imprisonment. Near the end, in late April, he wrote a highly-publicized letter to Moro's captors:

> "... on my knees I beg you, free Aldo Moro, simply, without conditions, not so much because of my humble and well-meaning intercession, but because he shares with you the common dignity of a brother in humanity, and because I would dare to hope that in conscience you would not want the cause of true social progress to be stained with innocent blood ...

> "Men of the Red Brigades, leave me, the interpreter of the voices of so many of our fellow-citizens, the hope that in your hearts, feelings of humanity will triumph ..."[26]

A few days later Moro's captors shot "a circle of bullets around his heart, which left him twenty minutes to drown in his own blood."[27] On May 9 his corpse was discovered in the trunk of a car. Paul could not believe the news. When it finally sunk in he was devastated. So were Moro's family, who accused the Christian Democrats of collaborating with the Communists to murder Moro. The confusion continued at Moro's funeral, where, according to at least one account, Paul publicly rebuked God for allowing Moro's death.[28] He left Rome in July 1978, and never returned there alive.

His plans were to rest at Castel Gandolfo, then visit for the first time the Holy Shroud in Turin, in September. On August 6, 1978, Paul assisted at Mass for the feast of the Transfiguration. He received Communion lying in bed. As the Mass ended he suffered a massive heart attack. "It is as though he had exploded from within," wrote Hebblethwaite.[29] He died hours later. There was no death agony, no last words. His last writing was in preparation for an Angelus he never recited. The final sentence read, "an incomparable destiny awaits those who have honored their Christian vocation."[30]

It was thought by many that Moro's death — and the manner of his death — killed Paul. It is hard to imagine an event more shocking to the preconceptions of the humanistic man of the left that Pope Montini was, or more likely to trigger soul searching in the man who helped found the Christian Democrat party in Italy. As a student Moro had been shaped by Montini. As an influential member of the Christian Democrats, he availed himself of the "opening to the left" to collaborate with Communists. This strategy was as close as the Christian left came to observing tradition; the "fathers" of this tradition, however, were Lammenais, Sangnier, and Maritain.

Alas for Moro, who in attempting to follow in the footsteps of the masters, not only failed to forge utopia but was murdered by his colleagues the Communists. The object lesson for Pope Montini was obvious enough. Like his encounter with Sister Lucy at Fatima, Moro's murder was one of those defining moments in the life of Giovanni Battista Montini. It was, perhaps, his last opportunity to examine his conscience, and to reach for grace.

It appears, however, that Pope Montini's heart gave out before he had a change of heart — about anything.

Who Was Pope Paul?

He died in the same bed as Pius XII. Unlike Pius, whose death was determined by a stethoscope, the death of Paul VI was determined by the more traditional silver hammer applied to the forehead. He is known best as "the Pope who banned the Pill", a reference to his encyclical *Humanae Vitae*, which repeated Church teaching that artificial contraception is immoral.

It is curious that this encyclical, and Paul, its reputed author, are thought "prophetic" for merely repeating Church teaching. In fact, Paul uttered many real prophecies throughout his pontificate. Unfortunately, he was invariably wrong, although his accuracy rose during the occasional lapses into his "prophet of doom" persona. The real achievement of his pontificate was that for seventeen long years he relentlessly implemented the gnosis of Vatican II, particularly the *Novus Ordo Missae*, on a Church that was flying apart due to the very reforms initiated by the Council. Events would have turned out far differently with any other Pope, and despite their criticisms of Paul, progressives know this.

Regarding Fatima, it is safe to say that Paul did not believe a word of it, and acted accordingly. He accepted the thesis of his close friend and arch-foe of Fatima, Father Edouard Dhanis, that Fatima was a simple message of prayer and penance. That this was undoubtedly true — on one level — added strength to the anti-Fatima campaign. So did Pope Paul's discreet and determined opposition, which surfaced in subtle ways during his 1967 visit — it was not a pilgrimage because he did not believe — to Fatima.

Those who have watched film of the Pope at Fatima claim he did not pray one Hail Mary.[31] He did not reveal the Third Secret either, or refer to the apparitions in any substantial way. His sermon was an impassioned hymn to the glory of man. Curiously, the Pope who so loved his fellow human beings demanded Lucy come to Fatima against her will, then refused to grant her the courtesy of an audience.

"I wish to speak with you alone," she told him again and again, words of grace splashing against a stone, against the rock of the papacy. Why did Pope Montini really want Lucy to come to Fatima? Was it merely for the sake of appearances? Or did the Pope wish to discretely scorn both her and Those she spoke for?

Perhaps that is too harsh, for it is certainly possible that the insistence on Lucy's attendance came not from Paul but from the Holy Ghost, who willed that Christ's Vicar on earth be afforded a chance at grace. Ever the model of discreet and determined opposition, Pope Montini refused the opening Sister Lucy presented to him. Had he not in fact already chosen his god, and very publicly so, at the close of the Second Vatican Council? It was there that Pope Paul VI declared:

> "The Church of the Council, it is true ... is much occupied with man, Man as in reality he presents himself to our era, the living Man, Man entirely occupied with himself, Man who makes himself not only the center of all that interests him, but who dares pretend to be the beginning and the ultimate reason of all reality. The whole phenomenon of Man, i.e. with the trappings of his innumerable appearances, is clothed standing before the assembly of the Council Fathers ...

> "Humanism, profane and worldly, finally has appeared in its

terrible stature and has, in a certain sense, defied the Council. The religion of God-made-man meets the religion (for such it is) of man-made-God. What has happened? A clash? A fight? An anathema? That could happen, but it didn't. The old story of the Samaritan has been the model for the spirituality of the Council. A sympathy without limits has completely overwhelmed it ... At least acknowledge this merit, you, modern humanists, who renounce the transcendence of higher things, and know how to recognize our humanism; we too have, more than anyone else, the cult of man."[32]

The analogy of the Samaritan is a false one that seeks to elicit even more "unlimited sympathy" for those "modern humanists", whom Paul depicts beaten, robbed, and forsaken on the road of life. In fact, the Twentieth Century has featured again and again the "religion of man who makes himself God" beating, robbing and forsaking the Church and Christians. The Pope was nothing if not consistent, however, for after the Council his sympathy for modern humanists appeared to remain unlimited. Paul's sympathy for orthodox Catholics, on the other hand, was at times quite limited.

For instance, in 1970 Paul told journalists, "We have confidence in man; we believe in this depth of goodness in every heart. We know the motives of justice, of truth, of renewal, of progress, of brotherhood, which are at the origin of so many fine initiatives and in so many disputes up to now, and unhappily, sometimes of violence."[33]

Remarkably enough, Paul may have been referring to Communism here, which Pius XI called "intrinsically perverse". Regarding "progress", "brotherhood", and "fine initiatives", in 1958 — only five years before Paul was elected — Pius XII said, "Today the Enemy of God has seized all the levers of command. We must raise ourselves and stand up against corruption and the corrupters."[34]

The closest Paul VI came to issuing an anathema was in 1966, when he publicly chastised the small group of confused and dismayed "traditionalist" Catholics: "Woe to those who remain aloof (from conciliar reforms), woe to those who are sad, to those who are indifferent and discontent; woe to those who lag behind!"[35]

This "strange sounding curse" belies the image (created by conservatives and progressives) of Paul as a conservative, or even a moderate. His "unlimited sympathy" for the traditional enemies of the Church was matched by his intolerance for "integrists". What woe did Pope Montini envision for those who were wary of the foul winds blowing through the Church's open windows? Were his words a charitable correction, or a hostile rebuke? Who was he speaking for? The saints? Heaven? If not them, then whom?

Montini was a man of the left who spent much of his career as a bureaucrat in the Secretariat of State. It was unusual that such a person would ascend to pro-Secretary of State under Pope Pius XII. From that position Msgr. Montini displayed considerable talent as a diplomat and deal maker. He also undermined Pius XII behind his back by maintaining forbidden communications with Soviet Russia, and using his position to give aid to theologians of dubious orthodoxy, and socialists.

Pius XII found out, and exiled Montini to Milan, emphasizing his displeasure by refusing to make him a Cardinal. It is extremely unusual that a man who has betrayed the Pope, and incurred that Pope's obvious displeasure, should be seen as such a desirable candidate for the papacy that Cardinal Roncalli was elected primarily to make Montini a Cardinal, so that Cardinal Montini could succeed him. What was it that made Montini such hot property?

His stock continued to rise when he drafted Pope John's speech that opened the Council. Cardinal Montini was given private quarters in the Vatican, a unique distinction that allowed him to consult continually with Pope John.[36] The transition from John to Paul was as seamless as a smooth baton exchange in a relay race. It almost seemed John had called the Council for Montini to manage.

As Pope of the Council, Montini's talent rested in appearing to be the moderator between conservatives and progressives while in reality giving away the store to the progressives. Not that it was all artfulness. Formerly a man of the left, and now a Pope of the left, it was only natural that Montini would honor his tendencies. He did so in a way that kept the conservatives signing documents, without affording them footholds for reaction.

Yet Paul VI probably does not deserve all the credit (or blame) for the lack of effective reaction by Council conservatives during and after the Council. There may be other reasons, like the Third Secret of Fatima. Indeed, does not the fact that traditional Catholicism was in a minority at the Council speak volumes on the state of the Church in the 1960's? Was this one of the signs that would make the Third Secret "clearer", to quote Sister Lucy?

The pattern Paul set at the Council, appearing as a moderator while in reality favoring the progressives, intensified during his pontificate. The stunning, disturbing symbolic acts he indulged in; the license he gave heresies in doctrine and novelties in liturgy; his attempt to completely suppress the Mass in favor of a liturgy written to encourage inter-faith worship — a liturgy that actually looks "conservative" today, at least when compared to the innovations and bad translations that encrust the *Novus Ordo Missae* like barnacles on a sunken ship — the wearing around his neck of a jewel that was an exact reproduction of the Ephod of the High Priest of Judaism; these and scores of other aberrations only make sense if they were performed by someone who had either lost his faith, apostasized, or was suffering from a "diabolical disorientation".

Why else would one address the United Nations as "the last hope for peace and concord", or as "the world's greatest hope for it is the reflection of God's design, a design transcendent and full of love"? Why else would one attend a session of the World Council of Churches (WCC) and engage in common prayer? Why would one chant:

> "Honor to man; honor to his thought; honor to his scientific knowledge; honor to his technical skill; honor to his work ... (etc.) ... honor to Man, king of the earth and today, prince of the heavens ..."[37]

Was Pope Paul VI an apostate? He certainly talked and acted like one, at times. Yet one could also catalogue a series of orthodox statements and acts by Pope Montini. Some were performed sincerely, others with mixed motives, still others from dry duty or necessity; yet one could say this about other popes. What sets Paul VI (and the other conciliar popes) apart from all other popes is the papal vision, the breathtaking panorama of universal brotherhood and world peace, the engine of which is a universal (catholic) religion that finally gives man his due, that finally recognizes the glory of man, a religion modern man can accept rather than fight against, a religion that used to be called Catholicism ... Oh, the popes who achieve this heaven on earth would truly be glorious!

It is all delirium; or, if you please, diabolical disorientation. The papal vision is the dream of Freemasonry and the "curse" of Fatima on an incredulous world and a stiff-necked papacy. Is it also the Third Secret coming true before our very eyes?

NOTES

1. Jacques Maritain, *The Peasant of the Garonne*, Holt, Rinehart and Winston, 1968, p. 57. Emphasis in the original.
2. As quoted in Siri, *Gethsemane,* op. cit., pp. 50-51.The modernism Paul was condemning was probably the extremism of Hans Kung who, like Joseph Ratzinger, was a student of Karl Rahner. The difference between Ratzinger and Kung was one of degree; Kung followed Rahner's thought to its logical, faith dissolving consequences. In so doing he has become a (at times convenient) scapegoat for the more "moderate" neo-modernists, like Ratzinger and Pope Wojtyla.
3. As quoted in *Si Si No No*, April 1994, p. 23.
4. Ibid., p. 17.
5. Amerio, op. cit., p. 257. This comment was prompted by Amerio's knowledge of an incident after Vatican II, where the French bishops included Karl Marx into a Sunday Mass booklet.
6. FIJWE, op. cit., pp. 33-34.
7. As quoted in TWTAF, Volume III, op. cit., pp. 750-751.
8. Ibid., pp. 752.
9. Ibid., pp. 752-753.
10. Ibid., pp. 752-758.
11. Ibid.
12. FIJWE, op. cit., pp. 272-273.
13. Discourse of December, 1968, as quoted in ibid., pp. 272-273.
14. Discourse of December 3, 1969, as quoted in ibid, pp. 272-273.
15. Discourse of June 29, 1972, as quoted in ibid., pp. 272-273.
16. CRC Journal No. 304, December 2997, p. 7.
17. As quoted in *Liber Accusationis in Paulum Sextum*, op. cit., p. 60. Comments the Abbe de Nantes, "It seemed, for one moment, as though the Church of Silence was going to disturb the silence of the Church."
18. Memoirs, op. cit., pp. 236-238, 242, 244-246, 335.
19. Ibid.

20. After announcing Mindszenty's "abdication," the Vatican lifted his excommunication of "peace priests," Hungary's version of French "worker priests," that is, Communists or Communist sympathizers who were also priests.

21. Memoirs, p. 242. Deleted was this paragraph: "The East (Communist governments) proclaims that there even the worst atheists have become gentle lambs. Do not believe it! You shall know the tree by its fruits. It is possible that in the East there are more churchgoers than in many a Western country, but that is not to the credit of the regimes, there, but of those Christians who manage to walk bowed down by the weight of the cross."

22. Carroll, op. cit., pp. 494-500. As usual, the Communists had formed a coalition of left wing groups to aid their rise to power. According to a Portuguese on the scene, one Alfonso Castelo, Communist allies consisted of the liberals, the democrats and non-communist socialists, the anarchists, Christian Democrats, Opus-Deists and the rest of the tribe..." Later, a similar "tribe" would constitute the Polish "trade union," Solidarity.

23. Ibid.

24. Ibid.

25. Gordon Thomas and Max Morgan-Witts, *Pontiff,* Doubleday and Company, 1983, p. 25.

26. Hebblethwaite, *Paul VI,* op. cit., p. 702-703.

27. Gordon and Morgan-Witts, op. cit.

28. This is at least Peter Hebblethwaite's version of events. See Hebblethwaite, *Paul VI,* op. cit., p. 706. Hebblethwaite doesn't quote Paul, but says Paul "upbraided" God for allowing this appalling deed to happen."

29. Ibid., p. 710

30. Ibid.

31. I.e., the Abbe de Nantes.

32. As quoted in Le Roux, op. cit., pp. 13-14.

33. Ibid., p. 16.

34. Ibid. It is likely the Holy Father was *not* referring to the papacy as one of the levers of command.

35. *Liber Accusationis in Paulum Sextum,* op. cit., p. 38. It was the Abbé de Nantes who termed it "strange sounding curses."

36. It is Father Francis X. Murphy (pen name "Xavier Rynne") who states that Cardinal Montini stayed at the Vatican during the Council. See James F. Andrews, Editor, *Paul VI: Critical Appraraisals,* The Bruce Publishing Company, 1970, p. 141.

37. The source for this quote, for Paul wearing the ephod, and Paul's quote at the U.N., is *Liber Accusationis in Paulum Sextum,* op. cit., pp. 12, 16, 63.

Chapter Seventeen

The Consecrations of Pope John Paul II

Much ink has been spilled over one of the shortest pontificates in the history of the Church, the thirty-three day reign of Pope John Paul I, Albino Luciani, the former Cardinal of Venice.

He has been embraced by traditionalists as a martyr-pope — even though he chose a name combining the two popes responsible for the not-quite-traditional Second Vatican Council. He has been hailed as a ramrod of orthodoxy — even though he urged Pope Paul VI to erase the Church's ban on artificial contraception. Incidentally, by way of response Paul visited Venice and, amidst the cheers of onlookers, gave Luciani his papal stole as a gift.[1] It was another of those very symbolic public gestures Paul liked to make; it also seemed he liked giving things away — especially things that didn't belong to him.

Anyway, Paul's gesture was a clear enough signal that Luciani had, at the very least, the approval of a Pope who was steadily and surely squeezing the last pockets of traditionalism out onto the very margins of Catholicism. As Paul would not have given his papal stole to a "pre-conciliar" Cardinal, neither would a conclave of Cardinals picked by Pope John and Pope Paul have so quickly elected Luciani unless they were satisfied he would follow the post-conciliar script.

Moreover, Luciani's speedy election was subject to a new rule enacted by Paul VI that barred Cardinals over 80 years of age from having a vote. This seemed to be added insurance against the election of a "pre-conciliar" pontiff. Did Luciani fool everybody? Was he really a traditionalist mole? He didn't live long enough to answer the question, and people have been guessing at his true colors ever since. Part of the fascination stems from his unusual death.

The official cause, heart failure, was disputed by Luciani's family, and the evidence. The Vatican press office didn't help matters by issuing conflicting reports about the death scene and the medical evidence. Adding to the confusion was the regrettable fact that members of the dead Pope's entourage actually tampered with evidence at the death scene. Also unusual was the rush to embalm the Pope's body — it was done just hours after his death. In spite of the loud clamor for an autopsy, one was never performed; or if it was, it was done secretly and the results were never publicized.

What made things even more curious is that the Vatican had some experience dealing with heart attack victims; Pope Paul's death by heart failure two months previously was remarkably uncontroversial. Part of the controversy over John Paul I's death was that the physical evidence, although subtle, tended to indicate poisoning as the cause of death. This was not, and probably never will be, proven. (The point to the controversy over the quick embalming is that this made it almost impossible for an autopsy to detect poison).

Who would have wanted to poison Luciani, and why, has fueled several books and countless conspiracy theories on the left and the right. Did John Paul I really intend to overturn *Humanae Vitae*? Was he really going to expose the Vatican banking scandal and implicate the financial conglomerates of P-2 Masonry and Opus Dei? Or was he murdered for planning to consecrate Russia to the Immaculate Heart of Mary?[2] In 1977, the year before his death, Cardinal Luciani visited Sister Lucy at the Carmelite convent in Coimbra, Portugal. (At the time Cardinals were able to visit Lucy without requiring permission from Rome.) They spoke together, alone, in Portuguese, for almost two hours. He left the meeting impressed by Sister Lucy, and shaken by her words. After becoming Pope he spoke as if Sister Lucy had predicted his election:

> "It is most incredible, and yet Sister Lucia's prediction proved to be true. I am here. I am Pope. If I live, I shall return to Fatima to consecrate the world and the peoples of Russia in particular, to the Blessed Virgin in accordance with the indications She gave to Sister Lucia."[3]

It is not known whether Lucy told Luciani the Third Secret, or whether he read it during his short pontificate. As Pope he indicated several times that he didn't think he would live long. He was right.

"The Outsider"

John Paul's successor was Paul VI's "other favorite", Polish prelate Karol Wojtyla. The first non-Italian Pope in centuries dubbed himself "a man from a far country". After Paul's miserable last years, an "outsider" like Pope Wojtyla seemed a healthy change. In reality, however, few Churchmen were as "inside" as Wojtyla.

He was first noticed at Vatican II, where he argued against condemning Communism, and for that matter, atheism. "It is not the Church's role to lecture unbelievers," Archbishop Wojtyla lectured the Council Fathers. "We are engaged in a search with our fellow men ... let us avoid moralizing or the suggestion that we have a monopoly on the truth."

In fact for nearly two thousand years the Church taught that She did have a monopoly on the truth — and She had often taught this without "lecturing". According to his biographer Jonathan Kwitny, "Wojtyla put himself squarely on the side of the 'reformers' (sic) at the Council. The men he singled out for praise were mostly supporters of major change, among them Hans Küng ..."⁴ Wojtyla also adopted the "People of God" rhetoric used by Council progressives to "democratize" the Church. This exhausted the patience of Polish Primate Wyszynski, who expressed his disgust directly when he was alone with Wojtya and the Polish bishops.⁵ At the end of the Council, however, Wyszynski's request to delay implementing liturgical changes in Poland was denied by Paul VI; and when Paul personally insisted that Archbishop Wojtyla remain in Rome after the Council, it was clear that a star had been born.

Paul talked to Wojtyla about the birth control commission set up by Pope John to study the merits of artificial contraception (i.e., "the Pill"), and about Wojtyla's book on sexual ethics, *Love and Responsibility*.⁶ At the end of the conversation Paul asked the Archbishop to join the commission, and Wojtyla assented. In 1967 he became, at age forty-seven, the second youngest Cardinal in the world. The next year *Humanae Vitae* was issued, and Cardinal Wojtyla, one of its principal drafters, was its staunchest defender.

The issuance of *Humanae Vitae* triggered a collaboration between the world and much of the Church according to the prescriptions of Vatican II (and Jacques Maritain). Unfortunately, the purpose of the collaboration was to publicly ridicule Church teaching, and to berate and humiliate Paul. Given the circumstances, Pope Montini was understandably grateful for Wojtyla's support. "This episode bound Paul VI yet more closely to Cardinal Wojtyla, whom he regularly entertained in private audiences," write John Paul's biographers Bernstein and Politi. "Between 1973 and 1975 alone, the Archbishop of Cracow entered the Pope's study for private audiences eleven times."⁷ Some outsider.

In 1971 Wojtyla convoked a diocesan synod in Cracow to implement the Council, and wrote a book, *The Second Vatican Council and the Work of Theologians*. According to the Cardinal, the work of the theologians was, first, to recognize that the fundamental aspects of the Council were ecumenism and inter-religious dialogue; and next, to facilitate the "Adaptation of the pre-conciliar Church to the conciliar Church, and the conciliar Church to the modern world." The Cardinal, a professor of existential philosophy, saw this process not as a change of religions ("new ecclesiology"), and most certainly not as an apostasy, but as an evolutionary transformation through different "stages of consciousness".⁸

In 1974 Cardinal Wojtyla received the honor of heading the Bishops Synod in Rome. In 1976 Paul asked Wojtyla to give a Lenten retreat at the Vatican, for himself and the Curia. Retreat master Wojtyla's lectures, later published in a book, *Sign of Contradiction*, relied heavily on his interpretations of a few passages from conciliar documents he had helped draft (*Gaudium et spes* and *Lumen Gentium*). The lectures are dense and rather veiled, clothed as they are in the "pastoral language" of the Council. Everyone, including Pope Paul, was suitably impressed.

It may have been around this time that Paul decorated the chapel of the papal summer residence at Castel Gandolfo with a large painting depicting the Swedish army's Seventeenth Century siege of the Polish monastary at Czestochowa. "It will serve my successor," Paul is said to have remarked.[9] So while he was "from a far country," Wojtyla was one of the elite few who quickly advanced up the post-conciliar ladder, was regularly consulted by Pope Paul, and just as regularly bestowed with papal favors. It is unlikely Cardinal Wojtyla received these numerous benefits because he advocated the restoration of traditional Catholicism.

The Pope and Communism

If there were any doubts on this point, Pope Wojtyla's first encyclical (*Redemptor Hominis*) made it clear he intended to continue the "work of the Second Vatican Council and my great predecessors, who set in motion this new surge of life for the Church, a movement that is much stronger than the symptoms of doubt, collapse, and crisis."[10]

The "surge of life" Vatican II "set in motion" often appeared more like an axe hewing at the root of the Catholic faith. The Council coincided with a massive loss of faith among clergy and lay that statistics corroborated, but barely began to explain. In Italy in the early 1980's, for instance, only 20 per cent of Catholics went to weekly Mass, and 405 out of every 1,000 babies in this predominantly Catholic country were killed by abortions, the second highest rate in Europe (Denmark was first).[11]

If Vatican II can not directly be blamed for the massive apostasy that coincided with it, then at the very least it could be said that not only was the post-conciliar Church utterly ineffective at combating the apostasy, it seemed at times to be encouraging it. As early as 1969, even the protege of Karl Rahner, Council *peritus* and progressive theologian Joseph Ratzinger, noted that:

> "... the Church of modern times has ... become, and will continue to become still more, the Church of pagans: no longer the Church of pagans who have become Christians, as She used to be, but the Church of pagans who still call themselves Christians. Paganism is at home today in the Church ..."[12]

Ratzinger would prove expert at making a diagnosis, and incapable of providing a real remedy. At times Pope John Paul II was also able to make a realistic assessment of the state of the Church, like his admission that "doubt, collapse, and crisis" were "symptoms" of Vatican II. Most of *Redemptor Hominis*, however, was equal doses of wishful thinking and cryptic neo-modernism, modestly veiled by "pastoral language" and conveyed through traditional religious terms that, after Vatican II, now admitted more than one definition. *Redemptor Hominis* made Pope Wojtyla seem an unlikely candidate for orthodox Catholics to pin their restoration hopes on.

Early on John Paul II rejected requests to consecrate Russia to the Immaculate Heart. A month after becoming Pope he was petitioned to consecrate Russia to the Immaculate Heart. The following year a "high ranking Roman prelate" handed John Paul a book by Father Alonso on Fatima. "I do not wish to hear about that," John Paul replied. "I am well-informed on the matter. I know what I have to do."[13] In 1980 he told a bishop that the consecration "would be considered by the Russians to be meddling in their internal affairs, and it would have political consequences."[14] The Pope then made light of the issue, jokingly inviting the bishop to "Go, win over for me all the bishops of the world to the idea of this consecration, and I will do it with them."[15] It did not seem a serious invitation.[16]

Having spent much of his life under Communist rule, it was difficult to gainsay the Pope when he continued Paul VI's policy of dealing with Soviet Russia diplomatically, even when he chose as his Secretary of State Cardinal Agostino Casaroli, of whom graffiti on walls near the Vatican proclaimed, "Excommunicate Casaroli, the Red Excellency of Compromise."[17]

Although John Paul proved more outspoken against Communism than John XXIII and Paul VI, his opposition to Communism (before and after becoming Pope) stemmed from its inability to appreciate man's dignity as fully as Christianity. This was a long way from Pius XI's condemnation of Communism as "intrinsically perverse." John Paul appeared unfamiliar with most of Pius XI's teaching; not just on Communism, but on marriage (*Casti Connubi*) and the incompatibility of Christianity and Socialism (*Quas Primas*) as well. Professor Wojtyla would tell his students, "Socialism isn't against the Church's teaching."[18] Well, it was, once.

Not all religious in the "Silent Church" in Communist occupied eastern Europe were anti-Masonic saints like Fr. Kolbe, or martyrs like Mindszenty, Stepinac, and the hundreds of Polish clergy who were murdered or exiled for refusing to "peacefully co-exist" with their new, secular masters. After the Allies gave Poland to Stalin at the end of World War II, Communists quickly took advantage of "peaceful co-existence" to infiltrate the Church and Polish culture. Polish intellectual Jozef Tischner observed:

> "Marxism in Poland ... became the essence of popular social consciousness ... Marxism was in the school textbooks, in newspapers, on radio and television, in the high schools, the universities ... Can one wander in a fog and avoid getting soggy? Everyone got a bit soggy — some more, others less; some willingly, others unwillingly. The various socialist dogmas kept seeping into one's soul ..."[19]

Tischner continues, "Marxism radiated. It radiated the hope of building a world more just than the world of yesterday ... Marxism could sink into the social consciousness like a warm knife into butter." Aside from orthodox Catholics (who were disposed of if they were too outspoken), the main opposition to Marxism was Polish Catholic humanism, which according to Tischner, was supplemented by the transplanting "onto Polish soil (of) Maritain's ideas of 'integral humanism' and the personalism of the school of Emmanuel Mounier." Tischner concludes that "his (Maritain's) 'integral humanism' became the basis of a Catholic dialogue with other currents of thought, among them Marxism."[20]

What Polish Catholics (including Wojtyla — and Wyszynski) and Marxists ended up wrestling over was not the divinity and rights of Christ the King, but "the concept of the person and an ideal of the rights of a person." This dialogue was applauded by the Polish socialist Kuczynski, who enthused:

> "something great is happening in Polish Catholicism ... And now it is our (Catholics and socialists) duty to the country to transform this theoretical meeting of the two humanisms ... into a great, creative sociocultural force. Let each humanism confirm its anthropological and historical theses in a practical, constructive rivalry for the common good of society, for building a truly humanistic society."[21]

Other eastern European countries responded to Communism by vigorously asserting their Catholicism. The Church led the way, which is why Cardinals Mindszenty and Stepinac were martyred. Poland took a different tack. In addition to emphasizing the rights of man, Poland, led by Cardinal Wyszynski (a self-professed "sociologist"), agreed to support Poland's new Communist government. This policy, viewed with great suspicion by Pius XII (and others), became known as the "Warsaw heresy". Suffering by comparison to Mindszenty and Stepinac, Wyszynski was accused of selling out the Church to the Communists. John XXIII and Paul VI, on the other hand, approved of the "peaceful co-existence" between the Church and government in Poland, and the humanistic dialogue between the two.

To question Wyszynski's strategy does not negate his courage, craftiness, and stamina in fighting the Communists, who routinely double-crossed the Primate, even imprisoning him for a short time. Had the Communists really wanted Wyszynski permanently removed, however, this would have been accomplished with dispatch. Instead, confusion was sown. Communist disinformation painted Wyszynski as an incorrigible reactionary, which made him a hero among western Christians, who compounded this mistake by confusing Wyszynski's nationalism for orthodoxy. In fact, it was Wyszynski's nationalism that caused him to make many religious concessions to the Communists in order to keep peace, and to protect Poland. Consequently the Church in Poland was honeycombed with infiltrators and subverters. "The teaching of Marxist doctrines was introduced in the senior seminaries of Wroclaw and Poznan," according to Albert Galter, author of *The Red Book of the Persecuted Church*. "In all the other seminaries Communist infiltration in the formation of clerics is an established fact."[22]

One of the consequences of Communist infiltration was that it became difficult to know who to trust. For years Wyszynski did not trust Bishop Wojtyla, calling him at one point "an opportunist." Part of his mistrust came from the fact that Wojtyla's friendships were primarily with progressives and socialists. He continued writing for *Tygodnik Powszechny*, even after it was taken over by "the editing house Pax, which the Communist government had handed over to the 'progressive Catholics.'"[23] In fact the 1958 appointment of Wojtyla as bishop was done behind Wyszinski's back.[24] Later, he fought against Wojtyla becoming a Cardinal, but Paul VI won that battle. Wyszynski knew that Wojtyla, while not overtly political, was philosophically a man of the left. He was also a member of *Znak* ("Sign"), a progressive Catholic publication (and movement) that tended to espouse liberal and socialist views. The *Znak* newspaper, to which Wojtyla was a contributing writer, often made Poland's primate grind his teeth.[25]

Yet *Znak* appeared centrist when compared to Pax, the Communist-operated publishing house for "progressive Catholic intellectuals". Pax leader and self-professed Catholic Boleslaw Piasecki spouted the Communist Party's line that Poland was destined by God to be the model for co-existence between Communism and the Church (a view shared by Pope John and Pope Paul), and also claimed:

> "In order that Poland may serve as a model, it is essential that Polish Catholicism becomes progressive as quickly as possible and collaborates increasingly actively in the construction of socialist economy. That is the daily task of our progressive movement."[26]

The 'pre-Conciliar' *L'Osservatore Romano* addressed the claims of Pax incisively:

> "According to a very widespread opinion, the possibility of 'co-existence' between Catholicism and Communism will be tested in Poland. To attain this end recourse is had to self-styled 'progressive' Catholics who are furnished with ample means for both domestic and foreign propaganda.

> "Moscow needs an apparent 'reconciliation' with Polish Catholicism, not for the purpose of consolidating its position in that nation which was made part of its sphere of influence at Yalta and Potsdam, *but to exert a disintegrating influence on the forces of Catholicism, which in countries still free act as a barrier to Communism.*

"In Poland the persecution has assumed a particularly insidious guise. *An effort is being made to despoil Catholicism of its effective content in such a way that seen from the outside it will still
appear unchanged. Even now an impossible Christian-Marxist
syncretism destructive of all true spirituality is being subtly introduced within the framework of Catholicism.*"[27]

Although Wyszynski rightly denounced Pax and their "patriot
priests", his policy of co-existence and, at times, actual support of the
Communist government, strengthened Pax. Moreover, like Wojtyla,
Wyszynski did not use his spiritual authority to condemn Communism,
disdaining the supernatural battlefield in favor of a naturalistic debate
as to whether Communism or Christianity better served mankind.

His unchosen understudy, Bishop Wojtyla, had an intimate view of
the struggle between Church and State in Poland. It was not surprising
then, that on becoming Pope, John Paul II would expand Wyszynski's
strategy to every point of conflict between Communism and Catholicism
in the world. One of Pope Wojtyla's premises was that Communism was
reformable, that it could evolve into something beneficial to mankind.
The issue with this opinion is whether it is a legitimate product of
Wojtyla's Catholic experience, or the product of the insidious Marx-
ist-Christian syncretism of Communist Poland warned of by
L'Osservatore Romano.

The left was far from displeased at Wojtyla's ascension to the papacy.
The earlier quoted socialist, Kuczynski, wrote that "the election (as
Pope) of a citizen (Wojtyla) of a socialist country (Poland)" continued
"above all, the leveling of the church (sic) and its opening to history that,
especially since Vatican Council II, has been taking place behind the
'Bronze Gate'"[28] (the formal entrance to Vatican City).

This is the context in which John Paul approached the problem of
Communism. The "Polish problem" was the primary focus of the first
decade of his pontificate. His behind-the-scenes diplomacy with the Polish government and the Solidarity movement is credited with breaking
the Soviet rule over Poland. Later, John Paul appeared to be the only
world figure capable of matching wits with Mikhail Gorbachev in the
high-stakes game of geopolitics. When the Soviet Union appeared to give
up the ghost, the world rejoiced. Had Russia been converted? Had
Fatima, already in twilight, been rendered obsolete by the contrary
events of history?

The Pope and Fatima

These questions began to be answered on May 13, 1981, the anniversary of the first apparition at Cova da Iria, when, while greeting thousands of well-wishers in St. Peter's Square, Pope John Paul was shot
and seriously wounded by Turkish assassin Ali Agca.

Initially Agca's act appeared related to a threat he made against the

Holy Father in 1979. Learning that John Paul was planning a visit to Turkey, Agca wrote "Western imperialism has ... dispatched to Turkey in the guise of a religious leader, the Crusade commander John Paul. Unless this untimely and meaningless visit is postponed, I shall certainly shoot the Pope."[29] Agca penned his threat shortly after having been smuggled out of jail, where he had been placed for killing a progressive Turkish editor — an editor of the same newspaper that published Agca's letter against the Pope.[30]

He was, in short, a classic Islamic terrorist who resented Western culture, saw the West and Western Christianity as decadent allies of Israel and enemies of Islam, and believed violence was an appropriate remedy for these problems. It is likely that these passions, coupled with an apparent mental imbalance, caused Agca to attempt to kill Pope John Paul II.

Later, Agca's connections with the Bulgarian secret service were discovered. It was commonly known that the Bulgarian secret service took its orders from the Soviet KGB. It was assumed that Soviet Russia was angry and alarmed not only at the election of Pope John Paul II, but at his criticisms of eastern European Communism, and the enthusiasm these criticisms created in Poles. Thus the theory that Russian Communists had used Agca as their agent in the attempted assassination of John Paul II became popular, and is generally believed today, at least by people who follow events like this.

The logical appeal of this theory for Catholics is obvious. The good Pope John Paul II, the bad Communists, the intervention of the Blessed Virgin (John Paul credited Her with saving his life), the Pope's grateful pilgrimage to Fatima to consecrate Russia to the Immaculate Heart, and then, the Communist withdrawal from eastern Europe. Yes, things should happen this way when God is in His Heaven. How encouraging it is to believe that the predictions of the Blessed Virgin: "the Holy Father will consecrate Russia to Me" and finally, "My Immaculate Heart will triumph", had indeed come to pass.

In spite of all this, it can be said with some certainty that Soviet Russia was not involved in Agca's assassination attempt. The authority for this is former KGB agent Anatoliy Golitsyn, who defected to the United States and has been exposing Communist disinformation plans ever since. Golitsyn, whose predictions on Soviet policy have proven remarkably accurate, has several reasons why Russia probably did not try to assassinate John Paul II. For example, the KGB generally didn't entrust high profile assassinations to religiously passionate, mentally unstable terrorists like Agca. The KGB preferred more discreet, less sensational methods, like lethal poisons that were almost impossible to detect, making it appear that the victim died of natural causes. The poisons were generally introduced to the victim via meals, or even body contact.

Golitsyn claims Agca's assassination attempt doesn't fit Soviet assassination policy, or method. Moreover, he quietly questions the assumption that Soviet Russia was angry or alarmed over Pope Wojtyla's activities in Poland. For if this were true, why would they allow John Paul repeated visits to Poland? (By contrast, in spite of his requests, Paul VI was not allowed even one visit in his pontificate of fifteen years).[31]

A plausible reply is that this may have been a calculated risk the Soviets took to avoid the danger of inflaming the Polish nation by not allowing her favorite son a visa. Yet this does not explain why Karol Wojtyla was so frequently allowed what appeared to be unrestricted travel around the world before becoming Pope, a privilege not enjoyed by any other Polish bishop. The logical inference is that Soviet Russia derived some benefit from the special policy they applied to Karol Wojtyla. It is entirely possible that this benefit was derived without Wojtyla's knowledge.

The philosophical and theological views of Bishop Wojtyla did not change when he became Pope John Paul II. Neither did Soviet Russia's policy: they afforded Pope Wojtyla the same easy access into and out of Poland that they afforded Bishop Wojtyla. These facts seem to contradict the theory that the KGB hired Agca to assassinate Pope John Paul II.

Is it possible the Soviets also derived a benefit from being thought to oppose Pope Wojtyla strongly enough to attempt to murder him? This impression would make the "surprising" influence of the Communist-infiltrated trade union, Solidarity, and John Paul II's continual interventions in Polish politics, appear to be opponents of Soviet Russia's long-term plans for eastern Europe, instead of (probably unintentional) facilitators of Soviet plans.

It is impossible to be dogmatic about any of this, due to what Golitsyn calls Soviet Russia's "sophisticated disinformation policies", and what Pope Pius XI called "propaganda so truly diabolical that the world has perhaps never witnessed its like before", propaganda that "penetrates into all classes ... with the result that few are aware of the poison which increasingly pervades their minds and hearts."[32] It was this worldwide system of terror, lies, and murder that the Second Vatican Council could not even bring itself to name, much less condemn.

Small wonder that Pope Wojtyla, who practiced "peaceful co-existence" with the Communists in Poland, and came of age during the Council, would ignore Pius XI's warning that "no one who would save Christian civilization may collaborate with it in any undertaking whatsoever." Also consigned to the cobwebs was Pius' exhortation:

"When the Apostles asked the Savior why they had been unable to drive the evil spirit from a demoniac, Our Lord answered: 'This kind is not cast out but by prayer and fasting.' So, too, the evil which today torments humanity can be conquered only by a worldwide holy crusade of prayer and penance ... Let them implore also the powerful intercession of the Immaculate Virgin who, having crushed the head of the serpent of old, remains the sure protectress and invincible 'Help of Christians.'"[33]

Pope Ratti spoke these words from bitter experience; one can almost see black ash from his failed Ostpolitik on his forehead. Pope Wojtyla, it seems, believed he had built a better mousetrap. He would go to Fatima to "implore the intercession of the Immaculate Virgin", and continue the same Ostpolitik of dialogue and "peaceful co-existence" with Soviet Russia he had practiced in Poland. But would he really be able to serve two masters? Would they allow him to?

The 1982 Consecration

His brush with death on May 13 awakened John Paul II's interest in Fatima. From his hospital bed, the Pope studied documents on the apparitions at the Cova da Iria. Less than a month after the attempt on his life, the Holy Father entrusted the human family to the maternal protection of Mary.

The Pope renewed this act on the Feast of the Immaculate Conception, December 8, 1981. When asked why he had used the word "entrust" rather than "consecrate", John Paul replied, "There are still some theologians who doubt that we can make a consecration to anyone other than God Himself."[34] This was one of the arguments Father Dhanis used to undermine Fatima. While John Paul may have been sincerely confused on this point, Louis de Montfort and Maximilian Kolbe (Pope Wojtyla was familiar with the writings of both) would have been stunned by Dhanis' argument. Both saints strongly believed that a personal consecration to Mary increased a soul's consecration to Jesus.

Meanwhile, the Blue Army worked tirelessly to present petitions to the Holy Father requesting the consecration of Russia to the Immaculate Heart. John Paul studied them. In March, 1982, he ordered Portugal's Apostolic Nuncio to interview Lucy. Lucy explained to the Nuncio the requirements of the consecration and offered suggestions on how it could be accomplished.[35]

John Paul II decided to make a pilgrimage to Fatima on May 13, 1982. According to a letter from Cardinal Casaroli to the bishops in April, the Pope's reason for going to Fatima was to "thank the Holy Virgin for saving his life" from the assassination attempt and to renew "in spiritual union with all the bishops of the world, the two acts of consecration done by Pius XII."[36] Before leaving Rome John Paul read the Third Secret and consulted a Portuguese bishop in Rome on the nuances of the Portuguese language.

On May 13 John Paul II and Sister Lucy met for the first time. The Pope greeted her warmly. Lucy gave him her memoirs, which she had written during a retreat just before the Pope arrived at Fatima. Then they talked privately for twenty-five minutes. Lucy told John Paul that

God wanted the Third Secret revealed. He replied that it was "neither necessary nor prudent to reveal now the contents of that Secret, seeing that the world would not understand it."[37]

Lucy asked about the consecration of Russia. The Pope answered that he would discuss "all those things" at the 1983 Bishops' Synod. Lucy asked about the beatification process for Francisco and Jacinta, and the Pope was non-committal: "Pray, my daughter, that this may be achieved during your life and during mine."[38]

True to his word, John Paul II renewed Pius XII's consecration of the world to the Immaculate Heart of Mary later that day. For Lucy and the Fatimists it was an anti-climax. The Pope did not mention Russia, or order the participation of the world's bishops in similar ceremonies in dioceses across the world. It was clear even before the actual consecration that the requests of Our Lady of Fatima would not be satisfied.

From his reading of the Third Secret, his personal research, and his conversation with Lucy, it can fairly be assumed that John Paul II understood the real Fatima Message. Yet his public remarks at the Cova da Iria made it clear that John Paul would interpret Fatima according to his own lights. "You want me to teach you a Secret?" he asked in his first speech. "It is simple, and that is already not a secret anymore. Pray a great deal; say the Rosary every day."[39]

Such was John Paul's response to requests to reveal the Third Secret. It was not much of an improvement over Pope John's anonymous press release. Granted, telling Catholics to pray a lot and say daily Rosaries is good advice; it was recommended by the beautiful Lady at Cova da Iria. But John Paul's implication that the Third Secret concerned *only* prayer was misleading. In fact, his attitude towards the Fatima Message, while not openly scornful, was not particularly reverent either. Again, as with Pope John, one wonders why a Pope just couldn't come out and say something like, "We know you want to know the Third Secret, but we have decided not to reveal it for the following reasons ..."

(Not that the Pope is required to give reasons. But isn't it unusual that none of the Popes of the pastoral Second Vatican Council have been the slightest bit pastoral about the Third Secret of Fatima? From a psychological standpoint, mustn't it be obvious to them that their extreme sensitivity towards the Third Secret only increases curiosity?)

Instead John Paul II used his sermons to subtly subvert the Message of Fatima according to the theories of Father Dhanis. "The Message of Fatima is, in its fundamental nucleus, the appeal to conversion and penance as found in the Gospel," the Pope declared. He ignored those parts of the Message outside this "fundamental nucleus", commenting only that the language of the Fatima Message was "simple, in proportion to their (the seers) capacity to understand."[40]

To be a bit more precise, the language of the Secret is not only remarkably concise and direct, it is also richly theological, far beyond the ken of illiterate peasant children. Whatever else the Pope may have been implying does not seem geared towards encouraging belief in what the Blessed Virgin said to the children. His words almost appear to belittle the Fatima Message and the seers.

John Paul also took the liberty of publicly reinterpreting the prayers Our Lady and the Angel had given the children, going so far as to delete the words "committed against the Immaculate Heart of Mary" from one of the Fatima reparatory prayers.[41] And he implied that Pius XII's consecration of the world to the Immaculate Heart satisfied Our Lady of Fatima's requests, when he rhetorically asked, "Has he (Pius XII) not, by this consecration, given satisfaction to the evangelical repercussion of the appeal from Fatima?"[42]

Well then, if everything has already been accomplished, why hadn't Russia converted? Why wasn't the world in the "period of peace" promised by the beautiful Lady? The Pope did not tie up these loose ends, but he made it clear that he only came to Fatima "to accomplish once again what my predecessors have already done: entrust the world to the Heart of Mary ..."[43]

On returning to Rome the Holy Father concluded matters: "I have sought to do everything which could be done ..." The Bishop of Fatima agreed, and Catholics were told to stop pestering the Holy Father about Fatima. Worse, lies began about Sister Lucy. An alleged interview was published wherein Lucy supposedly claimed that John Paul's consecration totally fulfilled Our Lady of Fatima's requests. A year later the Portuguese nuncio was persuaded to interview Lucy about her alleged interview. Did Lucy really think John Paul's consecration fulfilled Heaven's request?

"The consecration of Russia is not done as Our Lady has demanded it," Lucy answered, because Pope John Paul did not specifically consecrate Russia, and the consecration was not in union with the world episcopate. "We can expect some benefits" from the Pope's consecration, Lucy said, "but not the conversion of Russia." Why hadn't Lucy refuted the phony interview? "I did not have the permission of the Holy See," Lucy replied. The forged interview appeared to be the work of a high-ranking member of the Blue Army, apparently done out of zealous over-obedience to Rome.[44]

Lucy also told the Nuncio she had written John Paul about the problems with the 1982 consecration. Later that summer Lucy told her relative, Maria do Fetal:

"I am old, I am seventy-five, I am preparing to see God face to face. I have given all my texts to Holy Church. I shall die tranquil. But, if they want my opinion, here it is: The Consecration of Russia, as Our Lady has asked for it, is not done."[45]

The 1984 Consecration

Although the Holy Father had indicated his satisfaction with the 1982 consecration, he nevertheless repeated the consecration in 1983, at St. Peter's Square during the Bishops' Synod.

Later that year, during Advent, Pope John Paul II preached at a Lutheran church in Rome on the occasion of the five-hundredth anniversary of Martin Luther's birth. In the first papal statement about Luther since Leo X excommunicated him in 1521, John Paul praised Luther's vision and prophesied that he (the Pope) could see "from afar the dawn of the restoration of our unity."[46]

Later that month, two days after Christmas, John Paul, accompanied by bodyguards and a photographer, visited Ali Agca in his cell. They met alone, and from film of the meeting it appeared Agca was asking forgiveness. The Pope was asked later if Agca confessed his sins:

> "'No,' Pope John Paul smiled. 'Agca is a very superstitious person. He learned in prison that the assault took place on the same day as the revelation at (sic) Our Lady of Fatima. And he started reading about this. As he imagined it, it was some kind of mysterious force that made his (assassination) plans fall through. He was living in fear that he would be harmed by this mysterious force. And I said that Our Lady of Fatima would not try to take revenge on him. I was trying to calm him. He was not confessing his sins.'"[47]

John Paul did not say if he tried to convert the "very superstitious" prisoner to Christianity. Less than two months later, however, *L'Osservatore Romano* published a letter the Pope had sent to the world episcopate announcing he would repeat the 1982 consecration at Rome, on March 25, 1984. In the letter, which was originally sent on December 8, 1983, John Paul wrote: "The words of the act of consecration and offering which I am sending you enclosed, is the same Act which I pronounced at Fatima on May 13, 1982, with some slight modifications." He invited the bishops to "renew this act at the same time with me, in the manner in which each of you judges most suitable."[48]

March 22 was the celebration of Lucy's seventy-seventh birthday. She was asked about the upcoming consecration. Lucy, who had read the text of the consecration, replied, "That consecration cannot have a decisive character,"[49] because once again Russia was not mentioned. The consecration, or "Act of Offering" as the Pope called it, occurred in St. Peter's Basilica. The Pope knelt before the Pilgrim Virgin statue and repeated the 1982 consecration, pledging: "In a special way we entrust and consecrate to You those individuals and nations which particularly need to be entrusted and consecrated." Departing from his prepared text, the Pope added: "Enlighten especially the people whose consecration and entrusting You are awaiting from us ..."[50]

This was an obvious reference to Russia, and an equally obvious allusion that the Pope knew his act was insufficient, precisely because he did not specifically consecrate Russia. Later he said he feared that naming Russia "would be interpreted as a provocation by Soviet leaders."[51] Most Fatima scholars agreed with Sister Lucy and Pope John Paul that the 1984 consecration had not satisfied the request made at Cova da Iria. In fact, on March 27, 1984, the Italian Catholic bishops' newspaper *Avvenire* reported that the Holy Father, on March 25 at 4:00 in the afternoon, *three hours after* he consecrated the world, prayed at St. Peter's, asking Our Lady to bless "those people for whom You Yourself *are awaiting* our act of consecration and entrusting". Thus he admitted that the Consecration of Russia remains unfulfilled.

The Other Consecration

You've got to give the Pope credit for trying to do the consecration, and wonder at his inability, or unwillingness, to perform the consecration correctly.

It has often been said, in the Holy Father's defense, that he did not enlist the world episcopate in the consecration because he knows he does not have their support for the consecration. If this is true, it is also true that when Pope Wojtyla has really wanted something, he has been very effective at getting it.

Despite the obvious attraction John Paul had to Fatima, at least for a few years, it was also clear that John Paul II had so little sympathy for the spirit of reparation inherent to Fatima that he publicly changed the prayers given the children by the Blessed Virgin and the Angel. Moreover, he never mentioned the vision of hell the children had, and made only the vaguest of allusions to the seal of divine authority given to the Fatima apparitions — the Miracle of the Sun.

Instead of revealing the Third Secret he made a joke about it, and then (in all likelihood) misrepresented what the Secret contained, stating it was a message to pray the Rosary. This is very unlikely, since the Blessed Virgin openly told the children to pray the Rosary at each of Her visits to them. Why then would She repeat Herself, and make the repetition a Secret?

The other difficulty John Paul II had with Fatima was the difficulty of all progressives — Fatima's anti-Communism. The Blessed Virgin spoke of converting Russia by consecrating it to Her Immaculate Heart. Pope Wojtyla was more accustomed to the humanistic anti-Communism of Poland's intellectuals, and he was obviously uncomfortable with making an issue out of the need to convert to Catholicism.

Having said all this, it is fair to ask just what Pope John Paul II's attraction to Fatima was based on. Certainly not the Message. Perhaps the Rosary, as John Paul seemed less opposed to praying the Rosary than he was to the rest of the Fatima Message.[52]

It is likely, however, that the Pope's primary attraction to Fatima from 1981 to 1984 sprang from his belief that Our Lady of Fatima had aligned Herself to his efforts to free Poland from Communism. This belief was born on May 13, 1981, when John Paul very narrowly escaped death from an assassin's bullets. John Paul publicly thanked the Blessed Virgin for saving his life, studied the Fatima Message, met Sister Lucy, and repeated Pius XII's consecration of the world to the Immaculate Heart of Mary.

According to his biographers Bernstein and Politi, "The Pope experienced the great upheaval in the Soviet Union as a kind of mystery play, in which, as he saw it, Our Lady of Fatima had played a major role. In March 1984, when Solidarity seemed doomed, the Pope ordered that the original Fatima statue, three and a half feet tall, be specially shipped from Portugal to the Vatican. The Pope had given orders to set it in his private chapel ... On the night of March 24-25, the feast of the Annunciation, he spent long hours in prayer before the statue ..."53

Melodrama aside, John Paul may well have thought Our Lady of Fatima intended to help him save Poland, the focus of his pontificate in the 1980's. This belief may have provided enough incentive for him to suffer the rest of the Fatima Message, pre-conciliar as it was, in order to free Poland from Russian rule (which for most Poles, was just as annoying as Communist rule). Of course, while he was willing to pay homage to Our Lady of Fatima, he couldn't openly insult the Russians — particularly the Russian Orthodox — by making an attempt to convert them, since the papal vision he inherited from his predecessors demanded the participation of the schismatics — as schismatics, not converts ...

Whether John Paul believed (or believes) any of the Fatima Message is debatable. After all, he is not "a very superstitious person", like his would-be assassin Agca, who allowed himself to be shaken by Our Lady of Fatima. Pope John Paul II, on the other hand, has inherited and accepts as his own the papal vision of his predecessors. This adherance of Pope John Paul II constitutes a prior commitment that, due to its nature, supersedes any contrary consecration. For the real consecration, the one that really stuck, was the wedding of Pope Wojtyla's considerable gifts and talents to the furtherance of the papal vision of his predecessors.

This is why he did not properly consecrate Russia to the Immaculate Heart of Mary. He had already consecrated himself to another master.54

It will be seen how the merciful blessing of Fatima, when spurned, became a curse, leaving Pope Wojtyla with the bitter fruits of his grace-deprived efforts. Failing to rise above the spirit of the world, he would prove to be as destructive to the Church and to the world as his star-crossed predecessors.

If the chastisement of apostasy spread through the Church because the successors of St. Peter defied the Fatima Secret, this would explain Jacinta's anguished preoccupation with the Holy Father, and her pleas for all to "pray, pray very much for the Holy Father."

NOTES

1. Bernstein and Politi, *His Holiness, Pope John Paul II and the Hidden History of Our Time*, p. 112.
2. David Yallop's bestseller, *In God's Name, An Investigation Into the Murder of Pope John Paul I* (Bantam Books, 1984) advances the theory that the Pope was murdered by P-2 Masonry, who, thanks to Paul VI, had their hands all over the Church's money. Yallop says the motive for the murder was Luciani's intention to expose the arrangement. John Cornwell was hired by the Vatican to refute this argument. In his book, *A Thief in the Night*, he theorizes that Luciani was at the point of death when elected, and Vatican negligence concerning Luciano's health caused his death. The Abbé de Nantes is the main (I think only) proponent of the "Pope John Paul I was secretly a traditionalist saint" theory.

   For what it's worth, I think that Yallop, who admired John Paul I because he thought he would "overturn" *Humanae Vitae*, is mostly right about the Vatican's financial scandals – but his portrayal of Luciano as a crusading financial reformer is unlikely. Even more unlikely is Cornwell's theory of John Paul I's frail health and bum ticker. It just isn't so. Regarding the third theory, if Luciano (an understudy to Angelo Roncalli) was a traditionalist he was a very late bloomer. There is little evidence of this quality, excepting his involvement with and apparent admiration for Sister Lucy. It is certainly possible that Luciano was converted from conciliarism by Sister Lucy, because all things are possible with God. What I'm saying is that the Abbé's theory requires a miracle …
3. While disagreeing with all these theories, I have no theory of my own to advance. I don't know how John Paul I died, or why.
4. Kwitny, op. cit., p. 188.
5. Ibid., p. 189.
6. At Wojtyla's request, Henri de Lubac wrote the book's Introduction.
7. Bernstein and Politi, op. cit., p. 113.
8. As quoted in Father Johannes Dormann, *Pope John Paul II's Theological Journey to the Prayer Meeting of Religions in Assisi*, English translation by Angelus Press, 1994, pp. 15-19.
9. Kwitny, op. cit., p. 247. Castel Gandolfo was also equipped with a Polish alarm clock at Paul's bedside. As Peter Hebblethwaite tells it, the clock was notoriously unreliable. It rang madly – and very unexpectedly – at the exact moment Paul died.
10. His Holiness Pope John Paul II, *Redemptor Hominis*, Vatican translation published by the Daughters of St. Paul, 1979, Sec. I, Par. 5.
11. The statistics on Italy are from Kwitny, op. cit., p. 493. Statistics and polls documenting the loss of faith and vocations are omnipresent. A representative sample, now slightly dated, is found in Appendix VIII of Michael Davies' *Pope John's Council*.
12. As quoted in Dormann, op. cit., p. 86.
13. *CRC* No. 335, Nov.-Dec. 2000, p. 22.
14. *FIJWE*, Vol. IV, op. cit., p. 151.
15. Ibid.
16. In 1966 Archbishop Wojtyla declined an invitation by Bishop Venancio to make a pilgrimage to Fatima, saying it would be impossible for him to go there (*FIJWE*, op. cit, p. 146). Subsequent to this refusal, however, Wojtyla reportedly twice signed petitions for Pope Paul VI to consecrate Russia to the Immaculate Heart.
17. Kwitny, op. cit., p. 242.
18. Bernstein and Politi, op. cit., pp. 77-78. In *Quas Primas* Pius XI had said it was impossible for a man to be both a good Christian and a true socialist. He was one of a long list of Popes to condemn socialism.
19. Jozef Tischner, *Marxism and Christianity in Poland*, English translation published by Georgetown University Press, 1987.
20. Ibid.
21. As quoted in Ibid., pp. 108-109
22. Galter, op. cit., p. 290.
23. Ibid., p. 292.
24. According to Wojtyla's long-time friend, Father Malinski. See Kwitny, op. cit., p. 159. Kwitny adds, "Wojtyla's identification with the radical Catholics at *Tygodnik Poweszechny* and *Znak* would have sealed the case (ie, the episcopal appointment) against him. (p. 159)"
25. For the relationship between Wyszynski and Wojtyla, see Kwitny, op. cit., pp. 158-159, 173, et. Seq.
26. The word 'communist' could easily, and more correctly, be used than 'progressive.' This quote

by Piasecki was included in Cardinal Wyszynski's report on Pax to the French Episcopate in 1963. It was reproduced in Vicomte Leon de Poncins, *Freemasonry and the Vatican*, Christian Book Club, 1968, pp. 208-209.

27. As quoted in Galter, *The Red Book of the Persecuted Church*, op. cit., p. 293. Emphasis supplied.

28. As quoted in Tischner, op. cit., pp. 108-109.

29. Kwitny, op. cit., p. 346.

30. Ibid.

31. Anatoliy Golitsyn, *New Lies For Old, The Communist Strategy of Deception and Disinformation,* Dodd, Mead & Company, New York, 1984, pp. 351-354.

32. From his 1937 encyclical on Atheistic Communism.

33. Ibid.

34. *FIJWE*, Vol. IV, op. cit., p. 154.

35. See ibid., pp. 156-157. Lucy stressed the importance of the involvement of the world episcopate: "In order that the bishops of the world be united to the Pope during the Consecration of Russia to the Immaculate Heart of Mary, the Pope would have to ... order the Bishops of the entire world to organize, each one in his own Cathedral, a public and solemn ceremony of reparation and of Consecration of Russia to the Holy Hearts of Jesus and Mary."

36. Ibid., p. 158.

37. Sister Lucy reported these words to Cardinal Oddi during a conversation with him in May, 1985. As quoted in Ibid., p. 159.

38. Ibid.

39. Ibid., p. 160.

40. From his sermon on May 13, 1982, as quoted in Ibid., pp. 161-162.

41. Ibid., pp. 160-161.

42. Ibid., p. 162.

43. Ibid.

44. Ibid., pp. 163-164.

45. Ibid.

46. Kwitny, op. cit., p. 491.

47. Ibid., p. 491.

48. As quoted in *FIJWE*, Book IV, op. cit., p. 167.

49. Lucy's words were reported to Father Caillon, who relayed them in writing to Frère Michel in a letter dated March 30, 1984. It was Mrs. Pestana, a friend of Lucy's, who verbally reported Lucy's words to Father Caillon. The Pestana family had known Bishop da Silva very well, and knew Lucy ever since she left Fatima for Tuy. See Ibid., p. 168, fns 129 and 159 on pp. 226-227.

50. Ibid., pp. 169-170.

51. Ibid., p. 172.

52. The Rosary appears to have been an acquired gift, as Pope Wojtyla had not been known for praying the beads.

53. Bernstein and Politi, op. cit., p. 479.

54. Matthew 6:24. This is explained in future chapters.

Chapter Eighteen

The Other Master ...

Since 1960, when the Third Secret was supposed to have been revealed but was suppressed instead, Sister Lucy has spoken of a "diabolical disorientation" in the Church. It is a reference to the apostate words and deeds of consecrated religious, but more than a few lay folk appear disoriented as well, particularly in their views of the conciliar popes. For instance, progressives tend to see Paul VI as a "conservative", and John Paul II as a "reactionary" who is attempting to "turn back the clock" to pre-conciliar days.

The progressive's supposed opponents, conservative Catholics, have similar views. They have rallied around *Humanae Vitae*, and tried very hard to ignore the rest of Paul's fifteen-year pontificate, his ignoble career as "junior pope" to Pius XII, and the file kept on Archbishop Montini by the Milan police. Although John Paul II's decision to allow female altar boys blunted the enthusiasm of a few conservatives for his person, he is generally seen as attempting to restore the Church to orthodoxy. The reason there is some evidence to support this has less to do with John Paul II's traditionalism than St. Pius X's observation on "the methods of modernists", whereby "one finds some things which might well be approved by a Catholic, but on turning over the page one is confronted by other things which might well have been dictated by a rationalist."[1]

That "on turning over the page" John Paul II looks, sounds, and acts a lot like a neo-modernist is one of those dirty little secrets conservatives would rather dump into the same "deep, dark well" Cardinal Ottaviani declared the Third Secret had been pitched into. Of course, John Paul is much more than a mere neo-modernist, who are a dime-a-dozen these days anyway. Many of them call themselves conservative Catholics, and would never dream a Pope could lead them astray.

To stay in line with the Pope conservatives have had to redefine orthodoxy to include abominations like John Paul kissing the Koran,[2] or organizing and hosting the prayer meeting of religious at Assisi, a milestone in ecumenism that featured the placement of a statue of Buddha on top of the tabernacle at the high altar of St. Peter's Basilica in Assisi.[3] Conservatives have provided cover for the liturgical revolution as well, by "conserving" the often scandalous innovations and aberrations of the progressives, and attacking traditional Catholics who criticize the revolution. Some of these "conservatives" have no idea how far they've slipped. Others don't want to know. And some know perfectly well what they have done, and why.

The other faction of note is a cluster of traditionalist Catholic groups, who have a reputation for being pious, ill tempered, and critical of virtually everything and everyone. On the other hand, traditional Catholics are capable of adhering with holy obstinacy to the truth. In these days of "diabolical disorientation" the rare appearances of truth serve as a lightning rod for calumny and detraction from "the blind and their blind guides", to paraphrase Sister Lucy.

Yet if traditionalist Catholics were consistently operating under the grace of the Holy Ghost they would be far less prone to the bickering and backbiting that at times obscures their fidelity to Tradition. Another anomaly is the variety of opinion among traditionalists regarding the conciliar popes. Some traditionalist Catholics, like conservatives, prefer not to criticize the popes. Others go so far as to argue that Paul VI was (literally) *the* anti-christ, or that none of the popes after Pius XII are valid popes. Still others fluctuate between these two poles.

Since 1988 the Church has attempted to incorporate traditionalist Catholics into the "plurality of Catholic religions," or at the very least, *out of* the Society of Saint Pius X. The vehicle for this dubious effort is the Indult Mass. In exchange for the Mass of the Ages, traditionalist Catholics are expected to stop being pious, ill tempered, and hyper-critical, and become care-free know-nothings and de facto apostates instead. Although traditionalists vary in their reactions to this snare, the majority of them may prove too independent[4] to be corralled by anyone for very long. It is already evident that, in at least some cases, the "weapon" of the Indult has been turned against its wielder.[5]

The Ratzinger Interview

After Pope John Paul II had repeated Pius XII's consecration of the world to the Immaculate Heart of Mary in Rome in 1984, he went on vacation. An avid skier, His Holiness headed for the mountains with Sandro Pertini, the Socialist president of Italy. Pertini was asked by reporters what he and the Pope talked about. He replied, "I said to the Pope, 'What is God for you, is for me the conscience.' And the Pope replied, 'That is because the conscience is transcendent.' I have always found in this Pope a great respect and sensitivity for my socialist faith."[6]

It was around this time (fall, 1984) that an interview with Cardinal Ratzinger was published in an Italian journal. The interview was conducted by Vittorio Messori, and entitled "Here is Why the Faith is in Crisis." When asked, Ratzinger stated he had read the Third Secret of Fatima. Why had three popes refused to reveal the Secret? "According to the judgment of the popes," Ratzinger answered, "it would add nothing to what a Christian must know from Revelation: a radical call to conversion, the absolute seriousness of history, the dangers threatening the faith and life of the Christian, and therefore the world. And also the importance of the last times."[7]

The Prefect for the Congregation for the Doctrine of the Faith continued:

> "If it is not published — at least for the moment — it is to avoid confusing religious prophecy with sensationalism. But the things contained in this Third Secret correspond to what is announced in Scripture, and are confirmed by many other Marian apparitions, beginning with the Fatima apparitions themselves in their known contents. Conversion, penance, are essential conditions of salvation."[8]

Later the interviews were published as *The Ratzinger Report*. The section of the book containing Ratzinger's comments about Fatima were significantly altered from the original interview. Many of his earlier statements about the Third Secret were deleted or modified. The Cardinal had said too much. Yet he had also said too little. Like Cardinal Ottaviani's attempt to justify Paul VI's refusal to reveal the Third Secret in 1967, Ratzinger's explanations rang hollow. For instance, he stated that the Third Secret was not revealed because it added nothing a Christian shouldn't already know. Using that logic, how would the Cardinal explain the Church's publication of a new Catechism?

It was surprising that Ratzinger said anything about the Third Secret. He certainly didn't need to, since his purpose in granting the interviews was damage control. In contrast to the present Pope's boundless, occasionally surreal optimism, Ratzinger acknowledged a few of the many obvious areas of crisis within the Church.

To this teaspoon of reality a false scapegoat was added: the crises in the Church were solely the fault of a few radical theologians. This is partly correct, but had the Cardinal seen fit to drop the other shoe he would have admitted that the conciliar popes had protected and encouraged the radical theologians, and even made them Cardinals (particularly John Paul II). This was not mentioned, however, because the purpose of Ratzinger's interview was to take heat off the Vatican for the abysmal mess the Church was in.

So why did Ratzinger, a progressive, talk about Fatima at all? Well, having recently read the Third Secret, perhaps he was torn between a sincere desire to warn Catholics of the content of the Third Secret, and a mandate from the Pope to keep silence. Consequently, the Cardinal gave clues about the Third Secret in one breath — it concerned "the dangers threatening the faith and life of the Christian and therefore the world, and also the importance of the last times" — and in the next breath declared that revealing the Secret would be repetitious, and encourage "sensationalism."

Life After the Consecrations

Pope John Paul II also appeared conflicted in his efforts. While publicly reinterpreting the Fatima Message and minimizing its importance, the Pope nevertheless attempted three times to effect the consecration of Russia to Mary's Immaculate Heart. Perhaps his efforts, like those of Pope Pius XII, found some favor with Heaven. While this certainly may be hoped for, it does not appear that John Paul II accepted the profound immediacy of the Fatima Message.

Instead, John Paul tried to slot Russia — and the rest of the world — into the Second Vatican Council's version of religious liberty. Similar to the Council, and unlike Fatima, the Pope's vision of universal brotherhood did not stress conversion to the one true faith.[9]

Consequently, after 1984 Fatima was officially ignored. Pope John Paul II made persistent ecumenical overtures to the Russian Orthodox Church, whose hierarchy was a veritable "Who's Who" of the Soviet KGB. One of the conditions for dialogue with the Russian Orthodox was to ignore the Orthodox persecution of Ukrainian Catholics, who went underground to survive.

In March, 1985, Mikhail Gorbachev became secretary general of the Communist Party, and declared the Kremlin, like the Church, was finally opening its windows to the world. For veteran Soviet watchers, Glasnost and Perestroika were the latest in a long line of Soviet public relations stunts. In the 1920's Lenin announced that the Communists were becoming capitalists. In 1936 Stalin announced the same thing. In 1956 Khrushchev announced "peaceful co-existence". In 1970 Brezhnev announced "detente". Through all these announcements international Communism continued its work of infiltrating and subverting non-Communist governments. Now Gorbachev was announcing that Russia had reformed itself, an idea that appealed to many in the West — and in the Church.

In 1989 Gorbachev met with John Paul II at the Vatican. After talking privately for one and one-half hours, John Paul announced that he and Gorbachev had discussed promoting "a common bond in favor of peace and collaboration in the world." John Paul went on to say that the Catholic Church "associates itself today, more than ever, with all those who want to serve the cause of man and contribute to the progress of nations."[10] The Pope seemed satisfied that Gorbachev was acting in good faith. So did much of the rest of the world, thanks in part to a remarkable worldwide press campaign on behalf of the miraculous Mr. Gorbachev.

Had Russia been converted? The Vatican pressured the Blue Army to promote the idea that Gorbachev was a Christian, and that Perestroika was proof that Russia had finally converted. A certain priest active in the Fatima cause in the midwestern United States began circulating what he said were letters written and signed by Sister Lucy, attesting that the 1984 consecration of the world to the Immaculate Heart had fulfilled the requirements. According to Frère François and others who have examined these documents, they are, without exception, forgeries. As with the 1982 forgery, Lucy was not allowed to respond publicly to the latest disinformation campaign.

During a 1989 visit with the Archbishop of Boston, Cardinal Law, however, Sister Lucy said the consecration of Russia had not been done. "The Holy Father speculates it has been done," she said, "done in the best possible way under the circumstances. Done on the narrow road of the collegial consecration that She has demanded and has been wanting? No, that has not been done."[11]

In 1991 John Paul II announced his plans to go to Fatima on May 13. Lucy told her Carmelite Superior she did not wish to meet the Pope at Fatima. On hearing this, John Paul ordered Sister Lucy to Fatima, and she obeyed. Once again the Pope and the seer met on May 13. Lucy gave John Paul a handmade rosary and the "Book of Our Lady." They spoke privately. No account has been given of this conversation. It is likely that if Lucy had privately congratulated John Paul on successfully consecrating Russia to the Immaculate Heart, the Pope would have mentioned this during his public remarks at Fatima. During his two day visit, however, the Pope never mentioned his visit with Sister Lucy. In fact, he didn't mention her at all.

Instead, in his May 13 homily, John Paul claimed that the Blessed Virgin had come to Fatima in 1917 to call "all of humanity to conversion and prayer." The Pope continued, "Seventy-five years later, numerous elements have undergone a change in the European and world panorama, and many events have happened in the course of this century, above all in these last years." This was a reference to the apparent failure of Communism in eastern Europe.

Stating that "My predecessors and myself have always turned our glance towards the Virgin of Fatima," the Pope recalled his 1984 consecration of the world to the Immaculate Heart of Mary, linking it contextually to the break-up of Communism, which, according to John Paul II, marked "a veritable historical turning ... with the disappearance of division between the two social blocs based on ideological and socioeconomic principles that are opposed."[12]

In passing, it must be said that this is a remarkable assessment. John Paul appears to reduce the battle between Christianity and Communism to one of opposing "ideological and socioeconomic principles", instead of a spiritual battle upon which millions of souls hung in the balance. After all, did not the enormous stakes bring down from Heaven the very Mother of God to console and instruct Her Son's Church?

To reduce this shattering confrontation to a squabble between "two social blocs" is to introduce a sense of unreality, even falsehood, into the history of the Twentieth Century. Would the tens of thousands of Christian martyrs to Communism in eastern Europe have agreed with the Pope's characterization, and with his assertion that there was no longer a division between Communism and Christianity? Indeed, if there is no longer a division between Communism and Christianity, is this cause for celebration?

Returning to John Paul's remarks on Fatima, the most obvious reading is that he believes the fall of Soviet Communism is the result of his 1984 consecration of the world to the Immaculate Heart of Mary, a consecration that, at the time it was made, was unanimously believed not to fulfill the requirements of Fatima, as it did not explicitly mention Russia, and did not involve the world episcopate in any meaningful fashion. Since there was no meeting of the minds between the Holy Father and Sister Lucy on the consecration of Russia, it is plausible to conclude that the Pope ordered Lucy to Fatima in 1991 to give the impression that Lucy agreed with the Pope. Put more bluntly, and not unkindly, Lucy bolstered John Paul's credibility. Yet her silent, discreet lack of enthusiasm for John Paul spoke volumes. So did the presence, in the very sanctuary of Fatima, of Mr. Guennadi Guerassimov, the Soviet ambassador to Portugal, and former spokesman for Mikhail Gorbachev. As he and Lucy listened to John Paul's remarks, it must have been clear to both of them whose side the Pope was on.

In 1992 and 1993 there was another flurry of propaganda to the effect that Sister Lucy had "approved" the Pope's 1984 consecration. In 1994 the Pope spoke of Fatima and Russia again. In his book *Crossing the Threshold of Hope*, John Paul ignored the Third Secret, and reduced the Fatima Message to "Russia will convert" and "in the end My Heart (sic) will triumph." The Pope concluded, "It happened just as they (the children) had said."[13]

Then he appeared to contradict this point. According to John Paul, stressing the role of Divine Providence in the fall of Communism was "simplistic": Communism "fell by itself, because of its own weaknesses."[14] The Holy Father's thinking on Fatima then, appears to go something like this: the consecration of Russia has been properly done and Russia has converted, but Communism would have failed anyway, with or without Heaven's help.

It is likely that the "inevitable failure of Communism" theory is closer to John Paul's real thinking than any significant reliance on Our Lady of Fatima he is alleged to have. Having spent decades under Communist rule, the astute Bishop Wojtyla had a bird's-eye view of Communism's very real deficiencies. This is to be distinguished from "Russia's errors", however, which were two. First, the intrinsically evil nature of Communism, which made Bolshevism irreformable, humanly speaking. Second, the Orthodox Church's continuing schism: instead of bowing to Peter, the Orthodox bowed to Czarism, and then Bolshevism. The remedy for

Russia's errors was its conversion via consecration to the Immaculate Heart.

I contend that Pope Wojtyla never accepted that Russia's errors were those expressed above. For him, Communism was "deficient" because it did not honor man's dignity. The remedy was for Communism to convert to the idea that religious faith was an important human need. Russia needed a political conversion as well, from an oppressive totalitarianism to a democracy that observed man's religious liberty and honored man's freedom of conscience. John Paul's premises are entirely different than those of the Blessed Virgin — and they both know this, even if pilgrims to Fatima do not.

The world, of course, is oblivious. For them, the role of the Polish Pope in the fall of Communism in eastern Europe is assuming legendary — one might say mythical — proportions. And why not? For this Pope was a true prodigy who accelerated both the revolution within the Roman Catholic Church and the dissolution of Soviet Communism. The apparent transformation of these worldwide organizations from irreconcilable enemies to allies with a common cause is nothing less than a feat of magic. The result has intensified the pace of the march towards universal peace and brotherhood signified by the Event at Assisi — yet another milestone, and one the Pope happily (and quite correctly) claims credit for.

Left choking on the dust rising from this forced march away from the God of Revelation and towards the God of the future were a very small number of incorrigible anti-Communists, some of whom were Catholics clinging to the forsaken Message of Fatima. They were left with nothing but their faith, as objective circumstances seemed to contradict everything they believed. Even more confusing, their Pope appeared to be a friend of the Blessed Virgin and an opponent of the Fatima Message, at least as it had always been understood prior to Pope Wojtyla. Was the Holy Father right?

The Pope and Fatima, 1997

The safest answer is yes, John Paul was right according to his view of things. The problem is that this sort of logic legitimizes everything; after all, Josef Stalin had his point of view too. But concerning Fatima the differences are too stark. One must either accept the message of a Church-approved apparition with a public message for the whole world, or believe instead the most popular and best known Pope to ever have reigned. The choices are mutually exclusive, and to choose is not optional, at least according to Sister Lucy, who in 1957 said to Father Fuentes, "from now on we must choose sides. Either we are for God or we are for the devil; there is no in-between."

It can be argued that only a false argument could oppose the Blessed Virgin and Christ's Vicar on earth. Surely they are on the same side;

only a Protestant would think otherwise. Yet since 1960 this divergence between the Blessed Virgin's will as expressed at Fatima and the will of the conciliar popes is too obvious to avoid. The problem, not merely with John Paul II, but with his conciliar predecessors and the monstrosity of a Church they are erecting, is that they are attempting to serve two masters, with the same results forecasted by Our Lord in Matthew 6:24:

> "Either he will hate the one and love the other: or he will sustain the one, and despise the other. You cannot serve God and mammon."

Which brings us to the message the Holy Father sent the pilgrims at Fatima on October 13, 1997, on the occasion of the eightieth anniversary of the Miracle of the Sun. It was a short message, but notable because the Holy Father actually mentioned "the prodigious 'dance of the sun'" that "took place in the sky." Of all the signs of the times in the Twentieth Century, "the sign of Fatima appears to be one of the greatest," continued John Paul, "because its message predicts a number of signs that were to follow and it invites us to live out their messages as well."[15]

The signs were four, or rather four pairs, each presented by the Pope as a problem followed by a solution. For instance, the first pair of signs was the "two World Wars, but also the great gatherings of nations and peoples under the sign of dialogue and peace (a probable reference to Vatican II and the Event at Assisi)." The next sign the Pope noted was "the oppression and anxieties that different peoples and countries have lived through," a likely reference to Communism in eastern Europe. This problem is trumped by "the voice that has been given to peoples and individuals and which, in these times, has made itself heard in the international forum"; this is a reference to Solidarity, and perhaps to the Pope's belief that Russia has been converted. Note that the Holy Father's first two "signs" — the World Wars and Communism — are probably intentional allusions to the Fatima Secret. The cryptic allusions to the Fatima Secret continue in the last two signs. The third set of signs concerns "the crises, the desertions and the numerous sufferings of the Church's members, but also renewed and more intense, the sense of solidarity and reciprocal dependence in the Mystical Body of Christ, which is currently growing stronger amongst all those who have been baptized, in accordance with their vocation and their mission ..."

Crises and desertions "of the Church's members" is a description of apostasy in the ranks. To this very concrete and demonstrable sign the Pope opposes a rather vague intangible: "the sense of solidarity, etc." which he believes "is currently growing stronger". Certainly the Pope, with his large view of people and events, would be in a position to know this. It is equally true, however, that his statement is incapable of being proved or disproved; it seems as much an assertion as a sign. The last set of signs the Holy Father describes concern:

"the withdrawal from God and His abandonment at the hands
of individuals and societies, but also a bursting forth of the Spirit
of Truth in hearts and communities, leading to sacrifice and martyrdom in order to preserve the image and likeness of God in man
(cf. Gen 1.27)."

The individual and societal abandonment of God is another description of apostasy. To this concrete, demonstrable sign the Pope opposes
"the Spirit of Truth", and rightly so, for the Holy Ghost opposes apostasy with the truth of Revelation. However, the Pope's characterization
of the Holy Ghost "bursting forth in hearts and communities" lends itself to misinterpretation, since traditional theology denies the Holy
Ghost can be possessed by non-Catholic "communities". Moreover, his
implication that man has retained the image and likeness of God after
the Fall is also difficult theologically, since such a retention would make
Christ's redemptive death on the Cross irrelevant to man's salvation.
Refusing to recognize the permanency of original sin, or to suppose, as
the Pope seems to, that a purely manmade sacrifice or martyrdom can
somehow "preserve the image and likeness of God in man" (which was
destroyed in the Fall) is characteristic of someone who holds to the theory of universal salvation.[16]

The more immediate point, however, is that this address, along with
some remarks made by John Paul during the 2000 beatification ceremony of Francisco and Jacinta Marto, is as close as he has come to revealing the Third Secret of Fatima – including the supposed revelation
of the "entire" Third Secret in June, 2000. In both instances, John Paul
made veiled allusions to religious apostasy and a crisis of faith.

Against this crisis of faith he proposes his own solutions — Vatican II,
Assisi, perhaps even universal salvation — as remedies, while remaining
silent on the remedy demanded by Heaven: true devotion to the Immaculate Heart of the Mother of God. Since the Pope has studied Fatima it
is fair to assume he knows the difference between Fatima's message and
his own. Yet he consistently attempts to replace the Fatima Message
with his own. Is he intentionally defying the divine message? Is he trying to "neo-modernize" Fatima? Or does he simply not believe there is
anything heavenly about the Fatima Message (as opposed to the actual
apparitions — Father Dhanis' false distinction)? Can any of these atti-
tudes be reconciled with the Pope's motto, Totus Tuus — his public
pledge to the Blessed Virgin that he is "totally Hers"? Can one claim to
belong "totally" to the Blessed Virgin and then not only ignore Her message, but seem to consistently attempt to subvert it? Should these be
called acts of devotion to the Blessed Virgin, or acts of hostility? Acts of a
beloved son, or a committed enemy?

It is hoped readers will pardon the pointed quality of these questions.
No hostility or impertinence towards the Holy Father is intended. Yet
facts are facts, and here are two more. During John Paul's pontificate

the feast of the Immaculate Heart of Mary has been lowered to the rank of a simple optional memorial, a demotion even a staunch ally of John Paul called "deplorable." The counterpart to this liturgical scorn is John Paul's complete silence regarding the Immaculate Heart of Mary in his Marian encyclical *Redemptoris Mater* (Mother of the Redeemer, 1987).

The intention here is not to belabor Pope John Paul II. He is certainly not the only Pope to be either indifferent to or opposed to Fatima. The point is that there are differences between John Paul II's version of Fatima and the actual message as given by the Blessed Virgin that are so crucial a choice is demanded. This is an unenviable choice to have to make. The reason for the choice is the Pope's other master.

NOTES

1. His Holiness Pope Pius X, *Pascendi Dominici Gregis* (On the Doctrines of the Modernists), 1907, republished by the Daughters of St. Paul, Boston, Massachusetts, p. 23.
2. Yes, it really happened, on May 14, 1999. See *Fides* (International Fides Service, Dossier Indonesia) report, June 4, 1999 – No 4151 – NE 312.
3. This really happened too. According to an account by Cardinal Oddi: "On that day ... I walked through Assisi ... and I saw real profanations in some of the places of prayer. I saw Buddhists dancing around the altar, upon which they placed Buddha in the place of Christ and then incensed it and showed it reverence. A Benedictine protested and the police took him away. There was obvious confusion in the faces of the Catholics who were assisting at the ceremony." ("Confissoes de um Cardeal," Interview granted to Tommaso Ricci, in *30 Dias*, November 1990, p. 64.) Oddi's account is quoted in Atila Sinke Guimarães, *Quo Vadis, Petre?*, translated and edited by Marian Therese Horvat, Ph.D., Los Angeles, Tradition In Action, 1999, pp. 5-6.
4. Some might say stiff-necked — but not me.
5. While some Indult Catholics are content with their position, for others the Indult has merely proved a stepping stone, a more 'respectable' entrance into Tradition.
6. Kwitny, op. cit., p. 504.
7. As quoted in *TWTAF*, Volume III, p. 822.
8. Ibid, pp. 822-823.
9. It is certainly true that on occasion the Pope *has* stressed the necessity of the Church for salvation, but these affirmations are invariably placed beside contrary exhortations to dialogue and religious liberty. *Redemptoris Missio* is a good example of this, but by no means the only one. The bottom line with John Paul II is that conciliar novelties have pride of place over traditional Church teaching.
10. *FIJWE*, op. cit., p. 181.
11. Ibid., p. 190, fn 211 on p. 229.
12. As quoted in Ibid., p. 213.
13. His Holiness Pope John Paul II, *Crossing the Threshold of Hope*, Alfred A. Knopf, 1994, pp. 131-132.
14. Ibid.
15. The Pope's 1997 address to Fatima pilgrims was originally published by *La documentation catholique*, November 16, 1997. It was reprinted in the English translation of CRC Journal No. 304, pp. 3-4, from which all the following quoted extracts in this section come from. I diverge somewhat from the analysis of the Pope's address given by the Abbé de Nantes in No. 304.
16. On John Paul II and universal salvation, see Johannes Dormann, *Pope John Paul II's Theological Journey to the Prayer Meeting of Religions at Assisi*, op. cit., pp. 86-87.

Chapter Nineteen

... And the Conversion of Russia

In his eventful twenty-five year pontificate Pope Wojtyla has used Vatican II to consolidate the union between the post-conciliar Church and the world on a level never dreamed of by his forerunners, two of whom were Felicite Lammenais and Marc Sangnier.

Granted, there are surface differences between Karol Wojtyla and the aforementioned Frenchmen. Unlike Pope Paul VI, Wojtyla was more attracted to German philosophy and theology. It is likely that, for the pre-papal Wojtyla, the appeal of French Jesuit Henri de Lubac was the similarity of his theology to the anonymous Christianity (i.e., universal salvation) of the German theologian, Karl Rahner. Another apparent difference is that where Lammenais and Sangnier sought (at least for a while) to Catholicize the revolution, Pope John Paul II has sought to merge secular society with Christianity through two organizations: Opus Dei and Solidarity.

Consequently, although the Holy Father has repeatedly attributed the fall of Communism in Poland (and Russia) to the consecration of the world to the Immaculate Heart of Mary, there is considerable evidence that John Paul's involvement with Fatima was secondary, and subordinate to, a political/religious problem that for over a decade consumed the best energies of the Pope: the unraveling of the Gordian knot binding Poland to its Communist government.

Pope John Paul II's primary focus was not the Cova da Iria, but the intense pirouettes performed by the Communist government in Poland and Moscow, the socialist-democratic trade union, Solidarity, and Opus Dei. The dance ended in a temporary withdrawal of Communist government from Poland. Pope John Paul II was intimately involved with all parties. His long-standing relationships with them, his vast objectives and his enormous ambitions offer an instructive counterpoint to Heaven's emphasis on devotion to the Immaculate Heart.

The following brief, and admittedly "non-infallible" synopsis of the relationship these three organizations have had with each other, and with Pope John Paul II, is intended to shed some light on whether Russia really has converted, and if so, exactly what it has converted to.

Opus Dei

John Paul's relationships with Solidarity and Opus Dei preceded his election to the papacy. "Poland was Opus Dei's first deep-penetration operation," according to investigative journalist Robert Hutchison,[1] who states that Opus' home base was Vienna. By coincidence, an influential community of Polish intellectuals-in-exile also resided in Vienna, and they were actively recruited by Opus.

During this time, the early to mid 1970's, Cardinal Wojtyla frequently visited Vienna. According to Hutchison, "it was rumored inside Opus Dei that Wojtyla had been inducted as an associate into the Priestly Society of the Holy Cross ..."[2] The Society was a "corporate subsidiary" of Opus Dei. Wojtyla's visits to Vienna then, could have been to visit the Polish intellectuals, some of whom were close friends, to visit Opus' home base, or both.

John Paul's biographers Bernstein and Politi declare:

"Opus Dei had supported Karol Wojtyla since he was Archbishop of Crakow. He had frequently been invited to address its members. In the days just before the conclave that elected him Pope, Wojtyla went to pray at Escriva's (Opus' founder) tomb."[3]

Escriva, who died in 1975, would later be canonized by Pope John Paul II. Less than a month after his election as Pope, John Paul declared that "the transforming of Opus Dei into a Personal Prelature" was "a necessity that can no longer be delayed."[4] In this he departed from his namesakes. Popes Roncalli and Montini had thought this question far from a necessity, and repeatedly delayed Escriva's insistent requests.

Given the new Pope's zeal for the Father (as Escriva was called) and his Work, it was hardly surprising that when John Paul made his first papal visit to Poland in 1979, "he was accompanied by an Opus Dei staff, including his personal secretary, Father Stanislaw Dziwisz," according to Hutchison, who adds:

"Opus Dei's *milites Christi* brought to Poland the financial means to form a Catholic underground that would act, if not in outright defiance of, at least in parallel to the government."[5]

Few orthodox Catholics would quarrel with a Catholic organization attempting to subvert a Communist government. The problem was that Opus also acted "if not in outright defiance of, at least in parallel" to the Church in Poland.[6] And although this is not unusual for Opus, the point is that after 1978 they may have been doing so on orders from Pope Wojtyla. The other organization he was closely connected with was Solidarity. The level of John Paul's involvement with this "spontaneous" trade union caused Italian Cardinals to criticize "the Pope's preoccupation with Polish political events."[7]

Solidarity

The exact origins of Solidarity are disputed, but it was undeniably influenced by a lesser known organization, the Worker's Defense Committee (in Polish, *Komitet Obrony Robotnikow*, or KOR), an illegal underground group of socialists, Marxists, and left-wing Catholics who agitated against Poland's Communist government. Many KOR members were familiar to Cardinal Wojtyla from his days as a writer for the "liberal-socialist" newspaper, *Znak*. According to John Paul's biographer Tad Szulc, "Wojtyla quickly established close ties with KOR, which already was linked with the Catholic Intellectuals' Clubs (KIK), and the so-called (sic) progressive wing of the Church, politically identified with the Cardinal (Wojtyla), played a significant role in the great events to come in Poland."[8]

After Wojtyla became Pope, KOR agitprop displayed a painting of John Paul II, "muscled like an athlete, hands clenched under his chin — one a fine intelligentsia hand, the other a gnarled worker's hand."[9] It was probably the first time socialist art had presented a Pope in a favorable light. KOR's underground newspaper incited Poles against the Communist government, and planned and executed nationwide strikes. Unrest grew.

One of the strikes occurred at the Lenin shipyards in Gdansk. The workers were protesting the firing of a shipyard employee, when the strike was hijacked by an unknown named Lech Walesa, whose dramatic raising of the stakes turned a local issue into an international one. And wouldn't you know it — Walesa singlehandedly made the Communists back down, just like in the movies.

The Gdansk strike is generally thought to be the beginning of Solidarity, but this isn't quite true. Solidarity was never simply an organization of Gdansk shipyard employees. It was an intentionally revolutionary movement steered from the beginning by KOR members, who filled most of the upper level positions, and no one was more aware of this than Pope John Paul II. Surprisingly, the other oar propelling Solidarity's boat may have been the Polish government. According to former KGB agent Anatoliy Golitsyn,

> "...there were 1 million Communist Party members in Solidarity. Forty-two out of the 200 members of the (Polish Communist) Party's Central Committee in 1981 were Solidarity members. Bogdan Lis, Walesa's deputy, was a Central Committee member. Zofia Gryzb, another Solidarity leader, was a member of the Politburo.

> "These leaders were not expelled from the Party for their membership in Solidarity. On the contrary, Solidarity recognized the leading role of the Party and the Party recognized Solidarity's existence ... Solidarity enjoyed access to the state-controlled media. Obstacles were not placed in the way of Walesa's extensive foreign travels, (etc.) ..."[10]

In other words, Poland's Communist government treated Walesa the same way they had treated Cardinal Wojtyla. It is likely that the pre-papal Wojtyla came to know, if only by reputation, many of the Communists in Poland's government; after all, a lot of them were Catholics too. As Pope John Paul II, his involvement with Solidarity and KOR was at a sufficient level for him to realize the Communist infiltration (if it can be called that) of Solidarity. Although it is certainly possible the Pope was unaware of all this, it is difficult to imagine a subtle and shrewd geo-political player like Pope Wojtyla being so oblivious of the politics and alliances of his own country.

Although the Holy Father was enthralled by Solidarity, Cardinal Wyszynski was still Poland's Primate, and he was far less enthusiastic. In fact Wyszynski, although dying, publicly sided with the Communist government against Solidarity, as he feared the demands of the "union" would lead to violence. Siding with the Communists was not an unusual position for the Primate to make; he had been splitting the difference with the Communists for decades. But now Wyszynski's strategy upset Pope John Paul II, who according to Bernstein and Politi, responded to Wyszynski's statements "with irritation and disappointment: 'Oh, this old man ... this old man,' he sighed to two Polish priests who were passing through Castel Gandolfo."[11]

To further undercut the authority of Poland's ailing Primate, John Paul invited Walesa and his family to Rome (they had no trouble coming or going) and publicly praised both him and Solidarity. For such a young, spontaneous trade union, Solidarity had a large budget from the very beginning. Where did the money come from? A small amount came from European socialist trade unions. Much of it seems to have come from the Vatican. Shortly before his death Vatican banker (and Freemason) Roberto Calvi wrote: "I must be repaid the $1,000 million that I furnished at the express wish of the Vatican in favor of Solidarity ..."[12] Granted, Calvi is not the most reliable source; yet he is not the only one to claim the Roman Catholic Church generously subsidized Solidarity. And for what it's worth, it is claimed by those who have studied the situation that Opus Dei, not the CIA, was Solidarity's cash cow. Wherever the money came from, there was enough not only to finance Solidarity operations in Poland, but to open an international Solidarity headquarters in Brussels.

John Paul's Grand Convergence

It was around this time that Agca shot John Paul in St. Peter's Square, and the Pope apparently became convinced that Our Lady of Fatima wanted him to live in order to continue ... his collaborations with Solidarity, Opus Dei, and the Communists?

Wyszynski died while John Paul was recuperating. The Pope reluctantly accepted Wyszynski's request that the Primate's secretary, Jozef

Glemp, be his successor. By this time it didn't much matter who the Primate was, because much of Church policy in Poland was being directed from Rome. Nevertheless, Glemp didn't fit in from the beginning. He was accused of anti-Semitism because he mistrusted the Jewish intellectuals (like Adam Michnik) from KOR who were so influential in advising Solidarity. Noting that "Workers from Solidarity even restored desecrated Jewish monuments," Jonathan Kwitny diplomatically adds, "there was still a perception that KOR was primarily Jewish, though the leadership was at least equally composed of John Paul's old Crakow Catholic intellectual group."[13]

In 1982 Glemp visited Rome twice, and according to a Roman Cardinal, was "bawled out" both times by John Paul for criticizing Solidarity. (He would go back in the doghouse in 1996 for saying Communism was still alive, and a threat to Poland). It would be incorrect to conclude from this that John Paul's ardor for Solidarity resulted from his anti-Communism. His encyclical *Labored Exercens* (On Human Work, 1981) was more than sympathetic to Communism, which detracted from his criticisms of capitalism. The Pope went so far as to call Communism a "protest in the face of injustice ... a protest on the part of the great world of workers, which then became an ideology."

This characterization is not only historically inaccurate, it is morally appalling. Russian Bolshevism was anything but a workers' movement. The Communists hunted down Russian peasants and workers and slaughtered them by the thousands, worked them to death by the tens of thousands in the gulags, and starved them to death by the millions by manufacturing famines. Yet after calling these cold-blooded massacres a "protest in the face of injustice", the Pope declares that "this protest has also become part of the teaching of the Church."[14]

What the Pope appears to be doing here is attempting to complete what he sees as a convergence between Communism and Christianity. The synthesis of the two is Solidarity, to which John Paul makes unmistakable allusions to in the same encyclical. Without taking the time to present this step by step, it can fairly be said that John Paul's ambition is to synthesize Communism and Christianity into a third entity comprising both "spent" creeds. The catalyst for this alchemy is humanism, with liberal doses of the New Theology of Vatican II applied as religious gloss.

So what? Well, getting back to Fatima, the point to all this is that it has nothing to do with Fatima, except perhaps as another example of the spread of Russia's errors — or an example of the Third Secret. As for the papal motto *"Totus Tuus"*, this may be better applied to Solidarity (or for that matter, Opus Dei) than to Our Lady of Fatima. No one can serve two masters, not even a man as gifted as Pope John Paul II. He will, as Our Lord said, love one and hate the other. The object of the Pope's devotion, attention, and concern during over half of his pontificate was not the Immaculate Heart of Mary. His devotion was to his collaboration with the socialist, Communist, left-wing Catholic and Jewish intellectuals in Solidarity, relationships that preceded by many years Wojtyla's election to the papacy.

The public premise of Solidarity was very similar to the Sillon of Marc Sangnier. The Sillon was a "non-denominational" social change organization that sought to elevate the dignity of the working man. In condemning the Sillon Pius X warned it would lead to socialism. The leadership of Solidarity were, if not avowed socialists, certainly on speaking terms with the theory.[15]

It must be understood that Solidarity was never intended just for Poland. Solidarity was — and is — the civil religion John Paul wants the entire world to adopt in anticipation of the "new advent of humanity" he thought he could see coming. It is the working model of his "civilization of love": non-violent, morally principled, concerned with the dignity of man, and committed to ensuring a fair distribution of surplus wealth. These principles were able to unite Catholics, Jews, Communists, socialists, and other atheists to a common cause. All the Catholics had to do was disregard all those divisive Christian dogmas that separate peoples. What unites us is greater than what separates us, Pope John had said. Funny how these and other conciliar expressions have taken on new meanings over time.

The civilization of love is John Paul's cure not just for "Russia's errors", but for the entire apostate world. It all sounds wonderful, of course. Much better than the Blessed Virgin's insistence on prayer, penance, reparation, and sacrifice. Unfortunately, the Pope's appealing vision does not appear to be Catholic in any real, substantial sense. There is no precedent in Scripture or Tradition for utopia on earth, except when it is offered by the devil as a temptation. In the hard, real world of universal apostasy, the "civilization of love" seems little more than a bizarre joke, a utopian what-if, a secular escape for Christians who have forsaken Christ and His Cross, and don't want to be reminded about it.

With this section as a backdrop, the claim that Russia has been converted can now be examined.

Russia's Conversion

Between 1985 and 1991 Mikhail Gorbachev implemented in Russia the well known political reforms of glasnost and perestroika. Glasnost ("openness") supposedly granted Russians freedoms of speech and association unknown under Stalin. Perestroika ("restructuring") sought to introduce economic reforms which would allow Russia to compete with other capitalist countries. The introduction of these reforms were accompanied by fond hopes that Russia had truly converted as Our Lady of Fatima had promised it would. These hopes were encouraged in no small measure by the Vatican and by Pope John Paul II.

When the Blessed Virgin spoke to Lucy of Russia converting, She was not referring to a political conversion from Communism to democracy. To save souls, "God wishes to establish in the world devotion to My Immaculate Heart," the Virgin had told Lucy. The conversion will be a radical return to the One True Faith preserved by the Holy Roman Catholic Church. It will be a miraculous religious conversion, so that all may understand and venerate the divine role of the Immaculate Heart of Mary in the economy of salvation. This is how Sister Lucy has always spoken of it.

With that in mind let us examine Russia today. After all, big oaks from small acorns grow. If the Holy Father said in the 1980's that Russia was converted, surely there will be signs of this ten years later.

Article 14 of Russia's 1993 constitution declares: "the Russian Federation is a secular state. No religion may be established as the state religion or a compulsory religion." The Russian Orthodox religion remains the primary religion in Russia. Its main competitors are a galaxie of Protestant sects, and Islam. Also represented are the Jehovah's Witnesses, the Mormons, the Quakers, the Hare Krishnas, the Moonies, the Unification Church, and the Church of Scientology.

While it is true that Russia has "religious liberty," the Russian Orthodox Church has taken decisive action to ensure its primacy. Aligning itself with nationalist politicians who decry the "sterile and decadent" religions of the West, the Orthodox Church has helped enact a variety of laws restricting missionary activity and the purchase of land and buildings by non-Orthodox religions, who must also register with the government and be "approved" before being given religious liberty.

Regarding Catholicism, the Church in Russia has agreed not to proselytize in Orthodox "territories." Since about seventy-five per cent of Russia is Orthodox, that doesn't leave a lot of room to move. Obviously, there has been no mass conversion to Catholicism as implied by the Message of Fatima.

Yet Pope John Paul II insists that Russia has converted. In 1994 the Holy Father stated, "we can affirm it is happening, especially in Russia. How? Above all in the return to the traditions and practices of the Orthodox Church." The Pope also noted, with apparent approval, that "Protestant communities" were "also enjoying a renewal there (Russia)."[16] So it seems that "conversion" for John Paul is a return not to Catholicism, but to any religion. Clearly, this is not the same type of "conversion of Russia" spoken of by the Blessed Virgin through Lucy.

Well then, perhaps the apparent stability of the Orthodox Church and the Protestant sects in Russia have initiated a gradual conversion of morals which we should view with hope and encourage with patience. What has happened in Russia in the last ten years?

In Russia in the 1990's, ten years after it was claimed that Russia had converted, abortion is the primary means of birth control. According to U.S. government researchers:

"Russia continues to have the highest abortion rate in the world, as did the Soviet Union. In the mid-1990s, the Russian average was 225 terminated pregnancies per 1000 births and ninety-eight abortions for every 1,000 women of childbearing age per year — a yearly average of 3.5 million. An estimated one-quarter of maternal fatalities result from abortion procedures."[17]

Regarding divorce, the researchers conclude:

"In the 1980s the divorce rate in the Soviet Union was second in the world only to that of the United States, although 'unofficial divorces' and separations also were common ... In the first half of the 1990s, the conditions contributing to the majority of Russia's divorces did not change, and the divorce rate increased."

Identified as "major causes" of divorce were infidelity and drunkenness. Regarding alcohol, researchers concluded:

"Russia's rate of alcohol consumption, traditionally among the highest in the world, and rising significantly in the 1990s, is a major contributor to the country's health crisis ... alcoholism has reached epidemic proportions, particularly among males ... A 1995 Russian study found that regular drunkenness affected between 25 and 60 per cent of blue-collar workers ... In 1994 some 53,000 people died of alcohol poisoning, an increase of about 36,000 since 1991."

There is additional evidence that instead of a moral conversion, Russia has suffered a moral relapse in the 10 years since she has supposedly "converted": "In 1995 an estimated 2 million Russians used narcotics, more than twenty times the total recorded ten years earlier in the entire Soviet Union, with the number of users increasing 50 percent every year in the mid-1990s."

Then there is "the Crime Wave of the 1990s":

"In the first half of the 1990s, crime statistics moved sharply and uniformly upward ... the crime rate nearly doubled between 1985 and 1992. By the early 1990s theft, burglary, and other acts against property accounted for about two-thirds of all crime in Russia. Of particular concern to citizens, however, was the rapid growth of violent crime, including gruesome homicides."

Space does not permit a description of the massive organized crime network in Russia (the "*mafiya*"), the introduction of pornography and gay rights into Russian culture, and the subsequent increase in cases of sexual violence and AIDS.

Remember the defeat of Communism? Today the Communists are a force in the Russian Parliament, and despite billions and billions of dollars of Western aid, Russia gets sicker and sicker, thanks in part to a toxic dose of our own cultural pathology. Even *Time* magazine is starting to worry again about "all those nuclear weapons" that belong to "an increasingly desperate, belligerent Russian state ..."[18]

Such are the facts, as reported by secular sources. Meanwhile, people who should know better claim that Russia has "converted", either to Catholicism or "religious liberty". It does seem true that Russia, for a time, has adopted a modest version of religious liberty. This change coincided not with a moral conversion, but a moral relapse. And not just in Russia.

As for the assertion that Russia has converted to Catholicism, this cannot be seriously maintained by any rational adult.

NOTES

1. Hutchison, op. cit., p. 355.
2. According to Huchison (p. 149), Wojtyla made three appearances and his talks were bound into a book entitled *La fede della Chiesa*.
3. Bernstein and Politi, op. cit., p. 394.
4. Hutchison, op. cit., p. 258.
5. Ibid.
6. Ibid.
7. Kwitny, op. cit.
8. Tad Szulc, *Pope John Paul II, The Biography*, Scribner, 1995, p. 203.
9. Kwitny, op. cit., p. 368. The painting of the Pope was displayed at a highly controversial, very well attended art exhibit in Crakow in 1980.
10. Golitsyn, op. cit., pp. 329-333.
11. Bernstein and Politi, op. cit., p. 245.
12. Hutchison, op. cit., p. 331. Calvi's letter was an attempt to recoup for the Vatican some expenditures he had made as their banker. Calvi was certainly no boy scout, but neither were any of the other financial advisors, and Cardinals, that were implicated in the Vatican Banking Scandal. Spokesmen for Opus Dei denied any illegal involvement by their organization. The alleged stonewalling (some call it a cover-up) of John Paul II in the scandal is beyond the scope of this story, as is the exact nature of Pope Wojtyla's relationship with Opus Dei. At the very least he appears to have been their client.
13. Kwitny, op. cit., p. 386.
14. Extracts from the Pope's encyclical were drawn from *Crossing the Threshold of Hope*, op. cit, pp. 130-142, and Kwitny, op. cit.
15. Besides the Sillon, the other historical parallel with Poland and Solidarity is, believe it or not, the Spanish Civil War. Remember the coalition of leftist groups who were all eventually co-opted by the Communists. Anatoliy Golitsyn argues that Solidarity, despite being full of the Pope's friends, is a Communist front organization seeking to broaden Communism's base among trade unions and the working class, and to fool Western governments into thinking Soviet Communism is moribund. In 1984 Golitsyn predicted "ex-Communists" would eventually rule Poland again under the guise of a coalition government. This came to pass in the 1990's. See Golitsyn, op. cit., pp. 328-337.
16. *Crossing the Threshold of Hope*, op. cit., pp. 175-176.
17. All the information on the state of Russia appearing in this section is taken from *Russia, A Country Study*, researched and published by the Federal Research Division of The Library of Congress of the United States, 1998, pp. 158-161, 209-216, 250-258, 268-273, 571-575. Also used was the CQ (Congressional Quarterly) Researcher for 3/95, 12/96, and 9/97.
18. *Time* Magazine, September 7, 1998.

Chapter Twenty

The Living Secret

(Author's note: My premise, which may not be shared by all readers, is that the Vatican has yet to reveal the entire Third Secret of Fatima. I maintain this despite the fact that in June, 2000, the Congregation for the Doctrine of the Faith (CDF) issued the document The Message of Fatima, *which purported to contain the entire Third Secret. Yet* The Message of Fatima *does not account for the one phrase of the Third Secret we* do *know: "In Portugal the dogma of the Faith will always be preserved etc." Sister Lucy, in her Fourth Memoir, attributes these words to the Blessed Virgin, words that Fatima experts have for decades thought to have been part of the text of the Third Secret.)*

Although the exact text of most of the third part of the Fatima Secret is unknown, much can be deduced from the first two parts of the Secret, and the known text of the Third Secret. Of primary importance are references Sister Lucy has made to the Third Secret. The research on Fatima done by Father Alonso, and the elaboration on his work by Frère Michel and Frère François of the CRC are also very important. Of further assistance are statements by Cardinal Ratzinger and other Churchmen, and the signs of our times.

First, a review of the known parts of the Fatima Secret. The first part of the Secret is the terrifying vision of hell the Blessed Virgin showed the young seers. The message: Hell is real, and because of man's continual offenses against God innumerable souls are going there. The second part of the secret reveals God's designation of devotion to the Immaculate Heart of Mary as the spiritual remedy for the Twentieth Century. If the Virgin's requests concerning the establishment of devotion to Her Heart are heeded by the Church, Russia would convert and another World War would be avoided. We are living through the consequences of the Church's failure to heed the Blessed Virgin's requests. The temporal chastisements from the second part of the Fatima Secret will cease when the Pope, in union with all his bishops, solemnly consecrates Russia to the Immaculate Heart of the Blessed Virgin Mary, and gives proper importance to the devotion of the Five First Saturdays. Until Russia is consecrated her errors will continue to spread, causing wars, famines, and persecutions of the Church.

Our Lady also prophesied that "various nations will be annihilated" and that "the Holy Father will have much to suffer." It is the opinion of the Church's official expert on Fatima, Father Joaquin Maria Alonso, C.M.F., that the "annihilation" of nations and the sufferings of the Holy Father announced by the Blessed Virgin have not yet occurred.

The Third Secret

Grammatically speaking, the text of the Fatima Secret has a definite pattern. Like prophecies in Scripture, the Fatima Secret is a series of alternating promises, warnings, and predictions of consequences if the warnings are not heeded. It is reasonable to assume the last part of the Secret, which presently is unknown, also follows the rhythm of the first two parts.

It is also reasonable to assume the Third Secret mentions the Holy Father. This would be consistent with the prominent role the Holy Father has in both the second Secret, and the revelation to Lucy at Tuy, where Mary requested that the Holy Father consecrate Russia to Her Immaculate Heart. It would also confirm a statement made by Father Schweigl, who served as Pius XII's envoy to Sister Lucy in the 1950s. In 1952 Pius XII instructed Father Schweigl to interrogate Lucy. Based on this interrogation, Father Schweigl later confided that the Third Secret "has two parts: one concerns the Pope."[1] Moreover, since it is known that the Third Secret mentions "the dogma of the faith", it would be unusual for the chief Shepherd of the Faith not to be mentioned as well. It is possible that the hidden text even mentions the Pope by name, like Pope Pius XI was named in the second Secret.[2]

Like the first two parts, the third part of the Secret is concise, about twenty handwritten lines on a single sheet of paper. It begins: "In Portugal the dogma of the Faith will always be preserved etc." It ends, "In the end, My Immaculate Heart will Triumph. The Holy Father will consecrate Russia to Me, and she will be converted, and a certain period of peace will be granted to the world."[3]

Father Alonso was appointed by the Bishop of Leiria-Fatima "to prepare the critical and definitive study of Fatima and its message."[4] Alonso was an internationally known theologian and scholar who held a Doctorate in philosophy and theology from the Gregorian in Rome. In compiling his twenty-four volume history on Fatima, Father Alonso was allowed unlimited access to published and unpublished Fatima documents. For a time he was even allowed unrestricted access to Sister Lucy. He initially agreed with the decisions of popes not to reveal the third part of the Secret, declaring that speculation on the hidden text was "impertinent." Before the end of his life, however, Alsonso declared:

"If 'In Portugal the dogma of the Faith will always be preserved,' it can clearly be deduced from this that in other parts of the Church these dogmas are going to become obscure or even lost altogether."[5]

A Consensus

Dr. Alonso was not given to rash speculations, so when he also wrote that it was "completely probable" that the Third Secret contains "concrete references to the crisis of faith within the Church," and to "grave pastoral negligence of the upper hierarchy,"[6] he was probably being as discreet as the truth would allow him to be. If he was off the mark with these conclusions, Lucy would surely have set him straight during their consultations together. Yet not only did Lucy not correct Father Alonso, she echoed him, in her interview with Father Fuentes, and in her letters to her priest-nephews. She repeatedly spoke of a "diabolical disorientation"; of "disoriented souls" in the Church being "fooled by false doctrine"; and "a great disorientation in so many persons who occupy places of responsibility ... They are blind men guiding other blind men."[7]

In passing, let it be remembered that since her childhood Lucy has been a model of discretion and prudence regarding the Fatima Message. If there were any kinder, less blunt way for her to tell the truth here, surely she would have done so. Father Alonso, the official expert on Fatima, and Lucy, the last living seer who received the Fatima Message directly from the Blessed Virgin, are consistent in implying that the Third Secret deals with a widespread, perhaps universal, apostasy in the Church. Alonso's exhaustive study of Fatima may have led him too close to the actual content of the Third Secret. According to Frère François, in 1975 Fatima Bishop do Amaral was pressured by the Vatican to forbid publication of Father Alonso's twenty-four volume study of Fatima.[8] No official expert on Fatima was appointed to replace Alonso after his death in 1981.

Father Alonso joins the company of Cardinal Ratzinger, who was also censored about his remarks on the Third Secret. Prior to being edited, the Cardinal, who has read the Third Secret, said the Fatima Message involved "a radical call to conversion." This corresponds to the first part of the Secret, the vision of hell so vivid the children were terrified. The Cardinal then described the Secret involving "the absolute seriousness of history." This corresponds to the second part of the Secret: the prophecy of the Second World War and the role of Russia as God's scourge, spreading error, causing wars, and persecuting the Church. Then the Cardinal spoke of "the dangers threatening the faith and life of the Christian, and therefore the world. And also the importance of the last times."[9] Following the methodical progression of Ratzinger's remarks, these statements should refer to the third part of the Secret. Progressive theologians are by habit obscure, but Ratzinger was direct enough here not only to be censored, but to confirm the conclusion of the Fatima expert, Father Alsonso, and the veiled statements of Sister Lucy, that the third part of the Fatima Secret deals with an apostasy in the hierarchy of the Church. After all, apostasy would qualify as a "danger threatening the faith and life" of Christians. And the Cardinal's allusion to "dangers threatening the faith" coincides with the topic of the Third Secret: "the dogma of the faith."

Sister Lucy's remarks concerning the Third Secret are of particular importance. Since 1957 — the same year the Vatican requested the written text of the Third Secret — Lucy has been making veiled references to its content.

She told Father Fuentes in 1957 that the Blessed Virgin had indicated to her that these were the last times of the world; that "the devil was about to wage a decisive battle with the Blessed Virgin"; that the devil will focus on overcoming "souls consecrated to God", which would leave "the souls of the faithful abandoned by their leaders"; that our last two remedies, offered by God Himself through the Blessed Virgin Mary, are the Holy Rosary and devotion to the Immaculate Heart; and that rejection of this remedy would terminate divine forgiveness because "we will have committed a sin which the Gospel calls the sin against the Holy Ghost." According to Sister Lucy, "This sin consists of openly rejecting, with full knowledge and consent, the salvation which He offers."[10]

In her letters Lucy described a "diabolical disorientation" in the Church that had caused many to be "blinded to the point of being incapable of seeing error." The Rosary was "the prayer Our Lady recommended the most" at Fatima, wrote Sister Lucy, "as if to arm us in advance, foreseeing these days of diabolical campaign." Lucy further declared that the devil had succeeded in infiltrating "evil under the cover of good," and that the diabolical disorientation was rampant in "persons who occupy places of responsibility." Being "fooled by false doctrine," they became "blind men guiding other blind men."[11]

It is highly unlikely these statements are mere personal prophecy. This would be out of character for a religious with as disciplined (and lengthy) a career as Sister Lucy. It is a virtual certainty that her statements allude to the hidden text of the Fatima Secret. Her remarks concern the topic "the dogma of the Faith." They fit Father Alonso's conclusions that the Third Secret speaks of apostasy in the "upper hierarchy" of the Church. And Lucy's remarks coincide with Ratzinger's comment that the Third Secret deals with "dangers threatening the faith." Therefore, it can be said that there is a consensus on the topic of the Third Secret by Sister Lucy, Father Alonso, and Cardinal Ratzinger.

This consensus can be broadened to include Brother Michael and Frère François of the CRC, who have thoroughly examined the evidence in the CRC's multi-volume work on Fatima. The consensus also includes the former Bishop of the diocese of Leiria-Fatima, Dom Alberto Cosme do Amaral. In September of 1984, during an interview at the University of Vienna, Bishop do Amaral stated: "The Secret of Fatima speaks neither of atomic bombs nor nuclear warheads ... its content concerns only our faith. To identify the Secret with catastrophic announcements or with a nuclear holocaust is to deform the meaning of the message. The loss of the faith of a continent is worse than the annihilation of a nation; and it is true that the faith is continually diminishing in Europe."[12]

Later Bishop do Amaral denied saying this. He was interviewed again in 1995 by Frère François, who reported that "Msgr. do Amaral had just retired and he was no longer subject to reprimand for having spoken too openly about the Third Secret ... he confided to me (that he):

> "'had consulted Lucy, and had obtained her assent before af-
> firming at Vienna that the contents of the Third Secret relate
> only to our faith, the loss of the faith.' It was astounding: Mgr. do
> Amaral had completely forgotten the denials he made in January
> 1986."[13]

Another "admission-retraction" occurred in 1997, when the well known Marian theologian Abbé Rene Laurentin was reported to have said that the Third Secret "concerned deviations from the faith that would arise in the Church after Vatican II." Laurentin was also reported as declaring that "the faith is disappearing"; that "one may observe a serious crisis at the heart of the Church herself"; and that "the Third Secret does not predict a cosmic cataclysm but the crisis of the faith, the apostasy, that has supposedly struck the Church since the Second Vatican Council."[14]

These remarks were broadcast on Italian television on October 13, 1997, the 80th anniversary of the dance of the sun, and the following day in the Portuguese and Italian press. The Vatican responded immediately. Cardinal Ratzinger declared Laurentin's remarks were "fantasies and twaddle. Three popes have been acquainted with the Secret, and if none of them judged it opportune to publish it, it is because they will have had good reasons. The whole content of the Fatima apparitions is based on the request of the Madonna for 'Prayer and Penance'. It is there that the essential lies."[15]

In passing, let it be noted that Ratzinger has several "essential" versions of the content of the Third Secret — and each one contradicts the other. Back to Laurentin, however, who, getting the hint, quickly retracted his earlier admissions. Perhaps Ratzinger, when he retires, will emulate Bishop do Amaral and resume his former frankness regarding the content of the Third Secret. For now, it is reasonable to conclude that Ratzinger, do Amaral, and Laurentin were silenced by the only man who could do so: Pope John Paul II. Speaking of popes, can the consensus on the content of the Third Secret be broadened to include a Pope? The future John Paul I visited Sister Lucy at the Carmelite convent in Coimbra, and later supposedly told his friends, "The Secret, it's terrible." In his subsequent writings Cardinal Luciani urged recitation of the Rosary to avoid, in his words, "the apostasy."[16]

The Secret Visible

Lucy wished the Third Secret revealed by 1960 because the Blessed Virgin had told her "it would seem clearer." This means that since 1960 we have been living in the time of the Third Secret. According to Frère François, Lucy confirmed this in the 1970s when she declared, "The chastisement predicted by Our Lady in the Third Secret has already begun."[17]

This statement of Lucy's, and the consensus by informed parties that the Third Secret concerns apostasy in the Church is confirmed by ... the apostasy in the Church since 1960. Surely Lucy took no satisfaction in warning of "disoriented souls" in the grips of a "diabolical disorientation", but the state of a majority of consecrated religious today fits her description exactly. The progressive Council Fathers at Vatican II chided the conservative minority for failing to heed "the signs of our times." Let us do so, and be mercifully brief: Weekly Mass attendance in the U.S. has declined from 71 per cent of all Catholics in 1963 to only 22 per cent in 1993 — an astonishing 50 per cent decline since the Council. The situation in Europe is even more catastrophic, with Mass attendance having declined since the Council to single digits.

In 1960 the annual number of converts made in the U.S. was 140,000. By 1995 the number was only 75,000 - 80,000. In 1965 there were some 57,000 priests in America. By 1995, after 30 years of population growth, the number of priests had declined to only 49,000, leaving 8,000 fewer priests than there were 30 years ago. Many of the remaining priests are nearing retirement age. In fact, the number of priests per 10,000 Catholics has declined from 7.87 in 1965 to 5.46 in 1995, which means that there are 30 per cent fewer priests available today than there were in 1965. At the close of Vatican II in 1965, there were approximately 12,000 brothers. By 1995 there were only 6,000. At the close of the Council there were approximately 180,000 sisters. By 1995 there were only 100,000. Some 4,200,000 students attended Catholic elementary schools in the Council's final year. By 1995 there were only 1,800,000. That's for America. The situation is equally disastrous in the world as a whole. According to *L'Osservatore Romano*, by the end of 1995 there were actually 44,000 fewer priests in the world than there were 25 years ago — despite a doubling of the world's population in that time.[18]

The objective statistics are catastrophic, almost unbelievably negative. By any measure the objective statistics are bitter news, and interesting fruit for a Council Pope John described as a "new Pentecost." Fortunately no one has died holding their breath in anticipation of the "great renewal" Popes John and Paul solemnly assured everyone the Council was ushering in. This utterly false papal prophecy is still making the rounds. More recently John Paul II solemnly assured everyone that a *"new springtime of Christian life"* would "be revealed by the Great Jubilee, if Christians are docile to the action of the Holy Spirit."[19] There was a time not so long ago when popes were pretty fair prophets. Not anymore. The conciliar popes have all been competent, highly intelligent, in many ways remarkably gifted men. Yet they haven't been able to predict the weather. Far more serious, the popes have been unable to stop the apostasy which is steadily mutating into ever more perverse forms. Even worse, apostasy has become normalized, and in many American dioceses and seminaries has become the new orthodoxy. In other words, prominent parts of the Catholic Church are actively destroying the faith of Catholics. Occasionally the conciliar popes have been forced to allude to the utterly devastated condition of the Church God gave them to shepherd. Paul VI said "the confusion" among "those exercising the highest authority" had created "a crisis of faith." Even John Paul II, in his otherwise resolutely optimistic Apostolic Letter, *Tertio Millennio Adveniente*, unexpectedly jack-knifed into the following passage:

> "It cannot be denied that, for many Christians, the spiritual life is passing through *a time of* uncertainty which affects not only their moral life but also their life of prayer and the *theological correctness of their faith* (which) is sometimes disoriented by erroneous theological views, the spread of which is abetted by the crisis of obedience vis-a-vis the Church's Magisterium."[20]

John Paul's use of the word "disoriented" recalls Lucy's references to "diabolical disorientation"; it has been speculated that this phrase (along with Paul VI's expression "the smoke of satan") is in the text of the Third Secret. Also of interest is the Holy Father's description of "erroneous theological views", which matches Lucy's reference to "false doctrines." Of further note is John Paul's implication that the false doctrines are spreading, not diminishing. Last, the Holy Father uses what has become Vatican code for apostasy, "the crisis of faith." This term was also used by Pope Paul VI and Cardinal Ratzinger in describing the post-conciliar Church. Ironically, the Pope's words contradict his claim that Russia has been converted. Our Lady has linked Russia's conversion with "a time of peace." It is quite obvious there is no peace, either in the Church or the world. The conclusion seems inescapable: the hidden text of the Third Secret almost certainly concerns a nearly universal apostasy from the faith by the Church hierarchy.

The Vatican's response to the Third Secret, and to the "signs of our times", does not rebut this conclusion. In 1960 the Vatican refused to reveal the Third Secret and began to restrict Sister Lucy's visitors and her public and private statements. Vatican justifications for not revealing the Third Secret have ranged from the incoherent ("Sister Lucy is still living") to the nonsensical ("The Vatican knows the content of the Third Secret") to the intentionally misleading (the Third Secret is insignificant, it is too sensational, it is a message of hope, and so on). One wonders at the presumption of declaring that a message from the Blessed Virgin concerning the dogma of the Faith is insignificant. But let's say the presumption is correct. If the Third Secret is in fact insignificant, why doesn't the Vatican simply reveal it, reproach everyone for their impertinence, and move on to important matters? If the Third Secret is merely pleasant, say, an exhortation to please Mary by praying the Rosary a lot more, why did it take Sister Lucy an agonizing three months, and finally the intercession of the Blessed Virgin, to write twenty lines on a piece of paper? If the Third Secret is such a small matter, why has Sister Lucy been silenced for decades? Why has the Vatican not allowed her to publicly contradict those in the Church who falsely claim she has said the consecration of Russia has been done?

How have the popes who have read the Third Secret responded to Lucy? Pope John XXIII never spoke to her, and never publicly mentioned her name or made any reference to the Third Secret. Pope Paul never publicly referred to the Third Secret, and refused to speak privately with Sister Lucy after insisting on her attendance at the Fatima Jubilee in 1967. Pope John Paul II has met privately with Sister Lucy several times. In their first meeting the Pope tried to persuade Lucy that the Third Secret shouldn't be revealed because people would not understand it. Nothing is known of the content of their second meeting, but there is considerable evidence that Sister Lucy continues to contradict the Pope's claim that the consecration of Russia has been done. In short, not only has the Vatican been unable to refute a convergence of evidence that strongly indicates the Third Secret concerns an apostasy of the Church hierarchy, statements by popes and Cardinals have unwittingly confirmed the evidence.

Shortly before his death Father Alonso explained things this way:

> "An inopportune revelation of the text would only have further exasperated the two tendencies which continue to tear the Church apart: a traditionalism that would believe itself to be assisted by the Fatima prophecies, and a progressivism which would have lashed out against these apparitions, which in such a scandalous manner would seem to put the brakes on the conciliar Church's forward progress ..."

Alonso concluded the conciliar popes "did not consider the moment had come to lift the veil of mystery, in circumstances where the Church has still not overcome the frightening impact of twenty post-conciliar years, during which the crisis of the Faith has installed itself at every level."[21]

These are prudent, guarded conclusions. Alonso is certainly correct that pastoral concerns may have played a part in the conciliar popes' decision not to reveal the Third Secret, even though such concerns, while valid, would seem to be subordinated to the will of Heaven. Yet there were other reasons, and another line of reasoning concerning the popes' silence that Father Alonso avoided discussing, again for very good reasons. It has to do with how far may one extend the implications of the Blessed Virgin's words: "In Portugal the dogma of the faith will always be preserved etc." The cautious Alonso felt bold enough to implicate the "upper hierarchy" in apostasy, but did not specify whether the "upper hierarchy" included the papacy. This raises a specter no one wishes to (publicly) pursue, since it could lead to a conclusion that the popes did not reveal the Third Secret because they themselves were (are) victims of the "diabolical disorientation."

Perhaps (this argument might run) the popes — that is, John XXIII, Paul VI, and John Paul II — were quite literally unable to recognize themselves and the state of the Church described by the Blessed Virgin in the Third Secret. This amounts to a "temporary insanity" defense. Another possibility, and this is the worst case scenario, is that the aforementioned popes were not victims but agents of delusion, who deliberately buried the Secret in order to collaborate with radical theologians and non-Catholic periti in the implementation of a decades-long series of reforms that are not only un-Catholic, but will inevitably be shown to be non-Christian as well. It is not being said here that this is in fact what happened, only that the nature of the Third Secret and the state of the Church at present make even this scandalous scenario a possibility.

At any event, we behold a situation that has no precedent in a Church that has seen everything. Except, perhaps, the fulfillment of part of the Apocalypse. Cardinal Ratzinger and Sister Lucy have said the Third Secret concerns the end times. The Cardinal said the Third Secret involves "the importance of the last times," and added that it "corresponds to what is announced in Scripture." Lucy told Father Fuentes the Blessed Virgin had made her understand "that we are living in the last times." In response to a question about the content of the Third Secret Lucy replied, "It is in the Gospel and the Apocalypse, read them!" Later, Lucy specified Apocalypse chapters 7-13.[22]

There are numerous references linking apostasy with the last times in the New Testament (see I Tim. 4:1-2; II Tim. 3:1-5; II Tim. 4:3-5; Jude 1:18; II Peter 3:3-9; II Thess. 2:3).[23] All these references, and the statements concerning the end times made by Our Lord, find their climax and fulfillment in the Apocalypse. Does the Third Secret of Fatima as well?

NOTES

1. *TWTAF*, Volume III, pp. 336-339, 710.
2. The vision of the Third Secret released by the Vatican in June 2000, with its central figure an aging pope, seems to confirm this analysis. We await the release of the *text* of the Third Secret to see if a pope is mentioned by name. Wouldn't it be likely, however, if the text of the Third Secret identified John Paul II as the pope in the vision of the Third Secret, that John Paul himself (or the CDF) would have called attention to this?
3. The words of the Blessed Virgin Mary in Her apparition to the three seers, July 13, 1917.
4. From the jacket of the English translation of Father Alonso's *The Secret of Fatima*, cited below.
5. Joaquin Maria Alonso, C.M.F., *The Secret of Fatima, Fact and Legend*, Ravengate Press, 1990 Revised Edition, p. 80.
6. These comments of Father Alonso, as quoted by Frère Michel in *TWTAF*, Volume III, p. 704, are from the Spanish language *The Secret of Fatima*. Curiously, they are absent from the English translation of the same work, at least in its 1990 Revised edition.
7. *TWTAF*, Volume III, pp. 754-761.
8. *FIJWE*, op. cit., p. viii.
9. *TWTAF*, Vol. III, pp. 820-823.
10. Ibid., pp. 504 et seq.
11. Ibid., 752-760.
12. *FIJWE*, op. cit., p. 243.
13. *CRC* Journal No. 304, pp. 6-7
14. Ibid.
15. Ibid. To the assertion of Cardinal Ratzinger that the essential message of the Third Secret is prayer and penance, Frère François replies, "If the Third Secret contained nothing but an invitation to prayer and penance, it is difficult to understand why the Pope would obstinately refuse to divulge it. Nor is it clear why Our Lady should have ordered the three shepherds to keep secret a message which Her public message on the 13th October supposedly repeated word for word."
16. *FIJWE*, op. cit., pp. 143-144.
17. Ibid.
18. The statistics are from a variety of credible sources, as quoted in Christopher Ferrara's *The Third Secret of Fatima and the Post-Conciliar Debacle*, Catholic Family News Reprint Service, pp. 13-14. There are many other sources I could have also used to confirm the disaster, but it would have been overkill; nobody is really debating the point anymore.
19. Emphasis in the original text of the Apostolic Letter of His Holiness Pope John Paul II, *Tertio Millennio Adveniente, On Preparation for the Jubilee of the Years 2000*, Vatican translation, published by Pauline Books & Media, Boston, Massachusetts, par. 18
20. Emphasis in original, Ibid., par. 36.
21. As quoted in *TWTAF*, Vol. III, pp. 704-706. Father Alonso has also said this of the Third Secret: "Were this text known today by the faithful, it would bring them immense spiritual benefit, and it would even dissipate certain doubts that many enemies of Fatima spread about in order to damage its message. (*CRC* Volume No. 304, p. 6)" A sign of our times is that these "enemies" of Fatima include the conciliar popes, including Pope John Paul II.
22. *FIJWE*, op. cit., p. 279.
23. The Douay-Rheims *New Testament*, translated from the Latin Vulgate, published by Catholic Treasures, Monrovia, California.

Chapter Twenty-One

Beyond Assisi:
The Papal Vision

Patmos is a small, sparsely populated Greek island in the Aegean Sea. In 95 A.D. St. John the Evangelist was exiled there by the Roman Emperor Domitian. Tradition has it that John prayed and fasted in a cave on Patmos, over time carving a cross into the cave rock with his bare hands.

It was in this cave (similar to the dwelling tradition says Our Lord was born in) that the Eternal Word imparted to His beloved disciple the visions contained in the Book of the Apocalypse. The power of the revelation created a huge triple fissure that split the dense cave rock into three parts.

And John beheld a great sign appearing in Heaven:

"A woman clothed with the sun, and the moon under her feet, and on her head a crown of twelve stars. And being with child, she cried travailing in birth, and was in pain to be delivered." (Apoc. 12:1-2)

The woman symbolizes both the Blessed Virgin Mary and the One, True Church.

"And there was seen another sign in heaven: and behold a great red dragon having seven heads, and ten horns, and on his heads seven diadems. And his tail drew the third part of the stars of Heaven, and cast them to the earth." (Apoc. 12:3-4). The great dragon is "that old serpent, who is called the devil and Satan, who seduceth the whole world." (Apoc. 12:9).

Do these Scripture passages apply to Fatima? The woman and the dragon recall Lucy's declaration to Father Fuentes that "the devil is about to wage a decisive battle with the Blessed Virgin." As with all of Lucy's comments, this brings us back to the Fatima Secret, specifically the first part, the vision of hell. The devil had been so successful in sending souls there that God, in His infinite mercy, offered man a remedy: devotion to the Immaculate Heart of the Blessed Virgin Mary.

The Fatima Secret announces the battle between the Blessed Virgin and the devil over souls; what Lucy calls the devil's "decisive battle with the Blessed Virgin." This corresponds to the battle between the woman and the dragon in Apocalypse 12. Both battles were foretold in Genesis

3:15, where God said to the serpent: "I will put enmities between thee and the woman, and thy seed and her seed. She shall crush thy head, and thou shalt lie in wait for her heel."

In his fight against the Blessed Virgin and the Church, the Red Dragon raises from the waters a beast. From his cave on Patmos, John saw:

> "a beast coming up out of the sea, having seven heads and ten horns, and upon his horns ten diadems, and upon his heads names of blasphemy ... and the dragon gave him his own strength, and great power." (Apoc. 13:1-2).

This beast is usually interpreted as political power that persecutes the Church. In St. John's day it was the Roman Empire. In our day it is a gradation of evil: secular humanism that lapses into the institutionalized militant atheism, commonly called Communism. It is also known as atheistic humanism, and as Marxist materialism. By any name, today's beast has spread its errors far beyond the borders of Russia. This has accelerated the secularization of the West — formerly Christendom — and produced an official hostility towards (and suppression of) Christianity. The correlation between this passage of the Apocalypse and the second Secret of Fatima is clear enough.

John continues: "And it was given unto him (the first beast) to make war with the saints, and to overcome them: and power was given him over every tribe, and people, and tongue, and nation." (Apoc. 13:7). The universal nature of the political power of the first beast implies an atheistic universal (or "one-world") government.

Then the apostle "saw another beast coming up out of the earth, and he had two horns, like a lamb, and he spoke as a dragon. And he executed all the power of the former beast in his sight: and he caused the earth, and them that dwell therein, to adore the first beast, whose deadly wound was healed.

"And he did great signs, so that he made also fire to come down from heaven upon the earth in the sight of men. And he seduced them that dwell on the earth, for the signs which were given him to do in the sight of the beast, saying to them that dwell on the earth that they should make the image of the beast, which had the wound by the sword, and lived." (Apoc. 13:11-14).

Later in the Apocalypse (Apoc. 16:13; 19:20; and 20:20), St. John calls the second beast the "false prophet." Combining this with his description of the second beast having "two horns like a lamb" but speaking "as a dragon," the most obvious interpretation is that the second beast is a religious figure or power that is completely in the service of the first beast (e.g., an atheistic world government). Presently, the only universal religious power of the scope implied in the Apocalypse is the Roman Catholic Church, and the only religious figure of the stature implied in the Apocalypse is the Pope.

In the last times the diabolic continues to mimic the Triune God, erecting a satanic trinity (dragon, beast from the sea, and beast from the earth) that is worshiped by virtually all mankind. If Sister Lucy is correct that the Third Secret is contained in the Apocalypse, the most likely correlation is with the second beast, the "false prophet": a satanic caricature of the Holy Spirit that leads souls to apostasies and idolatrously worship the first beast. Eventually this leads to worship of the Father of Lies himself. The result is eternal damnation, the vision of hell shown three small children by a sad, beautiful Lady, on a Portuguese hillside in 1917.

The Prophets

Since the Third Secret began being fulfilled in 1960, and Lucy has indicated the Third Secret is found in the chapters of the Apocalypse detailed above, it is reasonable to expect some evidence, even if only in silhouette, of the mystery of iniquity of the Apocalypse: the false prophet misleading souls to worship the first beast.

A natural temptation is to attach a name to the figure of the false prophet in the Apocalypse. On a superficial level the popes of the Second Vatican Council may even seem to fit the bill. John XXIII predicted the Second Vatican Council would be a "second Pentecost". Paul VI believed the same thing, even after detecting "the smoke of Satan" in the post-conciliar Church. The prediction of John Paul II that the millennial year would usher in a new Springtime in the Church has also gone awry. May these predictions be considered prophecies? If so, does the tragic inaccuracy of these prophecies make one or all of these popes the false prophet of the Apocalypse?

I'm certainly not the one to answer this question, but my hunch is the answer is No. Popes have been mistaken in the past, and will err in the future; this only means they are men. Another error, respectfully, of Popes John and Paul was an unCatholic overconfidence in the inherent goodness of man as proof against error and evil. Moreover, the conciliar popes have seen collaboration with Communism and secular society as not only a positive good, but as essential to developing the cult of man Paul VI announced at the close of Vatican II. These tendencies recall the relationship between the false prophet and the first beast: the false prophet causes the world to worship the beast, the political power that persecutes the Church.

Yet this convergence does not appear exact enough (at present) to warrant an accusation. Furthermore, the false prophet in the Apocalypse is generally thought to be an individual, not a series of individuals like the conciliar popes. Perhaps all that can be said about this highly controversial topic is that the conciliar popes have proclaimed false prophecies, and by their actions and inactions have encouraged anti-Christian organizations around the world, but not on the scale to make any or all of them the false prophet. Obviously, this is not a rousing endorsement of the conciliar popes, for even if they — thankfully — are not the false prophet, they resemble (and perhaps prefigure) him.

A Mystery of Iniquity

In contrast to the non-fulfillment of papal prophecies concerning the efficacy of Vatican II, the fulfillment of the Fatima prophecies is a matter of historical record. The puzzling, obstinate determination of conciliar popes to completely suppress the Fatima Message — particularly in light of the devastated condition of the Church — surpasses a merely prudential decision; can it be best explained as a mystery of iniquinty?

If so, the clearest present indication we have of this mystery of iniquity involves the papal vision that spawned Vatican II, and continues to operate in its wake. The mystery of iniquity and the papal vision are intertwined, like a serpent around a tree. It seems that the fallen angel of light has been allowed to tempt a succession of popes with a rapturous illusion that they have spent themselves — and the Church — striving for, without being able to grasp. It is a vision so radiant that conciliar popes appear to have deemed the destruction of the Catholic faith secondary — perhaps even necessary — to attainment of the consuming vision.[1] This papal vision appears remarkably similar to the Masonic dream of a universal non-Catholic religion.

Pope John XXIII saw a 20th Century Pentecost that would unite the world in the peaceful bonds of brotherhood and mutual charity. Through the operation of the Second Vatican Council the light of the Holy Spirit would descend on mankind and dissolve all religious and political differences that prevented a radical, never before achieved unity among men. Because man would, in John's vision, spontaneously turn towards God and away from error, the Church need only receive her wayward children with open arms. The days of the admonishing mother were over.

Pope Paul's vision encompassed John's vision and expanded on it. To further worldwide unity and universal charity, the Church began to accommodate Communists, Protestants, and other children of God who resolutely remained outside the fold of the One True Church. Tolerance was replaced by religious liberty and heresy was ennobled. The dogma that there is no salvation outside the Catholic Church became a scandal and, like a mad aunt, was locked in the cellar. To become the servant of man's fallen nature, pleasing lies were substituted for Catholic truth, since modern man, despite his high opinion of himself, still preferred darkness to light.

In fidelity to the new object of the Church's worship, the Eternal Sacrifice was also transformed to embrace the cult of man. A sincere, woefully misguided charity assumed Heaven would reward the

Church with good fruit for her efforts to make the Church comfort-able for the world. The eyes of misguided charity made the "tempo-rary" fudging of Church dogma and doctrine appear enlightened rather than deviant.

These preliminary concessions are the cornerstones of the papal vi-sion that has unleashed plagues of tragic, unforeseen consequences on the Church, and therefore the world. The plagues are generative, and compound geometrically. The most obvious example is the Novus Ordo Mass, which routinely undergoes scandalous and faith-diminishing revi-sions. Catholics fancying themselves loyal because they defend these re-visions are headed for despair, and worse, because the transformation of the Mass will not be complete for another generation.

The theology of the Novus Ordo is nominally Catholic, but a day may come when the divorce becomes complete, and Catholic liturgy will become completely alien to Catholic faith. Those left around to recognize this will have to choose yet again between defending the Novus Ordo and defending the salvation of their souls. These trans-formations, so contrary to faith and tradition, are preparations for the consummation of the papal vision that since 1960 has replaced the Fatima Message.

Pope John Paul II's vision is a highly charged synthesis of his prede-cessors, and the basis for his remarkably optimistic view of the Church and the world. His first public words as Pope, "Be Not Afraid!", were not an indication that John Paul intended to restore the ravaged post-conciliar Church, but a signal that Pope Wojtyla had inherited the papal vision.

The Second Vatican Council was the defining moment of John Paul's religious life. His self-professed mentors, Yves Congar and Henri de Lubac, were described by Pius XII as being "in the ranks of those who deny God." John Paul II must have disagreed, since he made them both cardinals without requesting a retraction from either one. The enormously prolific Pope continually harkens back to the Council and Council documents to impress upon his audience the impression the Council left on him. Vatican II confirmed for John Paul II the cor-rectness of his pre-existing mystical vision of Christ, the Church, and the world. He proclaimed his vision in his first papal encyclical and has tirelessly toured the world to make his vision a reality.

It is for qualified theologians to debate whether or not the Pope is an adherent of final restoration ("universal salvation"). Here it can only be said that universal salvation appears to be the logical conclusion of his personal theology, wherein John Paul believes that God the Son united Himself physically to every man, woman, and child who ever would be born, and that Christ's redemption "definitively restored" man's dig-nity. This, it is alleged, is code for universal salvation, the idea that ev-eryone goes to Heaven.

Consequently, the mystical Body of Christ is much larger than the members of the Catholic Church who are in a state of grace. The mystical Body of Christ is the entire world. Hell, the sacraments, and even the Catholic Church would no longer be essential to attaining the beatific vision. A belief in universal salvation would explain why John Paul rarely, if ever, speaks of hell. It would also explain, among other things, the Pope's kissing of the Koran, and his unabashed approval of the events at Assisi, truly scandalous affairs the Pope not only organized, but asserted grew out of the Second Vatican Council.

The Pope had high hopes his ecumenical ambitions would be consummated at the Great Jubilee during the year 2000, an event he spoke of in his first encyclical. The passage of years only made the Holy Father more impatient. "The time must come for the love that unites us to be manifested!" he declared in 1994 in *Crossing the Threshold of Hope*. He blamed the failure to realize his vision sooner on "the idea that one can have a monopoly on the truth."[2] Yet this "idea" had been a constant teaching of the Church until 1965.

John Paul II's vision — an intensified version of the vision of his predecessors — will in all likelihood be amplified by his successor. If the Third Secret is found in the Apocalypse as Lucy has implied, at some point, perhaps in the near future, the second beast — the lamb who speaks like a dragon, the false prophet — will consummate the papal vision.

The Queen of Peace

The consummation will not require another Council, merely a further stretching of the impressively elastic documents of Vatican II. After all, if a Pope can claim Vatican II legitimizes a scandal like Assisi, the sky is the limit, and any deviation from orthodoxy can be "reconciled" with tradition.

Here is the present state of convergence. Even atheists admit man benefits from religious beliefs. Religious beliefs are therefore good, not because they honor God, but because they benefit man. The problem remaining is to craft a religion that will meet man's needs without causing religious conflict. Religion must bring peace, not to give glory to God, but so that man's dignity, and his kingdom on earth, is not soiled by violence. The means towards this end are ecumenical gatherings like Assisi, and the millennial Jubilee. Both events were sponsored by the Roman Catholic Church.

Moreover, the Event at Assisi is commemorated annually by John Paul II and the "Community of Saint Egidio", a fifteen thousand member Catholic organization supposedly independent of the Vatican, that holds annual inter-religious gatherings in order to reduce war and increase peace. According to *Inside The Vatican* (November 1996), Saint Egidio's methods consist of:

"interreligious dialogue, with each religion firmly maintaining its own faith and characteristics ... international prayer gatherings ... (and) the undertaking of joint charity and relief activities, with a stress on solidarity (sic) and concrete projects."

In other words, Saint Egidio is John Paul's religious version of Solidarity. In 1996 he spoke to the annual interreligious gathering of world leaders (organized by Saint Egidio) and praised "those present who generously commit themselves to keeping the spirit of Assisi alive so that it may reach a growing number of men and women." He continued, "In this world, like a global village, we desire that every religious tradition be like a fountain of peace."[3]

Pope John said what unites mankind is greater than what separates it. Pope John Paul seems to believe that what unites mankind is its plethora of religious traditions, and that this commonality is greater than the contradictions and lack of truth that distinguish all these religious traditions from Roman Catholicism. There is nothing transcendent in such a view of the world. The "spirit of Assisi" is not only naturalistic, it is more of a sentiment than a religious doctrine. What logic there is, is upside-down: unity, rather than being based on truth, is emphasized at the expense of truth.

As might be expected, the unity at the Saint Egidio's annual interreligious gatherings is primarily among liberal world religious leaders. Concerning the advancement of peace, to date it cannot be claimed that the annual interreligious gatherings since Assisi have stopped any armed conflicts. Civil wars continue to erupt around the world at roughly the same rate as the increase in world democracies. The violence — in Bosnia, Rwanda, Kosovo, East Timor, and any number of other places — is barbaric, even satanic; a blood-soaked sign of contradiction to the claim that Russia has been consecrated, has converted, and that an era of peace has begun.

In a letter John Paul II sent to the annual gathering of world religious leaders, he wrote:

"History teaches us how precious and fruitful are the encounters between peoples, and how important it is firmly to eliminate conflicts, divisions, and oppositions, in order to replace them with a culture of tolerance, accommodation, and solidarity (sic). This peace process must experience an acceleration, now that there are only two years before the dawn of the new millennium ...

"To vanquish the so numerous misunderstandings that separate men and set them against one another is the urgent task to which all religions are called! ... It is the task of every believer to be an active artisan of peace, especially at the historic moment through which humanity is now living, on the threshold of the third millennium."[4]

Now that we are in the new millennium, it is evident how inconse-

quential these interreligious meetings are to world affairs. The new millennium has not revealed the springtime of the new humanity spoken of
so glowingly by the present pontiff. It has revealed, if anything, a sicken-
ing escalation in violence and terror, as witnessed by the World Trade
Center attacks and suicide bombers in the Middle East, and a leprous
spread of decadence and immorality in the Catholic clergy and episcopate, which was revealed shortly after John Paul's 2002 reprise at
Assisi.

The ostensible goal of all this interreligious mucky-muck is a laudable
one — peace. And the Pope appears to sincerely believe that a show of
unity among the world's religious leaders will decrease the violence in our
de-Christianized world. Typical of some other strictly man-made efforts,
such a show of "inter-religious solidarity" is wasted effort directed at rein-
venting the wheel. For how can peace be had without the Queen of Peace?

She Herself had said it, "If what I say to you is done many souls will be
saved and there will be peace." She said again, "If My requests are
heeded Russia will be converted and there will be peace; if not she will
spread her errors throughout the world ..." And a third time: "In the
end, My Immaculate Heart will triumph. The Holy Father will consecrate Russia to Me and she will be converted, and a period of peace will
be granted to the world."

This triple reference to peace by the Blessed Virgin was answered by a
triple denial by Popes John, Paul, and (thus far) John Paul II, who have
not only preferred their own designs to the designs of Heaven, but have
attempted to masquerade ambition and self-will as tradition. Yet is any of
this really so scandalous? In Sacred Scripture Our Lord warned Peter:

> "Simon, Simon, behold Satan hath desired to have you, that he
> may sift you as wheat: But I have prayed for thee, that thy faith
> fail not: and thou, being once converted, confirm thy brethren."
> (Luke 22:31,32).

The weakness of Peter, his humanity, was not a scandal to Pope Leo
XIII, who in 1888 penned a prayer to St. Michael. The short version was
suppressed after Vatican II. In the long version Leo calls the devil "this
wicked dragon", and accuses Satan and his "apostate host" thusly:

> "These most crafty enemies have filled and inebriated with gall
> and bitterness the Church, the spouse of the Immaculate Lamb,
> and have laid impious hands on her most sacred possessions.

> "In the Holy Place itself, where has been set up the See of the
> most holy Peter and the Chair of Truth for the light of the world,
> they have raised the throne of their abominable impiety, with the
> iniquitous design that when the Pastor has been struck, the
> sheep may be scattered."

As mentioned previously, there was a time — unlike today — when
popes were pretty fair prophets. What more sacred possession has the

Church than the Mass of the ages? As for Leo's warning of the presence of Satan's apostate host in "the Holy Place itself", the "Chair of Truth", one is tempted to shudder in agreement. Yet who knows? Perhaps Leo's plea for Michael to "bring help against the attacks of the lost spirits" was answered when the Angel of Portugal — commonly thought to be St. Michael — appeared to three Portuguese children to prepare them for the assistance of the Blessed Virgin.

As in the Apocalypse, the battle between the Virgin and the dragon has been joined. The outcome is known, but at present a mystery of iniquity has led a series of popes away from not only the Fatima Message, but from the gospel message that Fatima and the continual teaching of the Church embodies.

The Virgin has foretold Peter's repentance, and his compliance with the demands of Heaven. Until this occurs, however, the Church and the world will be rocked with the concussive force of divine wrath. One recalls Jesus' lament over Jerusalem not knowing the hour of its visitation, and the dreadful consequences of this willful ignorance. Alas, we echo the perfidy of the Jews. Sowing the wind of the spirit of the age, we have reaped the whirlwind. The price will be paid in souls.

NOTES

1. This was written in 1998. For a thoroughly documented confirmation that the destruction of the Catholic Faith was, and is, deemed essential by leaders of the Church, see Atila Sinke Guimarães, *Animus Delende – I (Desire to Destroy)*, Volume IV of the Collection: *Eli, Eli, Lamma Sabacthani?*, Translated and edited by Marian Therese Horvat, Ph.D., Los Angeles, Tradition In Action, 2000.
2. Both quotes are from *Crossing the Threshold of Hope*, op. cit.
3. *Inside The Vatican*, November, 1996.
4. The letter, officially sent to Cardinal Roger Etchegaray, then President of the Holy See's Justice and Peace Council, was written in 1997.

Chapter Twenty-Two

The Third Secret Revealed?

Here is the Third Secret of Fatima, according to the Vatican: "At the left of Our Lady and a little above, we saw an Angel with a flaming sword in his left hand; flashing, it gave out flames that looked as though they would set the world on fire; but they died out in contact with the splendor that Our Lady radiated towards him from Her right hand: pointing to the earth with his right hand, the Angel cried out in a loud voice: 'Penance, Penance, Penance!' And we saw in an immense light that is God: 'something similar to how people appear in a mirror when they pass in front of it' a Bishop dressed in White 'we had the impression that it was the Holy Father'. Other Bishops, Priests, men and women Religious going up a steep mountain, at the top of which there was a big Cross of rough-hewn trunks as of a cork-tree with the bark; before reaching there the Holy Father passed through a big city half in ruins and half trembling with halting step, afflicted with pain and sorrow, he prayed for the souls of the corpses he met on his way; having reached the top of the mountain, on his knees at the foot of the big Cross he was killed by a group of soldiers who fired bullets and arrows at him, and in the same way there died one after another the other Bishops, Priests, men and women Religious, and various lay people of different ranks and positions. Beneath the two arms of the Cross there were two Angels each with a crystal aspersorium in his hand, in which they gathered up the blood of the Martyrs and with it sprinkled the souls that were making their way to God."[1]

There are some obvious difficulties posed by the grafting of this vision onto the first two parts of the Secret. Before going into all that, let it be noted that the vision may well have been written by Sister Lucy. The writing style is simple and descriptive, and the vivid details are allowed to speak for themselves. Lucy writes like that.

The centrality of the Cross in this vision of the Third Secret is reminiscent of another vision of Lucy's, the vision of the Crucifix at Tuy in 1929, when the Blessed Virgin, in fulfillment of Her prophecy at Fatima, came to ask for the consecration of Russia to Her Immaculate Heart. This happened while Lucy was keeping her Thursday night holy hour in the small chapel of the Dorothean Order she belonged to. Prostrate on the floor near the Communion rails, she repeated over and over the prayers the Angel of Peace taught her. Except for her habit she could have been the nine-year-old shepherdess prostrate in the fields, praying again and again until night fell: "O Most Blessed Trinity, Father, Son, and Holy Ghost, I adore Thee ..." Suddenly "the whole chapel was illumined by a supernatural light, and above the altar appeared a Cross of light, reaching to the ceiling". Above the Cross was God the Father, and "upon His breast was a dove of light," the Holy Ghost. Below was Jesus, nailed to the Cross. To His side Lucy saw "a chalice and a large host suspended in the air, onto which drops of blood were falling from the face of Jesus crucified and from the wound in His breast. These drops ran down over the host and fell into the chalice."[2]

In the vision the Vatican claims is the Third Secret, angels with crystal aspersoriums were positioned under the Cross to collect the blood of martyrs — including the blood of a dead Pope. At Tuy a host and a chalice under the Cross collected the Blood of the first Martyr. Also under the Cross at Tuy was the Blessed Virgin Mary. As Lucy described it: "Under the right arm of the Cross was Our Lady, with Her Immaculate Heart in Her hand ... Under the left arm (of the Cross) some big letters, as it were of crystal clear water running down over the altar, formed these words: "Grace and Mercy." Then the Blessed Virgin spoke:

> "The moment has come when God asks the Holy Father to make, in union with all the bishops of the world, the consecration of Russia to My Immaculate Heart, promising to save it by this means. So numerous are the souls which the justice of God condemns for sins committed against Me, that I come to ask for reparation. Sacrifice yourself for this intention and pray."[3]

It is clear from this that God's will was not to set up democracy or a plurality of religions in Russia, but to establish in Russia (and the world) devotion to the Immaculate Heart of the Blessed Virgin Mary. The CDF document on Fatima, *The Message of Fatima*, claims the Holy Father's 1984 consecration of the world to the Immaculate Heart of Mary satisfied Our Lady of Fatima's request, and even quotes Sister Lucy to this effect.[4] In due course these claims will be examined.

The vision at Tuy, and the Blessed Virgin's request, were written down by Lucy in obedience to her confessor. Fourteen years later she would sit in the same modest chapel and write down the text of the Third Secret. This was also done under obedience; unlike the writing of the vision of Tuy, however, the writing of the Third Secret was an ordeal.

It began in September, 1943, when Bishop da Silva, alarmed when an attack of pleurisy (and several relapses) nearly killed Lucy, thought it prudent for her to commit the Secret to writing. Lucy wished to obey but did not feel an interior confirmation from Heaven to do so. As she did not want to take responsibility for writing down the Secret, she told the bishop that if he would issue her a formal order to write the Secret, she would obey. After the bishop, in October, commanded her under obedience to commit the Secret to paper, she still went through several months of intense inner conflict. Then on January 2, 1944, the Blessed Virgin appeared to Sister Lucy. She confirmed that Heaven willed Sister Lucy to write down the Third Secret, and assisted Lucy in doing so. On January 9, 1944, Lucy wrote Bishop da Silva, saying she had written down the Third Secret and placed it in a sealed envelope, *and* in her notebook.[5]

Lucy had the Secret hand-delivered to Bishop da Silva on June 17, 1944. In 1957 the Holy Office (now the Congregation for the Doctrine of the Faith, or CDF) requested all of Lucy's writings, including the Third Secret. Da Silva's auxiliary, Bishop Venancio, begged him to either read the Secret or make a copy of it before turning it over. Although da Silva was authorized to read the Secret, he refused to do so. Finding himself alone with the Third Secret, Venancio held the envelope holding the Secret up to the light. Inside the envelope was a smaller envelope, and inside that was a small piece of paper with handwriting on it. Venancio examined it, and estimated the Third Secret took up twenty to twenty-five handwritten lines on a small, margined piece of paper. If this (admittedly rough) estimate is reliable, the Third Secret would be about as long as the Second Secret.[6]

Both Lucy and Bishop da Silva said repeatedly (because they were asked repeatedly) that the Secret could not be revealed until 1960. When asked why, Lucy replied: "Because the Blessed Virgin wishes it so."[7] In 1955 Cardinal Ottaviani of the Holy Office visited Lucy and asked her the same question. She replied that the Secret should be read in 1960 "because then it will become clearer (*mais claro*)".[8] It was assumed that the Secret would be opened *and* read to the world in 1960. Pius XII may have assumed so too, for although he received the envelope containing the Secret in 1957, it remained unopened at his death in 1958.

Not that Pope Pacelli was uninterested in Fatima. Quite the contrary. Earlier that decade he sent a secret envoy to interrogate Lucy, who had left Tuy to join the Carmelite convent in Coimbra, Portugal. The envoy, an Austrian Jesuit named Father Schweigl, returned to Rome and gave his report to the Holy Office, which refused to publish Schweigl's interrogation of Lucy, or her answers. Father Schweigl was favorably influenced by his meeting with Lucy, for in 1963, a year before his death, he presented to the Council Fathers of Vatican II a paper entitled *The Immaculate Heart of Mary and Russia*. Father Schweigl also proved good at keeping secrets. He never revealed what Pius XII asked Lucy, or what she answered, despite being questioned about it for years. He did, however, confide the following to a colleague: "I cannot reveal anything I learned at Fatima about the Third Secret, but I can say that it has two parts: one concerns the Pope. The other, logically — although I must say nothing — would have to be the continuation of the words: "In Portugal the dogma of the Faith will always be preserved".[9]

This provocative sentence — or fragment of a sentence — first appeared in Lucy's fourth memoir, which was written in December, 1941. Although Lucy's memoirs, like all her writings, were done under obedience, the express purpose of the fourth memoir was to assist the cause of Francisco's beatification by Lucy's recollections of his spiritual life. Lucy's third memoir, written in August, 1941 had attempted to assist Jacinta's beatification in the same way. In each of these memoirs Lucy included the first two parts of the Fatima Secret, explaining that she felt an inward confirmation from Heaven to do so. The versions are very similar except that in her fourth memoir, after relating the end of the Fatima Secret ("In the end, My Immaculate Heart will triumph. The Holy Father will consecrate Russia to Me, and she will be converted, and a period of peace will be granted to the world.") Lucy discreetly tacked on another sentence that did not appear in her third Memoir. In this new sentence Our Lady of Fatima appeared to change subjects, declaring: "In Portugal the dogma of the Faith will always be preserved; etc. Do not tell this to anybody. Francisco, yes, you may tell him."[10]

Lucy offered no explanation for the new sentence. Every Fatima scholar, without exception, considers the Blessed Virgin's words, "In Portugal the dogma of the Faith will always be preserved; etc." to be the beginning of the Third Secret, and place it after the end of the Second Secret, where the Blessed Virgin warned of the consequences of Russia not being consecrated to Her Immaculate Heart: "The good will be martyred, the Holy Father will have much to suffer, various nations will be annihilated. (In Portugal, the dogma of the Faith etc. ....)"[11]

Ironically, it came to light not when Lucy wrote down the Third Secret, or when the Secret was transferred to Rome, but as part of her efforts to get her cousins beatified. The Third Secret was officially buried in 1960, when Pope John, after reading it, authorized the issuance of a communiqué implying he had not read it. The communiqué declared, in pertinent part: "It is most likely that the letter will never be opened, in which Sister Lucy wrote down the words which Our Lady confided as a secret to the three little shepherds in the Cova da Iria ..."[12]

It would not be until the actual beatifications of Francisco and Jacinta where yet more cryptic information on the Third Secret would be released, without warning, and as unlooked for as the "In Portugal" hint dropped by Lucy in her memoir about Francisco. Does it not appear that Lucy's two cousins were intervening on her — and our — behalf? Have no fear if popes delay, for there are always the prayers of the little *pastorinhos* ...[13]

The Beatifications

Pope John Paul II made his third appearance at Fatima his briefest, barely one day. He arrived the evening of May 12 and left on May 13 after beatifying Francisco and Jacinta Marto. The long-awaited beatifications confirmed another declaration of Our Lady of Fatima, who on June 13, 1917, said, "I will take Jacinta and Francisco soon."

Francisco died in Fatima on First Friday, April 4, 1919, at age ten. Jacinta died at a Lisbon hospital on February 20, 1920. She was nine. Their bodies were moved to the Basilica of Fatima in the early 1950's. When Jacinta's body was moved it was discovered that after thirty years her face was still perfectly recognizable. On May 13, 2000, with their beloved friend and cousin, 93-year-old Lucia dos Santos, and about 600,000 pilgrims looking on, Jacinta and Francisco were declared Blessed, the next step to their canonization. Many of the families in attendance dressed their children as shepherds, in imitation of — and homage to — the Fatima seers.

In keeping with his brief visit to Fatima, the Pope's homily was also brief, but sprinkled with clues. In describing Our Lady of Fatima, he quoted passages from the Apocalypse — the very passages Lucy herself has related to the Third Secret: "According to the divine plan (said the Holy Father), 'a woman clothed with the sun' (Apoc. 12:1) came down from Heaven to this earth to visit the privileged children of the Father. She speaks to them with a mother's voice and heart: She asks them to offer themselves as victims of reparation, saying that She was ready to lead them safely to God. And behold, they see a light shining from Her maternal hands which penetrates them inwardly, so that they feel immersed in God just as — they explain — a person sees himself in a mirror."[14]

Those last words were taken — almost word for word — from the vision the Vatican later released as the Third Secret. In his beatification sermon, however, the Pope used the words to describe the first apparition of the Blessed Virgin on May 13, 1917. It should be noted, however, that Our Lady of Fatima did not say "She was ready to lead the children safely to God." She told them: "You are going to have much to suffer, but the grace of God will be your comfort."[15] Moreover, although the Holy Father said the children only *felt* like they were immersed in God, their testimony indicates they literally *were* immersed in God. Like the grace that streams like light from the wounds of the risen Savior, so from Our Lady's hands came, as Lucy explained: "... a light so intense that as it streamed from Her hands, its rays penetrated our hearts and the innermost depths of our souls, making us see ourselves in God, Who was that light, more clearly than we see ourselves in the best of mirrors."[16]

The following month the Blessed Virgin would open Her hands and again communicate to the seers "rays" of an "immense light" that immersed them in God. This time Lucy saw that "In front of the palm of Our Lady's right hand was a Heart encircled by thorns which pierced it. We understood that this was the Immaculate Heart of Mary, outraged by the sins of humanity, and seeking reparation."

The sermon of His Holiness Pope John Paul II did not contain the words "Immaculate Heart". Yet he would quote again from the *Apocalypse*: "Another portent appeared in Heaven; behold, a great red dragon." (Apoc. 12:3) For the Pope this recalls "the great struggle between good and evil". The "Message of Fatima," said the Pope, "is a call to conversion, alerting humanity to have nothing to do with the 'dragon' whose 'tail swept down a third of the stars of Heaven, and cast them to the earth.'" (Apoc. 12:4)[17] A common interpretation of this passage is that the "third of the stars of Heaven" are souls consecrated to God who apostatize.

May 13 is also the anniversary of Ali Agca's assassination attempt. The Holy Father credited "the Lord's goodness to me" with being "saved from death after being gravely wounded," and thanked "Blessed Jacinta for the sacrifices and prayers offered for the Holy Father, whom she saw suffering greatly." This was probably another reference to the vision later released as the Third Secret, which John Paul interprets as pertaining to him personally. Here is how he ended his sermon: "My last words are for the children: dear boys and girls, I see so many of you dressed like Francisco and Jacinta. You look very nice! But in a little while or tomorrow you will take these clothes off and ... the little shepherds will disappear. They should not disappear, should they?! Our Lady needs you all to console Jesus, who is sad because of the bad things done to Him; He needs your prayers and your sacrifices for sinners. "Ask your parents and teachers to enroll you in the 'school' of Our Lady, so that She can teach you to be like the little shepherds, who tried to do whatever She asked them. I tell you that 'one makes more progress in a short time of submission and dependence on Mary than during entire years of personal initiatives, relying on oneself alone'." (St. Louis de Montfort, *True Devotion to the Blessed Virgin Mary*, n. 155)[18]

How easy it is to love the Holy Father when he feeds the faithful with solid spiritual food.

The Message of Fatima?

After the beatification Mass the Vatican Secretary of State, Angelo Cardinal Sodano, wished the Holy Father a happy 80th birthday, then explained to the startled multitude that the Third Secret of Fatima was in fact a symbolic vision of the 1981 assassination attempt on John Paul II, and that the Fatima Secret as a whole "concerns above all the war waged by atheist systems against the Church and Christians."

The Vatican continues to have difficulty saying the word "Communist," but the real tough one is "Immaculate Heart." Sodano had no more success than John Paul on this score. Yet at least the Holy Father did not seek refuge in double talk, like Sodano's memorable explanation of the Third Secret: "That text contains a prophetic vision similar to those in Sacred Scripture which do not describe with photographic clarity the details of future events. They synthesize and condense, against a unified background, events spread out over time in a succession, and a duration, which are not specified. As a result the text of this third part of the secret must be interpreted in a symbolic key."[19]

Huh? Well, here's Sodano's point: The Third Secret has already happened, it happened to the Pope, and only the CDF could properly explain things to everyone. After a month of delays the CDF released a forty-page document containing the Third Secret, with photographic reproductions of the Secret in Lucy's handwriting, other correspondence, and a theological commentary on Fatima by Cardinal Ratzinger that made Cardinal Sodano sound lucid.

Like Pope John's 1960 press communiqué, the release of the CDF's *The Message of Fatima* aimed to put Fatima to rest forever. Appearing to view Fatima as similar to patriotism — the last refuge of scoundrels — the CDF document gave the motley crew of Fatimists precious little room to move. The choices left to the Fatima crowd — mostly die-hard anti-Communists and traditionalists convinced the Third Secret was about apostasy in the Church hierarchy — were to either move even further out onto the fringes of the establishment Church, or to find their respective places in the Advent of the New Humanity, and proceed in blissful lockstep toward the Civilization of Love.

Of course, one can make a case that a significant number of the Church hierarchy have departed from orthodox Catholicism whether or not this fact is mentioned in the Third Secret. Only the actual text of the Secret can clear that up. Beyond that, however, there are some things about all this that just don't make sense. For instance, although Cardinal Sodano stated that the Third Secret contained "events spread out over time in a succession and a duration which are not specified," the Vatican is nevertheless able to conclude that the Third Secret has already happened. How? The answer appears to be "because the Pope says so". There is a modicum of evidence to support John Paul II's belief that he is the Pope mentioned in the vision. Like the Pope in the vision (and several other Popes in the 20th Century) the Holy Father often dresses in white. Like the Pope in the vision, the present Holy Father at times, appears "half trembling with halting step, afflicted with pain and sorrow," although more so in recent years than in the physical vigor of his early pontificate. The description of the faltering Pope in the Fatima vision would not have fit John Paul II on May 13, 1981, when Agca shot him. Even after the shooting he remained, for the most part, an energetic, fit man who skiied mountains and made frequent triumphal pilgrimages around the world.

One cannot recall a pilgrimage to a Cross on a steep mountain where he was murdered, however. The circumstances of the Holy Father's life just don't match up with the Fatima vision, but because the Pope apparently believes it does, the CDF brain trust were left with an unenviable task: to argue that a lone gunman's assassination attempt of a healthy, heroic Pope in cheering St. Peter's Square was the equivalent of a frail Pope scaling a lonely "steep mountain" only to be murdered under a Cross, along with unnumbered "bishops, priests, men and women Religious" by a "group of soldiers" firing bullets and arrows.

It cannot be seriously maintained that the Fatima vision matches Agca's 1981 wounding of John Paul, where no one was killed, unless we blur the lens of reason and reality by "interpreting" the vision "symbolically." But by this incoherent standard one could argue that the Pope in the vision fits the description of any Pope after 1917. The Vatican's interpretation is therefore meaningless, and offers no proof that the Fatima vision has already occurred. This problem led "very senior Vatican officials" to argue against publishing the Secret, as it "would highlight the difference between the document's words and the Pope's interpretation of them," reported the *London Daily Telegraph* on June 27, the day after publication of the Secret. Marco Politi, an Italian journalist and co-author of a biography of John Paul II, declared that "the vision of a Pope being killed by soldiers with guns and arrows has nothing to do with the assassination attempt" of 1981.

Vatican expert and biographer of John XXIII, Giancarlo Zizola, claimed that John Paul's interpretation emphasized the Pope's "view of himself as a messianic figure, one called upon — and saved — by Providence," a view that "has created many problems," according to the progressive Zizola. Ratzinger responded to charges that John Paul was being vainglorious or just plain wrong in his interpretation of the Fatima vision by backpedaling. "It seems to me that the Pope sees here an account of his own suffering," he admitted, adding, "The Church does not want to impose an interpretation" on the Fatima vision.

This was a sure signal the Cardinal felt on shaky ground — not so shaky that he stopped maintaining the Fatima Secret only referred to the past, however. And contrary to his words, the publishing of *The Message of Fatima* most certainly *is* a concerted effort to impose an interpretation, which negative press attention will delay but not prevent. Here is the Vatican's interpretation: Fatima, like Russian communism, is finished, thanks to John Paul II's consecrations, and now, the release of the Third Secret. There is no more controversy. There is nothing left to say. It is over.

Sorry Cardinal Ratzinger. Sorry, Cardinal Sodano. Sincerely sorry, Holy Father, but its not over until Heaven says so, or at least until the actual *text* of the Third Secret is revealed, and Russia is consecrated to the Immaculate Heart of the Blessed Virgin Mary. In the interim, please explain something. If the Pope was convinced the Third Secret referred to his 1981 assassination attempt, why didn't he reveal the Third Secret in his 1982 trip to Fatima? If the Third Secret is really just a prophecy about the 1981 assassination, why wait nineteen more years to reveal an event that was already history in 1982? What better time and place to reveal it than while in Fatima in 1982?

What a dramatic revelation that would have been, what grace it could have brought down from Heaven. Instead of a dramatic triumph, however, Pope John Paul II went to Fatima in 1982 and privately told Sister Lucy that it was "neither necessary nor prudent to reveal now the contents of that Secret, seeing that the world would not understand it."[20] Moreover, in his public remarks John Paul almost seemed to make fun of the Secret. "Do you want me to teach you a Secret?" he asked his audience. "It is simple, and that is already not a secret anymore: pray a great deal, say the Rosary every day."[21] This was excellent advice, but why was it made at the expense of the Third Secret? Such incidents could lead one to wonder whether the Pope really saw himself in the Third Secret, or to wonder whether Our Lady of Fatima's interpretation of the vision of the Third Secret was the same as John Paul II's.

What the Pope told Lucy was neither necessary nor prudent to reveal in 1982 was deemed timely enough in 1960, the date the Blessed Virgin gave Lucy for the revealing of the Secret. Part of the CDF document contains a summary of an interview with Sister Lucy, wherein she allegedly recants this testimony.[22] This is very surprising since in matters concerning Fatima Lucy has been a model of constancy. The point, however, is this: how could a vision of a martyred Pope have been timelier in 1960 than in 2000?

Even though the vision released as the Third Secret has, like the vision of hell, a certain timeless quality to it, the Fatima Message has always had an element of timing, as witnessed by Our Lady of Fatima's mention of Russia's errors, the summer prior to the Bolshevik Revolution of 1917, and Her 1929 appearance to request the consecration of Russia after Russia had begun to "spread her errors". The timing made sense, so when the Blessed Virgin indicated to Lucy the date 1960 for release of the Third Secret, there was probably an element of timing involved. If the Third Secret of Fatima is nothing more than the vision released by the Vatican, it would appear that the Blessed Virgin was mistaken in Her calculations. In fact, it really wouldn't have mattered when this vision was released, 1960, 2000, 3000, or 1917. Who is in error here?

One also wonders how the writing down of the Third Secret, as released by the Vatican, caused a three-month spiritual ordeal for Sister Lucy so significant that the Virgin Herself assisted with the writing of the Secret. The vision she recorded is certainly dramatic, but it is nowhere near as terrifying as the vision of hell she saw as a child, which she had no difficulty recording at the proper time. Incidentally, it appears that either the careful Bishop Venancio was way off in his estimate of the length of the Third Secret, or there is more than one text. His visual examination revealed twenty-five handwritten lines on one piece of paper, while the photographic reproduction in the CDF document is several pages, or sixty-two lines. How many Third Secrets are there?[23]

The real problem with the Third Secret as revealed by the Vatican, however, is not *what* is missing; it's *who* is missing. Where is the narrator of the Fatima Secret, the sad, beautiful Lady who came from Heaven to a rocky country hill in the middle of nowhere, who lighted on a small holm oak tree, showed three illiterate children Her Immaculate Heart, and gave the 20th Century the lifeline it needed to survive the assaults of the red dragon?

When the children were shown a vision of multitudes of souls falling into hell the Blessed Virgin comforted them and explained why She showed them the vision. When She showed them a vision of Her Immaculate Heart She explained how God wished to establish devotion to it in the world. Are we to believe that She could supply visions and explanations of the first two parts of the Fatima Secret, begin to tell the third part — "In Portugal the dogma of the Faith will always be preserved etc." — and then fall mute, allowing the children to endure a vision of the Holy Father being martyred with no explanation? This seems impossible.

Why has the Congregation for the Doctrine of the Faith hidden away in a cryptic footnote the very words the Blessed Virgin introduced the Third Secret with? Why can they not bear to place Her words in their proper place? The authors of *The Message of Fatima* seem to seek to obscure more than Her words; they also avoid Her title — the Immaculate Heart. This is baffling, since the heart of the Fatima Message is not, as Cardinal Ratzinger maintains, "Penance, Penance, Penance," — although this is certainly a very important aspect of Fatima. The heart of the Fatima Message is the Immaculate Heart of the Blessed Virgin Mary, Mother of God and Queen of Heaven, destroyer of heresies and Mediatrix of all Graces. "God wishes to establish devotion to My Immaculate Heart," She told the children in Her simple, direct way. This is the Message of Fatima.

In contrast, *The Message of Fatima* according to the CDF appears to be an effort to silence the voice of the very Queen of Heaven by revealing a vision that is probably part of The Third Secret, but hiding the words following the Virgin's somber declaration. Is this a cynical analysis? Perhaps. Unfortunately, *The Message of Fatima* itself invites such a conclusion by the authors' inexplicable, simultaneous disclosure and concealment, a tactic that seems calculated to deceive ... to deceive the very elect?

Moreover, the deception — if that is what it is — is becoming predictable. There seems to have existed in the Vatican — even before 1960, but more obviously after this date — a certain malevolence towards Fatima that has manifested itself in a series of "revelations and concealments," from John XXIII's communique to Pope Paul VI's declaration (through his mouthpiece, Ottaviani) that the Secret had been pitched into a "deep, dark well," to the simultaneous silencing of Sister Lucy and publishing of false remarks attributed to her, to the suppression of the multi-volume work on Fatima by Father Alonso, to the Vatican campaign to convince everyone that John Paul II had consecrated Russia to the Immaculate Heart.

Now there is a document called *The Message of Fatima* that reveals a vision associated with the Third Secret, but conceals the words of the Blessed Virgin that would explain the vision, and in all likelihood, much more. What sort of intelligence would so dare to obscure — and in truth, despise — an apparition approved by the Church, a message hand-delivered by the very Mother of God, and solemnly given the divine seal, the (literally) earth-shaking miracle of the Dance of the Sun? The answer may lie in a reprobate audacity, or the "diabolical disorientation" Lucy said was afflicting "so many persons who occupy places of responsibility" in the Church.[24] One could even speculate that the perpetrators of this spiritual piracy act as much out of desperation as malevolence.

God is the judge of the rulers of this present darkness. Yet perhaps it is permissible to wonder: when these men contemplate their eternal welfare, do their reflections ever make them shudder?

NOTES

1. *The Message of Fatima*, The Congregation for the Doctrine of the Faith, p. 17.
2. Frère Michel de la Sainte Trinité, *The Whole Truth About Fatima*, (hereinafter referred to as *TWTAF*) Immaculate Heart Publications, 1989, Volume II, pp. 463-464.
3. Ibid., p. 464.
4. *The Message of Fatima*, op. cit., pp. 6-7.
5. *TWTAF*, Volume III, pp. 44-47 for an account of the writing of the Third Secret.
6. Ibid., p. 481.
7. Ibid., p. 472.
8. Frère François de Marie des Anges, *Fatima: Tragedy And Triumph*, (hereinafter referred to as *FIJWE, Volume IV*), Immaculate Heart Publications, Volume IV, p. 43.
9. *TWTAF*, Vol. III, pp. 336-339, 710.
10. Fr. Louis Kondor, SVD, Editor, *Fatima In Lucia's Own Words, Sister Lucia's Memoirs*, 9th Edition, The Ravengate Press, 1995, p. 162.
11. Ibid., p. 162.
12. Father Joaquin Maria Alonso, C.M.F., *The Secret of Fatima, Fact and Legend*, Revised Edition, The Ravengate Press, Cambridge, 1979, pp. 55-56.
13. Portuguese for shepherd children.
14. *L'Osservatore Romano*, English Language Edition, May 17, 2000, p. 1.
15. *TWTAF*, Volume I, p. 113.
16. Ibid., pp. 113-114.
17. *L'Osservatore Romano*, May 17, 2000, p. 1.
18. Ibid., p. 3.
19. Ibid., p. 2.
20. *FIJWE*, Volume IV, p. 159, 226-227.

21. Ibid., p. 160.

22. *The Message of Fatima*, op. cit., p. 22.

23. Andrew M. Cesanek argues for the existence of two original manuscripts of the Third Secret, one the text of the Blessed Virgin (a continuation of "In Portugal the dogma of the Faith will always be preserved ...") and the other the vision of the Third Secret, which he deduces was written in Lucy's notebook. This was released as the entire Third Secret by the Vatican on June 26, 2000. See "Are There Two Original Manuscripts on The Third Secret?", *The Fatima Crusader*, Summer 2000 issue.

24. *TWTAF*, Volume III, pp. 757-760.

Chapter Twenty-Three

"The Message of Fatima"

I t is remarkable that the Congregation for the Doctrine of the Faith (CDF) document *The Message of Fatima* (June, 2000) contains neither the word "apostasy," nor the conciliar Pope's euphemism, "crisis in the Church." While it is silly to be dogmatic about a Secret one hasn't read, it has long been the assumption of Fatima scholars that the Third Secret concerns apostasy in the Church. Some defenders of the status quo seek to dismiss such opinions as the bitter rants of disenfranchised traditionalists. This is a false depiction for two reasons. First, these defenders would have to include Sister Lucy and Father Alonso in the ranks of the malcontents. Second, there is a super-abundance of evidence supporting the theory that the Third Secret treats of apostasy in the Church.

For example, in 1957 Sister Lucy was interviewed by Father Augustine Fuentes, the vice-postulator of the beatification causes for Francisco and Jacinta. In their conversation Lucy referred to "the third part of the Message of Our Lady which will remain secret until 1960."[1] She told Father Fuentes:

> "The devil is in the mood for engaging in a decisive battle against the Blessed Virgin. And the devil knows what it is that most offends God and which in a short space of time will gain for him the greatest number of souls. Thus the devil does everything to overcome souls consecrated to God because in this way, the devil will succeed in leaving the souls of the faithful abandoned by their leaders, thereby the more easily will he seize them.

> "That which afflicts the Immaculate Heart of Mary and the Heart of Jesus is the fall of religious and priestly souls. The devil knows that religious and priests who fall away from their beautiful vocation drag numerous souls to hell ... The devil wishes to take possession of consecrated souls. He tries to corrupt them in order to lull to sleep the souls of lay people and thereby lead them to final impenitence."[2]

Lucy is describing an apostasy inside the Church, and linking it to the Third Secret of Fatima. Although the subject of apostasy does not seem directly related to the vision of the Third Secret released by the Vatican, which presents images of martyrdom, not apostasy, the two are reconcilable if Father Schweigl was correct that the Third Secret: "has two parts: one concerns the Pope. The other, logically — although I must say nothing — would have to be the continuation of the words: 'In Portugal the dogma of the Faith will always be preserved'."[3]

According to Father Fuentes, Lucy said the Blessed Virgin told her and Francisco and Jacinta that "God is giving two last remedies to the world. These are the Holy Rosary and Devotion to the Immaculate Heart of Mary. These are the last two remedies, which signify that there will be no others."[4] Lucy told Fuentes that God had offered the world the Blessed Virgin Mary as "the last means of salvation," and declared: "If you despise and repulse this ultimate means we will not have any more forgiveness from Heaven because we will have committed a sin which the Gospel calls the sin against the Holy Spirit. This sin consists of openly rejecting with full knowledge and consent the salvation which He offers. Let us remember that Jesus Christ is a very good Son and that He does not permit that we offend and despise His Most Holy Mother ...

"The Most Holy Virgin in these last times in which we live has given a new efficacy to the recitation of the Rosary ... There is no problem I tell you, no matter how difficult it is, that we cannot resolve by the prayer of the Holy Rosary ... we will save ourselves ... console Our Lord and obtain the salvation of many souls ...

"Finally, devotion to the Immaculate Heart of Mary, Our Most Holy Mother, consists in considering Her as the seat of mercy, of goodness and of pardon and the certain door by which we are to enter Heaven."[5]

Father Fuentes' version of his conversation with Lucy was later published, with the approval of the Bishop of Leiria.[6] Afterwards, however, unauthorized, inaccurate versions sprang up in several different languages. The Coimbra chancery issued a blistering press release, blasting Father Fuentes for making "sensational declarations of an apocalyptic, eschatological and prophetic character," and quoting Sister Lucy to the effect that Father Fuentes had misrepresented her. Branded as a liar, Fuentes lost his position as postulator for Francisco and Jacinta.

Did Fuentes lie? Father Alonso, the official Church historian of Fatima, was willing to believe so, until he studied the matter, and talked with Sister Lucy.[7] Alonso ended up exonerating Father Fuentes, declaring that: "The genuine text, *the only one that can be justly attributed to Father Fuentes,* does not, in my opinion, contain anything that could give rise to the condemnatory notice issued from Coimbra. On the contrary, it contains a teaching most suited to edify the piety of Christians."[8]

As for the Coimbra press release, Alonso noted that it "made no distinction between the genuine text which can alone be justly attributed to Father Fuentes, and the vast 'documentation' to which we have already referred. An error of judgment was thus committed (by the chancery), for everything was included in one single all-embracing condemnation."[9] Fuentes' replacement, Father Luis Kondor, who also was able to talk to Lucy, described Fuentes as indiscreet rather than dishonest.[10] Well then, were the statements attributed to Sister Lucy in the Coimbra chancery's press release true? Did she really believe Father Fuentes misquoted her? If one may rely on the informed opinion cited here, the evident answer is no.

There are two points to be made here. First, Lucy's words on the Third Secret correspond in content to the known words of Our Lady regarding the Third Secret. Both imply a loss of faith, an apostasy inside the Church, a topic the CDF document on Fatima ignores completely. Second, ever since her interview with Father Fuentes it has been very difficult to determine whether or not statements attributed to Lucy are things she actually said. Instead of detailing the contentious history of this,[11] let us explore the issue as it relates to statements attributed to Sister Lucy in the CDF document, *The Message of Fatima*.

The Importance of Lucy

There are some remarkable statements attributed to Lucy in *The Message of Fatima*, remarkable in that they either contradict her previous statements, or are not spoken in her "tongue." For instance, there is a description of a meeting between Sister Lucy, Archbishop Tarcisio Bertone, Secretary of the CDF, and the Bishop of Leiria-Fatima, Serafim de Sousa Ferreira e Silva. The authors of *The Message of Fatima* claim that during this meeting Sister Lucy "repeated her conviction that the vision of Fatima concerns above all the struggle of atheistic Communism against the Church and against Christians."[12]

If true, this is a stunning change of opinion. For eighty years prior to April 27, 2000, the day of this interview, Lucy's singular conviction, as manifested by her words and actions, has been inseparable from her unchangeable mission: to spread devotion to the Immaculate Heart of the Blessed Virgin Mary. There is not one statement in Lucy's memoirs to corroborate *The Message of Fatima's* assertion that Lucy is convinced Fatima is primarily about Communism and the Church.[13] Instead one finds complete fidelity to the mission given Sister Lucy by Heaven: "Jesus wishes to make use of you to make Me known and loved. He wants to establish in the world devotion to My Immaculate Heart."[14]

This was the reason Lucy was left behind, while Francisco and Jacinta were drawn into Heaven, where she could pray to them and beg their intercession. Year after year, decade after decade, Lucy has taken every opportunity, not to tell everyone of the evils of Communism, but to spread devotion to the Immaculate Heart of the Beautiful Lady who gave Lucy Her Heart as a sure refuge. We have many of Lucy's writings available. In none of her memoirs or letters does she express the belief she is said to have expressed to Archbishop Bertone.

The same may be said of another statement attributed to Lucy in this interview, namely, her alleged denial that the Blessed Virgin fixed the date of 1960 for revealing the Third Secret. After Archbishop Bertone raised the issue of the date, Lucy is quoted as saying: "I fixed the date because I had the intuition that before 1960 it would not be understood, but that only later would it be understood."[15] This contradicts consistent, fully documented testimony by Lucy and Bishop da Silva that the Blessed Virgin had set the date of 1960 for the revealing of the Third Secret. At stake here is the Vatican's claim that the vision of the Third Secret is the 1981 assassination attempt against Pope John Paul II. Such a claim is made even more improbable if the Blessed Virgin wanted the Secret to be revealed in 1960,[16] twenty-one years before the Pope was shot!

Perhaps the most disturbing contradiction attributed to Lucy in *The Message of Fatima* concerns her alleged opinion on the efficacy of John Paul II's 1984 consecration of the world to the Immaculate Heart of Mary. The introduction of *The Message of Fatima* contains the text of this consecration, after which Bertone declares: "Sister Lucy personally confirmed that this solemn and universal act of consecration corresponded to what Our Lady wished ('*Sim, esta feita, tal como Nossa Senhora a pediu, desde o dia 25 de Marco de 1984*': 'Yes it has been done just as Our Lady asked, on March 25, 1984': Letter of November 8, 1989.) Hence any further discussion or request is without basis."[17]

That last sentence by Bertone is what the Vatican has maintained since the late 1980's. The Holy Father himself has implied that his consecration caused the fall of Communism in Eastern Europe and Russia in 1989. Several of the Pope's biographers agree with him. So does a portion of the secular media. Moreover, the timing of events certainly makes it appear that there is a connection between the 1984 consecration and the apparent fall of Russian Communism several years later. This plausible scenario is very appealing to Catholics, as evidenced by the success of the Blue Army and Father Fox in disseminating the notion that the Pope's 1984 consecration has ushered in the reign of Mary's Immaculate Heart.

These and other agents of influence, namely, the Fatima authorities, have offered as supporting evidence a series of letters they say were written by Sister Lucy, wherein she supposedly confirmed that John Paul had performed the consecration as Heaven requested. The "Catholic Counter-Reformation" (CRC) has examined the letters, and in a series of detailed expositions have offered proofs that the letters are forgeries. Without entering into the details of the controversy, it can fairly be said that the CRC — actually, the Abbé de Nantes — exposed some clumsy, "un-Lucy" like statements in her supposed letters that tended to discredit them. One of these questionable letters contains the quotation "Yes it (the consecration) has been done just as Our Lady asked, on March 25, 1984" cited by the CDF's *The Message of Fatima.*[18]

This document's questionable legitimacy (supposedly a letter from Sister Lucy to one Walter Noelker on November 8, 1989) may explain why the authors of *The Message of Fatima* do not cite the source for the "Yes it has been done just as Our Lady asked ..." quote they attribute to Lucy.[19] Had the entire letter been quoted readers would quickly understand why Fatima experts do not take the letter seriously.

First, the author — Lucy? — refers to a consecration made by Pope Paul VI during his 1967 visit to Fatima. There was no such consecration, and Lucy should know, because she was there. Second, the author — Lucy?? — declares the consecration of Russia could not be done during the course of a Council.[20] In fact, Lucy and other Fatima experts are of the opinion that a gathering of the world episcopate is an ideal setting for the consecration of Russia to the Immaculate Heart,[21] and several (unsuccessful) attempts were made during Vatican II to have Paul VI perform the collegial consecration (he refused). It appears, therefore, that when the Abbé de Nantes denounced this letter as a clumsy forgery, he was probably right.[22]

Which makes its inclusion in a document issued by the Congregation for the Doctrine of the Faith a scandal, pure and simple. Worse, the authors appear to have guilty knowledge of their deed. There is no footnote or other effort to identify the source of the quote they lifted, and no attempt to rehabilitate a tainted document of dubious origin. This is the *only* proof that Russia has been successfully consecrated offered in the entire document. Yet so convincing does the CDF find this lone statement that Archbishop Bertone summarily concludes: "Hence any further discussion or request is without basis."

Well, not quite. Perhaps there could be further discussion on how pathetic it is that the highest office in the Church, the one charged with safeguarding our faith, dares to issue a document like *The Message of Fatima* with a straight face. It is a measure of their desperate plight, and the importance of Lucy. They have silenced her, *and it is her silence that now condemns them*. We know she has corresponded with the present Holy Father,[23] and had several face-to-face meetings with John Paul. Yet after all the letters and meetings, John Paul has never been able to claim that Lucy told him Russia had been consecrated to the Immaculate Heart. The most logical reason for the Pope's silence is that Lucy has dared to tell him that he in fact has not consecrated Russia according to the wishes of Heaven.

When the Pope forced the issue during the beatifications of Francisco and Jacinta, the CDF had to resort to an apparently apocryphal letter. Let's suppose however, that against all reasonable evidence, Lucy really did write this gentleman in 1989 and approve of the 1984 consecration. Why did it take her five years to decide the consecration was valid? Once she finally figured it out, why did she confide this important realization, this great good news, to a gentleman she didn't even know — *and to no one else?* Why didn't she tell the Pope, her bishop, or her Mother Superior?

It makes no sense. The simplest, most logical solution is that she did not believe the Holy Father's 1984 consecration complied with Heaven's requests. Supporting this assertion are actual, verifiable statements (attested to by numerous eyewitnesses) of Sister Lucy. For instance, prior to the 1984 consecration, Lucy received and read the Holy Father's text. When asked by an old friend, Mrs. Maria Eugenia Pestana, about the upcoming consecration, Lucy made a negative gesture and replied, "This act of consecration cannot be decisive because Russia does not appear in it as the sole object of the consecration."[24] The other difficulty was the failure to expressly include the world episcopate in the consecration.

These are not technicalities. They were express conditions given by Heaven for specific reasons. All evidence indicates that Russia is to be the stage where the heel of the Virgin crushes the head of the serpent in decisive, unmistakable fashion, thus demonstrating to the world the glories of the Immaculate Mother of the Son of God. And if it pleases God to so showcase the Queen of Heaven, does it not follow that He expects the same solemn veneration, the same affection, the same love for His Mother from His ministers, the bishops of His Church? Does He not have the right to request, nay, command this of them? And if they do not comply by performing a collegial consecration, is one to distort or discount the Message of Fatima in order to accommodate their stiff necks? Or is one to ask our shepherds their reasons for not responding to the Blessed Virgin and Her Son with the fidelity and love due Them?

At any rate, confirmation of Lucy's belief the 1984 consecration was insufficient came from a relative who attended Lucy's eightieth birthday celebration in 1987. Lucy was questioned about the consecration but refused to respond. Then, "There came the turn of a certain cousin, who lives in Fatima ... and who, above all, knew very well what had to be asked and under what conditions it had to be said. That cousin wanted to hear from the very mouth of Sister Lucy of Fatima if the consecration of Russia to the Immaculate Heart of Mary was truly done, according to the specifications of Our Lady. The reply came clean, like a cannon ball and in a sudden manner: 'No!' "[25]

Moreover, in 1989 Cardinal Law visited Lucy and asked her about the consecration of Russia. She told him the consecration had not been done. "The Holy Father speculates that it has been done, done in the best possible way under the circumstances," Lucy told Cardinal Law. "Done on the narrow road of the collegial consecration that She has demanded and has been wanting? No, that has not been done."[26]

This difference of opinion explains Sister Lucy's reluctance to meet John Paul during his 1991 visit to Fatima. That she sought to avoid a chance to return to Fatima was remarkable enough to make the Portuguese newspapers.[27] In the end she had to be ordered to attend. At Fatima Lucy had a brief, private meeting with John Paul. No details of their conversation were made public. Later, in his numerous remarks to pilgrims, journalists, and the Portuguese hierarchy, the Pope didn't mention Lucy's name. Had Lucy privately congratulated the Pope on his successful 1984 consecration, would this remark have remained shrouded in silence?

It is likely Lucy's present opinion on the consecrations of John Paul II is the same as her opinion in 1991 and 1984: that Heaven is still awaiting the consecration of Russia to the Immaculate Heart. The statements attributed to Lucy in the CDF document The *Message of Fatima* really must be questioned, inasmuch as they fail to correspond to this reality: in matters concerning Fatima, Lucy does not waver, does not hesitate, and does not change her mind.

The Conversion of Russia

The importance of Lucy in interpreting the *real* message of Fatima cannot be underestimated; surely it is why Heaven has kept her on earth for ninety-six years. Yet it must be admitted that she is only one yardstick, albeit a crucial one. If John Paul's 1984 consecration of the world to the Immaculate Heart truly did cause Russia's conversion, or, like Pius XII's consecration, brought down some grace without relieving the necessity for the real consecration, there should be some evidence in the past nineteen years to indicate this.

Between 1985 and 1991 Mikhail Gorbachev implemented in Russia the well known political reforms of *glasnost* and *perestroika*. *Glasnost* ("openness") supposedly granted Russians freedoms of speech and association (what we call civil rights) unknown under Stalin. *Perestroika* ("restructuring") sought to introduce economic reforms which would allow Russia to compete with other capitalist countries. The introduction of these reforms, occurring so quickly after the 1984 consecration, kindled hopes that Russia had truly converted as Our Lady of Fatima had promised it would. These hopes were encouraged in no small measure by the Vatican and by Pope John Paul II. The validity of their viewpoint depends largely on what one means by "conversion."

When the Blessed Virgin spoke to Lucy of Russia's conversion, She was not referring to a political conversion from Communism to democracy and capitalism. To save souls, "God wishes to establish in the world devotion to My Immaculate Heart," the Virgin had told Lucy. Conversion, as understood in the real Message of Fatima, involved a radical return by Russia — *as a nation* — to the one religion that venerates the Mother of God in a way that is truly pleasing to God — the One True Faith preserved and transmitted by the Holy Roman Catholic Church.

The real Message of Fatima involves the radical, sudden conversion of an entire nation. Sound miraculous? That is precisely the point. The conversion of the Russian nation to Catholicism will rival, and perhaps surpass, if that is possible, the miraculous conversion of Mexico by Our

Lady of Guadalupe. This is how Sister Lucy has always understood and spoken of the conversion of Russia. Her interpretation is faithful to the essence of the Fatima Message: God wishes to establish in the world devotion to the Immaculate Heart of Mary, so that all may understand and venerate the divine role of the Immaculate Heart of Mary in the economy of salvation — or have no excuse not to.

Russia has not yet experienced the mass conversion to Catholicism guaranteed by Our Lady of Fatima ("The Holy Father will consecrate Russia to Me, and she will convert"). The Russian Orthodox religion remains the primary religion in Russia. Their chief competition is a galaxy of Protestant sects, and Islam. In the recent climate of "religious liberty," the Orthodox Church has taken decisive action to ensure its primacy. Aligning itself with nationalist politicians who decry the "sterile and decadent" religions of the West, the Orthodox Church has helped enact a variety of laws restricting missionary activity and the purchase of land and buildings by non-Orthodox religions, who must also register with the government and be "approved" before being given religious liberty.

Regarding Catholicism, the Church in Russia has agreed not to "proselytize" in Orthodox territories. Since about seventy-five per cent of Russia is Orthodox, that doesn't leave a lot of room to move. Catholicism has the status of a sect among sects, including Jehovah's Witnesses, the Mormons, the Quakers, the Hare Krishnas, the Moonies, the Unification Church, and the Church of Scientology. Despite the plurality of religions, the loosened tether they presently enjoy, and the prominence of the Orthodox religion, Article 14 of Russia's 1993 constitution declares: "the Russian Federation is a secular state. No religion may be established as the state religion or a compulsory religion."

Yet Pope John Paul II insists that Russia has converted. In 1994 the Holy Father stated, "we can affirm it is happening, especially in Russia. How? Above all in the return to the traditions and practices of the Orthodox Church." The Pope also noted, with apparent approval, that "Protestant communities" in Russia were "also enjoying a renewal ..."[28] So it seems that "conversion" for John Paul is a return not to Catholicism, but to *any* religion. Clearly, this is not the same type of "conversion of Russia" spoken of by the Blessed Virgin to Lucy — or for that matter by any Pope, prior to, say, 1960.

Well then, perhaps the religious liberty enjoyed by the Orthodox Church and the Protestant sects in Russia has initiated a gradual conversion of morals which we should patiently encourage, with the hope that this will, over time, evolve into a national adherence to the Catholic Faith. Is there any evidence that this evolution has begun?

In Russia in the 1990's, ten years after it was claimed that Russia had converted, abortion is the primary means of birth control. According to U.S. government researchers:[29]

"Russia continues to have the highest abortion rate in the world as did the Soviet Union. In the mid-1990s, the Russian average was 225 terminated pregnancies per 1000 births and ninety-eight abortions for every 1,000 women of childbearing age per year — a yearly average of 3.5 million. An estimated one-quarter of maternal fatalities result from abortion procedures."

Regarding divorce, the researchers discovered: "In the 1980s the divorce rate in the Soviet Union was second in the world only to that of the United States, although "unofficial divorces" and separations also were common ... In the first half of the 1990s, the conditions contributing to the majority of Russia's divorces did not change, and the divorce rate increased."

Identified as "major causes" of divorce were infidelity and drunkenness. Regarding alcohol, researchers concluded: "Russia's rate of alcohol consumption, traditionally among the highest in the world, and rising significantly in the 1990s, is a major contributor to the country's health crisis ... alcoholism has reached epidemic proportions, particularly among males ... A 1995 Russian study found that regular drunkenness affected between 25 and 60 per cent of blue-collar workers ... In 1994 some 53,000 people died of alcohol poisoning, an increase of about 36,000 since 1991."

In the ten years since the alleged conversion of Russia, there has also been a sharp increase in illegal drug use: "In 1995 an estimated 2 million Russians used narcotics, more than twenty times the total recorded ten years earlier in the entire Soviet Union, with the number of users increasing 50 percent every year in the mid-1990s."

Then there is "the Crime Wave of the 1990s": "In the first half of the 1990s, crime statistics moved sharply and uniformly upward ... the crime rate nearly doubled between 1985 and 1992. By the early 1990s theft, burglary, and other acts against property accounted for about two-thirds of all crime in Russia. Of particular concern to citizens, however, was the rapid growth of violent crime, including gruesome homicides."[30]

Space does not permit a description of the massive organized crime network in Russia (the "mafiya"), the introduction of pornography and gay rights into Russian culture, and the subsequent increase in cases of sexual violence, sexually transmitted diseases, and AIDS.

Despite many billions of dollars of Western aid, Russia gets sicker and sicker, thanks in part to a toxic dose of our own cultural pathology. The democratic hero of yesterday, Boris Yeltsin, has been replaced by former KGB agent Vladimir Putin. Putin has made no secret of his Communist past or his Orthodox faith. Time will tell whether the "religion card" is more than an appeal to nationalism, and whether Putin is more than a transitional leader. Meanwhile, the Communist Party is alive and well, and the instability of the great nation has even *Time* magazine expressing anxiety about "all those nuclear weapons" that belong to "an increasingly desperate, belligerent Russian state ..."[31]

Such are the facts, as reported by secular sources. The evidence points towards a nation as bankrupt morally as it is financially. Although there is precious little evidence of any religious renewal, people who should know better claim that Russia is in the process of converting to Catholicism. This cannot be seriously maintained by any rational adult. It is bad enough that Churchmen have for decades ignored and misrepresented the Blessed Virgin's Message at Fatima. Must insult be added to injury by implying that the human decadence, wretchedness, and barbarism cited above is proof of this poor nation's consecration to Her Immaculate Heart?

John Paul the Magnificent?

Slightly less offensive is the plausible notion that Russia has converted to the "religious liberty" model espoused by Vatican II. It is indisputable that she has, for the moment, allowed a modest version of religious liberty (rendered even more modest by the Orthodox Church). This change from hard-line atheism to a grudging religious liberalism, however, has coincided not with a moral conversion, but a moral collapse. Whether or not this is a coincidence is an interesting question.

Shortly after authorizing the release of the vision of the Third Secret, Pope John Paul II was yet again denied permission to visit Russia, a request he has made innumerable times. The Orthodox Patriarch is miffed because there are some Russian Catholics who, against the express orders of the Vatican, have tried to convert the Orthodox. Yet he who has been given credit for the "fall" of Russian Communism continues to be barred from entering the nation of his most spectacular political triumph. For in the final analysis Pope John Paul II's triumph is political, not religious. A religious triumph would have established in the world devotion to the Immaculate Heart of the Blessed Virgin Mary, the conversion of Russia as a nation to Catholicism, and a period of peace in the world: a peace that is noticeable by its absence, yet another (negative) proof that the real consecration of Russia remains to be done.

It is a little known fact that the Church's strategy against Communism, particularly in Poland, was the primary responsibility of Pope John Paul II, not that *bete noire* of traditional Catholics, Cardinal Casaroli.[32] John Paul's implementation of his "Polish Strategy," as it was known, relied heavily on the funds and manpower of Opus Dei, and the international alliance of leftist and socialist intellectuals (many of whom were personal friends of the Pope) known as Solidarity.

The 1981 assassination attempt convinced John Paul that Our Lady of Fatima was his ally in his geopolitical battle against Communism. When 1984 brought dark days to the Polish struggle for freedom, John Paul resorted to spiritual weapons, bringing the Pilgrim

Virgin statue to Rome and repeating his 1982 consecration of the world to the Immaculate Heart. He specifically did not mention Russia, he later said, for fear of provoking them — against his native land. John Paul's motive in making the 1984 consecration, then, was not so much the conversion of Russia as the revival of Solidarity and the freeing of Poland from Communist rule.[33]

Let it be duly noted that his motives were not unworthy. Perhaps Heaven even rewarded John Paul for his consecration by freeing Poland, eastern Europe, and Russia from Communism (although this freedom may be conditional, and therefore temporary). The old adage about being careful what you pray for applies here, however. John Paul's beloved Poles used their newfound political freedom to legalize abortion. It was a bitter trial for Pope Wojtyla, who for several years became estranged from his countrymen.

Worse than that, however, was his playing politics with the Fatima Message. Was the political freedom of Poland more important than the conversion of the Russian nation to Catholicism? What was to be gained by ignoring the wretchedness of post-Communist Russia, and claiming instead that the Blessed Virgin had triumphed there? Was the Pope truly content with the present state of affairs, or do we have here a matter of legacy building? These and other questions may have prompted Sister Lucy's remark in 1988 — during the Vatican's campaign to convince everyone that Russia was at that moment converting, thanks to Pope John Paul II — that "As for the consecration of Russia, we must wait for better times."[34]

We are assured that better times will come. A Pope will consecrate Russia to the Immaculate Heart. Meanwhile, the present Holy Father appears to have survived his brush with the Sorrowful and Immaculate Heart of the Blessed Virgin Mary with his neo-modernist sensibilities intact. Moreover, he has taken the extraordinary — some say extraordinarily arrogant — step of inserting himself as the main character in the Third Secret of Fatima. It may be the final gem in the tiara of a pontificate that is viewed by the world, and many in the Church, as magnificent, and viewed by faithful Catholics as magnificently beside the point.

NOTES

1. *The Whole Truth About Fatima*, (*TWTAF*), Volume III, p. 504.
2. Ibid., pp. 505.
3. Ibid., Volume III, pp. 336-339, 710.
4. Ibid., p. 507.
5. These excerpts quoted by Frère Michel are taken from the Spanish version of Father Alonso's *The Secret of Fatima*, op. cit., as found in *TWTAF*, Volume III, pp. 507-508. In the English translation Fr. Alonso notes that the excerpts are an "abbreviated translation": so abbreviated that much of what is quoted here is not present.
6. It was entitled *A Message from Lucia*, although it is not clear that Sister Lucy intended for her remarks to Father Fuentes to be published. On Father Fuentes' behalf, he was doubtless shaken by his conversation with Lucy, and intended to sound a warning for the good of souls. In addition to receiving the approval of the Bishop of Leiria, Fuentes' original version received the imprimatur of Archbishop Sanchez of Veracruz, Fuentes' diocesan bishop (see *Fatima, In-*

timate Joy, World Event [FIJWE], Volume IV, p. 37, n. 68).

7. This is the surmise of Frère François, *FIJWE*, Volume IV, p. 32. Unlike virtually everyone else, Alonso had, for a time, easy access to Sister Lucy. This makes his conclusions and opinions all the more significant, and explains, perhaps, why his multi-volume work on Fatima appears to have been buried in the same "deep, dark well" that was once said to have also contained the Third Secret.

8. Alonso, *The Secret of Fatima*, op. cit., p. 112, emphasis in original.

9. Ibid., pp. 112-113. An "error in judgment" with international consequences for Fatima, and the muddying of an honest priest's reputation.

10. *FIJWE*, Volume IV, op. cit., p. 38, n. 76.

11. The most well-known battleline on this issue pits the *CRC* against Father Robert Fox, but reports of what Lucy said are, like Elvis sightings, ongoing.

12. *The Message of Fatima*, op. cit., p. 21.

13. For example, Lucy said to Father Fuentes in 1956, "... My mission is not to indicate to the world the material punishments which will happen if the world does not pray and do penance." No! My mission is to indicate to everyone the iminent danger we are in losing our souls for all eternity if we remain obstinant in sin." (See *FIJWE*, Volume IV, p. 28.)

14. Words of Our Lady during Her apparition on June 13, 1917, from Alonso, op. cit., p. 5.

15. *The Message of Fatima*, op. cit., p. 22.

16. Apart from the suddenly contradictory testimony of Sister Lucy, there is the possibility that there are "two parts" to the Third Secret: the written text and the vision released by the Vatican which probably relates to part of the written text. Yet in the interview with Bertone, the "letter" Lucy refers to is the text of the Third Secret, while the "secret" Bertone refers to is the vision that he or someone else is trying to represent as the Third Secret. Are things muddled enough yet?

17. *The Message of Fatima*, op. cit., pp. 6-7.

18. See *FIJWE*, Volume IV, p. 231, n. 224, the reference to Lucy's response to a Walter Noelker, dated November 8, 1989, the same date as the letter cited in *The Message of Fatima*.

19. *The Message of Fatima*, op. cit., p. 7.

20. See *CRC* May 1990, p. 2, and *CRC* August 1990, *Fatima Inquest* by David Boyce.

21. See *CRC* No. 318g, April, 1999, p. 12.

22. The Abbé de Nantes and the *CRC* were not the only ones to claim that an entire series of letters attributed to Sister Lucy were forgeries. See *FIJWE*, Volume IV, pp. 194-195.

23. A portion of a 1982 letter is reproduced in *The Message of Fatima*. One longs for the day when all of Sister Lucy's letters to the popes will be published, *unedited*.

24. See *CRC* August 1990, *CRC* February 1990, *FIJWE*, Volume IV, pp. 167-168.

25. *FIJWE*, Volume IV, pp 188-9. The story continues: "The cousin added: 'It seems that the Holy Father believes that the consecration of Russia is done?' Then Lucy neither answered yes or no. In the testimony of her relatives, Sister Lucy kept quiet 'out of respect for the Pope.' She remained silent and lowered her head. (p. 189)"

26. Ibid., p. 190.

27. Ibid., pp. 197-204.

28. His Holiness John Paul II, *Crossing the Threshold of Hope*. Edited by Vittorio Messori, Alfred A. Knopf, 1994, pp. 175-176.

29. *Russia, A Country Study*, researched and published by the Federal Research Division of the Library of Congress of the United States, 1998.

30. The preceding quoted paragraphs are from *Russia, A Country Study*, op. cit., pp. 158-161, 209-216, 250-258, 268-273, 571-575. Also used was the *CQ* (*Congressional Quarterly*) *Reporter* for 3/95, 12/96, and 9/97.

31. *Time*, September 7, 1998, p. 34.

32. This is maintained by Jonathan Kwitny in his biography of John Paul II, *Man of the Century, The Life and Times of Pope John Paul II*, Henry Holt and Company, New York, 1997. Perhaps he overstates it some, but Casaroli was often in the role of fulfilling orders, rather than dictating policy.

33. See Carl Bernstein and Marco Politi, *His Holiness, Pope John Paul II and the Hidden History of Our Time*, p. 479.

34. *CRC*, No. 318, April, 1999, p. 12.

Chapter Twenty-Four

Fatima and Cardinal Ratzinger

When the Catholic Bishop of Moscow, Msgr. Tadeusz Kondrusiewicz, came to Fatima in 1996, he painted a glowing portrait of a nation converted to the Immaculate Heart of the Virgin Mary:

> "'In the end, My Immaculate Heart shall triumph and Russia will be converted.' These words were pronounced at Fatima in 1917, the same year that our country fell under the domination of an atheist system. Today, eighty years later, we have seen Our Lady's prophecy fulfilled under our eyes: after long years of persecution, faith has been reborn in Russia and the crucified country is risen. We have waited long for this day, when Mary's statue will come to visit the peoples of the East as Her messenger ... Mary sings with us today the Magnificat. Welcome, Mary, to Russia and to Kazakhstan!"[1]

What Bishop Kondrusiewicz neglected to mention in his inspiring speech was that his diocese of Moscow had been particularly hard hit by Russia's "crime wave of the 1990's." All violent crime increased in Moscow: rape, murder, violent burglaries, even serious crimes by teenagers.[2] White-collar crime reached epidemic proportions: a 67.2 percent increase in swindling, and a 37.5 percent increase in extortion in 1995.[3] Moscow was the nation's center of automobile theft, with a daily average of fifty stolen cars. The Russian Mafia responsible for most of these thefts also engaged in high volume drug dealing, and contract murders (and terrorist bombings) of Moscow business leaders, politicians, and journalists.[4] Most of these high-profile crimes remained unsolved by the police.

Moreover, Moscow has the highest proportion of gays and lesbians in Russia, the highest incidences of AIDS, and the lowest birth rate of a national birth rate that is so alarmingly low that one commentator calls it "the quiet suicide of a nation."[5] Interestingly, the birth rate plummeted in the 1990's, *after* the fall of Communism and the alleged religious conversion of Russia.

But the hundreds of thousands of pilgrims at Fatima in 1996 didn't hear about any of this. Nor did they hear from Cardinal Glemp, the Primate of Poland, who had also been invited to Fatima. At the last minute Glemp was uninvited by the Vatican, and replaced by Cardinal Ratzinger. The likely reason for the switch was Glemp's outspoken opinion that Communism was still alive and well in Poland and Russia; this contradicted the Vatican's line that Russian Communism was history. Equally unwelcome was Glemp's dismissal of Solidarity, the apple of the Pope's eye, as "a mixed bag" of "Marxists, Trotskyites and (Communist) Party members."[6] An additional observation, that the Solidarity leadership contained a high proportion of Jews, earned Glemp a trip to Rome where he was bawled out in person by John Paul II.[7]

If Glemp could not be trusted to toe the (Vatican) party line on Fatima, his replacement would not make the same mistake — although once even Cardinal Ratzinger had said too much.

Ratzinger and Fatima

In 1984, in the course of an interview entitled "Here Is Why The Faith Is In Crisis," Ratzinger said he had read the Third Secret. His interviewer, Vittorio Messori, asked why the Secret was not revealed, if only to quiet some of the more fantastic speculations as to its contents. Ratzinger replied:

> "Because, according to the judgment of the Popes, it would add nothing to what a Christian must know from Revelation: a radical call to conversion, the absolute seriousness of history, *the dangers threatening the faith and life of the Christian, and therefore the world. And also the importance of the last times ... the things contained in this Third Secret correspond to what is announced in Scripture.*"[8]

Ratzinger's explanation for not revealing a message from Heaven — because it adds nothing to Revelation — is startling in its arrogance. By his logic we may consider ourselves fortunate that the apparitions of the Sacred Heart did not occur during the post-conciliar years — we may have never heard about them, since they don't add anything to Revelation either. Funny, the apparitions at Fatima did *seem* important. After all, there was the Miracle of the Sun, witnessed by tens of thousands, Catholic and Freemason alike, even at a distance of many miles. Was Heaven guilty of melodrama in punctuating a "repetitious" message with an earth-shaking miracle? If we accept Ratzinger's explanation, the evident answer is yes.

The rest of Ratzinger's answer, however, seemed a precise description of the entire Fatima Secret. His reference to a "radical call to conversion" related to the first Secret, the vision of hell. The reference to the "absolute seriousness of history" aptly described the second Secret: the spread of Russia's errors, the wars, the martyrdom of the good, the sufferings of the Holy Father, and the annihilation of nations. That left the "dangers threatening the Faith and life of the Christian, and therefore the world," and "the importance of the last times" for the Third Secret. Ratzinger's additional comment, "the things contained in this Third Secret correspond to what is announced in Scripture," is believed by many Fatima experts to be a reference to the Book of the Apocalypse.

Messori tried to follow up on Ratzinger's answer, but the Cardinal clammed up. Perhaps he knew he had said too much. The following year a significantly edited version of his interview with Messori was published in *The Ratzinger Report*. Missing were the "Crisis In Faith" title, and Ratzinger's original explanation of the Third Secret.[9] We are left with the knowledge that the Cardinal, who would later accuse Fatima followers of "sensationalism," once linked the Third Secret to "the importance of the last times."

Also guilty of sensationalism is Sister Lucy, who, like Cardinal Ratzinger, has linked the Third Secret and the last times. She reportedly told an inquisitive relative the Third Secret could be found "in the Gospel and in the Apocalypse, read them!"[10] On another occasion Lucy specified chapters 7 to 13 of the Apocalypse.[11] Let those with ears hear the prophecies of the woman clothed with the sun — *"We saw a Lady all dressed in white, more brilliant than the sun,"* Lucy said[12] — with the moon under Her feet, and on Her head a crown of twelve stars. It is the figure of the Church, and the Blessed Virgin, destroyer of heresies. She who will crush the head of the great red dragon of the Apocalypse appeared, at Fatima, to be no more than eighteen years old, and stood barely five feet high, according to Lucy.[13] So close to Her that they knelt in the light radiating from Her glorified body, the children heard Her begin the Third Secret with the words, "In Portugal the dogma of the Faith will always be preserved etc."

If the Third Secret concerns the last times and is in the Gospels, as Cardinal Ratzinger and Sister Lucy have maintained, we cannot overlook St. Paul's statement that a "revolt," or apostasy, from the true Faith *(2 Thess. 2:3)* would occur during the "last times,"[14] which is taken to mean "a great falling off of great numbers from the Catholic Church and Faith, in those nations where it was professed before."[15] Like post-modern Europe, perhaps. Bishop Venancio, in a 1966 pastoral letter, called the Third Secret "difficult and even perilous," and warned:

> "Fatima has not said its last word ... Fatima cannot be reduced to sensational prophecies of frightful wars ... Fatima is something much more serious than all that. Fatima, really, in this too, 'actualizes' the whole evangelical meaning of a Church launched eschatologically towards the future which is, to be sure, most assuredly in God's hands; but which, however, is continually threatened by the mystery of iniquity 'which is already at work' *(2 Thess. 2:7)*."[16]

This Scripture passage describes the presence of anti-Christs and the coming of *the* Antichrist. Venancio never read the Third Secret, but maybe he didn't need to. He knew Lucy very well, and had spoken with John XXIII and Paul VI about Fatima. It is likely, therefore, that Bishop Venancio chose his Scripture verse carefully. Perhaps he, like Cardinal Ratzinger in 1984, felt weighed down by its contents. Perhaps both men even felt a moral obligation to leak out some information, cryptic as it may seem.

By 1996, however, it was clear that Cardinal Ratzinger, like John Paul II, had little interest in Fatima, except perhaps for the opportunity it provided for catechizing the 600,000 to 800,000 pilgrims in the rubrics of post-conciliar consciousness. The pilgrims seemed slow to catch on to the new rules, however, which may explain Ratzinger's temper tantrum at a press conference during his appearance there. The nerve of those Portuguese, questioning the Vatican's representative in Fatima on October 13 about the Third Secret! Ratzinger snapped:

> "I've had enough of speaking about that. The message transmitted by Sister Lucy, and not yet revealed, concerns neither the history of the world in general nor individual facts in particular. The Lady does not enter into details about the future. The Secret contains nothing new, it foretells no tragedy for humanity, nothing apocalyptic and nothing essential for the faith. The Lady simply opens a path, and this path leads to conversion and to faith. In a certain sense, the Second Vatican Council was the realization of the Virgin's message and, in summoning it, Pope John XXIII did the essential in answer to the Virgin's Message."[17]

When the actual text of "the Virgin's Message" is finally released, we will see how accurate these statements are. For now, see how far Cardinal Ratzinger has come in twelve years: no more talk about the Third Secret concerning "the importance of the last times," and "the dangers threatening the faith and life of the Christian, and therefore the world." Had the message changed? Or had Ratzinger changed?

Moreover, if the Second Vatican Council really was "the realization of the Virgin's Message" in the Third Secret, are we to conclude that the Blessed Virgin wanted a Council that refused to condemn Russia's errors, that initiated the Protestantizing of the Holy Sacrifice of Her Son, and that coincided with a defection of priests and faithful so massive the Church is yet to recoup her losses? And if Vatican II really was "the realization of the Virgin's Message," why would the Vatican have spent the last forty years stubbornly refusing to reveal Her endorsement of the post-conciliar Church?

Equally absurd is Ratzinger's defiance of history in his claim that Pope John's convening of the Council was the "essential answer" to the Third Secret. In fact, John's answer to the Third Secret was to bury it with an anonymous press release that cast suspicion on the three children. To claim that Pope John's refusal of the Blessed Virgin's request to reveal the Third Secret in 1960 was really the "essential answering" of it is neo-modernist double talk. It is evident the Cardinal was being less than candid in his answers.

The same may be said of Ratzinger's Theological Commentary on what he now calls "the text of the so-called third 'secret' of Fatima."[18] It appears the years of deception have hardened his heart, and erased from his mind any whisper of relevance the Secret of Fatima had for him in 1984. Declaring that the vision of the Third Secret released by the Vatican was the Third Secret "in its entirety,"[19] Ratzinger primes his readers with a series of questions, seemingly calculated to plant seeds of doubt:

> "Is this what the Mother of the Lord wished to communicate to Christianity and to humanity at a time of great difficulty and distress? Is it of any help to us at the beginning of the new millennium? Or are these only projections of the inner world of children, brought up in a climate of profound piety but shaken at the same time by the tempests which threatened their own times? How should we understand this vision? What are we to make of it?"[20]

To make a long story short, here's what Ratzinger makes of the vision of the Third Secret.

First, "the concluding part of the 'secret' uses images which Lucy may have seen in devotional books and which draw their inspiration from long-standing intuitions of faith."[21] In other words, the vision is not from Heaven, it sprang out of Lucy's head.

Second, "we must affirm with Cardinal Sodano ... the events to which the third part of the 'secret' of Fatima refers now seem part of the past."[22] In other words, the vision refers solely to the attempted assassination attempt of John Paul II in 1981, and has no future relevance.

Third, "what remains was already evident when we began our reflections on the text of the 'secret': the exhortation to prayer as the path of 'salvation for souls' and, likewise, the summons to penance and conversion."[23]

In addition to neglecting to mention Our Lady of Fatima's repeated admonitions to pray the Rosary, Ratzinger neglects to mention devotion to the Immaculate Heart — until his final paragraph, when he recalls "... another key expression of the 'secret' which has become justly famous: 'My Immaculate Heart will triumph.' What does this mean? The Heart open to God, purified by contemplation of God, is stronger than guns and weapons of every kind. The fiat of Mary, the word of Her Heart, has changed the history of the world, because it brought the Savior into the world — because, thanks to Her yes, God could become man in our world and remains so for all time."[24]

Note how the paragraph begins by recalling the triumph of the Immaculate Heart, and ends with devotion to the Immaculate Heart becoming the hole in the donut — it disappears! We have here an attempt to use one truth to hide another. The Cardinal is certainly correct that a grace-filled heart "is stronger than guns and weapons." Recall, however, that God sent the Blessed Virgin to Portugal not to establish devotion to Mary's fiat — as worthy a goal as that would have been. Rather, God sent the Blessed Virgin to establish devotion to Her Immaculate Heart. Devotion to the Immaculate Heart, and the Rosary, are the remedies for souls falling into hell, for Russia's errors, and for the present apostasy in the Church. God Himself emphasized the importance of this message by performing a solar miracle seen for miles by tens of thousands of people, skeptics and believers alike, a stupendous prodigy that unaccountably escapes mention by the authors of *The Message of Fatima*.

For Cardinal Ratzinger, however, here are the essentials of the Third Secret. The two angels in the vision of the Third Secret[25] don't really exist; they are figments of Lucy's pre-conciliar conditioning. The murdered Pope in the vision is John Paul II (who miraculously survived — it is pleasant to see the Cardinal believes in *some* miracles); and the triumph of Mary's Immaculate Heart occurred at Her *Fiat*! One can only marvel at how determined the post-conciliar hierarchy is to bury Fatima, even while claiming to reveal it.

In addition to penning a theological commentary unique in the history of Christianity, Cardinal Ratzinger continues to contradict himself on Fatima. In 1984 he said the Third Secret concerned dangers to the faith and "the last times." But in 1996 he mentioned none of this, saying instead that the Third Secret concerned "neither the history of the world in general nor individual facts in particular." Now in 2000 he tells us the vision of the Third Secret *does* concern "the history of the world", *and* "individual facts in particular," namely the 1981 assassination attempt on John Paul II. Yet in *The Ratzinger Report*, published in 1985, he claimed that "Lourdes and Fatima have their precise place in the development of the life of the Church in the last century."[26] That would be the 1800's. Any bets on what His Eminence will say about Fatima next year?

"Fog Over Fatima"

That the CDF document *The Message of Fatima* is in fact a concerted effort to bury the real Fatima Message will seem fantastic to some, and scandalous to others. In addition to evidence already cited, why else would Cardinal Ratzinger speak at length (and quite correctly) about the limits of "private revelations", but then neglect to mention the public miracles at Fatima, and that the Message was *intended* to be publicized, particularly within the Church? To buttress these omissions Ratzinger cites "the Flemish theologian, E. Dhanis, an eminent scholar in this field."[27] An eminent scholar on Fatima Father Dhanis most certainly was *not*, at least in the estimation of his peers. Ratzinger's name-dropping, however, offers a glimpse at the man responsible for much of the darkness presently blanketing the Fatima Message.

From 1942 to 1952 Jesuit Father Edouard Dhanis was notorious for his attacks against Fatima, a fact surely known to Father Joseph

Ratzinger, who at the time traveled in the same neo-modernist circles as Dhanis. Like Cardinal Ratzinger in 2000, Father Dhanis in the 1940's implied that Lucy invented the Fatima Secret, which for Dhanis was distinct from the apparitions of 1917. He based this division on the gap of time between "Fatima I" in 1917, and "Fatima II" (the Fatima Secret), which became publicized in the 1940's. Dhanis maintained that Lucy, although pious, was so ill equipped to deal with realities like the Spanish Civil War that she overcompensated by creating "Fatima II", which Dhanis called an "unconscious fabrication" and a "hallucination."[28]

All this was phrased rather elegantly, and qualifications were added to give a veneer of reasonableness. Dhanis' work was a sophisticated stiletto designed — like Pope John's 1960 communiqué and Ratzinger's commentary — to cast doubt on Lucy's veracity, and ultimately, on Fatima. For if Lucy was as addled as Dhanis insinuated, her incapacities logically called into question the 1917 apparitions as well. But if Sister Lucy was indeed prone to "unconscious inventions," one wonders why this personality defect was unnoticed by everyone who knew Lucy, and observed only by Father Dhanis — who never met her. The reason is because it was not Lucy, but Father Dhanis who was inventing things.

For instance, the time "problem" between "Fatima I" and "Fatima II" is more apparent than real. The Blessed Virgin had promised at Fatima that She would come again to ask for the consecration of Russia, and twelve years later She did so at Tuy. Even before this, however, Lucy had written down the Secret in 1927, at the request of her confessor.[29] In 1924 the presence of a Secret was revealed when Lucy was interrogated as part of the canonical process.[30] In addition to the Secret, Dhanis also thought Lucy's account of the angel that appeared to her and her cousins in 1916 was a later fabrication like the rest of "Fatima II"; yet Lucy told Canon Formigao about the angel's apparitions in 1917.[31] Note that all this occurred well before the Spanish Civil War.

Nor were these facts secret information. Had Father Dhanis bothered to really examine the Fatima documentation, or visit Coimbra to question Lucy, as he was often invited to do (he always declined), he would have realized that his thesis was built on sand. Perhaps he did not wish to know this. Dhanis' perseverance in his blatant errors for a decade, even after being publicly corrected and refuted by Fatima experts, suggests an anti-intellectualism born of stubborn malice, no less determined for being veiled.

The new theologians flocked to Dhanis' standard, and his critiques of Fatima — such as they were — were translated into several languages and widely disseminated. The rebuttals of Dhanis by Fatima experts were largely unread, including a series of articles written by Hubert Jongen, a Montfort Father, in 1946. The series was entitled "Fog Over Fatima". After noting Dhanis' refusal to go to Portugal to examine the documents or talk to Sister Lucy, and his unswerving reliance on popular devotional books rather than the more serious works by Fatima experts, Jongen asked: "Is that really the mark of a sound critical mind?" He continued: "Uncertainty and doubt are more harmful in such an affair than a declared opposition. ... when someone merely expresses a doubt based on deficient information, one no longer knows what to believe. A study such as this by Father Dhanis can say too much or too little: too much for one to continue believing in Fatima and too little for one to condemn the entirety of these prodigious events. After reading him one feels very ill at ease. And for the piety of the ordinary reader, Fatima has lost all its significance."[32]

May not the same be said for Cardinal Ratzinger's theological commentary in *The Message of Fatima*?

Dhanis' opposition to Fatima opened doors, particularly after Pius XII died. In 1962 he was a consultor to the Holy Office. In 1963 he was rector of Gregorian University. He was a Vatican II *peritus*, and a member of the Council's theological commission. In 1967 Paul VI made Dhanis special secretary of the first Synod of Bishops.[33] Paul refused to block publication of the controversial Dutch Catechism, of which Dhanis was one of the main authors.

The Catechism was so wrongheaded a sixty-page addendum was added correcting the texts.[34] One of many problem areas was the Catechism's treatment of angels, and this may be traced to Edouard Dhanis who, like Cardinal Ratzinger, was skeptical of Lucy's accounts of the angels. Dhanis also complained the seer's depiction of the vision of hell was "exaggeratedly medieval," and wondered aloud "how Our Lady could present it this way in the 20th Century."[35]

Just what Dhanis *did* believe was not always clear, but it is safe to assume he had all his doubts about Fatima, angels, and hell answered definitively in 1978, when he left this world. *L'Osservatore Romano* described Father Edouard Dhanis, S.J. as someone Pope Paul VI had complete trust in.

The Real Fatima Expert

There is a saying in Portugal: God writes straight with crooked lines. Father Dhanis caused much harm to Fatima. His veiled malice and general skepticism were contagious, infecting not only Cardinal Joseph Ratzinger but conciliar Popes as well. It was these "crooked lines" that led Fatima's Bishop Venancio to commission Claretian Father Joaquin Maria Alonso to begin an exhaustive historical/critical study of Fatima. Alonso spent ten years analyzing, classifying and commenting on 5,396 documents concerning the apparitions of Fatima.[36]

By the mid-1970's Alonso's massive work was ready for publication, but Bishop Venancio was no longer Bishop of Leiria (the diocese containing Fatima). His successor, Bishop Alberto Cosme do Amaral, refused to publish the multi-volume opus. Alonso contented himself with writing short articles on the topic until his death on December 12, 1981. Although little of his work has been translated into English, it is known that Father Alonso was unimpressed with the theories of Edouard Dhanis. With all the documents at his command, Alonso dismissed Dhanis' theories as "lacking documentation," a polite way of saying the neomodernist Jesuit was being unfactual.[37]

Father Alonso learned far more about Fatima than Dhanis — or anyone else, except Lucy. Unlike Dhanis, Alonso was an internationally recognized historian. This was precisely why he was commissioned to critically examine the Fatima apparitions. So why has the Church for twenty-five years refused to publish his results?

It is likely that Alonso's study of Fatima remains unpublished because of his conclusions about the contents of the third part of the Secret. After examining all the documents and enjoying, for a time, unlimited access to Sister Lucy, Father Alonso had some very interesting things to say on this subject. Unfortunately, the objective, informed insights of the *real* Fatima expert are — like the Miracle of the Sun, the Rosary, the Five First Saturday Reparatory Devotions, and the known words of the third part of the Fatima Secret — conspicuous by their absence from CDF's *The Message of Fatima*.

NOTES

1. *CRC* No. 289, October, 1996, p. 15.
2. *Russia, A Country Study*, op. cit., p. 572.
3. Ibid., p. 572.
4. Ibid., pp. 572-573.
5. Ibid., pp. 268-269. Since this research, completed in the mid 1990's, the trend has continued. "Birth-rates in Russia have been cut in half since 1988 from just over 2.5 children per family on average to 1.3. Russia's population is plummeting at a rate of half a million per year." (*The Wanderer*, August 17, 2000).
6. Jonathan Kwitny, *Man of the Century, The Life and Times of Pope John Paul II*, Henry Holt and Company, New York, 1997, p. 506. That there were a lot of Polish Communists in Solidarity is also asserted by former KGB agent, Anatoliy Golitsyn, *New Lies For Old, The Communist Strategy of Deception and Disinformation*, Dodd, Mead, & Company, 1984, pp. 331-332. Noting the high percentages of Communists in Solidarity, and Solidarity members in the Polish Communist government, Golitsyn concluded Solidarity was little more than a front for Communist disinformation. The Holy Father appears to have viewed Solidarity as a non-violent solution to Communism, as well as a foundation stone of his "Civilization of Love".
7. After the Pope made him wait three days for the meeting. For his part, Glemp resented John Paul's "interference" in Polish affairs, and his second-guessing of Glemp's decisions. See *Man of the Century, The Life and Times of Pope John Paul II*, p. 506, and notes on p. 717.
8. Ratzinger's original answer in the Italian religious journal, *Jesus*, published in November, 1984 (emphasis supplied), as quoted in *The Whole Truth About Fatima (TWTAF)*, Volume III, pp. 770-771, 822.
9. See *TWTAF*, Volume III, pp. 818-840, for a detailed analysis of the two interviews.
10. *Fatima: Intimate Joy, World Event*, op. cit., p. 279.
11. *Fatima: Intimate Joy, World Event*, op. cit., p. 279. By an interesting coincidence Pope John Paul II read and commented on passages from chapter 12 in his sermon for the beatifications of Francisco and Jacinta.
12. *TWTAF*, Volume I, p. 142.
13. Ibid., p. 141.
14. 2 Thessalonians, 2:3. The "last times" being the time just before the appearance of Antichrist.
15. See Commentary to ver. 3-4, p. 1563 of *Douay Rheims* New Testament, reprinted by Catholic Treasures, 1991. This is not the unanimous view of the Church Fathers, however.

16. As quoted in *TWTAF*, Volume III, p. 778.

17. *CRC* No. 289, October, 1996, p. 9.

18. *The Message of Fatima*, op. cit., p. 25. In fact, the text of the Third Secret is precisely what the Vatican has *not* released.

19. Ibid., p. 25. This declaration, and the rest of Cardinal Ratzinger's theological commentary fails to account for the known words of the Third Secret spoken by the Blessed Virgin, "In Portugal the dogma of the faith will always be preserved, etc..."

20. Ibid., p. 25.

21. Ibid., p. 35.

22. Ibid., p. 36.

23. Ibid., p. 36.0

24. Ibid., p. 37.

25. "Each with a crystal aspersorium in his hand, in which they gathered up the blood of the Martyrs and with it sprinkled the souls that were making their way to God."

26. As quoted in *TWTAF*, op. cit., Volume III, p. 838.

27. Ibid., p. 28.

28. *TWTAF*, op. cit., Volume I, pp. 394-411, and generally Part 2, Chapters 1 and 3.

29. Ibid., p. 490. The text was burned. Lucy offered the names of her confessors to Fr. Dhanis so that he could corroborate her statement, but Dhanis declined to investigate.

30. Ibid., p. 491. This also contradicts Dhanis' insinuation that the Spanish Civil War (1936) provoked "Fatima II."

31. Ibid., p. 492.

32. As quoted in *CRC* No. 318, April 99, p. 11.

33. *TWTAF*, op. cit., Volume I, pp. 392-393.

34. Peter Hebblethwaite, *Paul VI, The First Modern Pope*, Paulist Press, 1993, pp. 490-491.

35. *TWTAF*, Volume I, op. cit., p. 399.

36. *Fatima: Intimate Joy, World Event*, op. cit., Volume IV, pp. vii-viii.

37. Ibid., p. 434, note 56.

Chapter Twenty-Five

This Present Darkness

In addition to refuting Father Dhanis' objections to Fatima, Father Alonso developed the case that the Third Secret announced "the crisis of faith in the Church" and "deficiencies among the Church's upper hierarchy."[1] Smart money has it that this very thesis doomed Alonso's twenty-four volume *Fatima: Texts and Critical Studies* to the conciliar Church's Index of Forbidden Books. Placed there in 1976, it languishes there today in lonely exile.

The actual text of the Third Secret written down by Sister Lucy remains in the conciliar Church's Index of Forbidden Letters. It was not included in *The Message of Fatima* released by the Vatican on June 26, 2000. How do we know this? Because Lucy, in writing her fourth Memoir in 1944, quietly revealed the first sentence of the Third Secret: "In Portugal the dogma of the Faith will always be preserved, etc. "

The speaker was the Blessed Virgin Mary, and the "etc. " signified the rest of Her message concerning the dogma of the Faith, which Lucy said she wrote down on a single piece of paper. This was confirmed by one of the few people to have read the Secret, Cardinal Ottaviani, who said of Lucy: "She has written on one sheet of paper what Our Lady told her to tell the Holy Father."[2]

Bishop Venancio glimpsed the Secret through the envelope containing it, and saw twenty to twenty-five handwritten lines on a small sheet of paper.[3] Father Schweigl, Pius XII's envoy to Sister Lucy, said the Third Secret has two parts: "one concerns the Pope"; the other concerns "the continuation of the words: 'In Portugal the dogma of the faith will always be preserved'."[4] Even Pope John's 1960 press communiqué admitted the Third Secret concerned "the words which Our Lady confided as a secret to the three little shepherds in the Cova da Iria ..."[5]

In contrast to this unanimous consensus of those in the know, the Secret as released in June 2000 by the Vatican, contained no "words which Our Lady confided as a secret," as the Vatican itself described the Third Secret in 1960. The Secret released by the Vatican in 2000 does not contain "on one sheet of paper what Our Lady told her (Lucy) to tell the Holy Father," as Cardinal Ottaviani described the Third Secret. In the Secret released by the Vatican, Our Lady did not speak to the Holy Father or anyone else, and Her silence measured not twenty-five but sixty-two lines; not one sheet of paper, but four. What the Vatican released is a vision that corresponds to either the second or third Secret of

Fatima. It may even be the part of the Third Secret Father Schweigl said "concerns the Pope." Left hidden, however, are the words of the Blessed Virgin that follow Her declaration, "In Portugal the dogma of the Faith will always be preserved etc."

Yet in his commentary Cardinal Ratzinger called the vision "the text of the so-called third 'secret' of Fatima, published here in its entirety ..."[6] To add to the confusion, *The Message of Fatima* selects Lucy's third memoir to quote the Fatima Secret from. It was her fourth memoir that contained the revelation, "In Portugal the dogma of the Faith will always be preserved." In *The Message of Fatima* this key text is treated like an incidental detail, and buried in this footnote: "In the 'Fourth Memoir' Sister Lucia adds: 'In Portugal the dogma of the faith will always be preserved etc.'"[7] This grudging admission, disguised and burrowed away as it is, contradicts Ratzinger's claim that the Vatican has published the entire Secret.

The Message of Fatima's treatment of Our Lady's words is unique, to say the least. As Vatican II *peritus* and Fatima expert Father Alonso noted: "All authors have taken into consideration how Lucia, in the fourth Memoir, introduced the famous paragraph with the words: 'In Portugal the dogma of the Faith will always be preserved etc.' They have deduced as certain that the third 'thing' began there. These words introduce the revelation of the third part of the Secret."[8]

Since the Vatican document is silent as a thief on this theme, here is Father Alonso's elaboration: "The phrase most clearly implies a critical state of faith which other nations will suffer, that is to say, a crisis of faith; whereas Portugal will preserve its faith. That is why Lucia, in the enormous difficulty she experienced in writing this remaining third part, complained, saying that it was not necessary, for she had already said it so clearly."[9] So clearly did Lucy's clue illuminate the contents of the Third Secret that the clue had to be buried in a document with the ironic name of *The Message of Fatima*, a document that in fact is a disorienting compilation of mistruth and calculated deception.

The Pope of Fatima?

Although John Paul II has kept silence concerning the latest Fatima distortion campaign, his intentions in releasing the Third Secret and the CDF document were explained by Vatican spokesman (and Opus Dei member) Joaquin Navarro-Valls:[10]

> "The publication of the prophecy will provide *no papal support for the anti-ecumenical traditionalism* which has improperly seized hold of certain aspects of the Message of Fatima ... *the decision to publish it arose from the conviction that one could not allow Fatima to become hostage to a partisan position* ..."[11]

Prior to this press release (May 21), it seemed the Pope's May 13 announcement on the Third Secret at Fatima had caught everyone by surprise, including the CDF. According to papal spokesman Navarro-Valls, however, the release of the Secret was strategic, aiming at wresting Fatima from "anti-ecumenical traditionalists."[12] This seems a surprising tactic for a Pope whose motto is "Totus Tuus" — totally yours, Mary. Were he true to his motto one might expect John Paul to release the Secret to encourage devotion to the Immaculate Heart. Instead, he does so to seize turf from traditionalists.

Twenty years ago Father Alonso said of the Third Secret: "Were the faithful to know the contents of this text today, it would bring them immense spiritual benefits and would even dispel certain doubts that the many enemies of Fatima have sown against its message."[13] Time has proven John Paul II to be one of these adversaries. In his twenty year pontificate John Paul has not fulfilled any of the Fatima requests. He has not consecrated Russia to the Immaculate Heart. He has not released the (entire) Third Secret, and what he has released has been distorted by his (probably incorrect) self-insertion into the vision. He has not promoted the First Saturday reparatory devotions. His avoidance of the title "Immaculate Heart" is conspicuous, and consistent with the Church's disregard of this devotion during his pontificate. The CDF's *The Message of Fatima* is the most recent attempt to stifle devotion to the Immaculate Heart, and it has the Pope's apparent approval.

John Paul II silenced Cardinal Ratzinger when he was too frank in his comments on the Third Secret, and he has made Ratzinger toe the line for eighteen years. This has resulted in some of the most incoherent statements the Cardinal has ever made. John Paul also had Fatima Bishop do Amaral muzzled after the Bishop broke his ten year silence on the Third Secret. During a question and answer session in 1984 at the University of Vienna, do Amaral gave this answer to a question about the Third Secret:

> "Its content concerns only our faith. To identify the Secret with catastrophic announcements or with a nuclear holocaust is to deform the meaning of the message. The loss of the faith on a continent is worse than the annihilation of a nation; and it is true that the faith is continually diminishing in Europe."[14]

Bishop do Amaral had the courage to admit the obvious fact that Europe had apostatized from the faith. After his remarks linking this "loss of faith" to the Third Secret were published, however, Bishop do Amaral issued a retraction, denying he had said the Third Secret involved the apostasy of nations. Only the Vatican could have caused the humiliating about-face.[15] Upon retiring in 1995 do Amaral admitted in an interview with Frère François that he "had consulted Lucy, and had obtained her assent before affirming at Vienna that the contents of the Third Secret relate only to our faith, the loss of the faith."[16]

Frère François concludes that "the forced denial of the Bishop of

Fatima shows that under the pontificate of Pope John Paul II, the top hierarchical authorities always forbid saying or writing the truth on the contents of the Third Secret of Fatima."[17] That John Paul II is widely considered "The Pope of Fatima" is quite remarkable, given the outright deceptions concerning Fatima issuing from the Vatican during his pontificate. In fairness to John Paul, however, it didn't start with him. On Fatima, the papacy has been hitting below the belt for forty years.[18]

Many, probably most, people will contest this assertion, and the assertion that John Paul II is an adversary of Fatima. After all, he beatified Francisco and Jacinta. He has visited Fatima three times. He has talked to Sister Lucy. He has said many favorable things about Fatima. He was even saved from death by the Blessed Virgin Herself in 1981 — *on May 13,* of all dates. Surely that, if nothing else, qualifies him as a friend of Our Lady, and therefore of Fatima.

Most of this is true, more or less. Yet it is also true that for the past twenty years no one has done more to silence and subvert the *real* message of Fatima than John Paul II. The confusion over his position on Fatima is understandable, and anecdotes like the following clarify rather than resolve the difficulty:

> "... in Fatima (in 1982) John Paul burst, as if spontaneously, through police lines into a field of Portuguese peasants, shaking hands, defying his guards. But journalist Wilton Wynn later learned from security officials that the precise area of his departure from the road had been planned in advance and made safe. The same thing happened the next day, when the Pope, acting as if on a whim, left his route to kiss a child in a wheelchair: he knew where the wheelchair would be."[19]

It is no secret that Karol Wojtyla was an accomplished actor prior to being Pope. His theater background has contributed to the personality cult surrounding him. His charisma comes not just from his intelligence and attractive personality, but from his actor's sense of timing and taste for the dramatic. Given this background, then, *occasional* papal theatrics should be tolerated, even expected. Yet this propensity also raises awkward questions. Who does the Pope go to Fatima to encourage devotion to? The Blessed Virgin? Or someone else?

Whether he intended to or not, Pope John Paul II again took center stage (no pun intended) at Fatima in May 2000, grabbing more headlines than the Blessed Virgin, Blessed Francisco and Blessed Jacinta combined. Yet the Pope's revelation that he was the lead character in the Third Secret did not evoke the adulation that has become customary with papal announcements. "Dismayed, cheated and betrayed, that is how many people feel," reported *O Publico*, a Portuguese newspaper. "If the Vatican knew that it was not apocalyptic, why on earth did it make it public only now?" complained Portuguese Bishop Januario Torgal.[20] A monk blamed Lucy, claiming she lives in a "delirious world of infantile fantasies" and "religious hallucinations".[21] A letter writer may have gotten to the heart of the matter:

> "One would have to be in complete ignorance of the history of Fatima to believe in the version of the Third Secret that His Holiness Pope John Paul II gave us on 13 May ... In truth, it is strictly Vatican II that is brought into question in the contents of this Third Secret ... The Holy Spirit tells us: 'A lying mouth deals death to the soul.' (Ws. 1:11) And it is because I have the courage to state the truth that I speak. And I affirm, before God who will judge me, that never has any Pope, until our own day, uttered so great a lie as that of H.H. John Paul II concerning the Third Secret of Fatima."[22]

The Secret Visible

The indignant layman cannot prove the Third Secret even mentions, much less condemns, the Second Vatican Council, and wins nothing by blindly insisting so. He is correct however, that "one would have to be in complete ignorance of the history of Fatima to believe in the version of the Third Secret that His Holiness Pope John Paul II gave us ..."

Unlike John Paul and the CDF, who locate the Third Secret in the past, most Fatima experts[23] reckon the time of the Third Secret began around 1960, the year the Blessed Virgin wanted the third part of the Secret revealed, and will end with the triumph of Her Immaculate Heart and a period of peace granted to the world. In other words, the time of the Third Secret is now. Regarding the Secret's content, Frère Michel summed up Father Alonso's decade of study on Fatima thusly: "It is therefore completely probable that the text (of the Third Secret) makes concrete references to the crisis of faith within the Church and to the negligence of the pastors themselves." He (Alonso) speaks further of "internal struggles in the very bosom of the Church and of grave pastoral negligence by the upper hierarchy," of "deficiencies of the upper hierarchy of the Church."[24]

Father Alonso was no traditionalist. Yet after a thorough study of thousands of documents relating to Fatima, and several meetings with Sister Lucy, he began to sound like one. He stressed, however, that none of his conclusions were "foreign to other communications Sister Lucy has had on this subject."[25] Unfailingly discreet and prudent, Father Alonso nevertheless gives every indication that Lucy has privately confirmed for him what she also confirmed for Bishop do Amaral: the Third Secret concerns the apostasy of nations, and implicates the upper hierarchy of the Church.

The "communications Sister Lucy has had" on the Third Secret comprise more than her conversations with Father Alonso and Bishop do Amaral. "The devil is in the process of engaging in a decisive battle against the Blessed Virgin," she told Father Fuentes in 1957, explaining: "The devil does everything to overcome souls consecrated to God because in this way, the devil will succeed in leaving the souls of the faithful abandoned by their leaders, and thereby the more easily will he seize them."[26]

She has repeated the phrase "diabolical disorientation" so often one wonders if this phrase is part of the Third Secret. In a letter to her nephew, who was a priest, Lucy wrote: "People must recite the Rosary every day. Our Lady repeated this in all Her apparitions, as if to arm us in advance against these times of diabolical disorientation, so that we would not let ourselves be fooled by false doctrines, and that through prayer, the elevation of our soul to God would not be diminished."[27]

In addressing "the great responsibility of those who have the duty of leading" the Church, the following lament of Sister Lucy seems a direct echo of the Sorrowful and Immaculate Heart of the Blessed Virgin Mary:

> "Poor Lord, He has saved us with so much love and He is so little understood! So little loved! So badly served! It is painful to see such a great disorientation and in so many persons who occupy places of responsibility ...

> "It is because the devil has succeeded in infiltrating evil under cover of good ... he has succeeded in leading into error and deceiving souls having a heavy responsibility through the place which they occupy ... They are blind men guiding other blind men ... Gladly I sacrifice myself and offer my life to God for peace in His Church, for priests and for all consecrated souls, especially for those who are so deceived and misled."[28]

These statements could be multiplied, and annotated with copious real-life examples, but perhaps the point is made. After studying Father Alonso and Sister Lucy's comments on the Third Secret, and taking into account what conciliar popes have called "the crisis of faith" in the Church, it is understandable why most students of Fatima conclude that the Third Secret concerns apostasy of the hierarchy. This would also explain why it was so difficult for Lucy to communicate the Secret to her superiors.

Consider that because of the Fatima Secret Lucia dos Santos has been beaten by her mother, insulted and kicked by her neighbors, kidnaped and threatened with death by Freemasons, threatened with decapitation by soldiers of Portugal's Republican Army, and silenced for decades by the Church. Yet the hardest thing that Lucy — a consecrated religious who has seen both hell and the wounded Immaculate Heart — ever did was to write down the last part of the Blessed Virgin's message at Fatima. She said it left her "like a skeleton, stripped of everything."[29]

Knowing this makes one skeptical of the Vatican's inconsistent declarations on the Third Secret: that it merely contains exhortations to prayer and penance, or the latest explanation, the wordless vision. Compared to the real life traumas she suffered as a child, a vision of a murdered Pope, dramatic as it is, hardly seems something Lucy would break a sweat over, much less need an intervention from Heaven to commit it to paper. "How are we to understand Lucia's great difficulty in writing the final part of the Secret," asked Father Alonso, "when she had already written other things that were extremely difficult to put down?" He explains: "Had it been merely a matter of prophesying new and severe punishments, Sister Lucia would not have experienced difficulties so great that a special intervention from Heaven was needed to overcome them. But if it were a matter of internal strife within the Church and of serious pastoral negligence on the part of high-ranking members of the hierarchy, we can understand how Lucia experienced a repugnance that was almost impossible to overcome by any natural means."[30]

Fatima and the Council

Although Lucy rarely refers to the Second Vatican Council, it and the Third Secret are linked in time, if in nothing else. In 1959 John XXIII announced his plans for a Council. Some months later he read the Third Secret and declared it did not concern his pontificate. Instead of proving his point by revealing the Secret, he hid it by deceptive means in 1960, the very year the Blessed Virgin wished it revealed. Shortly after 1960, when Lucy said "things would be clearer" regarding the meaning of the Third Secret, the Second Vatican Council convened.

Forty years has been ample time to sniff out and deplore the neo-modernist gnosis emanating from the ambiguous phrases in Council documents. The orthodox passages interspersed through the documents proved useful in reassuring the nervous, but it was the ambiguities that were elevated, by progressives and Popes, to the status of doctrines in the post-conciliar Church. For example, in a speech to the Roman Curia John Paul II not only attributed the "great event" at Assisi to "the teaching of the Second Vatican Council," he declared that "we cannot remain content with the fact (Assisi) itself and its successful realization."[31]

It appears, then, that what the Council really said remains to be seen. "Developments" like the pan-religious prayer meeting at Assisi are defended by some as "living tradition." In fact they are aberrations that make an utter mockery of Tradition. Such a result should not be surprising when one examines the alliances Popes John and Paul forged before and during the Council with progressive Council Fathers and *periti* like Yves Congar, Karl Rahner (and his protégée Joseph Ratzinger) and Henri de Lubac (and his admirer Bishop Karol Wojtyla). The neo-modernism of Congar and de Lubac had been condemned in 1950 by Pius XII in *Humani Generis*. In the 1960's, however, these same theologians claimed that the Council that solicited their opinions was the infallible work of the

Holy Ghost. Pope Paul VI and John Paul II agreed with them,[32] neglecting the warning of their predecessor, Pope Saint Pius X, who called modernism in all its guises "the apostasy of modern times."[33]

Was the euphoria at the Council — at least among the progressives — the work of the Holy Ghost? If one looks at the fruits of the Council, the work of a different spirit emerges. In 1963 71 percent of American Catholics attended Mass. In 1993 only 22 percent attend Mass. Of them, less than half believe in the Real Presence of Christ in the Eucharist. In some European countries, the percentage of people attending Mass is in single digits. In France, there are as many Muslims as Catholics, and since the Muslims are less likely than Catholics to contracept and abort, France — the eldest daughter of the Church — may soon have more Muslims than Christians. *L'Osservatore Romano* reported that by the end of 1995 there were 44,000 fewer priests in the world than twenty-five years previous — a staggering decline considering that during this same time the world's population doubled.[34]

In other words, only the Black Plague in the Middle Ages wiped out more priests and laymen than the Second Vatican Council. Yet the present pontiff insists Vatican II was *"a great gift to the Church,"* a veritable *"seminary of the Holy Spirit."*[35] One shudders to think of the results had the Council been a failure.

Vatican II and subsequent disasters coincided with the non-release of a message from Heaven that experts believe speaks of a universal apostasy in the Church and the world. Defenders of the popes who have repeatedly refused to reveal the Secret accuse followers of Fatima of over-emphasizing the importance of the Third Secret. One could perhaps say the same for the conciliar popes, who have manifested a decades-long silence so stubborn and absolute that they appear to have forgotten basic human psychology: the more you hide something the more curious people become about what you are hiding.

Despite the papal policy of absolute secrecy about the Third Secret, at times what lawyers call "admissions against interest" have been wrenched from them. Only three years after the Council Paul VI spoke of "the auto-destruction" of the Church, where "It was as if the Church were beating herself."[36] Seven years after the Council Paul VI declared: "Through some crack the smoke of Satan has entered into the temple of God; doubt, uncertainty, problems, disquiet, and dissatisfaction have appeared."[37] A year before Paul's death Albino Luciani, Cardinal of Venice and protégé of Pope Roncalli — who chided "prophets of doom" — visited Sister Lucy at Coimbra and left a changed man. "The Secret, it's terrible," he told his friends. He began urging recitation of the Rosary to avert, in his words, "the apostasy." He was Pope John Paul I for thirty-three days.[38]

During the beginning years of the pontificate of John Paul II, Father Alonso tried to justify the papal policy of not revealing the Third Secret:

"An inopportune revelation of the text would only have further exasperated the two tendencies which continue to tear the Church apart: a traditionalism that would believe itself to be assisted by the Fatima prophecies, and a progressivism which would have lashed out against these apparitions, which in such a scandalous manner would seem to put the brakes on the conciliar Church's forward progress ..."[39]

Alonso's hints are intriguing. Why would revealing the Third Secret "put the brakes on the conciliar Church," unless the Council was mentioned in the Secret, even implicated with a "diabolical disorientation," a "crisis of Faith," or "the smoke of Satan entering the Church" after 1960?[40] Only the release of the Blessed Virgin's words can answer this question. One is left to ponder this cliff in the mist, this drama of the latter times in which the mystery of iniquity has entwined itself around the papacy like a snake around a tree. The mystery concerns the papal vision of the conciliar Popes. Pope Roncalli's vision of peace and universal brotherhood was the inspiration for convoking a Council. Paul VI continued Pope John's friendly overtures to Russian Communism, and de-Catholicized the Sacrifice of the Mass to accommodate unbelievers.

"Pope Paul VI judged it opportune and prudent to delay the revelation of the text" of the Third Secret "until better times," wrote Father Alonso. His successor, John Paul II, "did not consider that the moment had come to lift the veil of mystery, in circumstances where the Church has still not overcome the frightening impact of twenty post-conciliar years, during which the crisis of the Faith has installed itself at every level."[41] Yet what difference would releasing the Third Secret make if it only concerned an assassination attempt on John Paul II? It is obvious that the Fatima expert was occupied with other themes. Alonso is once more implying a connection between the content of the Third Secret and the Second Vatican Council. Moreover, his assertion that the apostasy had "installed itself at every level" of the Church would seem to include the upper hierarchy, and the papacy.

The Immaculate Heart and the Papal Vision

Pope John Paul II has done more than refuse to "lift the veil of mystery" concerning the Third Secret. For twenty years he has used the chair of Peter to communicate his own intensely personal version of the papal vision, wherein interreligious dialogue, interreligious prayer services, papal apologies, high-profile (and highly expensive) papal road shows, and even the kissing of the Koran are so many bricks in the altar of world peace and universal brotherhood. The Pope is building the "Civilization of Love," which he opposes to the "culture of death," otherwise known as Western Civilization. If the moral consequences of the apostasy of an entire civilization are mind-numbing, the slippage in the Church is so severe that many "good Catholics," including consecrated religious, are active agents of the death culture.

This profound apostasy, which seemed to accelerate rapidly after the Council, continues to mock the papal vision of the conciliar popes, buffeting them, striking their faces and taunting, "Prophesy, who is it that struck thee?"[42] Paul VI responded to the taunts by prophesying that Christianity would be reduced to a pitiful remnant. The present pontiff is either blinder or less easily daunted than his predecessor. By persuasion and photo opportunities, and through a volatile mixture of Polish messianism and neo-modernist mysticism, a physically enfeebled John Paul II still strives to render visible the papal vision of peace and universal brotherhood.

As a man with first-hand experience of war and Communist oppression, few could wish for peace more fervently, more sincerely, than Pope John Paul II. This makes his response to the Blessed Virgin's promise of peace at Fatima all the more baffling. It could have been so simple. Peace in return for the Consecration of Russia, and the development of the already existing devotion to the beautiful Lady with the wounded Heart: that admirable Heart whose blood nourished the infant Heart of the Redeemer; that Heart like a flame, pulsing in time with the Sacred Heart of Her Son; two Hearts inches away from each other in flesh, and inseparable in spirit: one the Heart of a God, the other a human Heart so graced by the Holy Ghost that it would not suffer one inch of distance between Her will and the will of the Father. This has caused Lucy to echo St. John Eudes in calling the Sacred Heart and the Immaculate Heart "one Heart." Completely absorbed in and by the Sacred Heart, the Immaculate Heart of the Blessed Virgin can only mirror the Blessed Trinity, and lead souls to a more intimate union with the Divine.

It is this Immaculate Heart, venerated for centuries by the Church, that Pope John Paul II has scorned, relying instead on Vatican II and his position as a world figure to consummate the papal vision by brokering a man-made truce with the enemies of the Church — men of blood who are the sworn enemies of truth and of real peace. That his toils in this arena mesh effortlessly with the long-range plans of Judeo-Masonry and world capitalism only strengthens the contention that the papal vision of John Paul II is part of the diabolical disorientation that gripped the Church hierarchy, including the papacy, halfway through the last century.

Confirmation of the gravity of the present plight of the Church comes from Pope Leo XIII who foretold a day in the 20th Century when: "In the Holy Place itself, where has been set up the See of the most holy Peter and the Chair of Truth for the light of the world, they have raised the throne of their abominable impiety, with the iniquitous design that when the Pastor has been struck, the sheep may be scattered."

Alas for our stricken Holy Father and his efforts at peace, for *there will be no peace without the Queen of Peace.* After Our Lord has once more allowed Satan to sift Peter like wheat, he will prove himself worthy, and confirm his brethren; Peter, that is. For we have it on Heaven's authority that God's will, as manifested at Fatima by the Blessed Virgin Mary, shall prevail — thanks to the Pope: "In the end, My Immaculate Heart will triumph. The Holy Father will consecrate Russia to Me, and she will be converted, and a period of peace will be granted the world." Meanwhile, we wrestle "not against flesh and blood, but against principalities and powers, against the rulers of the world of this darkness: against the spirit of wickedness in the high places."[43] In this bleak winter of the Faith, may the Immaculate Heart of the ever-Blessed Virgin Mary be our refuge and the road that leads us to God, and may She and Her Spouse, the Holy Ghost, illumine this present darkness foretold in the Third Secret of Fatima.

NOTES

1. See, *CRC* Oct.-Nov. 1990, *Fatima Inquest* by David Boyce, note 9.
2. Alonso, op. cit., p. 65.
3. *The Whole Truth About Fatima (TWTAF)*, op. cit., Volume III, p. 481.
4. Ibid., Vol. III, pp. 110, 336-339.
5. Alonso, op. cit., pp. 55-56.
6. *The Message of Fatima*, op. cit., p. 25.
7. Ibid., p. 40, fn. 7.
8. Alonso, op. cit., pp. 69-70.
9. Ibid., p. 70.
10. See Robert Hutchison, *Their Kingdom Come, Inside The Secret World of Opus Dei*, Doubleday, 1997, pp. 370-373, who writes: "John Paul II was increasingly surrounded by professional image-makers ... By the end of the 1980's Opus Dei's AOP (Apostolate of Public Opinion) specialists were responsible for overseeing the Vatican Radio, *l'Osservatore Romano*, the Vatican publishing house ..."
11. As quoted in August 2000 *CRC* online edition, www.crc-internet.org/aug00b.htm. Emphasis supplied.
12. "Anti-ecumenical" probably refers to the insistence of Fatimists that Russia needs to — and will be — converted to Catholicism.
13. *Doctrina y espiritualidad del mensaje de Fatima*, 1990, p. 45, as quoted in *CRC* August'00 online edition.
14. *Fatima Intimate Joy World Event (FIJWE)*, op. cit., Volume IV, pp. 243-244.
15. It is probable the Vatican also exerted pressure to prevent the publication of Father Alonso's work on Fatima, and prevented the replacement of Alonso upon the latter's death in 1981.
16. *CRC* No. 304, pp. 6-7.
17. *FIJWE*, Volume IV, p. 290, fn. 18.
18. Excluding the brief pontificate of John Paul I.
19. Kwitny, op. cit., p. 502. Kwitny, a mostly friendly biographer, notes that Fatima was not the only site of papal theatrics.
20. *London Times*, June 29, 2000.
21. Ibid.
22. A letter from Elichar Alesne, published in *Le Figaro*, Wednesday, 17 May 2000, as quoted in *CRC* June 2000 online edition.
23. That is, Father Alonso, Frère Michel, Frère François, Bishop Venancio, Father Messias Dias Coelho, Canon Galamba, Father Martin dos Reis, and so on: see *TWTAF*, Vol. III, pp. 686-688. In North America one would have to include the apostolate of Father Nicholas Gruner among the experts. All put great importance on Lucy's statements regarding Fatima and the Third Secret.
24. See *TWTAF*, Volume III, p. 704. Frère Michel is quoting from the Spanish translation of Alonso's *Fatima Fact and Legend*, which is far more revealing than the English translation, at least as it was "revised" in 1990 ...
25. *TWTAF*, Volume III, p. 706. Frère Michel notes that Alonso "can hardly be accused of being

an *a priori* 'integralist.'" (p. 705).

26. *TWTAF*, Volume III, op. cit., p. 746.

27. Ibid., p. 754.

28. Ibid., pp. 754-758.

29. Alonso, op. cit., p. 89.

30. Alonso, op. cit., p. 82.

31. Speech to the Roman Curia on December 22, 1986, Par. 2. In Par. 3 the Pope cites *Lumen Gentium* 1,9 and *Gaudium et Spes*, 42, in justification of Assisi, a claim that may have surprised even some progressive Council Fathers.

32. John Paul made them cardinals.

33. In *Editae saepe Dei*, as quoted in *TWTAF*, Vol. 3, pp. 804-805.

34. The statistics in this paragraph are from Christopher Ferrara's "The Third Secret of Fatima And The Post-Conciliar Debacle," *Catholic Family News* Reprint Service, pp. 13-14, except for "Muslim France", which is from a *Wall Street Journal* editorial, September 25, as quoted in *The Wanderer*, October 5, News Notes, p. 3.

35. Emphasis in original, His Holiness Pope John Paul II, *Crossing the Threshold of Hope*, Vittorio Messori, Editor, Alfred A. Knopf, New York, 1994, pp. 157, 159.

36. Papal discourse of December 7, 1968, published in *Doc. Cath.*, January 5, 1969, col. 12, as quoted in *TWTAF*, Volume III, p. 849, note 1.

37. Papal homily of June 29, 1972, published in *Doc. Cath.*, July 16, 1972, col. 658-659, as quoted in *TWTAF*, Volume III, p. 849, note 2.

38. See *CRC* online edition of August 2000. The *CRC* claims that in their meeting, Lucy predicted Luciani's ascendancy to the papacy, and that when he became pope Luciani vowed to return to Fatima to consecrate Russia to the Immaculate Heart.

39. *TWTAF*, Volume III, op. cit., p. 712.

40. Also of interest are Alonso's battlelines: traditionalists versus progressives. That curious muddle known as the "conservative" Catholic exists only at the margins of this struggle: complaining when progressives move too fast, but lashing out against serious attempts at restoration.

41. *TWTAF*, Volume III, p. 712.

42. Matthew 26: 67-68.

43. Ephesians 6:12.

Chapter Twenty-Six

A Missed Opportunity
The October 8, 2000
"Entrustment" to Our Lady

The largest gathering of bishops since the Second Vatican Council were in Rome in October 2000 to observe the Great Jubilee. In addressing the august assembly, Archbishop Giovanni Battiste Re noted that the bishops had gathered on "October 7, the Memorial of Our Lady of the Rosary, and the first Saturday of the month, both integral elements of the message of Fatima."

It was nice to hear someone at the Vatican get the Message of Fatima straight. In so doing Archbishop Re probably hadn't consulted *The Message of Fatima*, that woefully misnamed Congregation for the Doctrine of the Faith (CDF) document that ignored the Rosary and the First Saturday Communions of Reparation, among other things. The CDF made it easy to forget that at Pontevedra in 1925 the Blessed Virgin promised eternal salvation to anyone who "on the first Saturday of five consecutive months shall confess, receive Holy Communion, recite five decades of the Rosary, and keep Me company for fifteen minutes while meditating on the fifteen mysteries of the Rosary" with the intention of making reparation to Her Immaculate Heart.[1]

According to Sister Lucy, the principal condition was to perform the devotions with a "spirit of reparation" to the Immaculate Heart. It was fitting then, that the Pope, so often mentioned in the Fatima Message, should lead a worldwide Rosary on the First Saturday of October, the month of the Rosary. In so doing, however, Pope John Paul II did not mention First Saturday devotions, the title "Immaculate Heart" or the word "reparation." He also omitted the Fatima prayers customarily said at the end of each decade of the Rosary: "*O my Jesus, forgive us our sins, save us from the fires of hell,*" etc...

The next day the Pope and 1500 bishops prayed the Pope's "Act of Entrustment" of the future to Mary, of whom the Pope petitioned: "O Mother, You know the sufferings and hopes of the Church and the world: come to the aid of Your children in the daily trials which life brings to each one, and grant that, thanks to the efforts of all, the darkness will not prevail over the light."

Mary's children, it would seem, include worldlings, and the Pope appears to believe their efforts will help light prevail over darkness. Such a blending of the sacred and the profane is a far cry from Fatima, with its vision of these same worldlings falling into hell for lack of prayers and sacrifices on their behalf.

Absent from John Paul's Act of Entrustment were the words "consecration," "Russia," "Immaculate Heart," "conversion," "Fatima," and "eternal salvation." Thus were dashed the hopes of thousands around the world (including Robert Moynihan, Editor of *Inside The Vatican*) that the Pope and his bishops would finally consecrate Russia to the Immaculate Heart.

NOTES

1. Frère Michel de la Sainte Trinité, *The Whole Truth About Fatima*, published by Immaculate Heart Publications, Volume II, p. 247.

Chapter Twenty-Seven

Lucy and the Pirates

Few revelations have been as unconvincing as the Vatican's version of the Third Secret of Fatima. Those who thought, or hoped, that the June 2000 unveiling of the CDF's booklet, *The Message of Fatima*[1] ended matters are probably surprised by the recent tumult over Fatima in the press. There should be no surprise. For over forty years nearly every tactic — silence, intimidation, bad theology, disinformation, and hired liars —have been used to bury the *real* Message of Fatima. Yet the cork continues to bob to the surface. The terrorist attacks on September 11, 2001 triggered a chain reaction of Fatima stories. The buzz in the press and on the Internet was that the attacks were part of the Third Secret of Fatima.

How exasperating for the drafters of the CDF's *The Message of Fatima*, who insist the entire secret of Fatima is contained inside its covers. They simply are not believed, in part because they are not believable, but also because of a certain collective awareness, a shared sense of our impending doom. Deep down we know that a "Civilization of Love" is utopian nonsense. It has never existed and it never will. The real Message of Fatima implicitly confirms this: hell is real and many souls are going there because there is no one to pray and make sacrifices for them. Heaven's remedy is not well-publicized interreligious prayer rallies. Rather, it is devotion to the Immaculate Heart of Mary, and the Rosary. The real Message of Fatima is not a request for more papal apologies. It is a plea to Jesus to "forgive us our sins," to "save us from the fires of hell". We are not experiencing the new advent of humanity. We are on the Titanic as it slides into the blackness, and the world senses the impending doom even as it continues to heap judgment on itself.

This awareness can be the fruit of the perspective a Christian conscience brings. For most, however, it is merely an instinctive knowledge. Being primitive, it is easily fooled. Hence the credence given to the bogus Third Secret circulating on the Internet. The language in the false version — "We are close to the last minute of the last day and the catastrophe is near" — was assumed to refer to the September 11 attack on the World Trade Center. Another portion of the false text — "the Pope and the bishops are now awaiting another message, which speaks about repentance and prayer" — also struck many as credible. It is interesting that American Archbishop John C. Favalora publicly denounced this version of the Third Secret.[2] He was right to do so, but usually the official Church response on things Fatima is reserved to Cardinal Ratzinger or the Vatican Press Office (a pseudonym for Secretary of State Sodano).

Archbishop Favalora's rebuttal to the false Third Secret — "the secret of Fatima is already known, and the world has not ended" — would have been more convincing without the distinct echo of a company man toeing the Company line.[3] His Excellency's problem is that the Vatican has painted itself into a corner on Fatima, and their case is far from compelling. Not even venerable Vatican booster Mother Angelica believes the Vatican's claim that they have revealed the entire Fatima Secret. What few proponents there are of the CDF's *The Message of Fatima* seem to comprehend in it nothing more than a stick with which to belabor their more traditional co-religionists.[4] So it goes.

Less than a month after the September 11 terrorist attacks, and the bogus Internet Third Secret, came news that the Blessed Virgin had appeared again to Sister Lucy. According to one report, this apparition occurred on October 7, the feast of Our Lady of the Holy Rosary. It was said that the Virgin asked Lucy and her fellow Carmelites to pray the Rosary in order to avoid "the imminent bloodbath". This appeal was publicized primarily in traditionalist circles, where it was eventually determined to be false.[5]

Gaining wider circulation was a conversation Sister Lucy had with Italian priest Luigi Bianchi. According to the Italian daily *la Repubblica,* Father Bianchi revealed that: "Sister Lucy is very worried for the Pope. She says his life is endangered and she urges us to pray for him."[6] Father Bianchi's report of his conversation with Sister Lucy fueled existing speculation that Osama bin Laden or other unnamed Moslem "extremists" were plotting to assassinate His Holiness Pope John Paul II. It subsequently came to light that in recent years there have been at least three plots to kill the Pope.[7]

Several other Italian newspapers picked up the story of Father Bianchi's conversation with Sister Lucy. Some reports stated that Sister Lucy had sent a letter to John Paul II, warning him that his life was in danger. Other accounts included the claim that the Holy See had not revealed the entire contents of the Third Secret of Fatima. This was based on Father Bianchi's assertion that "When Cardinals Ratzinger and Sodano revealed the Third Secret of Fatima, they did it in a very watered down fashion" in order to "avoid creating a panic". According to Father Bianchi, "Sister Lucy agrees with this explanation."[8]

The Bianchi interview drew a response not only from Sister Lucy's bishop (Bishop Serafim de Sousa Ferreira e Silva of the Diocese of Leiria-Fatima), but from Cardinal Ratzinger as well. Bishop Ferreira denied that Sister Lucy sent a letter to John Paul telling him his life was in danger. Bishop Ferreira did not deny Father Bianchi's statements about the Vatican's "watered down" version of the Third Secret, however, and neither did Cardinal Ratzinger, who contented himself with

describing "rumors about this alleged letter" of Sister Lucy as "the continuation of an old polemic fed by certain people of dubious credibility,"
for the purpose of "destabilizing the internal equilibrium of the Roman
Curia and of troubling the people of God".[9]

If he was quoted correctly, Ratzinger seems to be implying a split in
the Roman Curia on the subject of Fatima. For a relatively minor story
such as Sister Lucy writing the Pope to "destabilize the internal equilibrium of the Roman Curia," one of two things is probably true. Either it is
normal for the Curia to be dangerously unstable or, more likely, there is
internal disagreement over the Vatican's external packaging of *The
Message of Fatima*. Given the Holy See's public insistence (since June
2000, anyway) that Fatima is a dead letter "belonging to the past," Cardinal Ratzinger's comments are a startling admission. Far from "troubling the people of God," however, the implication that some souls in the
Roman Curia may be resisting the neo-modernist straitjacket strapped
on Fatima during this pontificate is a real ray of hope in these dreary
days of "Son of Assisi".

The Plot Thickens

By the end of 2001, everyone from grocery store tabloids to the Vatican press office was weighing in with their own versions of reality concerning Fatima. On December 4, 2001, the *Sun* featured the Blessed
Virgin Mary on its cover with the headline "Fatima Miracle". The story
was about an American pilgrim at Fatima on October 23, who claimed to
see in the sky over Fatima a pillar of fire a mile high. "In the midst of
this inferno in the sky," the pilgrim reported, "I saw the face of Mary."
The image of Mary assumed full form, and She told the awestruck pilgrim, "Unto you I will reveal the future."

The future, according to this apparition that only the *Sun* seemed
aware of, consisted of Osama bin Laden smuggling himself into the
United States in order to wage war "for the souls of mankind". The ensuing struggle between bin Laden and the United States would result in
Christ's second coming. According to the American pilgrim, Mary declared that "God has chosen America to be His champion." No reasons
were given for this unusual choice. After a rather lengthy message from
Her pillar of fire, Mary allegedly concluded that mankind's future is not
only in God's hands, but "in the stars" as well.

To elaborate on this last point, the *Sun* introduced "the world's leading Jesuit authority on Fatima," one Father Adrian Forsyte, S.J. An obvious multi-tasker, Father Adrian was not only a Fatima expert but an
astrology whiz as well. After speculating that the Blessed Virgin had
designated Osama bin Laden as the Antichrist, Father Adrian presented
a "Personal Virgin Mary Astrology Chart" for all twelve signs of the Zo-
diac, based on the alleged apparition at Fatima on October 23. "Your car
may be your salvation," was Father Adrian's message to Scorpios.

Libras were advised to report any suspicious strangers to the police. For those born under the sign of Aries, Father Adrian had this bombshell: "Safety lies in prudent planning." At the end of the article was a last bit of advice: "Use your birth sign to lose those extra pounds, see page 31."[10]

Not to be outdone, on December 20, 2001, the Vatican issued the following document:

"Made public today was a communiqué regarding a meeting which took place at the convent of Coimbra, Portugal, on November 17, 2001, between Archbishop Tarcisio Bertone, S.D.B., secretary of the Congregation for the Doctrine of the Faith, and Sister Mary Lucy of Jesus and of the Immaculate Heart."

"Over the last few months," says the communiqué, *"and especially following the sad event of the terrorist attack of September 11, articles have appeared in various newspapers regarding presumed new revelations by Sister Lucy, announcements of warning letters to the Pope and apocalyptic re-interpretations of the Message of Fatima.*

"Moreover, emphasis has been given to the suspicion that the Holy See has not published the integral text of the third part of the 'secret,' and some 'Fatimid' (sic) movements have repeated the accusation that the Holy Father has not yet consecrated Russia to the Immaculate Heart of Mary. For this reason, in order to obtain clarification and information directly from the surviving visionary, it was considered necessary to organize a meeting with Sister Lucy. This took place in the presence of the prioress of the Carmelite convent of St. Teresa and of Fr. Luis Kondor S.V.D., vice-postulator of the causes of Blesseds Francisco and Jacinta; and with the permission of Cardinal Joseph Ratzinger, Prefect of the Congregation for the Doctrine of the Faith and of the bishops of Leiria-Fatima and Coimbra.

"The meeting, which lasted more than two hours, took place on the afternoon of Saturday, November 17. Sister Lucy, who will be 95 on March 22 next year, was in good health, lucid and vivacious. She first of all professed her love for and devotion to the Holy Father. She prays much for him and for the Church as a whole.

"With reference to the third part of the secret of Fatima, she affirmed that she had attentively read and meditated upon the booklet published by the Congregation for the Doctrine of the Faith and confirmed everything that was written there. To whoever imagines that some part of the secret has been hidden, she replied: 'Everything has been published; no secret remains.' To those who speak and write of new revelations she said: 'There is no truth in this. If I had received new revelations I would have told no one, but I would have communicated them directly to the Holy Father.' "

Sister Lucy was asked: "What do you say to the persistent affirmations of Fr. Gruner who is gathering signatures in order that the Pope may finally consecrate Russia to the Immaculate Heart of Mary, which has *never been done?" She replied: "The Carmelite Community has rejected the forms for gathering the signatures. I have already said that the consecration that Our Lady desired was accomplished in 1984 and was accepted in Heaven."*

"Is it true," the communiqué concludes, *"that Sister Lucy is extremely worried by recent events and does not sleep but prays night and day?" Sister Lucy replied: "It is not true. How could I pray during the day if I did not rest at night? How many things are attributed to me! How many things I am supposed to have done! Let them read my book, there are the advice and appeals that correspond to Our Lady's wishes. Prayer and penitence, accompanied by an immense faith in God, will save the world."*[11]

Although the format of the press release is confusing — it seems to be a communiqué about a communiqué — there was no mistaking the point: the Vatican was debunking all speculation, informed and otherwise, about Fatima, the consecration of Russia, and the Third Secret, and insisting that the CDF's *The Message of Fatima* was the final word on Fatima. Their authority was Sister Lucy.

Lucy's Confirmation?

And that must really settle things. What more could be said? Who could gainsay the only surviving visionary of Fatima about Fatima? The answer is: the only person who can gainsay Sister Lucy is Sister Lucy. She has lived for more than ninety-five years and has said many things about Fatima that are a matter of record. Virtually all Lucy's statements contradict the Vatican's version of Fatima, particularly as it relates to the consecration of Russia, the Third Secret, and devotion to the Immaculate Heart. This means that Lucy's published statements on Fatima contradict the CDF's *The Message of Fatima*. Consequently, it is difficult to accept as credible the contention that Lucy attentively read and meditated on *The Message of Fatima*, and "confirmed everything that was written there".

For this to be true, Lucy would have to agree with Cardinal Ratzinger, who in *The Message of Fatima* suggested that the apparitions of the Angel and the Blessed Virgin Mary were not objective appearances by Heaven's messengers. Instead, they were perhaps "the projections of the inner world of children".[12] Lucy's visions were not real, their true origin is from "images Lucy may have seen in devotional books".[13] Cardinal Ratzinger has a reputation as a traditionalist, but his interpretation of Fatima is classic neo-modernism. That is, there is no external, objective truth, be it dogma or actual heavenly bodies: all religion is subjective, emanating from the natural human soul, and developing and changing over time to meet the changing religious needs of evolving mankind.

In fact, Ratzinger's commentary on Fatima is pinched from the first neo-modernist arch-enemy of Fatima, Jesuit Father Edouard Dhanis. During the pontificate of Pius XII, his lone voice of velveted malice insinuated doubt against a series of heavenly apparitions approved by the Church hierarchy and embraced by the faithful. How satisfied Father Dhanis would be to see his subtle character assassinations smoothly parroted by the second most powerful man in the Roman Catholic Church.

Sister Lucy was aware of Dhanis' criticisms of Fatima. She invited the Jesuit to come interview her and examine the documents on Fatima. Dhanis declined; his mind was made up, even though it was obvious from his commentaries that he hadn't taken the time to study Fatima in any depth. Unfortunately, it appears Cardinal Ratzinger hasn't either. For how could he maintain that the visions of the Blessed Virgin were merely "interior visions" when hundreds of eyewitnesses saw the leaves and branches of the holm-oak tree She rested upon move and bend under Her? How could he explain the other objective phenomena accompanying Her visits and also viewed by eyewitnesses: the flashes of light, flower petals falling from the sky, or the little cloud that accompanied Our Lady of Fatima as She came and left the Cova da Iria? Above all, how does Cardinal Ratzinger explain the cataclysmic Miracle of the Sun? Was it merely a subjective, interior vision that predicted and produced a prodigy viewed with awe and terror by seventy thousand people, and reported in secular newspapers around the world? Cardinal Ratzinger cannot explain this, because his understanding of Fatima, borrowed from Dhanis, is too superficial to sustain the supernatural.

Are we really to believe Msgr. Bertone then, when he asserts that Sister Lucy has attentively read and meditated on the CDF's *The Message of Fatima*, including the faithless commentary cited above, and *"confirmed everything that was written there?"*

Lucy Versus Fatima

Suffice it to say that Lucy's statements on Fatima over the course of eight decades thoroughly contradict this assertion. It is also a matter of record that several times during the present pontificate considerable publicity has been given to false interviews with Sister Lucy. In 1982, *Soul Magazine* published an interview with Sister Lucy in which she supposedly stated that the consecration of Russia had been accomplished by John Paul II's 1982 consecration of the world to the Immaculate Heart. It was later established that this interview was bogus. In 1989, apocryphal letters attributed to Sister Lucy were circulated throughout the world. The letters were of very dubious quality. There were statements attributed to Sister Lucy that ranged from the curious to the ridiculous. One letter maintained that Sister Lucy believed the consecration of Russia had been accomplished, not by John Paul's 1982 consecration, but by his *1984* consecration of the world to the Immaculate Heart. This letter was the sole support for the claim in the CDF's *The Message of Fatima* that Lucy believed Russia had been consecrated to the Immaculate Heart.[14]

In 1992, another bogus interview was publicized as proof that Sister Lucy believed the consecration of Russia to the Immaculate Heart had been accomplished. This was a particularly stubborn interview that lingered, in various versions, for years. It contains more remarkable statements supposedly made by Sister Lucy, such as "the Virgin did not request the conversion of Russia to Catholicism". There was also an account (by Lucy?) of Mikhail Gorbachev kneeling on his knees before John Paul II to beg forgiveness for his sins. Speaking of John Paul, Lucy also allegedly declared that "He who is not with the Pope is not with God". Interestingly, another comment attributed to Sister Lucy in this interview was "the Third Secret is not meant to be revealed".[15]

Of course, in reality Lucy said none of these things. In fact, at various times she has said the exact opposite: that Russia's conversion *would* be to Catholicism, that the consecration has *not* been done as Heaven demands, and that the Third Secret *should* have been published in 1960. Although numerous attempts have been made during the present pontificate to pit Sister Lucy against the Fatima Message, none of the bogus interviews mentioned above were conducted by a Vatican prelate, much less published by the Vatican. The interview of Sister Lucy in the document of December 20, 2001, carries the unmistakable weight of authority of the Holy See itself. Yet it seems to contradict everything that may reasonably be believed about Fatima. What are we to believe?

The Communiqué

I won't tell anyone what to believe, but I will examine the December 20 communiqué, and compare some of Lucy's statements there with other things she has said on the subject of Fatima. Given human nature, it is not unusual for people to change their opinions, particularly over the passage of years. One of the notable traits of Sister Lucy, however, is how exact and unwavering she has been in relating the Fatima Message. Given this prominent trait, one would expect her present statements on Fatima to mirror her previous statements. With this in mind, let us examine the communiqué of December 20.

First, it is reasonable to believe that the communiqué is correct in describing Sister Lucy as being "in good health, lucid, and vivacious". Aside from some occasional bronchial difficulties, Lucy's only significant health problems occurred in 1943, when at the age of thirty-six she contracted pleurisy.[16] It is apparent from her letters at this time that Lucy thought she was dying. So did her bishop, who panicked because Lucy had not yet written down the Third Secret. It was this, her only serious illness, that led Bishop da Silva to order Sister Lucy to commit the Third Secret to writing.

Although over ninety-six, Sister Lucy has maintained good physical health. Her personality and character also appear as stable and consistent as our fallen human nature allows. Dutch Montfort Father Jongen observed: "Lucy does a great deal of good for the children and for all who approach her. There is nothing which attracts attention to her in the convent. She has wit, she loves gaiety. If she distinguishes herself despite everything, it is perhaps for her attitude during prayer, the punctual observance of her rule and her love for the Holy Virgin ... Here is what characterizes her: an ardent devotion for the truth. Her veracity goes together with her disdain for human respect."[17]

Lucy's love for the truth has been dearly bought. Her refusal to lie about the Blessed Virgin's appearances caused her mother to beat her, and some good citizens of Fatima to kick and taunt her. The Tinsmith threatened to boil little Lucy in oil, and Portuguese Republican Guards threatened to cut her head off, but Lucy never changed a word of her account of the apparitions. It has been decades since she has been allowed to speak publicly about Fatima, but occasional reports of private conversations with family members indicate that, concerning Fatima, Lucy remains steadfast. This is worth remembering as we return to the December 20 communiqué.

The assertion in the interview that Lucy's first remarks were a profession of "love and devotion to the Holy Father" smacks of the personality cult enveloping the present pontiff. As a rule, rather than professing love and devotion, Lucy's marked tendency throughout her decades of religious life is to be deferential and discreet with superiors. These tendencies would be even more pronounced regarding the Pope.

There is, however, a very good reason for *presenting* Sister Lucy as brimming with love and devotion for the person of John Paul II, and this has to do with the prominent position the latter has given himself in the vision of the Third Secret. If John Paul is really the Pope in the vision, then he has a significant role in the fulfillment of the Fatima Message. Consequently, it would be very odd if Lucy *did not* exhibit love and devotion to such a personage.[18]

In fact, over the years Lucy has kept her distance from John Paul, and their relations have been cool at best. She did not wish to come to Fatima during Pope John Paul's 1991 visit, and only consented when ordered to appear by the Pope himself. They met privately and talked for some ten minutes. After speaking with Lucy at Fatima in 1991, however, John Paul II remained unable to publicly affirm that Sister Lucy believed Russia had been consecrated to the Immaculate Heart of the Blessed Virgin Mary.[19] This noticeable reserve of Sister Lucy towards John Paul II appeared to vanish during the 2000 beatification ceremony of Lucy's cousins, the Blesseds Jacinta and Francisco.

But to return to the December 20 communiqué: the assertion therein that Lucy "prays much" for John Paul II "and for the Church as a whole" is most likely true. Such a posture is consistent not just with Lucy's past statements, but with those of Blessed Francisco and Blessed Jacinta as well. Their encounters with the beautiful Lady at the Cova da Iria seemed to infuse them with a preoccupation to pray continually — it is not much of an overstatement — for the Holy Father. Later, Lucy would often plead, in letters and conversations, with others to pray for the Holy Father.[20] Her concern for "the Church as a whole" is equally well documented.

Lucy Versus the Third Secret

The communiqué continues:

> "To whoever imagines that some part of the secret has been hidden, she replied: 'Everything has been published; no secret remains.' To those who speak and write of new revelations she said: 'There is no truth in this. If I had received new revelations I would have told no one, but I would have communicated them directly to the Holy Father'."

To dispose of the last sentence first, "those who speak and write of new revelations" is likely a reference to the false rumor of the Blessed Virgin appearing at Carmel and telling the Carmelites of the "imminent bloodbath". Lucy has said "There is no truth in this." Her next sentence, however, seems out of character. When Lucy received the revelations at Tuy and Pontevedra, she shared them with her confessors, and followed their instruction. She has never communicated any revelation directly to any Pope without first going through proper channels. To have done so would have been presumptuous, and this is a fault no one has ever accused Lucy of.

Consequently, it is difficult to accept that this last statement was really said by Lucy. Its presence in the communiqué, however, serves two purposes. First, it emphasizes again the significant role of the present pontiff in the Vatican's version of Fatima. Second, it once again presents Lucy and the Pope as allies, or at least as enjoying a special relationship with each other. That such a depiction challenges reality is not as important as its purpose, which is (I think) to again implicitly oppose Lucy and the Pope against the ne'er do wells (that is, traditional Catholics, and anyone else who understands the Message of Fatima as it has been traditionally interpreted by priests, theologians, and scholars).

If this is the strategy of the December communiqué, it represents a development on the CDF's *The Message of Fatima*. The purpose of the latter, according to the Pope's spokesman, was to "provide no papal support for the anti-ecumenical traditionalism which has improperly seized hold of certain aspects of the Message of Fatima" and to "not allow Fatima to become hostage to a partisan position".[21] It seems plain enough. The Vatican wanted control of the Fatima Message, to massage it into compatibility with the "New Evangelization". In this they have succeeded to a certain degree. But if the 2000 release of the Third Secret sought to seize the Fatima Message and subordinate it to the persona of Pope John Paul II, the December communiqué seeks to seize Sister Lucy and subordinate her in similar fashion. It is a chilling strategy, and will probably also succeed to a certain degree.

Even more audaciously, the communiqué seeks to pit Sister Lucy against the Third Secret, at least as it has traditionally been understood by Fatima scholars. The statement "Everything has been published; no secret remains" simply cannot be believed as coming from Sister Lucy. It is as characteristic of Sister Lucy's real thinking as her supposed comment in the 1992 interview, "God condemns no one to hell" — which is to say that it is utterly uncharacteristic. Neither assertion can seriously be attributed to Sister Lucy.

What Sister Lucy *has* said about the Third Secret is worth repeating. There are consistent references to Churchmen "being fooled by false doctrine"; to a "diabolical disorientation" afflicting "so many persons who occupy places of responsibility" in the Church; to "priests and consecrated souls" who "are so deceived and misled" because "the devil has succeeded in infiltrating evil under cover of good ... leading into error and deceiving souls having a heavy responsibility through the place which they occupy ... They are blind men guiding other blind men," and so on.[22]

When we combine Lucy's real statements with the conclusions careful scholars like Father Alonso came to about the Third Secret involving apostasy in the Church,[23] with inadvertent admissions by Churchmen like Bishop do Amaral, the former Bishop of Fatima,[24] and with what we can see with our own eyes and hear with our own ears about the appalling state of the Church and the world — having considered all this, if we are to maintain any grasp of reality, the only conclusion is *Res ipsa loquitur:* the thing speaks for itself.

The "thing" is apostasy, the apostasy of the upper hierarchy many believe is mentioned in the text of the Third Secret the Vatican has yet to reveal. Only this "thing", this apostasy, can explain the December communiqué which, like *The Message of Fatima,* is an intentional interweaving of truth and falsehood. Both documents are carefully calculated to deceive.

Good God in Heaven! What manner of wretched men are these who, not content with despoiling the Church, seek to rob even the few remaining faithful of whatever integral faith they still possess?

Lucy and the Pirates

They are pirates, the pirates of our faith. Their crimes have aroused the Angel who stands poised in the heavens, "a flaming sword in his left hand; flashing, it gave out flames that looked as though they would set the world on fire". He seeks to avenge Our Lady, but the burning justice of his sword "died out in contact with the splendor that Our Lady radiated towards him from Her right hand".

This is the vision of the Third Secret, the outstretched arm of the Blessed Virgin averting judgment on sinful mankind. Despite our infidelities, She withholds the penalties of our sins. Then, "pointing to the Earth with his right hand, the Angel cried out in a loud voice: 'Penance, penance, penance'." Immediately following this cry the children were shown a Pope, "afflicted with pain and sorrow". He and his followers were murdered in cold blood. The Pope in this vision cannot be John Paul II (in my view), but he may well be the Pope who by his bloody martyrdom does "Penance, penance, penance" — purging the papacy of the sins and infidelities of his predecessors, including John Paul — particularly in regards to Fatima and the systematic dishonoring of the Immaculate Heart of Mary.

That, after all, is the real Fatima Message: devotion to the Immaculate Heart of Mary, which includes the Five First Saturday Communion of Reparation, will save souls from going to hell. Consecration to Her Immaculate Heart will convert Russia and grant the world a period of peace. Despite all appearances to the contrary, the Vatican appears to believe the triumph of the Immaculate Heart has already occurred, that Fatima belongs to the past.[25] But what the sad, beautiful Lady told Lucy and her cousins so many summers ago was that the triumph of the Immaculate Heart would happen "In the end."[26]

Long before the September 11 attacks, Father Alonso said, "The final triumph of Mary's Heart is certain and it will be definitive. But it will take place in the end, that is to say after a terrible purification of sinful humanity, in a baptism of fire, blood and tears."[27] The purification was ratcheted up a turn or two in September 2001. In response, the present pontiff again called for the world's religious liberals to come to Assisi to pray — to something — for peace.

In Coimbra, Sister Lucy gives no outward indication that the present orientation of the Vatican towards Fatima is deviant. In fact, her exuberance at Fatima in 2000 was almost disquieting. Surely the cause of her radiance, and her new graciousness towards John Paul, was her happiness over the beatification of her two cousins. Yet she remained exuberant even in the face of Cardinal Sodano's version of the Third Secret, going so far as to make large, awkward gestures to the crowd.

It is difficult to interpret, and things will only get more confusing when Lucy goes to her reward, for surely after her death the number of false statements and bogus interviews will multiply like demonic loaves and fishes. And make no mistake, her tomb at the Fatima Basilica has been ready and waiting for some time now. "But I am not dead yet!" Lucy was said to have protested when informed of the efforts of her gravediggers.

No, Lucy is not dead yet, and sometimes even pirates can be patient, if the prize is worthy enough. When the beautiful Lady told little Lucia dos Santos that, "You are to stay here some time longer," she was sad.

The Lady explained that Jesus wished to make use of Lucy "to make Me known and loved". Rather than be reserved with the child for her failure to recognize the remarkable dignity of her mission, the Blessed Virgin — one can almost see Her leaning towards the teary girl to comfort her — the Blessed Virgin said: "Do you suffer a great deal? Do not be discouraged. I will never forsake you. My Immaculate Heart will be your refuge and the way that will lead you to God."

Then She opened Her hands, and Lucy was flooded with the light and grace that compose that dearest of all human things — the Holy and Sacred Immaculate Heart of the Blessed Mother of God. The "final remedy" offered by God is the Immaculata, the Queen of Heaven and Refuge of Sinners, whose heart has sustained and sanctified St. John, St. Luke, St. John Eudes, St. Catherine Labouré, the Ratisbonne Brothers, Blessed Pius IX, St. Maximilian Kolbe — how many thousands of others has She led to Her Son? How many more does She yearn to present to He Whose Sacred Heart was pierced by a lance?

Her own heart was pierced with a sword of sorrow as She regarded Her crucified Son. At Calvary Mary's heart was afflicted as She stood before the tree of the cross, but at Fatima Mary stood *atop* the holm-oak tree — a modest, discreet promise of Her eventual triumph.

May God in His mercy quicken this Triumph. Let us pray that just as Mary will never forsake Lucy or any of Her other children, may not one of Her children ever forsake Her.

NOTES

1. Published by the Congregation for the Doctrine of the Faith, the (CDF) booklet, *The Message of Fatima*, June 2000.
2. In a news release dated September 18, 2001, out of Florida, published by Zenit electronic News Services.
3. To give the Archbishop his due, he also stated that "catastrophic predictions are not necessary to understand that 'penance and prayer for the conversion of the world are even more necessary,' because there are 'even more insidious enemies, such as materialism, secularism and hedonism.'" This is certainly true, particularly in America.
4. It is a peculiar type of zeal that causes anti-traditional Catholics to compromise not only their credibility, but their consciences as well, all for the sake of — of what? Taking a bullet for the Holy Father? Or firing a bullet at their enemies? In either case, the truth about Fatima seems secondary to other considerations.
5. The October 2001 issue of *CRC* contained a sidebar (entitled "A Sinister Hoax") reporting as rumor that "the Blessed Virgin had appeared to Sister Lucy to ask for the Carmelites to say the Rosary in order to avoid 'the imminent bloodbath.'" *The Remnant* published an apparitionless version of the same story, with qualifications. Eventually the Superior General of the SSPX, Bishop Bernard Fellay, publicly declared the story was without foundation. Both he and the *CRC* noted that the Carmel of Coimbra also formally denied the story.
6. The November 2001 issue of *Catholic Family News (CFN)* contains a photocopy of the article in Italian, with an accompanying English translation. The original article was published on *la Repubblica's* web page on October 10, 2001.
7. According to a Zenit story from Rome, dated October 11, 2001, sources in the CIA and NATO, an Italian press agency, and ex-President Clinton described three separate assassination plots against John Paul II. All were hatched by Moslem groups.
8. November *CFN*, p. 3. Father Bianchi's statement was contradicted in the January 9, 2002 issue of *L'Osservatore Romano*, where it was reported that Sister Lucy did not agree that the Vatican had not revealed the entire Third Secret.
9. All quotations in this paragraph are from a *Zenit News Services* report from Vatican City dated

October 28, 2001, entitled "Bishop Denies Reports That Sister Lucia Warned Pope".

10. No, I'm not kidding. See *Sun*, December 4, 2001, pp. 10-11.

11. "Sister Lucy: Secret of Fatima Contains No More Mysteries", Vatican Information Service, December 20, 2001.

12. *The Message of Fatima*, p. 25.

13. Ibid., p. 35.

14. *The Message of Fatima*, p. 7. Yet so embarrassed were the drafters that they could not bring themselves to cite the bogus letter as their source for their claim.

15. There are numerous sources for the various false interviews/letters of Sister Lucy. A handy synopsis is found in *Chronology of a Cover-Up*, written by Father Paul Kramer and published by the Fatima Center. The infamous 1992 interview was done by Carlos Evaristo, who admitted doing some creative editing with Lucy's remarks. This "interview" was exposed at length in more than one *CRC* volume.

16. The disease that killed Blessed Jacinta.

17 Frère François de Marie des Anges, *FATIMA: Intimate Joy, World Event*, (*FIJWE*) Volume IV, Immaculate Heart Publications, pp. 10-11.

18. One might almost say that she *must*.

19. The date 1991 is interesting because it is claimed that in 1989 Lucy wrote one Walter Noelker a letter in which she declared that John Paul's 1984 consecration of the world satisfied the Blessed Virgin's request for the consecration of Russia. If Lucy really believed this in 1989, why in Heaven's name did she not inform the Pope, either in 1989 or when she met with him privately in Fatima in 1991? The only reasonable answer is that she did not so believe, and that her letter to Mr. Noelker was apocryphal (a forgery). Also of note is that at Fatima in 1991 John Paul did not reveal the contents of the Third Secret, even though according to the CDF's *The Message of Fatima* the Third Secret concerns the 1981 assassination attempt on John Paul — an event that happened ten years prior to John Paul's 1991 trip to Fatima.

20. Contrary to what some may assume, Lucy's concern for "the Holy Father" is generic, not particular. It includes not only John Paul II, but all of his predecessors from Benedict XV onwards. In a 1945 letter to Father Aparicio, a former confessor who was residing in Brazil, Lucy wrote: "Down there do they pray for the Holy Father? We must not cease praying for His Holiness. Great days of affliction and torment await him still. (*FIJWE*, Vol. IV, p. 9.)" This was a reference to Pius XII. In terms of the Fatima Message, Lucy often appears to view all popes in the same light.

21. As if the neo-modernist gobbledygook in the CDF's *The Message of Fatima* is *not* a partisan position. For the quote, see August 2000 *CRC,* on line edition.

22. These quotations are condensed from numerous letters Sister Lucy wrote in the early 1970's to two of her nephews who were priests, and to other religious she knew. See *The Whole Truth About Fatima*, Vol. III, pp. 754-758.

23. Father Alonso was appointed the official Church historian on Fatima. He had access to all Fatima documents, from which he crafted a multi-volume work which remains in large part unpublished, due to his conclusions about the Third Secret. Much of his early work involved consultation with Sister Lucy. We may reasonably conclude that she would have corrected his conclusions about the Third Secret involving the apostasy of the upper hierarchy if this was a false conclusion.

24. In a question and answer session at the University of Vienna in 1984, Bishop do Amaral gave this answer concerning the Third Secret: "Its content concerns only our faith ... The loss of the faith on a continent is worse than the annihilation of a nation; and it is true that the faith is continually diminishing in Europe." See *FIJWE*, Volume IV, pp. 243-244.

25. The CDF's *The Message of Fatima*, p. 36.

26. Father Louis Kondor, Editor, *Fatima In Lucia's Own Words*, Sister Lucia's Memoirs, 9th Edition, The Ravengate Press, 1995, p. 162.

27. *CRC*, August 2000, p. 30.

Chapter Twenty-Eight
The Apostle of Her Heart

At this writing Sister Maria Lucia of the Immaculate Heart is ninety-six years old. She remains at the Carmelite convent in Coimbra, Portugal. When last seen she was at Fatima, waving her arms about rather erratically — in response to John Paul's beatification of Francisco and Jacinta, or at Cardinal Sodano's version of the Third Secret, it is difficult to say.

Lucy's last visit to Fatima caused the Abbé de Nantes to remark: "Poor Lucy, she is so easily misunderstood." The numerous false interviews Lucy has fallen victim to over the years — including her "interview" with Msgr. Bertone — haven't clarified things. Over the course of her life, however, what has been striking about Sister Lucy is her fidelity, both to her religious vocation and to the Message of Fatima.

Even within her religious community, however, her life must have continued to have been a very lonely one, particularly without the physical presence of her dearest friends, Francisco and Jacinta. The three seers understood each other when no one else did, and Lucy missed them terribly as a girl. How she must have missed them during those dark days after 1960 when it became obvious the Church hierarchy had adopted a policy of deception towards Fatima and the Third Secret.

It is, however, easy to imagine the three close friends continuing their relationship during Lucy's sojourn on Earth. Indeed, if one recalls Jacinta's impetuosity, it is difficult to imagine Lucy's younger cousin being able to wait for Lucy's death to speak to her. Remember how Lucy used to pick wild flowers for a bed-ridden Jacinta? Perhaps now it is the younger cousin's turn to pick spiritual bouquets, and present them with a caress to a dear, aged friend who can only wander the Portuguese hillside in her memory.

Lucy's last words to Francisco were a sob-choked "Good-bye till Heaven." The young boy had promised Lucy he would pray for her in Heaven, and Francisco always took his promises seriously. Is it possible his calm presence, the quiet steadfastness he showed even when terrorized by the Tinsmith, has ceased to be a part of Lucy's life? It is easy to imagine Blessed Francisco's presence being so tangible that Lucy can almost see him once more: perched on a rock, quiet and serious, first blowing his flute for his cousins to dance to, now prostrate on the ground, murmuring the Angel's prayer over and over again ...

"You are to stay here some time longer," the Blessed Virgin told ten-year-old Lucy. "Jesus wishes to make use of you to make me known and loved. He wants to establish devotion to My Immaculate Heart."

Even though Francisco and Jacinta have reached Heaven and have been allowed to grace her with consolations, no doubt there have still been times when Sister Lucy has repeated the question she once asked of the Blessed Virgin: "Am I to stay here alone?" And surely the Blessed Virgin has repeated Her answer of June 13, 1917: "My daughter ... Do you suffer a great deal? Don't lose heart. I will never forsake you. My Immaculate Heart will be your refuge and the way that will lead you to God."

Lucy's life after the apparitions is proof of her journey to God through the Immaculate Heart of Mary. She immediately shunned the temptations to head a religious-political movement, or to be the subject of a personality cult. Perhaps an even greater temptation came after 1960 — the temptation to reveal the Third Secret "for" the Holy Father. How did Lucy react? "I must remain in silence, in prayer, and in penance," she wrote a friend during this period, adding: "In this way I can and must help you the most ... such is the part the Lord has chosen for me: to pray and sacrifice myself for those who struggle and work in the Lord's vineyard and for the extension of His kingdom ..."

This was not a new role. Lucy has been living the Fatima Message of sacrifice and reparation every day since 1917. Her life is yet another dramatic proof — if one were needed — of the authenticity of Fatima and its Message. This is what a life lived next to the Immaculate Heart of Mary looks like. For most of her life Lucia dos Santos ("light of the Saints") has immolated herself in imitation of the Blessed Virgin's immolation of Her own will as She stood under the cross. Her life refutes the claim that such a life is impossible — even today.

Lucy has been definite that the last two remedies offered mankind are the Rosary and devotion to the Immaculate Heart. "There will be no others," Lucy told Father Fuentes. The Blessed Virgin has given the Rosary "a new efficacy" such that "there is no problem, no matter how difficult it is ... that we cannot resolve by the prayer of the Holy Rosary." Devotion to the Immaculate Heart, Lucy insisted, "consists in considering Her as the seat of mercy, of goodness and of pardon and as the certain door by which we are to enter Heaven."

There is significant evidence that for the last four decades popes have exerted considerable pressure on Sister Lucy to bend the Fatima Message to fit the papal vision of the post-conciliar Church. To this end she has been silenced, and words have been put in her mouth. Pains have been taken to create the perception that Sister Lucy agrees with the present Vatican interpretation of Fatima. These efforts have been so zealous it causes one to wonder whether certain individuals in the Vatican presented Sister Lucy with a "*quid pro quo*" proposition prior to the decision to beatify Francisco and Jacinta.

Although at present this is only speculation, it is true that at times Sister Lucy herself has caused confusion, at least in allowing herself to be manipulated. Was this done under obedience? In response to direct order from the highest level of the Church? What were her mental reservations? Indeed, it is very easy these days to misunderstand Lucy.

No effort is made here to criticize her, or judge her participation in recent events. We are living in the time of the Third Secret, and the diabolical disorientation is formidable, and can color every perception; who is completely immune from its power?

If anyone could be, Lucy could. Any evaluation must consider her entire life, which is a model of fidelity to the Blessed Virgin and the Message of Fatima. One may reasonably assume she enjoys the special protection of Heaven. Such protection may not protect Lucy from occasional prudential errors. It has, however, allowed Lucy to live her life in admirable, even profound imitation of the hidden life of the Blessed Virgin. Mary has been her refuge, and Lucia dos Santos has been the apostle of Her Heart.

* * *

In coming years, decades, or centuries, the final prophecies of Fatima will be fulfilled. Lucy's assertion that we are living in the last times may sound fantastic to modern Catholic ears, yet she is in famous company. Pope Pius XII also believed that "the present hour is a dread phase of the events foretold by Christ. It seems that darkness is about to fall upon the world. Humanity is in the grip of a supreme crisis."

Pius XII's predecessor, Pope St. Pius X, had this vision: "I saw one of my successors taking to flight over the bodies of his brethren. He will take refuge in disguise somewhere; and after a short retirement he will die a cruel death. The present wickedness of the world is only the beginning of sorrows which must take place before the end of the world."

These "papal visions" are a stark contrast to the utopia imagined by the conciliar popes. Sadly, they are more consistent with human experience, and with Jacinta's visions, which provide further details of the landscape seen by Pope St. Pius X. She saw "highways and roads and fields full of people, crying with hunger and (having) nothing to eat." The Holy Father was in a crowded church "praying before the Immaculate Heart of Mary." In another vision, Jacinta saw the Holy Father "in a very big house, kneeling by a table, with his head buried in his hands, and he was weeping. Outside the house, there were many people. Some of them were throwing stones, others were cursing him and using bad language. Poor Holy Father, we must pray very much for him."

Jacinta's visions may well provide details concerning the fulfillment of the remaining known prophecies of the Fatima Secret: various nations will be annihilated and the Holy Father will have much to suffer. The suffering will be intense, for the Holy Father will finally cleave heart and soul to the Fatima Message, thus inciting a satanic frenzy against him by the world and his Church.

When this will happen is in the hands of God and we, as always, are completely at His mercy. Mary has given us the promise: "In the end, My Immaculate Heart will triumph. The Holy Father will consecrate Russia to Me, and she will be converted, and some time of peace will be granted to the world." Father Alonso wrote, "The final triumph of Mary's Heart is certain and it will be definitive. But it will take place 'in the end', that is to say, after a terrible purification of sinful humanity, in a baptism of fire, blood and tears."

On that day history will at last be pulled into conformity with the Divine Will. The chastisement of apostasy will cease. In the new dawn all will realize that the darksome nightmare we are living through did not vitiate Christ's promise that the gates of hell would never conquer His Church. Perfect mercy will follow perfect justice. Russia will be devotedly consecrated to the Immaculate Heart. The conversion of that tortured nation will be dazzling, blinding, as the perfect humility of the Immaculate will put the red dragon and his beasts to flight. Perhaps the conversion will be triggered by a profound apparition of the Blessed Virgin, as at Guadalupe. New legends will be born that will seed cultures with the will to base society on the Kingship of Christ. This will inspire a renaissance of Christian poetry and art. Man will remember anew the supernatural reality of the Holy Sacrifice of the Mass. With trembling reverence, we will once more kneel before the Almighty.

Until that glorious day our models are the seers. Like Jacinta, we must pray much for the Holy Father and offer our sufferings and intentions to this end. Like Lucy, we must obey our authentic religious superiors in all things licit, but never fear speaking the truth of our faith, even if this means contradicting the prudential judgments of the Holy Father. Devotion to the Immaculate Heart, recitation of the Rosary, and participation in the First Saturday reparatory devotion are essential for the light of the Holy Spirit to illumine this present darkness shrouding the world and the Church.

For it is not Fatima that is in twilight. Fatima is a beacon of faith, hope, and charity, a message as clear and uncompromising as the Gospel, shining on all souls stumbling in the twilight of the Church and the world, as both fade to black in the long hours before the dawn.

Shall we slumber through her passion as the Apostles slept through Our Lord's agony in the garden? Shall we renounce membership in our disfigured Church as our first Holy Father renounced Our Lord in His final hours? We must not. We must pick up our cross, chosen for us before the foundation of the world, and bear witness to the one true faith, and the Church created by Our Lord to preserve this truth, even unto the end of the world.

INDEX

For more copies of this book for your relatives and friends,
e-mail us at fatimaintwilight@westelcom.com or
visit our website at www.fatimaintwilight.com

Marmion Publications

In Canada:
P.O. Box 694
Niagara Falls, Ontario
L2E 6V5

In U.S.A:
M.P.O. Box 743
Niagara Falls, New York
14302

716-691-7091